Fighting for Hope

WAR/SOCIETY/CULTURE

Michael Fellman, *Series Editor*

Fighting for Hope

☆ ☆ ☆

African American Troops of the 93rd Infantry Division in World War II and Postwar America

ROBERT F. JEFFERSON

The Johns Hopkins University Press

Baltimore

© 2008 The Johns Hopkins University Press
All rights reserved. Published 2008
Printed in the United States of America on acid-free paper
2 4 6 8 9 7 5 3 1

The Johns Hopkins University Press
2715 North Charles Street
Baltimore, Maryland 21218-4363
www.press.jhu.edu

Library of Congress Cataloging-in-Publication Data

Jefferson, Robert F., 1963–
Fighting for hope : African American troops of the 93rd Infantry Division in
World War II and postwar America / Robert F. Jefferson.
p. cm.—(War/society/culture)
Includes bibliographical references and index.
ISBN-13: 978-0-8018-8828-1 (hbk. : alk. paper)
ISBN-10: 0-8018-8828-x (hbk. : alk. paper)
1. World War, 1939–1945—Participation, African American.   2. World War,
1939–1945—Campaigns—Oceania.   3. World War, 1939–1945—Veterans—
United States—Social conditions.   4. United States. Army. Division, 93rd.
5. United States. Army—African American troops.   6. African American
soldiers—Social conditions—20th century.   7. African Americans—Social
conditons—To 1964.   8. United States—Social conditions—20th century.
I. Title.
D810.N4J44   2008
940.54'03—dc22   2007052603

A catalog record for this book is available from the British Library.

*Special discounts are available for bulk purchases of this book. For more information,
please contact Special Sales at 410-516-6936 or specialsales@press.jhu.edu.*

The Johns Hopkins University Press uses environmentally friendly book materials, including recycled text paper that is composed of at least 30 percent post-
consumer waste, whenever possible. All of our book papers are acid-free, and
our jackets and covers are printed on paper with recycled content.

CONTENTS

During the sixtieth anniversary of the Japanese attack at Pearl Harbor and on the heels of the terrible events of September 11, 2001, Brent Staples, in an op-ed piece for the *New York Times*, struck a chord when he observed how Hollywood movies tended to adopt a multicultural lens to describe the American experience in World War II. Commenting on the motion picture film *Pearl Harbor* and the role of Doris "Dorie" Miller, played by Cuba Gooding Jr., Staples points out that "the movie ends with Miller smiling proudly over his Navy Cross, but it fails to note that the Navy declined to issue it for several months while the *Pittsburgh Courier* led the Negro Press in a scorching indictment of military segregation that threatened to drive black voters out of the Democratic Party." He went on to correctly assert that contemporary movies about the wartime period have recycled many of the misconceptions that have shaped the American experience in the war because they, like their predecessors, have consistently failed to grapple with the military racism that "makes black heroism all the more remarkable." "In doing so, the movies have left the mistaken impression that heroism in the 'greatest generation' came exclusively with a white face," Staples concludes.[1]

Although Staples was writing some sixty years after the end of the fighting, the Hollywood version of the heroic American World War II soldier that he describes epitomizes the titanic challenges of researching and writing about the history of African American GIs and their communities in World War II, as well as understanding the rich, contradictory legacy black veterans left behind. Far from appearing as "whitened heroes" or soldiers "missing in action," African Americans who stood in the ranks of the segregated army of World War II held their own notions of manhood and bravery that defy conventional wisdom and categorization. And it is the perceptions that black GIs held of themselves as fighting soldiers and the worlds that framed their identities as men that make up the subject of this book.

The sources that shaped this study beckoned me from the very beginning. What began as a stab in the dark to write a case study of the men who served in the U.S. 93rd Infantry Division ended with a deep plunge into the heady waters of social and cultural history. In the early 1990s, when I began researching the men who served in the division, there were few books that fully chronicled the division's contribution to the Second World War, let alone books that tried to capture the thoughts and actions of the men who served in its ranks. I was told over and over again throughout my graduate study at the University of Michigan that I might not be able to locate many of these soldiers "because they may not want to talk about their experiences." Undaunted, I set out to attack the subject on a number of fronts. Turning first to a series of rosters of the division members recorded between 1942 and 1945 secured from the National Archives and Records Administration, I contacted the Retired Officers Association, the Disabled American Veterans of America, and other veterans' organizations to see whether they had the addresses for the individuals who appeared on the lists. I also placed a number of op-ed pieces and plaintive ads in a number of black weeklies, hoping to locate surviving members of the unit. What I thought would yield only a few individuals soon produced a deluge of responses from the former division members themselves. Once my inquiries appeared in the pages of veterans' newspapers and journals, my mailbox and answering machine soon overflowed with letters, cards, and calls from veterans who wanted to talk with me about their wartime experiences.

At one point during this period, when I returned home from a week of researching the division's activities in the National Archives, my wife, Lisa, told me that our phone had been ringing off the hook with people wanting to talk with me. But what my wife and I failed to realize at the time was that the responses of the former division members would overtake our lives on a different front. On a weekly basis between 1990 and 1995, I would receive some three hundred pieces of correspondence from the veterans along with various artifacts that they wished to share with me. Among the items I received were scores of military service records, photographs, service-related memorabilia, unpublished narratives, and personal correspondence penned by the veterans to family members and friends during the wartime period. Soon, our small one-bedroom apartment in Ann Arbor, Michigan, began to resemble a museum commemorating the experiences of members of the U.S. 93rd Infantry Division and their families.

Once I identified the former GIs who served with the unit, I began to survey the veterans to retrieve their recollections of their World War II service, a process that was expensive and time consuming. I developed a ten-page questionnaire and mailed 584 copies of the survey to the self-selected veterans and received

226 responses. The survey began with questions about their family history, geographical origin, pre-war communities, education, and occupations and ended with queries about their assessment of their wartime experiences. This information was crucial because it allowed me to get a better sense of their lived experiences before the formal interview process. After sifting through this material, I arranged to meet with 130 veterans and their families; most of the interviews took place between 1991 and 2002 in areas as far ranging as Cleveland, Ohio; Asheville, North Carolina; the District of Columbia; Sierra Vista, Arizona; Chicago; Stockton, California; Milwaukee; Atlanta; Tampa; and Newark, Delaware.

I wanted to write a book about the men who served in the division, but I realized that the story encompassed much more. My interviewing sessions with the veterans were often emotion-filled episodes during which I learned a great many things about the men and women associated with the unit and their children and grandchildren. First, all the former GIs were very gracious in welcoming me into their home. But once I sat down with them in their living room or at their kitchen table, they sometimes disclosed more than they initially intended, often resulting in idiosyncratic interview sessions that took on lives and personalities of their own. For example, I met with one veteran who, upon recalling how he felt when he entered military service, quickly repaired to his bedroom only to return moments later fully dressed in his wartime military uniform with tears streaming down his face. He then told me the story of how, as a callow 18-year-old Detroit youth going through the paces of basic training at Fort Huachuca, Arizona, he met General Benjamin O. Davis Sr. for the first time. And in the process of telling the story, he recalled the pride he felt in knowing that he had contributed to something significant.

Second, the memories involving the experiences of the men who served with the 93rd were family enterprises, each invested with its own allegorical meaning. While meeting with the family members of a former GI in Milwaukee, my wife and I choked back tears when his widow bitterly recounted her husband's desperate efforts to rebuild his life after he returned from overseas duty in 1945. After providing us with vivid examples of his postwar struggles, she ended by looking at me and saying, "He was never the same afterwards. Remember, young man, war continues long after the firing ceases." It was these bittersweet memories rendered by former servicemen and their families, along with those provided by countless others along the way, that spoke to me and expanded my imaginative powers in ways that microfilm and archival collections could not with regard to the experiences and legacy of the soldiers who served in segregated units like the U.S. 93rd Infantry Division during World War II.

This book took much too long to write, and I've accumulated some enormous debts of gratitude to family, friends, colleagues, faculty, and archivists in the process. The staff in the interlibrary loan office at Harlan Hatcher Graduate Library at the University of Michigan provided timely materials at the most crucial moments. Many thanks also go to the dedicated staffs at the main and law libraries at the University of Iowa; YMCA-USO Archives in Minneapolis; the Douglas A. MacArthur Memorial Archives in Norfolk, Virginia; the Veterans History Project and Manuscripts and Periodicals Divisions of the Library of Congress and the Mary McLeod Bethune Council House in Washington, D.C.; the Hoover Institution on War, Revolution, and Peace in Palo Alto, California; and the Detroit Public Library. I am especially indebted to Joellen Elbashir, the manuscript curator at the Moorland-Spingarn Research Center at Howard University; Ann Allen Shockley at the Fisk University Library; and Diana Lachatenere at the Schomburg Center for Research in Black Culture at the New York Public Library. Richard Boylan, Kenneth Schlessinger, and David Pfeiffer at the National Archives and Records Administration in Washington, D.C., handled my periodic bouts of insanity and strange requests with considerable aplomb and expertise. The same can be said for Raymond Teichman and Robert Parks, the archivists at the Franklin Delano Roosevelt Presidential Library in Hyde Park, New York.

Special praise also goes to Mary Dennis, deputy clerk of the court at the United States Army Judiciary in Falls Church, Virginia, and Peggy Cox, chief of the Military Operations Branch at the National Personnel Records Center in St. Louis, Missouri. Each provided considerable skill and grace in using the numerous service numbers of veterans that I provided to locate court documents and reconstruct career files among their collections. Additional documentation on several prominent former GIs was obtained from the Congressional Liaison of the Federal Bureau of Investigation under the Freedom of Information Act. A special note of gratitude goes to James P. Finley, the archivist at the Fort Huachuca Museum Archives. In addition to providing material resources for the book, Finley took me on a tour of many of the existing World II–era barracks, chapels, and dwellings on the base, which helped me to envision the world in which African American World War II veterans and their families lived and labored. Finally, I would like to especially thank Ruth Hodge, Richard Sommers, Tom Sweeney, and William Stoft at the United States Army Military History Institute at Carlisle Barracks, Pennsylvania, for their generosity and resourcefulness in assisting my research.

Special thanks go to the Horace H. Rackham School for Graduate Studies at the University of Michigan for funding my graduate study and research. I am also grateful to Wayne State University and the University of Iowa for providing summer research support for additional research and travel needed to revise the manuscript. Both institutions also provided me with timely semester sabbaticals to work through major portions of the book. Finally, gratitude must be extended to the Obermann Center for Advanced Studies at the University of Iowa and the Franklin and Eleanor Roosevelt Institute for providing grants-in-aid and fellowships that greatly facilitated the research and writing of this book.

To the hundreds of 93rd Infantry Division World War II veterans and their families I owe the very existence of this book. I shall always be indebted to Thomas White, Benjamin T. Layton, Francis Ellis, Clarence Ross, Vincent Browne, Jean Hunton, Pauline Redmond Coggs, Walter Sanderson, John Marshall, and George Nicholas, all of whom passed away before the publication of this book. Over the years, an ever-widening circle of former GIs and soldier's family members contributed greatly to my thinking on black World War II veterans and their activities; among them are John Howard and family, Alvirita Little, Irma Jackson Cayton Wertz, Henry "Hank" Williams, Herbert Hall, James Whittico, Nelson Peery, Reuben Fraser and family, George Leighton, Leo Logan, General Jerry S. Addington, Freida Greene and family, Elliotte Williams, James "Big Jim" Queen, William Brooks, Colonel (Ret.) Major Clark, Jehu Hunter, Arnett Hartsfield and family, Julius Young and family, Robert Johnson, Julius Thompson, Bennie Etters, Asberry McGriff, Clarence Gaines and family, Willard Jarrett, Percy Roberts, Edward Carr and family, Raymond Jenkins, Teddie Kemp, and George Shuffer. The people in this group not only took the time to talk with me but also provided many personal documents, thoughtful commentary, and timely corrections. Quite a few even went to their own attic or basement and to city hall to retrieve precious material to share with me. And to the large number of veterans and soldier's family members whose names don't appear in this acknowledgment,

I hope they clearly see that their fingerprints are all over this book. It is dedicated to them.

Veterans organizations that were gracious enough to freely offer their time and encouragement include the Huachucans Veterans Association; the 93rd Infantry "Blue Helmet" Association; the Disabled American Veterans; the Washington, D.C., chapter of the 555th Parachute Infantry Association (the "Triple Nickles"); the American Veterans of World War II, Korea, and Vietnam; the American Veterans Committee; the Blinded Veterans Association; the Retired Officers Association; the Black Military History Institute of America; the 92nd Infantry Division Association; the Women's Army Corps Foundation; and the Organization of African American Veterans of the United States. The Huachucans deserve special thanks because they watched the research and writing of this book grow from an undeveloped idea to an unwieldy dissertation to, finally, a publishable manuscript.

Discussions with colleagues at the institutions at which I was employed contributed to the completion of the book. At Wayne State University, I benefited greatly from conversations with Allan Raucher, Christopher Johnson, Melvin Small, and Elizabeth Faue. After I moved on to the University of Iowa, examples of collegiality and fonts of moral support reached new heights, as I had the good fortune to befriend Kenneth Cmiel, Stephen Vlastos, Colin Gordon, Shelton Stromquist, Mark Peterson, Linda Kerber, Michaeline Crichlow, James Giblin, Allen Roberts, and Peter Nazareth. I owe special thanks to Leslie Schwalm, whose scholarship on war, race, and gender greatly influenced the reconceptualization of this book and whose office discussions are greatly missed.

Often mentorship and friendship are overstated. But I have had the best of both worlds. At the University of Michigan, I had the opportunity to work with a host of historians whose research and writing have served as examples of the finest scholarship in the profession. I reserve the greatest accolades for John Shy, Earl Lewis, and Robin Kelley because they taught me how to be a serious historian and careful scholar. John always advised me to let the "veterans see themselves" in the story. And I would like to especially acknowledge the "Master Storytellers" Earl and Robin, who taught me more about seeing and listening to the complex nuances of African American history than they will ever know. Roger Hackett, Thomas Collier, Jonathan Marwil, Thomas Burkman, Alfred Rollins, and Brian Linn stoked my curiosity about East Asian history, New Deal studies, and military studies and blanched my ambitions with a cold dash of reality when I tended to lose focus along the way.

Katherine Beard, Richard Breaux, Jennifer Harbour, Lionel Kimble, Junko Kobayashi, and Vanessa Shelton, former graduate students at Wayne State University and the University of Iowa, challenged me during our discussions of African American history and probably taught me more lessons about heeding the ironies of history than I imparted to them. Others who heard about or read more parts of the book and helped shaped its inner workings include Bernard Nalty, Craig Cameron, John Dittmer, Quintard Taylor, Gerald Horne, Marc Gallicchio, Nicholas Cullather, Susan Smith, Angelita Reyes, Jennifer Keene, Dale Wilson, Bruce Fehn, Kimberley Phillips, Joyce Thomas, and Selika Ducksworth-Lawton. In some cases, they saw chapters of the manuscript even when they consisted of only a paragraph. And I'm pleased to reserve special recognition for Deborah Gershenowitz, who played an important role in the development of this book, providing a careful reading and kind words of encouragement throughout the process. Finally, special gratitude goes to my circle of friends: Frank "Micki" and Irene Schubert, Ken Gatlin, Guthrie "Guy" Ramsey, Hurley "Lee" Freeman, and Claude Clegg, from whom I have gathered strength to press on when the book seem to stall or who simply provided precious moments of levity when it was needed.

I am grateful to my editor, Robert J. Brugger, and the fine copyediting staff at the Johns Hopkins University Press for displaying extraordinary patience with a work that took too long to complete. *Fighting for Hope* stands as a living testament to their enthusiasm, generosity, and understanding. Heartfelt thanks are reserved for Grace Carino and the anonymous reader for the Johns Hopkins University Press who gave the manuscript a meticulous reading, saving me from numerous embarrassing assertions and stylistic lapses. I offer much praise to this talented group of people. Despite the help and encouragement of all involved, I alone am responsible for any mistakes or weaknesses.

Finally, the loving words of thanks cannot even come close to expressing the deep, abiding appreciation I have for the lifeblood of my being: my family. Much joy and happiness go to my growing extended family of grandmothers, brothers, sisters, aunts, uncles, cousins, nephews, nieces, and in-laws. Special insight into the project was provided by my grandfather, whose endless stories about his World War II experiences captivated a young boy from South Carolina. I also wish to pay tribute to the memory of my father, Robert Jefferson Sr., whose dreams have now become a reality. And there will always be special place in my heart for my grandmother Queen Esther Douglas; my mother, Lillie Lane; and my aunt Lowarn Carter, whose love, inspiration, and wisdom have served as the guiding star in my intellectual development. Their examples have bolstered my spirit both in times of joy and happiness and through moments of loneliness and self-doubt. Since I began this project many years ago, my father-in-law and mother-in-law sustained me, nourishing my body and mind with good food and stimulating conversation. I benefited especially from the enthusiasm and adventurous spirit exhibited by my father-in-law, Henry Jessie, whose injunctions sent me into revision mode on countless occasions. My greatest thanks go to my wife, Lisa, who is my life partner, coauthor, and co-pilot, not to mention my staunchest ally and most tireless critic. Finally, to my son, Evan: the intellectual and personal odyssey that started when he was just a toddler has been a road marked by a thousand tour guides and very few maps. No more road trips, son, I promise!

AGCT   Army General Classification Test
AVC   American Veterans Committee
CCC   Civilian Conservation Corps
CID   Criminal Investigation Detachment
CMTC   Citizens' Military Training Camp
CPNND   Committee for Participation of Negroes in the National Defense
FBI   Federal Bureau of Investigation
G-1   Personnel section of the army, division staff level and higher
G-2   Intelligence section of the army, division staff level and higher
G-3   Operations section of the army, division staff level and higher
MP   military police
NAACP   National Association for the Advancement of Colored People
NCO   noncommissioned officer
ROTC   Reserve Officers' Training Corps
UNAVA   United Negro and Allied Veterans of America, Inc.
UNIA   Universal Negro Improvement Association
USO   United Service Organizations
WAAC   Women's Army Auxiliary Corps

Fighting for Hope

Introduction

Recasting the African American Experience in World War II

> The Negro's contribution to the winning of the war will never be properly evaluated. As I see it, there are two reasons. One is that those who have the facts do not consider it important enough to warrant separate study. The second reason is that Negro writers who have the interest, and who do think it is important to appraise the Negro's contribution to the war, do not have the intelligence to sift the important facts from the trivial.
>
> *George N. Leighton*

> Hope, if we keep fighting; fighting, as we keep hope.
>
> *W. E. B. Du Bois, 1943*

It was a moment filled with fellowship, tribute, and sobering reflection. In April 1969, fifteen former GIs and their families journeyed to the ranch-style home of George and Helen Higgins in Pasadena, California, to commemorate their wartime experiences. After the group settled on the well-worn wicker chairs and sofas in the modestly furnished living room, the former servicemen spent a long night revisiting their wartime experiences as members of the U.S. 93rd Infantry Division during the Second World War. As they huddled together that evening, proud and dignified in the midst of surviving family members and friends, they couldn't help but place their wartime memories in the context of their daily issues of concern.

Among the women, men, children, grandchildren, and friends who traveled to recount past trials and tribulations sat Walter Greene; his wife, Freida Bailey; and their sons, Walter III and Gregory. As for most of the service families present that day, World War II and the 93rd Infantry Division held special relevance for Walter and Freida. Born in Detroit in 1917, Walter Greene was the son of a promi-

nent Common Pleas Court constable and a seamstress. He graduated from a Detroit high school in 1941 and was then drafted into the army and ordered to Camp
Wheeler, Georgia, where he completed his basic training. After graduating from
Officer Candidate School at nearby Fort Benning, the newly commissioned second lieutenant moved on to California, where he joined the 93rd Infantry Division's 25th Infantry Regiment while the unit was undergoing maneuvers as part
of training in the Mojave Desert in July 1943. Greene later traveled with the regiment as it advanced throughout the Pacific theater of operations, where he and the
rest of his comrades participated in patrolling missions on Bougainville Island,
New Guinea, and Morotai Island, Indonesia.

In the Pacific, Greene and other members of his regiment fought not only the
hostile enemy and the treacherous terrain but also endless bouts of racism within
their own army. For example, he and other soldiers in his regiment were assigned
to unload ships while similarly seasoned white combat units advanced through
the areas toward Japan. Greene suffered further insult when he and nine other
black commissioned officers were ordered to attend a special officers training school
that was established for poor soldiers on a nearby island by division headquarters. Greene and other officers responded by waging what he called "the war within
the war," staging sit-down strikes and refusing to answer to roll call on a number of occasions. Although the rebellious actions taken by Greene and other black
GIs represented an ad hoc response to the numerous impossible conditions they
faced within the segregated army, they had a tremendous impact on his thinking
at the time. After being shipped home to receive treatment for dengue fever in
early 1945, Greene bitterly remarked: "You have to understand. Overseas, a man
has a lot of time to precipitate his thoughts. While serving over there, I learned
that segregation is fostered at the top. Those on the bottom go along because it
bolsters their ego. One thing is certain to me, however. The Negro soldier is going to be militant because he is looking for something—he expects something
better than the status quo when he gets home or the public will have a severe
problem on its hands."[1]

Greene returned home to Detroit to find that, although the racial climate in
the city had not changed at all, his outlook regarding social and political empowerment had been fundamentally transformed as a result of his Pacific experiences.
Shortly thereafter, he translated his political thoughts born in the wartime emergency into postwar action, working as an employment negotiator and adjudication officer for disabled former servicemen in the Veterans Administration and
as a field representative with the Michigan Fair Employment Practices Commission before becoming the acting director of the regional office of the contract com-

pliance program within the Department of Defense in 1967. In this capacity, Greene continued to fight for civil rights causes, demanding that the University of Michigan take bolder steps in its recruitment of African American students and faculty, adopting measures to increase the number of black women and men in city government, and later—as Detroit's first African American deputy mayor—railing publicly against corporations that decided to move their operations out of Detroit during the winter months of 1969. Traveling to Pasadena and seeing his former comrades in arms produced a flood tide of emotions for Greene as it became evident to him that the hard political lessons they learned from their struggles in the segregated army informed their present commitment to their respective communities. Looking back at his wartime experiences during the gathering, Greene leaned over to his longtime friends who were seated in the living room and remarked, "There is a certain comradeship among us for no one else can understand what we've been through and the sacrifices we made in the man's army."

Although Greene didn't realize it at the time, his life partner understood all too well the hardships endured by him and the other former division members who were in attendance that evening. But for the proud and dignified Freida Bailey, the gathering evoked a different set of memories, for she had her own story to tell about her husband's wartime past. Born in Oklahoma in 1918, Bailey was the product of a household of homesteaders who migrated from Mississippi and Tennessee to the western territories in the late 1870s in search of land, prosperity, and autonomy. During the late 1920s, Freida and her family moved to Detroit, where she worked as a waitress while attending Michigan State Normal School (now Eastern Michigan University) in nearby Ypsilanti before transferring to Detroit's Wayne University. Shortly after graduating with a bachelor's degree in elementary education, she secured sporadic assignments as a substitute teacher in the city public school system, where she met and married Walter Greene in early 1940. She had no sooner accepted a permanent teaching position in Detroit when Walter received a letter from his local draft board in 1941 informing him that he had been selected for induction into the U.S. Army.

Throughout Walter's training stint in Georgia and California, Freida and her husband, like so many young couples at the time, had to grapple with the difficulties in their relationship born of the demands made by the wartime emergency, military service, and white racism. Walter Greene's stateside training meant time away from his wife, siblings, and elderly parents. So it fell to Freida Bailey to keep the family going. Throughout 1942 and 1943, she spent much of her time traveling the considerable distances between Detroit and the Georgia and California training centers to see Walter and to keep him abreast of news affecting his family and hometown community. In December 1943, she journeyed to Needles, California, to urge her husband to hurry home after learning that Greene's father was dying.

But just as Greene waged "his war within the war" against racial discrimination in the segregated army, Bailey and other black service women, children, and men developed their own responses to the war. During one of her periodic visits to the Mojave Desert area, Bailey lived with Ethel Tabor, Vera Sarazen, Wilamina Biddieux, and other women whose husbands were training nearby, and they formed a social group. Calling themselves the "Poinsettia Club," Bailey and the other relatives gathered with soldiers on a number of occasions to openly debate the issues that shaped the daily experiences of black GIs and their families. The informal institution the service family members created and the issues and agendas they addressed made a lasting impression on Bailey and the other members of the group. Of the wartime organization they created and the sense of responsibility they felt toward each other as black military community members, she later recalled, "The house we lived in was made up of three boxcars, and it was important to the fellows because this gave them a chance to drive in every Saturday night, catch up on family news, and talk about things that happened in the division without worrying about being brought up on charges."[2]

The wartime experiences and recollections of the Greenes are more instructive than those of World War II GIs and families presented in other works because they illuminate the complex nature of the 93rd Infantry Division's campaign and the paradoxical struggles of African Americans who lived on the home front during the wartime period. On appearance, division personnel and their family members and friends bear only a slight resemblance to the group theory analyses of recent studies. For example, once arriving at a military base, new recruits— all sporting different hair and clothing styles—are marched off to a nearby supply depot and barbershop where they undergo a change in appearance upon which they all seem rather indistinguishable from each other. But appearances can be deceiving. While the recruits might appear the same, they are still fully embodied human beings, possessing a range of economic, work, social, family, and folk backgrounds as diverse as the regions from which they came, the military occupational specialties to which they are later assigned, and the wartime aspirations they express and hope to translate into action.

This book is not intended to be a traditional military history; rather, it examines the social experiences of black 93rd Infantry Division GIs and service-related communities and their relations with the U.S. military during the wartime period. Using archival records, oral histories, and personal correspondence, it explores the political and cultural boundaries of the African American presence in the 93rd Infantry Division during the Second World War and the extent to which both identity and community shaped the parameters of the black experience in the segregated army. In many ways, the experiences of the men who served in the 93rd Infantry Division epitomize the political motivations, purposes, and objectives that framed the black experience in general in World War II. First, the unit was the first segregated division created in that war and was composed of white senior staff officers and African American junior officers. Owing to the wartime emergency, nearly 55 percent of its nearly 20,000-man enlisted corps were draftees; they came from Texas, New York, Florida, California, Pennsylvania, South Carolina, West Virginia, and Illinois. Consisting of the 368th, 369th, and 25th Infantry regiments and an assortment of field companies, battalions, and special service units, the division saw limited action in the Pacific during World War II and spent much of its time relieving other units as they advanced toward the Philippines during the latter stages of the war. For much of the war, the unit was relegated to noncombat roles, and the accounts of its wartime contribution have been written from the standpoints of War Department officials and social scientists—people who were more interested in assessing the unit's combat performance, the racist connotations of army discipline and efficiency, and the degree of racial contact between black and white soldiers than in exploring the human element of the Jim Crow army during the period.[3] As a consequence, the perspectives of black servicemen themselves and the ways in which black enlisted men and officers constructed their identities as soldiers have been obscured.

Even groundbreaking works on the contributions made by black soldiers in U.S. history have not explored the attitudes of black service personnel and their families toward military service and citizenship and the ways in which their perspectives coincided and competed with state institutions like the armed forces and civil society.[4] Thus, instead of a fully constituted soldier whose identity is shaped by race, gender, class, and generation, we are presented with a soldier who is largely disconnected from American society. By shifting the perspective away from questions of combat efficiency and race relations, *Fighting for Hope* allows one to gain a fuller understanding of the making of African American soldiers during the Second World War and its immediate aftermath.

Second, the multifaceted dimensions of black World War II political culture and the class, gender, and spatial fissures within it have been muted in unity aphorisms and golden age sentimentality. For example, most scholars have used concepts such as "greatest generation," "watershed moments," and "double victory" in interpreting African American battlefront and home front attitudes and behavior during the Second World War.[5] However, these terms obscure, rather than reveal, the realities of wartime struggle. The experiences of black servicemen in the segregated American army and of their family members and military-community friends suggest that their thoughts and actions fluctuated widely according to time, place, and circumstance and were far more complex than we have ever imagined. For black 93rd GIs and their kith and kin, physical battles and struggles for dignity were fought on the same terrain: that of white racism and class antagonism. And although the conduct and character of black soldiers in the division came under fire from many policymakers and senior army officials, the unit also attracted widespread support from the white cadre of the segregated army during the period. Furthermore, just as the war and military service provided the vehicle through which broader discussions regarding democracy and citizenship could take place, they also reinforced the social hierarchy within African American society at the time.

What's more, the relationship between the state and African Americans during World War II as presented in most social histories dealing with wartime black political activism looks different when viewed from the vantage point of African American GIs and their loved ones. For example, although many policymakers within the War Department remained deeply committed to long-standing segregation policies with respect to black soldiers, they disagreed widely over how the measures were to be implemented during the wartime period. The resulting cleavages within the segregated army allowed African American GIs and service-related communities to frame, interpret, and define the contours of their World War II experiences in their own terms. For Walter and Freida Greene and other 93rd Division families and friends, however, efforts to negotiate and contest the shibboleths of Jim Crow society did not end with battles of World War II but continued well into the postwar period, against the ever-changing montage of twentieth-century American life. Indeed, the relationship between the state and the men who made up the 93rd Infantry Division and their loved ones is as much a portrait of grassroots political struggle and its victories and defeats during the war as it is a story of the emergence of the civil rights movement of the 1950s and 1960s.

Encompassing the fields of African American history, military history, and gender and sexuality studies, *Fighting for Hope* examines the ways in which black GIs in the 93rd Infantry Division shaped the boundaries of their World War II experiences; it does so by illuminating the conflicting encounters between the GIs, American society, and the state during the war and in its immediate aftermath. Reflective of W. E. B. Du Bois's incisive analysis of the African American struggles for equality in 1943, these relations, I contend, were tempered by experience and infused with hope as each group embraced opposing visions of citizenship. Nowhere was this tenuous connection more apparent than in the unique political worldview that informed the thoughts and actions of the black 93rd GIs who toiled in the training areas and theaters of operation during the wartime period. Created in black neighborhoods and communities long before they entered the military, this critical worldview was bound up in notions of race and gender and served as a vital conduit through which issues regarding American democracy and citizenship were openly discussed and hotly debated.

By the end of the 93rd Division's campaign in World War II, a political strategy enveloped in household and community concerns was dialogically fused with the barracks experiences of black GIs to form a unique political culture that reaffirmed their identities throughout their military experiences. The combined political perspectives of black soldiers and their families and friends were employed to negotiate and contest the state power and the images that senior army commanders, Roosevelt administration officials, and American society held of African Americans in uniform. And at the same time, the political culture devised by black 93rd servicemen and their loved ones, friends, and neighbors both challenged and reinforced notions that black spokespeople and organizations held of them as "African American fighting men." Once the shooting war ended, black 93rd veterans refashioned this worldview as they struggled to make sense of the social and political challenges that African Americans faced during the Cold War years of the late 1940s and the emerging civil rights movement. Indeed, throughout the immediate postwar period, this perspective carried contradictory and (in some instances) tragic consequences for the former servicemen and their families.

Fighting for Hope begins with an examination of future African American 93rd Division servicemen during the years of the Great Depression in order to firmly situate them within the worlds from which they came and the hopes they held for the future. Chapter 1 documents the political context in which the initial encounters between black 93rd GIs, American society, and the state had taken place. Chapter 2 focuses on the American mobilization during World War II and charts the attitudes of young African Americans regarding America's foreign involvement and their prospects for military service. It also illuminates the public debate that ensued between black civic and political leaders, labor and civil liberties groups, the Roosevelt administration, and military officials over the possibility of allowing African Americans to enter the ranks of the army. Chapter 3 reconstructs the stateside training experiences of black service personnel while division members were assigned to Fort Huachuca, Arizona.

Part Two illuminates the social and political contexts in which African American 93rd Infantry Division soldiers and their families articulated their visions of American citizenship and where their views stood in relation to the explosive soldier-civilian confrontations of 1943 and the insistent clamoring among segments of African American society to make full use of black troops in the armed conflict. This portion of the narrative illustrates the complexities of the public debate over the employment of black GIs. Adjusting the analytical lens a bit, Chapter 4 chronicles the development of local service-related groups, church organizations, medical societies, and newspapers among relatives of the division members in order to examine the manner in which the attitudes expressed by the family-community networks regarding American citizenship both coalesced and clashed with the views held by division members at the time. Chapter 5 documents the social and political debate that took place between black 93rd GIs, American society, and Washington officials over the eventual deployment of the division and the unit's movement to the South Pacific theater of operations.

Part Three focuses on the ways in which the social and political experiences of black 93rd Division members in the Pacific theater of operations reshaped their perspectives of race, citizenship, and American society. Chapter 6 chronicles the initial combat experiences of black 93rd GIs in the Solomon Islands and the discussions that black civic and political leaders and organizations and Washington officials held over their participation in combat and subsequent battlefield performances during the spring and summer months of 1944. It also demonstrates how the physical presence of black troops in uniform had both reconfigured and reinforced the army's and American society's racial and gendered markings of black bodies during various stages of the overseas campaign. Through a close examination of a chain of controversial events that occurred in the Southwest Pacific during the spring of 1945, Chapter 7 analyzes how race, sex, and international politics engulfed African American service personnel and their families.

Exploring the postwar lives of 93rd Infantry Division soldiers, the epilogue steps away from the narrative momentarily and discusses the extent to which the worldview developed among black veterans during the war changed yet again as veterans struggled to reestablish relationships with family members, neighbors, and friends. At the same time, their perspectives regarding state power, race relations, and gender conventions expanded beyond their immediate households to challenge the workplaces, schoolrooms, veterans administration offices, and statehouses of post–World War II America as American society and the state struggled to make sense of the enlarged claims to first-class citizenship that were being advanced by black 93rd servicemen from various parts of the country. As the epilogue demonstrates, however, the political culture that was born during the wartime emergency and the enlarged claims to citizenship that it engendered proved to be short lived as 93rd Division veterans found themselves facing subtle yet far more devastating forms of racial, class, and gender oppression during the latter half of the twentieth century.

Finally, I would like to say a few words about how the writing of unit histories as case studies might provide the "missing" chapters in a larger work reassessing the black World War II past. Many recent studies have documented the black experience in World War II, and several have drawn comparisons between the experiences of black GIs in the World War II Asian-Pacific and European theaters of operations.[6] These works have greatly facilitated our understanding of the African American experience during this momentous period. But not until we pay closer attention to the relationship between the activities of specific service personnel in particular locales and the communities and neighborhoods in which they lived and labored will we even come close to a more comprehensive portrait of the black World War II experience.[7] Then and only then will we be able to properly evaluate African Americans' contribution to the winning of the war.

PART ONE

THE CRUCIBLE

I desperately wanted to help my family and decided, if necessary, to join the army after high school graduation and
help with an allotment of pay. But my father strongly objected saying: "The army will corrupt you and turn you into
a beast; besides I need you to help on the farm." After much
praying and soul searching, I decided to slip away from
home without my father knowing. It took careful planning
and confidential coordination.

George M. Shuffer Jr., 1999

CHAPTER ONE

The Great Depression and African American Youth Culture

I think of the blessings that have come to American youth through the programs of the National Youth Administration and the Civilian Conservation Corps, displacing delinquency and crime by the green pastures of education and work. What has happened to Negro youth in a program like this? Thousands who have been asleep in shiftlessness and despair have been awakened to a life of usefulness and hope. No, "we'll never turn back no more," to the apathy of indifference; to the growing disintegration of youthful dreams and visions.

Mary McLeod Bethune, 1939

In 1934, 19-year-old Leo Logan faced an unsettling future. Born in Leavenworth, Kansas, in 1915, Logan was raised in a poor working-class family, his mother struggling to support him after the death of her husband and three children. After Leo graduated from high school in 1933, he spent much of his time working an assortment of jobs, ranging from short-order cook to custodian. Finding work in Leavenworth, a town that was deep in the throes of the Great Depression, was most difficult for the teenager: "The first job that I had was unloading sand from a railroad car on a hot Kansas summer day, which was hot, dusty, and sweaty work," he recalled. After failing to secure steady employment, he entered the Civilian Conservation Corps in 1934 and was able to send a portion of his monthly pay to his mother.

Although sketchy, Logan's experience in the CCC had long-term implications. He was deeply influenced by the military regimentation in the CCC, regaling in the wearing of uniforms and the sense of purpose within the organization. Furthermore, he was so deeply touched by the rhythmic tramping feet of his neighbors who marched in the Citizens' Military Training Camp parades held each summer that he entered the camp in 1937. He participated in the CMTC for two years while he attended Ottawa University. Yet despite his penchant for military training, Logan challenged the racist aspects of the segregated army and had frequently participated with other corps members in attempts to improve their treatment and working conditions. In his efforts to elicit a modicum of respect from the white cadre in the CCC and the CMTC, Logan faced charges of insubordination on numerous occasions after he protested against racial indignities of Jim Crow military life. He eventually enlisted in the army at Fort Leavenworth in 1941. Recalling his decision to enter the military years later, Logan stated, "I wasn't particularly patriotic and I volunteered for the service because I figured that I would be drafted sooner or later."[1]

Logan's pre-war experiences offer a window into the social and political spaces that young black people occupied during the Great Depression. Alarmed by the growing numbers of unemployed African Americans, federal government officials and civic leaders sought to direct black youth into military-like programs such as the Civilian Conservation Corps, the Citizens' Military Training Camps, and the Army Reserve Officers' Training Corps. For Leo Logan, however, organizations like the CCC were more than just a source of employment: they provided instruction in military training. To be sure, these organizations marked a transitional phase between the Great Depression and World War II for this generation of young Americans. But one must remember that the regional, race, class, and gender cleavages present in American society at the time also shaped these programs. Upon entering these organizations, young black men struggling to make sense of these issues in society at large also confronted them in the military-structured formations in which they stood. So in many ways the experiences of Leo Logan and others during the 1930s were, as Mary McLeod Bethune has explained, forged in both "despair" and "hope."[2]

The Civilian Conservation Corps

The life histories of young African Americans like Leo Logan were deeply mired in the economic crises of the 1930s. Between 1925 and 1930, the labor participation rate for black working-age males (those between 16 and 24) declined from 85 percent to 82 percent. By 1940, the proportion dipped even lower, to 67 percent, reflecting a loss of thousands of positions in the agricultural, service, and industrial sectors due to whole-scale layoffs and firings.[3] Although illuminating, these figures minimize the economic woes that African American youth faced during the 1930s.

But when examined more closely, relief figures enumerated for the mid-1930s tell another story about black youth unemployment. In January 1935, the Social Research Division of the Works Progress Administration reported that the number of black working-age males (those from 16 to 24) constituted approximately 36 percent of the 2,877,000 unemployed workers in the nation, reflecting a rate higher than that of all other working-age groups.[4] Furthermore, nearly 29 percent were on relief in urban areas, compared with just 14 percent in rural places.[5] By October, the numbers of unemployed black youth in rural areas dipped to 625,000 as many blacks were transferred from the Federal Emergency Relief Administration to the Resettlement Administration. In northern and midwestern industrial states like Michigan, New York, and Pennsylvania, the percentage of black youth nearly trebled their representation in the workforce.[6] In the District of Columbia, Georgia, Louisiana, North Carolina, South Carolina, and Texas, nearly 45 percent of the young black population received some form of relief.[7] By 1937, the percentage of young black relief recipients in metropolitan cities like Los Angeles, Chicago, Cincinnati, St. Louis, Chattanooga, New Orleans, and Cleveland hovered between 11 and 32 percent, reflecting a percentage close to or slightly above their proportions in the total population.[8]

These conditions made an indelible impression upon 17-year-old Henry L. Williams. Born and raised in a poor working-class family, Williams struggled to make a living after his parents died, working as a dishwasher, bellman, elevator operator, waiter, and chauffeur. When the depression hit Cleveland, he recalled, "there were very few opportunities for college." "So I worked as many jobs and as often as I could manage." Eventually landing work as a life insurance salesman, Williams continued to struggle until he was drafted into the armed forces in February 1941.[9]

Meanwhile in the rural hinterlands, the magnitude of black youth unemployment was greater. Working largely as agricultural and unskilled wage laborers in rural southern regions characterized by a feudal sharecropping system, low wages, and deplorable living conditions, future 93rd Division service personnel toiled with family members on nearby farms, planting and picking cotton, tobacco, berries, and vegetables during the summer and winter months throughout the 1930s. But once the harvest season ended, black youth, like their fathers, had little choice but to seek work in textile mills and coal mines in nearby cities and towns, often unable to gain employment. Such was the experience of 13-year-old

Raymond Jenkins. Born into a poor working-class family in 1924, Jenkins left his home in Memphis to roam the countryside in search of work. Hoping to supplement his mother's earnings as a domestic, Jenkins, who had previously landed work as a delivery boy and cotton picker, abandoned his search after failing to secure employment. In search of better employment opportunities, Jenkins made his way to Detroit, where he was drafted in 1943.[10]

As he entered the Motor City, Raymond Jenkins and other future division personnel stood at the doorway of a new life. Between 1933 and 1939, a small segment of future 93rd Division personnel participated in segregated CCC companies scattered throughout the country. Many black youth who were attracted to the wide array of opportunities that the CCC offered in early 1933 were denied entrance, however, despite the measure specifying that there would be no discrimination on the basis of race, color, or creed. Operating under the aegis of the departments of War, Agriculture, Interior, and Labor, the Veterans Administration, and CCC director Robert Fechner, CCC state agents and army corps area commanders adopted policies that restricted the selection of black enrollees to approximately 10 percent of the total enrollment; reflecting the proportional ratio of African Americans in the entire U.S. population.[11]

In some ways, paramilitary organizations like the CCC served as the midwives to the World War II experiences of many 93rd Infantry Division members. In March 1935, the army recruiting officer in Berks County, Pennsylvania, had refused to accept previously selected black enrollees, claiming that there "were no vacancies for colored men."[12] When Roy Wilkins of the National Association for the Advancement of Colored People and other leaders questioned the Labor Department's selection of blacks for the CCC on these occasions, personnel enrollment head W. Frank Persons, the CCC director, and War Department officials assured them that no discrimination of recruits had taken place while at the same time continuing to select them as replacements in all-black contingents—a clear violation of the nondiscriminatory clause in the CCC law.[13] Selection policies varied widely, however. Although selection agents in states such as Texas, New York, Georgia, Florida, Arkansas, Mississippi, and Alabama were reluctant to enroll an equitable proportion of black applicants, the enrollment of African Americans in South Carolina climbed to well over 35 percent in 1933, 10 percent more than their proportion of the state's population.[14] Yet by December of that year, there were only 15,425 black enrollees among the 279,300 enrollees in the CCC, less than 6 percent of the total enrollment.[15] To make matters worse, Civilian Conservation Corps officials followed local racist mores and practices and restricted black enrollees largely to isolated camps and areas throughout the country.

Between 1933 and 1934, approximately 1,514 black youths toiled in sixteen seg-regated CCC companies throughout the Third Corps area, composed of Virginia, Pennsylvania, Maryland, the District of Columbia, New Jersey, and Delaware.[16] Yet War Department and CCC officials experienced tremendous difficulties es-tablishing black camps throughout the Fourth Corps area because of local in-transigence. Fourth Corps area commander General George Van Moseley refused to place many black companies after receiving some criticism. For example, Mose-ley and other War Department officials changed their plans to place an all-black camp near an exclusive resort area previously closed to black residents in North Carolina after white locals protested loudly against the initiative in July 1935. Re-sponding to the rising tide of public criticism, Fechner advised the army to place black enrollees only in their states of origin.[17] As the CCC continued throughout the 1930s, this policy was strictly followed. As late as 1939, for instance, when lo-cal residents protested against the placement of a black camp in Ohio, War Depart-ment officials transferred it to South Bend, Indiana.[18] To further lessen public hos-tility, Fechner told the army to place some black companies at Fort Benning, Fort McClellan, and Fort Bragg, where they performed valuable conservation work.[19]

But for black youth who hurdled the bureaucratic obstacles of institutional racism and discrimination, the Civilian Conservation Corps offered vast em-ployment opportunities, vocational education, and a chance to challenge the im-balance of power that had circumscribed their lived experiences to that point. In CCC camps in Pennsylvania, for example, black youth linked race-conscious vi-sions of the past with their present-day concerns by adopting company names such as Charles Young, in honor of the first African American West Point grad-uate; Robert L. Vann, for the famous newspaper editor; and Paul Laurence Dun-bar, after the noted black poet.[20]

The race consciousness of CCC camps as well as efforts to evade poverty and unemployment held special significance for Percy Roberts, a future 93rd Division member. Born into a poor family in Lincoln, Illinois, in 1914, Roberts had first learned of the CCC while making his living as a butler for a prominent local farmer and industrialist after graduating from high school. In July 1934, he went to Chicago, where he applied for CCC selection at the Cooke County Relief Administration office. Because he had done so well in the preliminary interviews and examina-tions, Roberts was recommended for CCC selection days later and was assigned to Company 605 of the all-black CCC Skokie Valley Camp located near Glenview, Illinois. Roberts and other camp members, who were largely natives of Chicago's South Side, planted hundreds of acres of trees and constructed dikes, roads, and telephone lines. For his labor, he, like other CCC workers, received $30 a month, of which $25 was sent to supplement his mother's and father's earnings as a do-mestic and chauffeur, respectively. After work, Roberts participated in athletic and recreational activities such as baseball, softball, basketball, and boxing and took trips to Evanston. And it was in the ordered ranks and timed executions of regu-lation drill and after seeing the army reserve officers that Roberts became inter-ested in a military career. After spending three arduous years in the CCC, Roberts promptly enlisted in the army in 1937, arriving at Fort Huachuca, where he was assigned to the 25th Infantry Regiment, one of the triangular units of the 93rd Infantry Division. Recalling his CCC experiences, Roberts noted, "The CCC was a good preliminary move prior to joining the army, but I went in to help my fam-ily out who was struggling."[21]

The military overtones that held Roberts's attention were typical for CCC camps during the period. Although scholars have pointed out that War Department officials had not attempted to militarize the New Deal program because of an acute awareness of critics who were suspicious of their intentions, elements of military life may have pervaded its organization and administration.[22] Specifi-cally, discipline was emphasized: corps members wore uniforms, performed vari-ations of regulation drill, and were supervised by Regular Army or reserve cap-tains and first lieutenants. For example, when approximately 226 men between 18 and 25 years of age poured into Fort Howard, Maryland, during the spring of 1933, they received extensive training in military discipline under the watchful eyes of army officers. During the two-week period, they were issued green uni-forms, assigned to training units and barracks, learned to march to and from work in platoon formations, and had every free minute of their leisure time sched-uled. Although officers were white army personnel, camp leaders were selected from among the ranks by the men themselves to administer discipline. Shortly afterward, the recruits marched off to reserve station camps deep in the Mary-land forest.[23]

In January 1938, Eugene Boykin of the NAACP argued that black enlistment in the CCC should be encouraged because black youths needed to be educated as "citizens." "Merely to give youths employment in useful tasks, however that may be, is not enough," he stated.[24] Four months later, CCC educational director Howard Oxley wrote the adjutant general, arguing that "citizenship courses" should be in-augurated because "this would stem the radicalism of those who make trouble in the camps." Emphasizing camp responsibility, Oxley went on to argue that such courses "would make the men respect their superiors and reduce the total num-ber of desertions within the CCC." The U.S. Office of Education adopted this pro-posal, which was hardly contested, in July 1938.[25] As CCC participants received courses in "citizenship," black leaders and CCC officials made every effort to limit working-class identification within the companies.

Yet a strange irony emerged during this period. While CCC camp officials tried to stem "radicalism" among black youths, messages of race and class consciousness were communicated through the educational courses they received and the nature of the work they performed in the camps. Between 1933 and 1935, black CCC camp members at Texas's Camp Sam Houston, Illinois's Camp Skokie Valley, and Kansas's Camp Lone Star who later served in the 93rd received courses in African American history as well as vocational instruction from educational advisers.[26] Throughout Illinois, Pennsylvania, and Maryland, CCC workers read articles published in the *Chicago Defender,* the *Pittsburgh Courier,* and the *Baltimore Afro-American* that called attention to working conditions in other camps, and they were able to link their own working struggles to elements of the labor process that revealed themselves elsewhere. Facets of work culture were adopted as CCC company leaders were called foremen and directed the manual labor of their subordinates. In late 1934, for example, a company of CCC workers at Pennsylvania's Camp Benezett chose Pittsburgh-born Odell Edwards as their foreman and planted trees and bowers under his leadership. Edwards also assisted the camp commander in administering discipline, admonishing members when they violated camp regulations.[27]

Interestingly, camp officials and foremen promulgated discipline in the CCC in ways similar to those used by the armed forces—from the top down. And like army personnel, CCC workers who violated company regulations received administrative and dishonorable discharges. In 1933, for instance, six black workers were arrested and incarcerated for disorderly conduct, and thirty-four others were sent back to Harlem with dishonorable discharges after they rebelled against the rigid disciplinary measures of camp authorities in Preston, New York.[28] Two years later, CCC laborers at White Haven, Pennsylvania, received dishonorable discharges after they left the work site to protest against its deplorable living conditions.[29] Meanwhile, Percy Roberts witnessed fellow members of his Skokie Valley's CCC encampment express their discontent over camp conditions with their feet: close to four hundred received administrative and dishonorable discharges from the CCC for "absences without leave."[30] And in August 1940, twenty Skokie Valley enrollees were given dishonorable discharges after they refused to leave the mess hall to protest over the poor food they received.[31]

Intra-racial class cleavages in black-supervised camps also surfaced when CCC workers disagreed with the labor policies of their superiors. At Camp Benezett, CCC workers were given dishonorable discharges in October 1935 after they attempted to organize their fellow company members against Commander Oscar Pindle's running of the camp area, particularly the poor condition of the food and the heavy tasks they were required to perform.[32] In late 1938, twenty-three CCC workers revolted against the poor food and working conditions in a segregated camp located near Camp Skokie Valley. To make matters worse, tensions in the camp heightened when foreman A. W. Underwood dismissed the demonstrators as "Northern Negroes thinking themselves better than Southern Negroes." The protest ended several days later when camp authorities dismissed the black enrollees and transferred them back to their homes on Chicago's South Side.[33] The alarming number of CCC protests in the Skokie Valley area led Illinois District investigator Harold G. Chafey to express these thoughts: "It is the opinion of the undersigned that the camp does not have a complete enough orientation program."[34] Shortly afterward, CCC educational advisers included orientation classes among their subjects of instruction.[35] Despite the efforts made by CCC officials and camp administrators to stem discontent among CCC enrollees, however, the total number of AWOLs in the Skokie Valley area surged from 340 days lost in 1940 to 358 a year later.[36]

The army's role in the CCC and the labor processes that existed in the New Deal organization did not escape the attention of future 93rd Division members like William Fentress. Born in 1918 into a poor working-class family in San Antonio, Texas, Fentress entered a CCC camp near Fort Sam Houston, Texas, after graduating from high school in 1936. It was during his work building roads, planting trees, and toiling on wood-cutting details in the arid Texas heat that he came to realize the close relationship between civil and military policy—specifically, when he witnessed fellow company workers organizing to revolt against the insufficient amount of food being served in the camp. Recalling his experience years later, he stated, "My first job after high school was that of a CCC worker doing various jobs of common labor, and it was there that I got a vague idea of what military life could be like." "The CCC, like military service, was hard work, and I was neither proud or [sic] ashamed of it."[37]

The Citizens' Military Training Camps

The decade prior to World War II also witnessed the training of many young black men as members of the Citizens' Military Training Camps. Created during the Preparedness Campaigns of 1915, the CMTC was aimed at young people and linked military training to citizenship. Between 1935 and 1940, thousands of working-class youths attended the nearly one hundred Citizens' Military Training Camps scattered across the country. Similar to those who served in the CCC, black young men in the CMTC found themselves standing face to face with the class system of the military as they also tried to improve their material conditions. Just getting through the CMTC was a feat in itself, since great emphasis was placed on discipline and mental and physical fitness. What's more, black youths who applied and qualified for the CMTC's basic course in the Third and Ninth Corps areas had to be physically capable residents of Pennsylvania, Maryland, Virginia, the District of Columbia, and western states between the ages of 17 and 24. In addition, applicants faced stringent literacy and moral requirements. Once accepted by the CMTC corps area headquarters, applicants were encouraged to continue on to the intermediate (red) course only after they received an acceptable rating during the military training camps held during the summer. Once an applicant completed the required correspondence courses and graduated from the advanced (blue) course, he appeared before a board of Regular Army officers, at which point he had to take an examination on military tactics and military organization. Successful candidates received commissions into the U.S. Army Reserves.[38]

But as recruits soon learned, the process appeared more attractive on paper than in its application. From the moment the more than 250 black recruits from Washington, D.C., Virginia, Pennsylvania, and Maryland arrived at the Citizens' Military Training Camp at Fort Howard, Maryland, they were put through the physical and mental rigors of military training. During the thirty-day training period, they received extensive physical examinations from army medical personnel. They were also given crew haircuts; were issued gray uniforms, serial numbers, and equipment; and lived in tents. Officers from the 428th Infantry Reserves put black youths through a strict regimen of calisthenics, regulation drill, inspections, roll calls, kitchen duty, and various organized activities, scheduling every minute of their leisure time. On the firing ranges and during elementary tactics held near the bivouac areas, the cadre appealed to the intestinal fortitude of the enrollees.[39] As one young black enrollee noticed during his CMTC training, the "officers did not believe in half-stepping; cadets had to either come hard with it or not come at all."[40]

More often than not, leadership at the CMTC mirrored the class-status structures that existed in African American society. The officers who were assigned to Fort Howard read like a who's who of the Washington, D.C., metropolitan area. Among the camp officials were West Hamilton, a public school teacher and member of the city board of education, and Howard Queen, a Spring Garden Institute instructor.[41] Also among the black elites who made up the officer corps was

Claude Ferebee, a Columbia University–trained dentist and future standout 93rd Division medical officer. Born in 1901 in Norfolk, Virginia, Ferebee had received his B.S. degree from Wilberforce University in 1923 before he established himself as a prominent physician in Washington, D.C., as well as a faculty member in Howard University's School of Dentistry during the early 1930s. From 1932 to 1940, he opened and operated his own practice in the Northwest district while serving in the 428th's dental reserve. Shortly afterward, Ferebee received orders to report to Fort Devens, Massachusetts, for training with the U.S. 366th Infantry before joining the 93rd Infantry Division in May 1942.[42] A major proponent of racial solidarity, ethnic pride, and equality, Ferebee envisioned his service in the pre–World War II army as an extension of his services to the larger community. Describing his CMTC experience years later, he would articulate what many 428th reserve officers must have felt: "I had hoped to vindicate the cause to children and myself as well as to the profession which I represented and fostered."[43]

CMTC training was very popular among black youths in the Third and Ninth Corps areas. Most of the youths who attended the CMTC noticed the collective spirit that emanated throughout the camp. Particularly, the CMTC made a lasting impression upon teenagers like Benjamin Hunton. Born in 1919 in Washington, D.C.'s Northwest District, Hunton attended the CMTC after graduating from Dunbar High School in 1936. In the Citizens' Military Training Camp held that summer, he witnessed not only numerous episodes of racial class division and paternalism among his superiors but also elements of racial solidarity and spiritual uplift. Furthermore, Hunton found the unbending discipline and the self-empowering presence of the camp cadre so much to his liking that he completed the CMTC requirements, earning commission in the U.S. Army Reserves in 1940, a year earlier than scheduled. After graduating that same year, Hunton continued his education at Howard University in pursuit of an M.A. degree until he was called to active duty in March 1942.[44]

Others had more vivid memories of the camps. John Howard grew up in the Northeast District of Washington, D.C., where his father worked as Pullman baggage handler. After his father died, his mother continued to support him from her meager earnings as a domestic. In 1938, 15-year-old Howard attended the CMTC summer camp at the behest of Armstrong High School military science instructor Colonel Alonzo Ferguson, an officer in the 428th Infantry Reserves. The CMTC training and its similarity to army life so impressed Howard that he subsequently immersed himself in the correspondence courses, completing the requirements in 1940, more than two years earlier than army regulations allowed. After earning his commission a year later, he continued his education at Miner Teachers

College before being ordered to active duty in April 1942. CMTC summer camp allowed Howard "to fire heavy weapons such as the machine gun for the first time." "The black lieutenants who commanded the units were so clean cut and highly respected that I realized right then that this [military life] was for me."[45] As one of the nearly two hundred CMTC participants at Fort Riley, Kansas, during the period, St. Louis, Missouri, resident Reuben Fraser expressed similar sentiments: "The officers at the CMTC Camp at Fort Riley, Kansas, were so admirable that it was then that I started to think about the military as a career."[46]

Although not all the experiences of young CMTC participants were similar, the examples set by the all-black reserve officers who lived in their communities had a direct influence on the young men's later World War II service. It was through these officers that young working-class black men from Washington's Northwest District, the southern neighborhoods of Richmond, Virginia, and Philadelphia's West Germantown first became acutely aware of the linkages between African American national and local community concerns in a military setting. Yet, at the same time, the class inequalities they experienced in civil society were being reproduced in the CMTC. Furthermore, as many young black CMTC enrollees tried to emulate the reserve officers, they also felt alienated from their own communities. While participating at the CMTC camp during the summer of 1938, Howard recalled visits from several *Philadelphia Afro-American* and *Pittsburgh Courier* journalists to Fort Howard. During their visits, the reporters interviewed the several reserve officers about the CMTC but never bothered to talk to the young enrollees about their experiences.[47]

The Army Reserve Officers' Training Corps

As the storm clouds of war gathered in Europe, Africa, and Asia in 1939, programs such as the Reserve Officers' Training Corps also shaped black youth activity and served as a forceful instrument for self-empowerment for many young African Americans. Throughout the 1920s and 1930s, high school cadet detachments operated in high schools scattered throughout Chicago; Gary, Indiana; and Washington, D.C. In Washington, for instance, an average of 649 boys between the ages of 12 and 17 enrolled in Junior ROTC courses in Dunbar, Armstrong, and Benjamin Cardozo high schools alone.[48] There they received instruction in close-order drill, playing brass instruments, physical exercises, map reading, tactical problems, and first aid. Once a year, members of the high school cadet corps attended a two-week camp where they put into practice what they learned in the classroom under the scrutiny of officers from the U.S. 428th Infantry Reserves and the National Guard on days that normally ran from 5 A.M. until 9 P.M.

As in the CMTC, business and professional people dominated the instructorships in the Junior ROTC, reflecting a collapsing of civilian and military discipline. For example, high school military instructors like Alonzo Ferguson and Vance Marchbanks convinced young Washington, D.C., students that they received tangible benefits from military training. From 1919 to 1940, Ferguson, a career 428th Infantry reserve officer, had trained his students in the nuances of military science, emphasizing ethnic pride and individual responsibility. In the classroom and at summer bivouac sites, he appealed to Armstrong cadets to "strive to maintain the highest standards no matter what the adversity." Such encouragement struck a chord among young blacks in the ranks. By early February 1942, Ferguson would witness the nearly two hundred of his former students who were called to active duty emerge as the key platoon leaders in the major combat units of World War II.[49]

Dunbar High School cadets received similar instruction in military science from Captain Marchbanks, a career army officer of thirty-nine years. Marchbanks was major advocate of the Washingtonian principles of citizenship, hard work, and racial solidarity. He wrote to the NAACP in 1934 that military training provided the essential key to the final attainment of social and political equality by African Americans: "You and I know that the Negro needs training in citizenship and that is what he gets in the army." "We cannot hope to get economic, political, and social justice in civic affairs unless we are willing to accept responsibility in the scheme of our national defense."[50] Although one cannot determine whether this was a true patriotic impulse or political posturing, such views made an indelible impression upon future 93rd veterans. In the words of one former Armstrong High School cadet, "These men, more than anyone else, greatly influenced our direction early in our lives."[51]

But as the 1930s drew to a close, African American involvement in military organizations was not just restricted to Junior ROTC units. Many young black men who later served in the U.S. 93rd Infantry Division were enrolled in regular ROTC units at Lincoln University in Missouri, Wilberforce University in Ohio, and Howard University in Washington, D.C. As freshmen and sophomores, they were required to receive up to three hours a week of instruction as a prerequisite for graduation. Only one of these institutions, Howard University's ROTC, had somewhat steady enrollments, however. In 1927, at the height of the Reserve Officers' Training Corps movement, the Howard University ROTC detachment attracted an average of 359 and 34 cadets in its basic and advanced courses, respectively.[52]

By 1938, budgetary cutbacks and decreasing student enrollments at Howard University led to a 20 percent decline in the average number of basic course cadets. Yet an interest in military careers continued to grow among black youth throughout the late 1930s. Although the average number of basic course students in the Howard University ROTC program decreased, the average class enrollment of cadets selected for the advanced course increased to forty-one annually.[53] Meanwhile, the late 1930s witnessed a flurry of activity at black educational institutions that did not have ROTC programs as attempts were made to establish military detachments. In March 1937, John W. Davis waged a campaign to persuade West Virginia senator M. M. Neely to support West Virginia State College's bid for an ROTC unit. This movement resulted in a congressional resolution creating an organization less than a year later.[54]

In 1938 and throughout most of 1939, ROTC instructors placed a great deal of emphasis upon cultivating a complex sense of race and national loyalty among the cadet corps. In black ROTC detachments at Howard University, for example, cadets received government-issued gray uniforms and formed a battalion consisting of four companies. During the autumn and winter quarters of 1938 and 1939, an average of fifty-one cadets spent twenty hours a week attending lectures given by former reserve sergeants and warrant officers on African American history, military theory, and "citizenship" and performing variations of regulation drill. As winter faded into the spring of 1939, cadets received all their instruction from class-elected cadet captains who put them through the paces of physical exercises and military training.[55]

Like other military programs described above, the main focus of the Reserve Officers' Training Corps was military camps. At summer camps held at Camp Meade, Maryland, in 1940, selected ROTC members received instruction in firing various types of weapons, tactical warfare problems, and close-order drill while living in conditions that closely resembled those that existed in the Regular Army. Under the tight reign of Colonel Charles E. Howard, cadets observed the military oath, received crew haircuts, and endured endless bouts of physical and emotional stress. Camp officers, who were selected from among the cadets, supervised various group competitions and company punishments in order to force individuals to place the well-being of their companies above their own. The small coterie of officers selected to oversee camp operations during the summer of 1938 was an unusual group of individuals who inspired the corps of cadets by offering self-styled renditions of "John Brown's Body" and employing colorful language to exhort their fellow members to unprecedented levels of racial unity, manhood, and physical strength. After one exhausting afternoon of tactical training,

17-year-old Walter Sanderson, a Washington, D.C., resident recalled, "I heard some of our company members complain that they were not going to make it, but I pleaded with them that race men don't quit and called them Goldbricks to their faces." "Somehow, damn it, they all made it." The son of a schoolteacher and a career police officer, Sanderson had initially entered the Howard University ROTC in 1939 with great deal of apprehension. But the officer training camp that summer had changed all that; by June 1941, he soon graduated from Howard University with a B.S. degree in mathematics while simultaneously earning a certificate of commission into the 428th Infantry Reserves. Shortly afterward, Sanderson worked for a Washington, D.C., post office before being called to active duty in 1943.[56]

Another young man who held an ROTC leadership position that summer and who hoped to gain a U.S. Army Reserve commission was Washington, D.C., resident Vincent Browne. Born in 1917, Browne entered the Howard University ROTC program to fulfill a lifelong dream of being in the military and at the same time pursued a degree in government under the tutelage of noted political scientist Ralph Bunche. After earning a commission in 1940, Browne worked as research assistant for the Carnegie Corporation in New York before heading to Harvard University. There he continued his studies until he was called to active duty in March 1942. "I was always interested in military things," Browne recalled. "Howard ROTC enabled me to win a commission after I was unable to gain entrance into West Point."[57]

Browne's interest in the military, however, was also accompanied by a stronger sense of racial and class unity. In August 1940 Browne had penned an article in which he linked Jewish struggles against the Hitlerian threat in Europe and the Chinese rejection of Japan's call for a "New World Order" in Asia to the African American struggle for equality at home. He excoriated "the smug complacency of the Negro intelligentsia and the 'high-brows' of Negro society" and pointed out that "a heterogeneous state is most vulnerable to the vitriolic attacks of racial theorists if one of its groups lives in a state of social ostracism and economic depression." "The defense of a race against tactics of race hatred at home cannot be estimated in terms of guns and other instruments of warfare, for great issues are seldom settled on the battlefield . . . we must have a type of unity which has never been known before."[58]

In the months that followed, young black men like Vincent Browne had come to realize that their people's struggles had taken on an international dimension. The very nature of the Great Depression years of the 1930s forced African American youth to see the new decade through lenses tinged with multiple layers of consciousness. And as German troops proceeded to launch their assault on Europe with lightning force in 1940 and Americans looked on from afar, the attitudes of young black men toward military life were rooted in neither patriotism nor civic duty but were instead deeply enveloped in their efforts to scale the racial and class boundaries that had long existed in the country. So as the prospects of American involvement in the European conflict drew near, young African Americans found themselves standing face to face with ambivalent War Department policymakers who needed their participation in the war effort but questioned their fitness for duty and the communities that nurtured their worldviews. Indeed, the stage upon which the wartime encounters between these groups would take place was now set.

Why Should I Fight?

Black Morale and War Department Racial Policy

Throughout the entire literature on Negro morale, most writers
have noted the difference between the status system which fixes
the Negro's position, on the one hand, and his freedom to compete
socially, economically, and politically, within certain spheres of
social life, on the other. The question which faces every Negro
policeman and soldier, is "Am I a Negro first and then a policeman
or soldier second, or should I forget in any emergency situation the
fact that my first loyalty is to my race?"

Horace Cayton, 1941

As an individual the Negro is docile, tractable, lighthearted, care
free and good-natured. If unjustly treated, he is likely to become
surly and stubborn, though this is usually a temporary phase. He is
careless, shiftless, irresponsible, and secretive. He resents censure
and is best handled with praise and by ridicule. He is unmoral,
untruthful and his sense of right doing is relatively inferior. Bad
leadership in particular is easily communicated to them.

The Employment of Negro Troops, *1966*

The Great Depression experiences of black youth coincided with the growing
American involvement in foreign affairs during the late 1930s. By the early 1940s,
the linkage between their growing international awareness and their pre-war circumstances produced a variety of attitudes among young African Americans regarding possible American foreign involvement and the prospects of military
service, ranging from an enthusiastic race-conscious participation in U.S. initiatives in Europe and Asia, to indifferent feelings toward American war aims and

military service, to, finally, outright opposition to "fighting in another white man's war." Although some, like George Shuffer, perceived a possible stint in the army as a means of improving their material conditions in American society, others saw military service itself as a punitive institution. These divergent and sometimes overlapping attitudes manifested themselves along class, generational, and regional lines. And as the probability of American involvement in the war became more likely during 1941, many black males of draft age agonized over the question "Why should I fight?" As Horace Cayton so eloquently noted in one of the epigraphs to this chapter, a paradox of loyalty dogged the thoughts and actions of black youngsters at almost every turn.

Meanwhile, Roosevelt administration and War Department officials faced an equally serious dilemma. Between 1922 and 1938, army planners had conducted numerous studies that advocated the segregation of black troops and called for the proportional representation of black males to be the same as that in the general population of the country. Using World War I as a benchmark, these studies denigrated the intellectual capacities of African Americans and the leadership capabilities of black officers. And as a result, army policymakers relegated black troops to service support duties and imposed strict limitations on the number of black officers. But with the passage of the Selective Service Act of 1940 and the unprecedented nature of the presidential election that year, army officials found themselves facing rounds of criticism from many parts of African American community after it released its utilization plans in September 1940. In response to public pressure, War Department officials made many policy revisions. By the end of 1941, one of the decisions reached by army planners resulted in the creation of the U.S. 93rd Infantry Division. And as numbers of prospective black citizen-soldiers of the division began to descend on the training camps of the segregated army, most were well aware of the peculiar nexus of military racial policy and political expedience that would shape their encounters with American society at large and the federal government.

Discussions of War and Race

Even though most African Americans in the United States stood on the brink of economic collapse during the 1930s, black residents in cities and towns all over the country expressed a variety of opinions regarding events overseas. Communities that focused on American foreign policy expressed their interest with varying degrees of race consciousness and nationalism. For example, throughout the early 1930s, hundreds of blacks in Chicago, New York, Cleveland, and the District of Columbia participated in programs of the Universal Negro Improvement Association, an organization founded by Jamaican activist Marcus Garvey which advocated the formation of an independent black nation in Africa and offered a trenchant assessment of Europe. Led by Amy Jacques Garvey, the *Negro World* and UNIA leaders denounced the European and American involvement in Asia and Nicaragua.[1] This racial interpretation of international politics was not lost on prominent black intellectuals. After examining the impact of the UNIA in Chicago's South Side neighborhoods during the period, sociologist St. Clair Drake pointed out, "While the majority of the people in the Chicago Negro community were never enrolled in the Black Internationale, there is little doubt that a large segment of the community was sympathetic with the movement and followed it with interest."[2]

In the mid-1930s, news from Africa grabbed the attention of various segments of the African American community. In October 1935, Italy invaded Ethiopia, the only independent country in Africa during the period, and few blacks could ignore the international implications of the event. Ethiopia was one of the wealthiest nations on the continent and in many ways held a key place in biblical prophecy for African Americans.[3] Owing to efforts made by the Ethiopian ambassador to the United States, more than 115 African Americans migrated to the country.[4] In a matter of days, members of the black press, black churches, and civic organizations in New York, Chicago, Los Angeles, and Philadelphia rallied to the cause of Ethiopia and raised money for supplies and medical aid. In New York, more than a thousand members of the clergy, led by Abyssinia Baptist Church pastor Adam Clayton Powell, held prayer vigils for Ethiopia, and the newly formed Committee for Ethiopia distributed peace petitions to protest against the war.[5] In August, the International Council of Friends of Ethiopia was formed, and its executive secretary, Willis N. Huggins, traveled to Europe, where he sought without success monetary as well as military aid for the country from the League of Nations.[6] UNIA locals and cults in New York headed by Prophet K. Constonie, Father Divine, and Emmett Parker developed songs, slogans, and banners embracing the defense of Ethiopia.[7] And in Chicago, former UNIA members played an active role in both the Ethiopian World Federation and the Peace Movement of Ethiopia, expressing their dissatisfaction over the Italian invasion of Ethiopia.[8] Indeed, the interest among black African Americans in the conflict was so strong that one observer remarked that "no other event in recent times stirred the rank-and-file of Negroes more than the Italo-Ethiopian War."[9]

In late 1935 and early 1936, events that occurred in the United States as well as in Germany and other countries of central Europe attracted the attention of black communities in Philadelphia, Chicago, Cleveland, and New York. After knock-

ing out Max Baer during the fall of 1935, boxer Joe Louis continued his phenom-
enal rise, defeating a string of opponents and becoming the idol of many African
Americans as well as increasing the circulation of many black newspapers, particularly the *Pittsburgh Courier*. Specifically, black intellectuals and artists could not
help but notice the sentiments of ethnic pride and racial solidarity that Joe Louis
aroused in African American communities throughout the country. Moments after
Louis's victory, Richard Wright, later a prominent black author, described the actions and thoughts expressed by residents who lived on Chicago's South Side:

> Five minutes after the words "Joe Louis—the winnah" were yelled and Joe Louis'
> hand was hoisted as victor in his four-round go with Max Baer, Negroes poured out of
> beer taverns, pool rooms, barber shops, rooming houses and dingy flats and flooded
> the streets. "LOUIS! LOUIS! LOUIS!," they yelled and threw their hats away. They
> snatched newspapers from the stands of astonished Greeks and tore them up, fling-
> ing the bits into the air. They wagged their heads. Lawd, they'd never seen or heard
> the like of it before. They shook like a revival. Really there was a religious feeling in
> the air. Well, it wasn't exactly a religious feeling, but it was something, and you could
> feel it. It was a feeling of unity, of oneness.[10]

In many ways, Louis's victories served as a tangible means of refuting the racist
ideologies of African American inferiority that were being circulated both at home
and abroad. But most important, Joe Louis himself served as a benchmark in the
lives of some young African Americans who later entered military service. At the
time, longtime St. Petersburg, Florida, resident Frank Little had moved to South
Philadelphia, where he made a living as a budding professional boxer. Struggling
to make ends meet during the lowest depths of the Great Depression, Little recalled, "There were few jobs to be had and men, in fact whole families, wandered
across the country hunting for work." "I couldn't find a job and made do with what
I had." After heeding the advice of a neighbor who was a retired army sergeant
to "join the army," Little ventured west, heading to Fort Huachuca, Arizona, in
the hope of entering the 25th Infantry Regiment, eventually landing slot in that
regiment's H Company. After Little's first professional fight in Chicago, he met
Joe Louis and the two men became close friends. Describing Louis years later, Little recalled, "He was just a humble man and he was unfailing in his kindness
toward those around him." When Louis suffered his defeat at the hands of Max
Schmeling, Little remembered, "It was the most devastating news that I had heard
up to that point." "I can't recall when I had ever seen so many black men depressed
over anything." Louis's budding professional career would continue to resonate
in Little's life long after he entered the army. Less than five years later, the two

men renewed their friendship when the army assigned the Philadelphia resident to Louis as a trainer while the heavyweight champion served in the military during the early 1940s.[11]

The linkages between racist ideologies exposed by Adolf Hitler and the treatment of blacks within the United States also resonated with future 93rd servicemen, but in different ways. Reubin Fraser, who had first learned about the Nazi plan for African Americans while attending Sumner High School in St. Louis, he expressed no fear or hatred of Germany. "The way the Germans were operating was similar to the way blacks were treated in this country." "The cycle was complete as far I was concerned." Issues of social mobility, racial uplift, and self-empowerment dominated Fraser's life decisions relating to military service more than anything else, however. After attending the Citizens' Military Training Camp at Fort Riley, Kansas, from 1935 to 1938, he opted for military service despite objections raised by both his uncle, a World War I veteran, and his father. Fraser subsequently immersed himself in CMTC correspondence work while attending Lincoln University in Jefferson City, Missouri, during the late 1930s.[12]

Nelson Peery's perceptions of the events were rooted in a different past and an alternative view of the present. Peery was born in 1923 into a working-class family in Junction City, Kansas. His mother was the granddaughter of Kentucky slaves, and his father, a World War I veteran, was the son of a Kansas dirt farmer and a regular subscriber to the Communist Party's *Daily Worker*. Peery had grown up hearing endless stories about his family's efforts to maintain their dignity under the vestiges of slavery and about his great-grandfather, who had joined the Union army to secure his family's freedom. He also grew up hearing daily discussions among his neighbors about the Communist Party's efforts to free the nine black youths involved in the Scottsboro incident and had witnessed the ravages of the Great Depression firsthand as a hobo "riding the rails" from Junction City to Los Angeles. And in Wabasha, Minnesota, he observed countless bouts of racism and violence, but he also saw clear examples of ethnic pride and black solidarity.

Yet it was only after his family moved to Minneapolis in the mid-1930s that Peery found himself drawn to the Communist Party and its international vision for equality, employment, and social programs. Although he had never joined the Young Communist League, his consciousness of the party's struggles was raised to even greater heights through his acquaintance with feminist activist Meridel Le Sueur while participating in a neighborhood discussion group composed of university students, mill workers, and self-educated intellectuals. By the time Germany invaded the Soviet Union in 1941, 17-year-old Nelson Peery was fully aware of the national and international implications of that event: "I had to do something about it. The Soviet Union was all we had. If it was defeated, there was nothing left to defend us. You must understand, they would have hanged the Scottsboro boys if it weren't for [the] Soviet Union telling the whole world about it. They would've driven us back to slavery or worse." Peery promptly signed up for the Citizens' Military Training Corps in June 1941 and was ordered to report to Fort Riley, Kansas, a month later.[13]

In contrast, young tenant farmers like George Shuffer paid very little attention to international events, as the daily struggle to provide a meager existence for their families dominated their thoughts and activities. Residents of Palestine, Texas, Shuffer and his family roamed through Anderson County in 1936 in search of work after a series of poor crop yields pushed his family's farm to the brink of foreclosure. Shuffer recalled his indifference regarding world events: "I was so busy those days that I paid little attention to events that were occurring in Washington, D.C., . . . let alone what was happening in Europe." By 1940, however, Shuffer saw a sliver of opportunity in the ashes of despair. He graduated from high school and elected to enter the army even though he had received academic scholarships from Mary Allen Junior College, Lemoyne College, and Pennsylvania's Lincoln University. Throughout the late 1930s and early 1940s, Shuffer's allotment check of ten dollars a month, along with the checks earned by his two older brothers, who were also in the army at the time, provided the only meaningful sources of income for his family.[14]

African Americans across the country reacted in various ways to the outbreak of war in Europe in September 1939 and the German invasion of the Soviet Union in June 1941. During the first weeks of the European war, their initial responses ranged from cynical isolationism to rabid patriotism. George Schuyler, a noted columnist for the *Pittsburgh Courier*, expressed his belief that there were great similarities between the German invasion of Austria and British colonialism in Africa. "The war is a toss-up," Schuyler claimed in his newspaper column, and the Harlem-based Negroes Against War Committee urged blacks throughout 1939 and 1940 not to become interested in the events overseas. "Why should Negroes fight for democracy abroad when they are refused democracy in every American activity except tax paying?" they argued.[15]

Isolationist views were expressed by other prominent black individuals and groups across the political spectrum. For example, a member of the political Left, George Padmore, justified isolationism with this criticism: "If the British government or the French government were sincere in their war rhetoric, let them extend Democracy to their colonies."[16] Recalling bitter memories of World War I, many members of the American Communist Party and the Socialist Workers Party saw the European crisis as an imperialist war, and they urged blacks to oppose military and economic aid to Britain and France. For example, on 14 November 1939, twenty-two thousand members of the Communist Party met at a rally in Madison Square Garden to celebrate the twenty-second anniversary of the Soviet Union. During the celebration, party members heard speeches given by Earl Browder, general secretary of the party, and James W. Ford, the party's vice presidential nominee, excoriating both Britain and France. Arguing that the war to save democracy was futile, they concluded that there were forces in the United States that aimed to destroy the civil liberties of African Americans before the country became involved in the war and that the European war was being fought for the control of colonial peoples.[17] In a pamphlet entitled *Why Negroes Should Oppose the War,* noted Afro-Caribbean scholar and activist C. L. R. James argued that no matter who won the war, blacks would continue to face discrimination, police brutality, and poverty worldwide.[18] What's more, between 1939 and 1941, publications such as the *Annals of the American Academy of Political and Social Science, Scribner's Commentator, PM, Common Sense, People's Voice, Opportunity,* and black newspapers carried articles with captions such as "Should the Negro Care Who Wins the War?"; "Should Negroes Save Democracy?"; "What Have Negroes to Fight For?"; "Is This a White Man's War?"; and "A White Folks' War?"[19]

Black leaders specifically compared the Nazi racial policies of Adolf Hitler to racism in the American South. In a feature article in the *Chicago Defender* titled "Blitz over Georgia," sociologist St. Clair Drake and editor Enoch P. Waters offered a stinging critique of American racial relations as well as a sympathetic view of conditions in Nazi Germany. In their description of a possible invasion of the state of Georgia by German forces, they described the racial politics that evolved around the use of bomb shelters in southern cities: "No provisions for Negroes were made in white sections of the city. Many persons were killed running from the white to the colored sections of the city for safety. A story is being told here of a maid who ran past seven shelters in the white section of the city on her way to the black belt. A few minutes after she entered one of the Negro shelters it was struck by a bomb and she, with many others, were killed."[20] Less than six months later, Roy Wilkins of the NAACP penned an editorial in the *Crisis* that compared the white supremacist doctrine in the American South to the Nazi racial theory of blacks, highlighting their similarities. Even *Opportunity,* the otherwise conservative journal of the National Urban League, pointed to the comparisons.[21] Many black leaders felt that there was little difference between German and American racial policies. For example, when asked by a teacher in early 1942 whether conditions would be worse under Hitler, a young student at a prominent southern black college promptly answered, "They can't possibly be any worse than they are for Negroes in the South right now."[22] The morale of African Americans on the eve of Pearl Harbor was such that sociologist Horace Cayton noted, "That the Negro might be treated even worse than he is now by a victorious Germany does not seem to worry numbers of black Americans."[23] Although the sentiments expressed by Drake, Waters, and others may appear a bit extreme, they reveal the degree of disillusionment among segments of the African American community regarding the racial attitudes in the United States.

Still other black leaders and intellectuals saw a possible German victory in an even harsher light and advocated a different choice for African Americans: involvement in the fight for democracy. In September 1939, *Philadelphia Afro-American* columnist William Jones expressed his belief that a possible German invasion of the Western Hemisphere would result in the placement of African Americans in concentration camps, a greater degree of racial segregation, and the complete elimination of black newspapers and cultural institutions. "Once in power, Hitler could bring these things about by the stroke of a pen," Jones claimed.[24] In March 1940, Ralph Matthews of the *Baltimore Afro-American* railed against African American indifference to the fighting in Europe. "We perhaps do not know that we are faced with a fate almost worse than death itself," he wrote.[25] In mid-1940, A. Philip Randolph joined the Committee to Defend America by Defending the Allies after he had formerly been a member of the pacifist Keep America Out of the War Congress. Urging blacks to support military and economic aid to Great Britain, Randolph later argued that, "without democracy in America, limited though it be, the Negro would not have even the right to fight for his rights."[26]

Many of the wide-ranging views expressed by Randolph and other African American leaders across the country regarding the U. S. involvement in the European war stemmed from the debates surrounding black military service throughout 1939 and much of 1940. Before Germany extended its westward plunge into Denmark, Norway, the Netherlands, Luxembourg, and Belgium and Congress initiated debate on the Selective Service Act in 1940, segments of the black community held their own discussions regarding the matter, connecting it to other aspects of racism and poverty that blacks faced in the United States. In January 1937, prominent black leaders and spokespeople gathered in Washington, D.C., to attend a conference sponsored by the National Youth Administration on the problems of "the Negro and Negro Youth." Following three days of reports and open forums on matters affecting African American life such as education, health, housing, tuberculosis, lynching, disfranchisement, and civil rights in the District of Columbia, the group also examined black participation in the armed forces, resolving to demand proportionate representation at all levels within service branches as well as admission to the service academies.[27]

About a year later, *Pittsburgh Courier* editor Robert L. Vann penned an open letter to President Franklin Roosevelt, launching a campaign to remove existing racial barriers within the armed forces. Vann demanded equal representation for blacks in the armed forces and called for the creation and maintenance of an all-black squadron and infantry division.[28] Adopting a pragmatic stance, he opined that although black taxpayers furnished money for battleships, submarines, cannons, airplanes, rifles, and soldier's pay, they were being excluded from the various branches of the armed forces such as the Army Air Corps, the Signal and Tank Corps, the Corps of Engineers, and the Marines. An infantry division of fifteen thousand African American troops commanded by black officers, he reasoned, would "be one way for Negroes to get back some of the vast sums they pour into military budgets as taxpayers and inspire black American youth to share the benefits of service."[29]

Vann's 1938 campaign for greater military representation by blacks reflected the anxieties he and other black leaders expressed regarding the dismal state of affairs with respect to African Americans in the armed forces during the interwar period. Between 1931 and 1940, blacks accounted for fewer than 4,000 of the 118,000 men in the Regular Army as vacancies and promotions became extremely rare in most segregated units.[30] Thus, for many African Americans, entrance into the U.S. Armed Forces was next to impossible during this period. Stationed at Fort Benning, Georgia; Fort Huachuca, Arizona; and Fort Riley and Fort Leavenworth, Kansas, the four black regiments—the 24th and 25th Infantry and the 9th and 10th Cavalry—were reduced to grooming horses and performing other fatigue duties.[31] Furthermore, few opportunities to gain a commission in the Regular Army existed for black aspirants, as only one African American, Benjamin O. Davis Jr., had graduated from West Point between 1920 and 1940. Only five black commissioned officers were in the Regular Army—two line officers and three chaplains.[32] African Americans accounted for fewer than 400 of the 100,000 officers in the organized army reserves and were largely products of ROTC training at Howard and Wilberforce universities.[33] Finally, in the few National Guard and reserve units that survived during the pre-war period, such as New Jersey's 1st Battalion, New York's 15th, Massachusetts's 3rd Battalion of the 372nd Infantry, and Illinois's 8th Infantry, blacks received very little peacetime training and faced the constant threat of disbandment or conversion into labor organizations.[34]

Throughout much of 1938, the *Pittsburgh Courier* surveyed thousands of its readers for their opinions of Vann's proposal, and the black weekly's efforts proved to have been of great importance for several reasons. First, the survey sparked a fierce public debate over the nature of black participation in national defense, arousing a flood of responses from black teachers, labor organizers, members of the clergy, social workers, and urban and rural working-class youths across the country. Their comments tended to reflect myriad class and regional distinctions. For example, whereas President Ormonde Walker of Wilberforce University and NAACP executive secretary Walter White favored total integration, other segments of African American society as diverse as leaders of the Southern Negro Youth Congress and Howard University secretary-treasurer Emmett J. Scott supported Vann's proposal for an all-black squadron and infantry division for various reasons.[35] During the second annual meeting of the Southern Negro Youth Congress, held in Chattanooga, Tennessee, that year, nearly four hundred delegates pledged their support for the *Courier* campaign calling for greater representation in the army and navy. Linking the fascist ideologies of Germany and France to racist practices in the South, members of the Southern Negro Youth Congress heard national secretary Edward Strong claim that black youths in the South should have equal opportunity to participate in the national defense program along with all other rights of citizenship. "The worst scourge that we face today is fascist barbarism, waging war against democratic civilization, it is brazen in its disregard for the rights of man, destroys culture and has raised the mythical idea of racial superiority."[36]

Not long afterward, the *Courier* campaign reached the halls of Congress. In April of that year, Emmett J. Scott, Robert L. Vann, Oscar De Priest, George Schuyler, and Eugene Kinckle Jones formed a steering committee after New York congressman Hamilton Fish introduced three bills for greater black representation in the armed forces in the House Committee on Military Affairs.[37] The bills called for an end to discrimination in the army and navy by asking for the opening of all branches of the armed forces, an annual appointment by the president of two blacks to West Point and Annapolis, and the creation of an all-black army division. After months of rallying support for the measure, the bills died in the House Affairs Committee in October, as President Franklin D. Roosevelt, ranking committee members, and the NAACP failed to provide adequate encouragement.

Undaunted, the *Courier* formed the Committee for Participation of Negroes in the National Defense to work for the inclusion of blacks in the military establishment during the following year.[38] Its members included NAACP special counsel Charles Houston, *Pittsburgh Courier, Baltimore Afro-American,* and *Chicago Defender* correspondent Louis Lautier, and Rayford Logan. Throughout the 1939 and 1940 congressional debates on the size of the national defense program and the

Selective Service Act, CPNND members clamored loudly for greater black participation in the army by testifying before the House Committee on Military Affairs and the Senate Military Appropriations Committee, lobbying key members of Congress, working closely with the NAACP, and organizing local branches and committees throughout the country.[39] In September 1940, the CPNND leadership persuaded Congressman Hamilton Fish to introduce CPNND-sponsored legislation on the House floor.[40] Although Fish's amendment was defeated, the organization's efforts reached fruition when Congress passed Public Law 783, which contained two antidiscrimination provisions proposed by New York senator Robert Wagner.[41] Its legislative victory proved to be short lived, however. As Rayford Logan noted in his diary later, CPNND members felt that "the Wagner Amendment was virtually meaningless, because it outlawed discrimination only in cases of voluntary enlistment."[42] Furthermore, the question of whether land and naval forces would accept African Americans remained unresolved.[43]

The CPNND's campaign coincided with other efforts to achieve black self-determination within the armed forces, however. During late 1938 and early 1939, the NAACP continued its call for total integration, and the National Negro Insurance Association and the Southern Interracial Commission adopted measures against the army's policies regarding African American servicemen. At its April 1938 annual meeting, held at Tuskegee Institute in Alabama, members of the National Medical Association's executive board voted to endorse the *Courier* campaign as a part of the association's fight for greater black representation in the army's Medical Corps. After days of discussion of issues including the eradication of syphilis, greater opportunities for postgraduate study for black physicians, and the establishment of a national college of black surgeons and physicians, board members authorized chairman William McKinley Thomas to contact the president of the United States and Congressman Andrew J. May, chairman of the Military Affairs Committee, informing them of the association's decision.[44] As an outgrowth of their efforts, National Defense Committees established various subcommittees throughout the states that coordinated their efforts with the national body. Throughout much of the late 1930s and early 1940s, the National Medical Association, along with other black professional groups, employed a variety of tactics to dismantle the Jim Crow practices and white supremacy within the armed forces.

"Greetings": Black 93rd Youth and the Selective Service

Meanwhile black communities across the country expressed a variety of opinions regarding the status of African Americans in the armed forces. When the

Philadelphia Afro-American conducted a survey on compulsory military training in Philadelphia and Baltimore during the summer and fall months of 1940, fifteen black males of draft age responded positively for various reasons. Some stated that it afforded the best means of protection for black soldiers in the event of war. Others expressed the hope that their participation would enhance the political, economic, and social status of blacks in the country. Yet approximately 30 percent of 250 young African Americans interviewed in North Philadelphia and the southeastern sections of Baltimore opposed the idea, basing their arguments on the discrimination that had been practiced in civil society and the U.S. Army.[45] For example, one Baltimore native responded, "I do not favor it because I don't think colored people have anything to fight for." "They ought to take those who enjoy the privileges of this country." Several young Philadelphia residents expressed their opposition to the draft measure, stating that the discrimination they faced precluded any commitment to military service.[46] In Detroit, Michigan state senator Charles Diggs told members of the St. John Colored Methodist Episcopal, St. Peter African Methodist Episcopal, and Calvary Baptist churches that unless African Americans were accepted for training in all branches of the military service, they should refuse to fight if the United States entered the European war. "It is high time that the colored man wake up and tell America, in no uncertain terms, that we are not going to be targeted in a scientific conflict without knowing something about the science of war," Diggs argued.[47]

During the initial stages of the Selective Service Act, more than 1.8 million black males registered, reflecting roughly 14 percent of the total African American population. However, registration totals varied widely by area because of regional and rural-urban differences in population. For example, the percentage of black male registrants between the ages of 21 and 35 in the Midwest and Great Lakes region (Ohio, Illinois, and Michigan) who registered on 16 October 1940 and the percentage of blacks who registered in the Northeast (New York, Pennsylvania, and New Jersey) were remarkably similar, fluctuating between 5 and 6 percent of their total populations. In Chicago alone, nearly 500,000 black youths registered with their local boards, reflecting 14 percent of the city's black population.[48] During the July 1941 registration drive, more than 82,000 draft-age blacks entered the national lottery, reflecting 9.8 percent of their proportion in the general population.[49]

To be sure, efforts to create self-empowering strategies that had been made throughout much of African American society during the national defense debate motivated many future 93rd Division members. But for most of them, military service epitomized the ultimate dilemma that black youth faced at the time—

namely, how to remain close to grassroots efforts to secure democratic rights at home while maintaining a healthy distance from military service. Many of their thoughts and actions about the registration process provide examples of this conundrum. In Cleveland, for example, Thomas White had befriended a member of the all-black Cedar Avenue draft board in Ward 19 in the hope of gaining an occupational deferment. White supported the black struggle to gain equal treatment in the armed forces but was apprehensive regarding his own possible entrance into the military. "I had no desire to go into the army because the military was seen as a form of punishment," he recalled. "It was something to avoid." White's efforts were fruitless, however. Less than a year later, he received a letter from the same draft board informing him that he had been selected during the ward's first drawing in 1941 after he was given a 1-A classification. But after undergoing basic training at Fort Huachuca three weeks later, White developed a liking for military life and was selected for Officer Candidate School at Fort Benning, Georgia. Shortly afterward, in 1942, he was assigned as a lieutenant with a company in the 368th Infantry before being transferred to the 25th Infantry Regiment.[50]

Thomas White was not the only future 93rd Division member to express such sentiments. In North Carolina, where black draft-age males constituted approximately 28 percent of the state's total registrants, Asheville native Willard Jarrett approached his draft board with a great deal of foreboding. "Registering is when I first knew for sure that the possibility of military service was no joke." Jarrett's apprehensions regarding military service probably had more to do with his background and boyhood images of the military than with anything else. Born into a middle-class family in 1925, Jarrett grew up in a family with a long history of military service; his father, a contractor's assistant, had served as an enlisted man during the First World War, and his brother had spent some time in the U.S. Navy. "The armed forces was something that my father and brother used to discuss all the time," he recalled. "They resented the treatment of Negroes in it, but didn't try to persuade me either way." In less than a year, Jarrett dropped out of college and enlisted in the army, which assigned him to Fort Bragg in North Carolina; in August 1943 he received orders to report to the 93rd Division.[51]

Meanwhile, many African American men faced the immediate prospect of either being drafted or ordered to active duty. During the initial stages of the Selective Service process, the number of young black men notified for induction was 96,000, less than 5 percent of the total African American male population eligible for induction.[52] By the end of 1942, the figure nearly quintupled to 420,000, or 23 percent of the total population.[53] Many black youths expressed very little concern over the Selective Service process, however, because of the logjam caused by the War Department's system of racial quotas. Throughout 1941 and 1942, nearly 28,000 blacks were passed over. In midwestern and northern industrial centers, approximately 8,000 black registrants were selected, but thousands more awaited induction while the armed forces worked to build separate training facilities and train cadres.[54] In southern areas, the number of black registrants awaiting induction notices from local boards may have been higher. In southern states located within the 4th Corps area, more than 6,000 black selectees waited to be placed in army units, as less than 1 percent of the area's black population eligible for the draft received induction notices.[55]

In March 1941, nearly 200 black youths from Chicago reported to the 122nd Field Artillery Headquarters to be inducted after months of delay.[56] During the first waves of the induction process, local boards in cities throughout the Midwest and Great Lakes region, like Toledo, Columbus, and Milwaukee, called up hundreds of young black men who reported to army reception centers only to be told to wait for the creation of new units.[57] The backlog in the racial quota system became more apparent in the District of Columbia as selected African Americans awaited orders for induction while some 1,100 white men were called.[58] In New York, more than 900 black selectees who were drafted in January 1941 were sent home because of construction delays at Fort Devens, Massachusetts, where they were slated to receive basic training courses. Indeed, between January and September 1941, only 4,449 blacks were in the army. By early 1943, Selective Service officials estimated that approximately 300,000 blacks awaited induction after being notified of their selection.[59]

After receiving their induction notice, however, thousands of 93rd black youths finally faced the sobering possibility of military service. Nearly 400 black youths who lived in Cleveland's Seventeenth Ward appeared at the U.S. Army Induction Station at Central Armory, where they received extensive physical examinations and endured a battery of questions posed by psychologists about their relatives, work ability, and schooling. Shortly afterward, more than 70 percent of the inductees were shipped to Fort Huachuca, Arizona, after undergoing basic training at Indiana's Fort Benjamin Harrison.[60]

Among the selectees who stood in line for the army's physical examinations at the time were Charles Rabb, Milton Carnes, Carney Reynolds, James Hutchins, Thomas White, Henry Williams, and Clarence Gaines, all of whom became prominent members of the U.S. 93rd Infantry Division. After hearing unflattering stories about the treatment of African Americans in the army and growing increasingly aware of the mortal dangers that military service presented, each selectee expressed varying degrees of ambivalence and foreboding as he contemplated what he was going to do. For instance, although Clarence Gaines was reluctant to leave his job as a bellhop at a prestigious Cleveland hotel, he didn't want to avoid the draft. "I had no feelings one way or the other regarding the army," Gaines recollected. "I felt overwhelmed by the selection process until I realized that most of my friends had been summoned as well."[61]

Other black Clevelanders also linked their decisions to answer the call to service to ties of friendship. When Frank Smith, an erstwhile life insurance salesman, received the letter from his local draft board notifying him of his selection, he remembered thinking, "Since my buddies were signing on, it wouldn't be too bad." Smith was assigned to a company in the 368th Infantry in February 1941.[62] When Cleveland-born Henry Williams was drafted at the time, he also had not given much thought initially to its significance. Recalling his reaction to the letter he received from the local draft board on that fateful day, Williams stated, "I came home from a hard days' work as a cab driver, and there was a letter which read 'greetings' . . . , but I never thought much of it because I didn't know anything about soldiering." However, Williams's next statement reveals a few anxieties that he may have had over his impending military service. Referring to the tenure of service regulations of the 1940 Selective Service System, he remembered, "I didn't want to go, but after talking it over with my friends, I figured that I would do the one-year stint in the service and that would be it."[63]

The support networks that Williams and other future division members forged among close friends reached their fullest expression in their surrounding neighborhoods. For example, in efforts to assuage apprehensions felt by black recruits after they were inducted, black post members of the American Legion held farewell dances for them in the East End Community Center throughout the early months of 1941.[64] During the same period, nearly 100 black former National Guardsmen gathered at the Central Armory for entertainment provided by a Cleveland citizens committee as they prepared to leave for induction centers scattered throughout Ohio.[65] When nearly 200 inductees were called up a year later, they were cheered by hundreds of Clevelanders who crowded the streets leading to Union Terminal Station, delaying their departure for more than an hour.[66]

The activities of the black community in Cleveland in support of its selectees were hardly unusual. In Baltimore, where nearly 160 black youths received their draft orders in November 1941, members of the city branch of the NAACP provided free legal advice for the men before they headed to Fort Meade, Maryland.[67] After nearly 70 black men in Georgia's Fulton and DeKalb counties were summoned to a Fort Benning reception center during August 1941, they attended farewell parties given by neighbors and friends, where they heard toasts and lectures on topics relating to national defense.[68] When Jefferson County, Alabama, inductees reported to Birmingham's Terminal Station, policemen on motorcycles and a local high school marching band escorted them to the Negro Masonic Temple, where they listened to addresses given by prominent black city leaders and World War I veterans, notably Parker High School principal W. B. Johnson and NAACP branch president E. W. Taggart, urging them to "uphold the traditional fearlessness of the Negro soldier." Yet these speeches also exposed the class dynamics within Birmingham's black community as prominent black leaders used the event as a political and social vehicle to reaffirm their self-assumed positions of authority as well as to influence the innermost feelings of the young black men regarding military service. For example, Johnson told the audience, "Yours is the opportunity to prove that democracy is not dead." "If you are proud, so are we whom you represent." Shortly afterward, the black inductees marched down Fifth Avenue, where they boarded railroad cars for the trip to the Fort McClellan reception center. In the audience that day sat Harvey Herndon, Willie Lambert, Henry Jackson, Demus Ingram, and Albert Talley, all of whom entered the ranks of the 93rd Infantry Division.[69]

In contrast, some draft-eligible black men faced public censure when they openly sought to evade military service or to appeal their draft status. Throughout much of 1941 and 1942, draft boards and neighborhoods in major metropolitan cities like Cleveland, Chicago, and Detroit launched extensive searches to locate black youths who refused to comply with the provisions of the Selective Service Act. In Cleveland, for example, Anne Gibson, chief clerk of local draft boards in the Seventeenth Ward, conducted an extensive campaign during the fall of 1941 to round up delinquent inductees and registrants. "Every effort," Gibson declared, "would be made to locate the 'missing' registrants before the Federal Bureau of Investigation were put on their trails." To aid the draft board's search, the *Cleveland Call & Post* carried articles publicizing the names of the men who were sought.[70]

The resistive impulse that Cleveland draft board officials witnessed was not an isolated phenomenon, since many black youths openly opposed the draft order. During late 1940, nearly 500 African American selectees were shipped to labor camps in Jamaica after they were arrested and imprisoned at Leavenworth, Kansas, for refusing to comply with the Selective Service Act.[71] In Harlem and other New York City neighborhoods, draft boards reported high rates of delinquency. Between 1941 and 1943, of the total number of African Americans in New York City who had received their draft notice, nearly 1,000 (19 percent) refused to report to their induction boards. By 1946, the proportion of black draft violators in New York reached 18 percent of the total that were prosecuted and imprisoned throughout the war.[72]

In May 1943, fifteen black men were prosecuted and imprisoned in Detroit after they refused to register with their local draft boards.[73] Appearing before a local draft board in Wayne County, Michigan, at the time was 19-year-old Raymond Jenkins. Like so many black youths, Jenkins had strong reservations regarding his induction. The exploitative labor conditions and racial struggles of his family in the Deep South had a profound impact on his views of military service: "My grandfather [Will Mobley] was a slave in Mississippi, and he used to tell me how the masters used to treat them, working them all day from sunup to sundown." "They had no future, and for me military service was in so many ways similar to things he talked about." "I was sorely tempted to appeal my draft status for an occupational deferment because I couldn't see fighting for something that we didn't have," he recalled. After days of contemplation as well as seemingly endless lectures from his mother and other relatives, however, Jenkins reluctantly complied with his draft orders and was shipped to Fort Custer, Michigan.[74]

Meanwhile, other black youths who later joined the division saw entering the military in a different light. Although their motives varied, virtually all sought ways to maintain control over their own lives. For example, Leo Logan, a Leavenworth, Kansas, resident, decided to enter the army in August 1941 to preempt his being drafted. Logan remembered, "I volunteered for military service to get it out of the way before going back to college." "My number was high, and so I figured that I would be drafted sooner or later." After completing basic training at Camp Wolters, Texas, Logan was chosen for Officer Candidate School at Fort Benning, Georgia.[75] In Maysville, Kentucky, 22-year-old Durward Griffey faced a different set of circumstances. After graduating from high school in 1939, Griffey had spent much of his early adult life laboring in a wide assortment of jobs, most of which were characterized by low wages and horrendous working conditions. Faced with either being inducted into the army or continuing to make his living working at backbreaking, low-paying jobs, he decided to enter military service in February 1941. Recalling his decision, Griffey stated, "I thought it was necessary at that time because I had been unable to find suitable employment." "But I didn't want to be drafted by any circumstances."[76]

Logan's and Griffey's sentiments were shared, more or less, by other future 93rd servicemen. Harlem native Elliotte Williams failed to gain entrance into the U.S. Naval Academy in June 1940 and fully expected to be drafted that winter. Two months later, Williams elected to enter the army's Medical Department and was stationed at the all-black station hospital located at West Point, New York. On his decision to join the army, he recalled, "I thought enlistment would solve my financial problems and provide an opportunity to go to the U.S. Military Academy." After his stint at West Point, Williams was assigned as a noncommissioned officer to the famous all-black 366th Infantry Regiment commanded by West Hamilton, which was then training in Massachusetts. There he abandoned his dreams of attending the army's service academy in March 1942, when he was selected for Officer Candidate Training at Carlisle Barracks, Pennsylvania.[77] John Marshall, 24, a resident of St. Clairsville, Ohio, opted to enlist in early 1941 not only to preempt being drafted but also to evade the drudgery and hard labor of his job as a coal miner. "I thought it was a way of leaving my hometown so I volunteered to get the year out of the way," he recalled.[78]

Still others sought to pursue professional aspirations. Born in Atlanta, Georgia, in 1914, Edward Freeman worked as a principal in a nearby Cobb County public school after earning a degree at Clark College in 1939. In addition, he spent some time as a Baptist minister in a local church with a small congregation. Uncomfortable with his career as an educator and expressing a great deal of concern over the prospect of being drafted, Freeman sought the chance to pursue his ministry permanently. His opportunity came in February 1941 when Colonel William Arnold, chief of the army's Chaplain Corps, announced that forty-five black chaplains would be needed to fill its officer ranks. After agonizing over the decision for nearly a month, Freeman traveled in March 1941 to Hartford, Connecticut, where he joined the army. Recalling his decision, he stated, "I was glad to give up my vocation as a teacher in Georgia's public schools for the opportunity to serve as an officer because I didn't want to be drafted and felt that the Chaplain Corps would greatly enhance my ministry and it did."[79]

While prospective recruits like Freeman worried about their immediate draft notification, young black reserve officers faced different circumstances. Initially, the army's lack of consideration regarding the employment of black officers led many to believe that they would not be ordered to active duty. Their belief was justified. According to the War Department protective mobilization plans of 1937 and 1940, cadres for newly created segregated units were to be drawn from the nearly 340 black reserve officers who occupied grades from colonel to second lieutenant in the cavalry, Quartermaster Corps, and medical and chaplain sections.[80] More than 70 percent of these reserve officers were products of the Reserve Officers' Training Corps from Howard and Wilberforce universities and qualified for duty in primarily infantry units, however, with the remainder commissioned in the medical and dental reserves. As a result, because of the high number of combat support units (engineer, quartermaster, antiaircraft artillery, railroad, and gas supply) proposed under the War Department's plans, when mobilization began in late 1940, no black reserve officers were called to active duty even though their numbers hardly approached the total number of positions in the units officered by black personnel.[81] Even after Roosevelt issued Executive Order 8618 on 23 December 1940, federalizing African American components in the National Guard (the 369th Coastal Artillery, the 372nd Infantry Regiment, and the 184th Field Artillery), and the War Department announced its plans to form an additional black combat regiment the previous month, 150 still remained available for military duty.[82] By October of that year, the 222 black officers on active duty represented only half the total in the reserve officer ranks.[83]

This problem had not gone unnoticed by War Department officials, however. During his ten-month investigation into the status of black soldiers in the army, William Hastie, civilian aide to the secretary of war, noticed that National Guard commanders were reluctant to call up black reserve officers and that many black officer personnel were being relieved of command. Acknowledging the problems that black officers faced, Hastie observed that, "with most Negro troops concentrated in overhead installations, the quartermaster corps, and the Corps of Engineers, there is no policy or plan for utilizing Negroes to command any of these troops." In addition to recommending that black junior officers in the reserve be assigned to reception centers, replacement training centers, and positions related to morale, he advised the War Department to place black officers in branches of the arms and services other than overhead installations.[84]

For the civilian aide, the difficulties that the War Department faced in requisitioning black reserve officers stemmed from the limited number of black units available to them, the minimal numbers of African American prospects in officer candidate schools, and the army's long-standing tradition of racial segregation. He argued that "an extensive training program is prerequisite to the extensive use of Negro officers, yet the absence of extensive plans for their utilization leaves no presently apparent purpose for such an extensive training program and encourages those commanders in the field whose attitudes toward the selection of officer candidates is already conditioned by prejudice against the Negro as an officer."[85] Aware of the attitudes of black youth toward American society and the army, Hastie went on to warn War Department officials that "until the men in our army and civilians at home believe in and work for democracy with fervor and determination, we will not be an effective nation in the face of a foreign foe."[86]

However, many of Hastie's recommendations went largely unheeded. His demands for racial equality and opportunity for black servicemen were anathema to many army planners, and no one within the War Department wanted to abandon the army's racial division of labor. In early November, members of the Personnel Division and the Operations Division examined Hastie's memorandum to the secretary of war and expressed their belief that the army should focus on bolstering the nation's defenses and that the War Department should abstain from involvement in racial and social issues. Chief of Staff George Marshall agreed. Six days before Pearl Harbor, he claimed that Hastie's recommendations would require a social revolution and that this issue was one that he and other War Department officials should avoid at all costs. He wrote Secretary of War Henry Stimson: "A solution of many of the issues presented by Judge Hastie in his memorandum to you on 'The Integration of the Negro Soldier into the Army,' September 22, would be tantamount to solving a social problem that has perplexed the American people throughout the history of this nation. This Army cannot accomplish such a solution, and should not be charged with the undertaking."[87]

Significantly, Hastie's recommendations and the War Department's narrow response to them prefigured the relationship between black youth, sectors of African American society, and the federal government and the public debate over the very employment of African American troops in the wartime army. But the disagreements among army planners over how far the policy of segregation should be extended in the event of war presented yet another side to the relationship, and it is to this dimension that we must now turn.

Dilemmas of Troops and Race

The reservations that most African Americans expressed regarding the war effort, the army, and possible military service stemmed from the Jim Crow practices of the War Department and the branches of the armed forces. Immediately after the First World War, War Department officials began to develop utilization policies regarding black troops. During the early months of 1920, the army's General Staff College disseminated surveys to officers who commanded black soldiers during the war, requesting them to comment on the performances of black personnel and to make recommendations for their use in the event of war. Their responses were largely negative and reflected many of the racial mores of the period. Colonel Charles C. Ballou replied that the use of black soldiers during the Civil War up to 1917 revealed that they were liabilities rather than assets, and he used racist generalizations to suggest that black soldiers be placed in labor battalions and regiments commanded by white officers. Ballou contended that the black soldier "has little capacity for initiative, is easily stampeded if surprised, and is therefore more dependent than the white man on skilled leadership." Reflecting on his own experience as the commander of the U.S. 92nd Infantry Division in Europe, Ballou stated, "I simply forgot that the average Negro is a rank coward" and that "his faults and virtues stemmed from being children of people in whom slavish obedience and slavish superstitions and ignorance were ingrained." Furthermore, he denigrated the performance of black officers and dismissed the performance of the 93rd (Provisional) Division's regiments, claiming that the unit's success were tied to the replacement of its black officers by a white cadre. Advising against the formation of segregated divisions in future conflicts, Ballou recommended that the War Department limit the size of black units to no larger than a regiment.[88]

The other field-grade officers of the 92nd Division reached similar conclusions, employing racial stereotypes and popular sexual myths to demonstrate the lackluster performance of black personnel and to advise against the formation of all-black divisions. Responding to the General Staff College study in April 1920, former 92nd Infantry Division chief of staff Allen J. Greer wrote that "the average Negro is naturally cowardly and utterly lacking in confidence in his colored officer." "Every infantry and other combat soldier should possess mentality, initiative, and individual courage; all of these are, generally speaking, lacking in the Negro," he claimed. Greer went on to recommend the placement of black troops in service, labor, and pioneer units staffed by white officers, warning that organizations commanded by black officers would result in numerous cases of rape similar to those that had reportedly occurred in the 92nd during the war.[89] A white commander of one of the regiments of the 92nd during the war wrote, "My experience confirms in the belief that, with Negro officers, the Negroes cannot become fitted as combat troops." Like Ballou and Greer, he recommended the assignment of black troops to labor and pioneer units no larger than a regiment, arguing that "it would be unwise to place more than one such regiment in a division."[90] One commander of the all-black 368th Infantry claimed that African American soldiers lacked home training and commented that "the average Negro has the mentality of an overgrown child so naturally it takes longer to train them." Advising against the formation of all-black divisions, he argued that no part of the country would permit the assembly of black divisions without protest.[91] Reacting to the General Staff College survey around the same time, former 370th Infantry commander Major Thomas A. Roberts described the officers and enlisted men in the unit as untruthful, lacking in initiative and sense of responsibility, and illiterate. "I favor no larger unit than a regiment," he suggested.[92]

Not all commanders of black troops assessed the performance of black personnel in World War I as a failure. In late March, Vernon A. Caldwell, commander of black units in Cuba, the Philippines, and France, responded, "I think it a mistake to organize colored troops into units as large or larger than regiments, the largest unit of colored troops should be the battalion." Caldwell defended his position on the grounds that the separation of black troops into large organizations would result in wholesale resentment within the African American population. "Most military men recognize that national defense is no longer a matter of a regular army but that it is, and always had been when correctly grasped, a matter of being able to make full use of its entire manpower," he claimed. Emphasizing that black units fought best when serving in white regiments, Caldwell urged the War Department to place black companies in every regular army organization smaller than a division.[93]

In late November 1922, staff members of the War Department's Operations and Training Section also drew on the General Staff College survey to formulate policies for the employment of black troops in the event of war. Created on the premise that, as citizens of the United States, African Americans should be subject to all the obligations of citizenship—namely, military service—the 1922 policy resulted in a manpower utilization plan that limited black units to sizes no larger than regiments. The study echoed the judgments of Ballou and others by claiming that the performance of black combat units of World War I "constituted an unbroken record of failure" and placing the onus for their difficulties on their intellectual capacities and the leadership abilities of black officers. The study concluded that, in the event of war, "large numbers of Negroes will be found unsuited for combat duty, and for these, other parts in the mobilization must be found." Its suggestions therefore gave rise to new bureaucratic policies that reflected the prevalent belief that African Americans were largely poor soldiers.

Yet the 1922 mobilization plans developed by the Operations and Training Section staff also recognized the social implications of protest politics that emanated from segments of the black community during the period, and they foretold the dilemma policymakers would face years later: "The War Department has already received communications from prominent Negroes throughout the country indicating their dissatisfaction with the provisions thus far made. If the Negro element of this country does not get satisfaction from the War Department, it will undoubtedly turn to Congress, and it is sufficiently powerful politically to secure a full hearing there. In other words, it will be required to furnish a solution for the problem and to do so under the fire of Congress. The probability of arriving at a satisfactory solution under such circumstances is slight." Approving the G-3's recommendations a month later, Secretary of War John W. Weeks informed corps area commanders confidentially of the War Department's new policy days later, instructing them to mobilize approximately 50 percent of all black recruits available in the event of war.[94]

Subsequent mobilization plans made adjustments to the number of units under the table of organization based on the 1922 policy. In July 1923, the adjutant general informed corps area commanders that additional segregated units would not be allocated until black personnel presented themselves physically, and decisions regarding personnel transfers were left to the commanders' discretion.[95] Four years later, the G-3 expanded on the 1922 plan by establishing the percentage of black representation in the armed forces in the event of war at 10.73, reflecting the proportion of African Americans in the general population.[96] These plans were shrouded in secrecy, however, as no one outside the military establishment was made aware of their existence.

In 1937, members of the G-1, led by Brigadier General L. D. Gasser, conducted another mobilization study that resulted in a major revision of the previous plans. First, they pointed out that the 1933 War Department plan had not provided for an adequate proportion of black troops in the event of war and established the percentage of black troops in the first mobilization at 9.45, reflecting the 1930 census estimates of African Americans' proportions in the general population. Second, after examining the total number of black Selective Service registrants during World War I, the study recalibrated the number of mobilized black troops in ways that reflected the existing ratios of white and black soldiers within the armed forces. G-1 members reiterated the previous War Department and General Staff College studies of black servicemen in World War I, however, drawing on long-standing racist stereotypes to disparage their leadership and intellectual qualities. What's more, the study continued the War Department's policy of segregation.[97] Secretary of War Harry Woodring approved the G-1's findings and directed that copies of the plan be dispatched to corps area commanders. Despite several revisions, major portions of the 1937 plan remained in effect throughout the army's peacetime expansion of 1940. And the secrecy surrounding the army's policies regarding African American servicemen continued.

Not surprisingly, the War Department's expansion plans were deeply ingrained with the racist attitudes of army senior staff officers toward black servicemen from the previous war but cloaked with a high degree of secrecy. At the same time, the General Staff College courses of the 1920s and 1930s were attended by several generations of Regular Army officers who served in the First World War and would assume key army staff positions during the Second World War. The student officers could not help but imbibe the racist stereotypes that circulated throughout American society during the period. During General Staff College courses on the army's preparation for war that were held in middle years of the 1930s, field-grade officers who later formed the division's senior cadre received instruction on the employment of black troops from studies that reflected the racist attitudes of World War I commanders. Although it is unclear as to the impact the General Staff College courses had on the thinking of these Regular Army officers, most of the individuals who later held senior positions in the division had southern roots, had attended service academies, had fought in World War I as junior officers, and had virtually no experience dealing with African American troops.[98] By evoking popular imagery regarding African Americans, the General Staff College courses also perpetuated the prevailing racial stereotypes regarding black servicemen in the minds of these officers.

Reforming the Army

The manpower mobilization studies, which created a rationale for revising World War I guidelines regarding black troops, also corresponded with descriptions of African American males that were put forth by civilian institutions and professions. As early as 1909, American psychologists had developed individual intelligence tests based on models established by Alfred Binet. By the beginning of the First World War, however, staff members of the psychology division of the army's Medical Department had devised several intelligence tests to measure the recruit's knowledge of various occupations as well as to screen out soldiers thought to have been unable to perform military duties.

Two of the most prominent psychologists in the army's Medical Department and the Classification Division during the war were Lewis Terman and Walter Bingham. Terman, a Stanford University psychologist, had a longtime interest in the intelligence testing of African Americans. Between 1910 and 1918, he had revised Alfred Binet's French-language intelligence test to examine the mental capacities of black children in the American Southwest and relied on the results to develop the army's Alpha Tests for literates and Beta Tests for illiterates and non-English-speaking men during World War I. Both tests grouped inductees in eight classifications based on test scores measuring mental age. In 1919, Terman coauthored the National Intelligence Tests and the Stanford Achievement Tests, and after studying the intelligence of nearly fifteen hundred 10-year-old California youths, he determined that the average child had an intelligence quotient of 100.[99] In a similar fashion, Bingham, a University of Chicago–trained psychologist, served as a consultant to the army's Division on Personnel Classification from the summer of 1917 to the end of the war. As president of the Psychological Corporation and consultant to the Western Electric Company and the Personnel Research Federation during the 1920s and early 1930s, he worked to apply classification devices developed in the military service to American businesses, industry, and government agencies.[100] By mid-1941, these intelligence standards and quantification methods had dominated American psychology and would remain in effect until the eve of World War II.[101]

In May 1940, as soon as President Roosevelt asked Congress to expand the armed forces, Adjutant General Emory Adams appointed an advisory committee to develop aids to appraise and classify military personnel and named Bingham as its chairman. Among the distinguished psychologists named to this group were C. C. Brigham, H. E. Garrett, L. J. O'Rourke, and M. W. Richardson. During the initial advisory council meetings held that summer, staff members discussed the classification problems the army faced. After listening to a report prepared by Marion Richardson of the Personnel Testing Section that outlined the specifications of the new test, the group proposed that the new general classification test be devised to include non-English-speaking recruits and illiterates and be administered to recruits reporting to army reception centers. In their 1940 revisions of the First World War standards, Bingham and other framers of the testing methods to be used during mobilization dropped such outdated intelligence terminology such as "mental age" and intelligence quotient. Shortly afterward, members of the army's Personnel Research Section under the leadership of H. C. Holdridge and his executive officer Donald Baier constructed the first trial forms of what became known as the Army General Classification Test along with special tests for non-English-speaking recruits and women.[102]

Although a vast improvement over the Alpha examinations administered during the First World War, the AGCT reflected certain preconceptions that may have hampered its effectiveness. For example, the first AGCT test consisted of 150 multiple-choice questions and comprised sections that included the following: arithmetic reasoning, block counting, vocabulary, number sequences, synonyms and antonyms, all implying a certain degree of educational opportunity and a middle-class background. To make matters worse, members of the Personnel Section had scaled and standardized their testing methods by using a nonrandom sample that failed to take variables of race, socioeconomic status, and regional and cultural biases fully into account. When War Plans and Training Division psychologists administered the test to a sample composed of 3,790 Regular Army enlisted men, 600 CCC enrollees, and a few hundred graduate students and institutionalized men in September 1940, they collected results from white males between the ages of 20 and 29 who resided in the northeastern portion of the country, an area known for the highest rates of literacy in the nation. This collection method resulted in a skewed distribution of test results, adversely affecting the employment of black soldiers. For example, with 100 being the average score, nearly 75 percent of the sample had scored in the first three grades, while only 24 percent made scores in the last two grades.[103]

In contrast, because most black inductees came from communities that lacked adequate school facilities, many scored lower on the AGCT than did white inductees, occupying grades lower than the standardized scores gathered by army personnel technicians. For example, of the AGCT distribution of the 13,800 black soldiers who were assigned to the 93rd Division's 368th, 369th, and 25th Infantry regiments during the fall of 1943, fewer than 1 percent obtained scores in Grade I, 4 percent were in Grade II, 14 percent were in Grade III, and a disproportionately high percentage fell into Grades IV and V.[104]

These low scores made an indelible impression in the mind of many army corps commanders and arms and service branch chiefs during the early stages of the Second World War as some army officers used the low AGCT scores of black recruits to confirm racist assumptions regarding black intellectual abilities as well as to substantiate their claims that blacks made poor soldiers. For example, a letter written by 3rd Army commander General Courtney Hodges to army ground forces chief Lesley McNair in April 1943 provides a window into the dominant beliefs that many white Regular Army officers held with respect to the training of black servicemen. During his observations of conditions of the 93rd Division at Fort Huachuca, Hodges noted that the "limited ability on the part of colored junior officers and the fact that 85.85 percent of the enlisted personnel are in grades IV and V constitutes a real training handicap." "Experienced officers, who have served for extended periods with colored troops, estimate that it takes from 50 to 100 percent longer time to train colored troops than it does white," he claimed.[105]

Some of the difficulties that these low scores posed to the employment of black troops did not escape the attention of members of the advisory committee, however. Examining the grade distribution of men processed through army reception centers in November 1941, Bingham and other committee members discovered some of the biases inherent in the War Department's testing methods and used samples of black registrants to standardized subsequent versions of the AGCT. Realizing that the testing results might unfavorably affect training, Bingham and other members denied that the AGCT was an aptitude test and expressed fears that some nonpsychologists might use the test scores of black inductees as indi-

cators of innate intelligence.[106] Yet Bingham and other classification and replacement branch members contradicted their reservations when they linked the
AGCT scores to job assignments. At reception centers scattered throughout the
country, classification officers used the U.S. Employment Office's *Dictionary of
Occupational Titles,* which listed and defined nearly seventeen thousand different
civilian jobs, occupations, and professions, to identify particular duties for black
recruits after they received the results of their AGCT tests.[107] Thus, the military
job-classification process reproduced popular notions of work performed largely
by African Americans in the civilian sphere.

Fighting for the "Right to Fight"

Between 1940 and 1941, as plans were being made for war, a combination of
events occurred that exposed the Roosevelt administration to intense criticism from
sectors of the black community. Despite the passage of the antidiscriminatory measures in the Selective Service Act, black leaders and intellectuals made the army's
racial policies a key issue during the 1940 presidential election year. In June, branch
members of the NAACP from twenty states and the District of Columbia assembled
at its annual conference held in Philadelphia, and much of the discussion was
centered on the attitudes of blacks toward the armed forces and their relationship
to African American equality. Among the distinguished individuals in attendance
were William Hastie, Ruth Logan Roberts, Aubrey Williams, George Murphy Sr.,
and Dorothy Boulding Ferebee, a prominent District of Columbia physician and
wife of the future 93rd Division member Claude Ferebee.[108] There members listened to a speech given by association president Arthur Spingarn that declared,
"Democracy will not and cannot be safe in America as long as 10 per cent of its
population is deprived of the rights, privileges, and immunities plainly granted
to them by the Constitution of the United States." Spingarn viewed the military's
policies toward blacks as an extension of the racism in American society and stated:
"We must unceasingly continue our struggle against the attempt to weaken the
military strength of our country by eliminating from the military forces a tenth
of our population."[109] Following the event, legal counsel Charles Houston urged
association members to write letters to their representatives in Congress protesting the War Department's racial polices.[110]

Two months later, Mary McLeod Bethune, an influential adviser in the National
Youth Administration, reported that blacks were demanding the appointment of
a black adviser to the secretary of war and warned the White House, "There is
grave apprehension among Negroes lest the existing inadequate representation

and training of colored persons may lead to the creation of labor battalions and other forms of discrimination against them in event of war."[111] From June to October of that year, black newspapers, especially the *Pittsburgh Courier* and the *Baltimore Afro-American*, carried editorials excoriating Roosevelt's silence regarding discrimination against blacks in the armed forces and endorsed Republican Party presidential candidate Wendell L. Willkie—a well-known proponent of African American equality.[112] For example, *Baltimore Afro-American* editor Louis Lautier noted the restrictions placed on African American recruits in the armed forces during a period when the volunteers were eagerly sought by the services, and he claimed that, "in this regard, President Roosevelt not only forgot us but he neglected us, deserted and abandoned us to our enemies."[113]

After Congress passed the first Selective Service legislation in September 1940, members of the Socialist Workers Party's Political Committee gathered at a national conference in Chicago and adopted a resolution rejecting the measure. "The system of Jim Crowism in the armed forces demonstrates very clearly to the Negro the hypocrisy of slogans about 'war for democracy,'" they contended. Linking the status of blacks in the army to their social, economic, and political positions in civil society, party members criticized the Roosevelt administration's failure to obtain greater representation for blacks in all branches of the armed forces. Roosevelt, they concluded, "cannot wipe out Jim Crowism in the armed forces without endangering the whole system of Jim Crowism practiced in civilian life—in industry, civil service, on relief, at the ballot booth, in housing, theaters, and restaurants." "Stop using Negroes as laborers and lackeys," they declared.[114] Sentiments regarding black self-dignity also were prominent in the thoughts of Eugene Kinckle Jones, executive secretary of the National Urban League. In a fall letter to President Roosevelt, Jones pointed out that blacks' views of the discriminatory policies in the armed forces were grounded in their acute awareness of their amorphous positions in American society. In unambiguous terms, Jones reminded the president "that no healthy morale can be maintained and no really secure democratic national defenses can be built which do not protect the self-respect of all groups in our population. The racial policy of the War and Navy Department has actually, in this respect, been a threat to democratic ideology."[115]

While African Americans waged a constant struggle against the War Department's discriminatory policies, generational and class divisions hampered their attempts at gaining equality in the army. During the NAACP annual meeting in 1940, members of the association's youth delegation led by James H. Robinson elected to send Roosevelt a large postcard expressing their opposition to the impending conscription measure, the Burke-Wadsworth Bill, then being hotly debated in Congress. Their motion met with defeat when the organization's parent body refused to lend its support, however.[116] Intergenerational conflicts within the NAACP regarding the prospect of military service also surfaced in other areas. Two months later, a youth delegation led by National Negro Congress Youth Council secretary Louis Burnham, National Negro Congress finance secretary Julius Bostic, NAACP Student Conference chairman Anderson Davis, and Emergency Peace Mobilization Committee member Dorothy Strange appealed to Illinois congressman Arthur Mitchell for his support in their efforts to defeat the Burke-Wadsworth Bill. The youth leaders felt that the measure was discriminatory. Mitchell remained unconvinced, however. "You're wrong," he told the young leaders, adding that he would do all he could to see that the bill was passed.[117]

Meanwhile, members of the Operation and Training Division led by F. M. Andrews struggled secretly to adopt policies that would both quell potential discontent and continue its existing practices. In June 1940, G-3 staff members began to implement changes in the 1937 plan, increasing sizes of black combat units from battalions to regiments. But the G-3 called for the policy change because it felt that separate regiments would preempt demands by African American civilian organizations to create separate brigades of regiments and would greatly facilitate the army's problem of absorbing black officers during mobilization. The problem of achieving an equitable balance between black combat and service personnel also occupied the attention of the G-3 division. Members felt that the only way to resolve the problem was to require other branches of the arms and services to expand the authorization of units composed of black personnel. "Otherwise, there will be an insufficient number of units in the War Department Protective Mobilization Plan to absorb the Negro Personnel procured by voluntary enlistment and through selective service," the G-3 declared.[118]

Yet in their efforts to head off criticism from segments of African American society, War Department officials clashed over the policy changes. First, Andrews and other G-3 members exempted the Air Corps and the Signal Corps from the department's expansion proposals after Army Air Corps commander General Henry H. Arnold raised reservations regarding the plan. An unreconstructed segregationist, Arnold grounded his objections in policy adopted by Secretary of War Henry Stimson that allowed black pilots to receive training in the Civil Aeronautics Authority at schools in Chicago and other facilities used by the Army Air Corps. Besides that, he expressed his belief that G-3's manpower plan would disturb the division of labor within the army based on race and stir up racial antagonisms. "Negro pilots cannot be used in our present Air Corps Unit since this would result in having Negro officers serving over white enlisted men," Arnold claimed.

"This would create an impossible social problem."[119] Arnold also held preconceptions about blacks that made it difficult for him to envision them serving in units other than engineer, quartermaster, and service components. Linking reservations about blacks' military efficiency to questions regarding their intellectual abilities, he told Andrews, "In order to organize an all-Negro Air Corps unit, it would take several years to train the enlisted men to become competent mechanics."

Signal Corps chief Clyde Eastman echoed Arnold's reservations. Eastman recommended against employing black servicemen in Signal Corps units because he felt that it would be next to impossible to obtain adequately trained personnel such as radio electricians, telephone electricians, and radio operators. Eastman pointed to the creation of segregated divisions, however, as a viable alternative, claiming that the Signal Corps could make exceptions in the event that such a unit was organized. Although he felt that only way blacks would assume their proportion of battlefield casualties was through the creation of all-black divisions, he also believed that properly trained personnel could not be secured for black divisional signal companies.[120]

The viewpoints held by Arnold and Eastman were also embraced by higher-ranking War Department officials. In a diary entry recorded at the time, Secretary of War Henry Stimson observed, "Leadership is not imbedded in the Negro race yet and to try to make commissioned officers to lead the men into battle—colored men—is to work disaster to both. Colored troops do very well under white officers but every time we try to lift them a little bit beyond where they can go, disaster and confusion follows. I hope for Heaven's sake they won't mix the white and the colored troops together in the same units for then we shall certainly have trouble."[121] Expressing very little confidence in black servicemen, Stimson warned President Roosevelt on numerous occasions of the danger of "placing too much responsibility on a race which was not showing initiative in battle."[122] General George Marshall, army chief of staff, also expressed his reservations about black soldiers, citing their "low intelligence averages" and the evaluations of World War I commanders of black units to claim that the difficulties that black soldiers faced resulted from a lack of confidence in their commissioned and noncommissioned officers.[123]

But several members of the War Department's Personnel Division and the War Plans Division disagreed with Arnold's and Eastman's recommendations, arguing that black personnel should be employed in all branches of the arms and services, including the Air Corps and the Signal Corps. In drafting a reply to the G-3 assistant chief of staff, Brigadier General William Shedd argued that without black representation in the Air Corps the War Department would be hard pressed to obtain the proportion of black troops sought during initial mobilization.[124] Brigadier General George Strong took exception to Arnold and Eastman's claim that the Air Corps could not train black personnel, arguing that "Negro manpower can be as successfully employed in some capacities in both the Air Corps and the Signal Corps as it is in other Arms and Services."[125]

As the summer faded into the fall months of 1940, the Selective Service Act and the presidential election campaign accentuated the dilemma within the Roosevelt administration. On 5 September 1940, President Roosevelt expressed his dismay over the attention that the army's racial policies had drawn from black leaders and directed the War Department and the navy to prepare a statement publicizing the equal proportion of African Americans in the military.[126] At a cabinet meeting held a week later, Secretary of War Stimson informed the president that plans had been developed by the G-3 to organize several new black regiments in the army and to accept 10 percent of the total African American population during the initial stages of mobilization. What followed Stimson's announcement was a string of press releases aimed at assuring segments of the African American community that blacks would have proportional opportunities within the armed forces.[127] This was significant because the press releases represented the first time that the War Departments policies regarding black participation in the event of an emergency had been revealed to the public.

But more important, these statements allowed War Department officials to claim that they promoted equal opportunity for blacks in the army when, in fact, they had no intention of abandoning their racial polices. After the 13 September meeting with Roosevelt, Stimson told the army General Staff that he wanted an "exact statement of the facts in the case and . . . how far we can go in the matter."[128] In a late September letter to Senator Henry Cabot Lodge Jr., Marshall pointed out that, although political pressure had forced the Roosevelt administration to announce that African Americans would be accepted in the army on a proportional basis, the War Department's policies had not changed. "It is the policy of the War Department not to intermingle colored and white enlisted personnel in the same regimental organization." "The present exceedingly difficult period of building up a respectable and dependable military force for the protection of this country is not the time for critical experiments, which would inevitably have a highly destructive effect on morale—meaning military efficiency," he claimed.[129]

Although Roosevelt, during a conference held in late September 1940, had informed African American leaders Walter White, T. Arnold Hill, and A. Philip Randolph that black officers and enlisted men would be employed throughout the army and that black units would be organized in all branches of the armed services, he approved a press release prepared by Assistant Secretary of War Robert Patterson announcing the War Department's racial policies.[130] Left largely unrevised, the oblique policy regarding the status of black recruits would be carried forward into the following year with the creation of the U.S. 93rd Infantry Division.

The Making of the 93rd

Hastie's recommendation for the provision of higher-level units for black officer personnel echoed what had been debated within the War Department for some time, however. The civilian aide had not been informed that the War Department had planned to create an all-black cavalry division early in 1941. However, the organization and training of the unit was hampered by the slow construction of facilities and the War Department's adherence to racial segregation. Two months after William Hastie's memorandum on black units was submitted to Undersecretary of War Robert Patterson, deputy chief of staff General William Bryden met with the undersecretary to discuss measures to be taken in connection with Hastie's recommendations. Both men agreed with Hastie that new black units larger than regimental size were needed for the expansion of black cadres, pointing to the brigading of the famous 9th and 10th Cavalry regiments with the 2nd Cavalry Division as well as the creation of the 99th Pursuit Squadron and the development of all-black tank battalions as examples of the "new" types of organizations for African American officer personnel. "As expansion continues, this practice may be further extended if it is determined that the resulting divisional organizations would represent the strongest possible combinations of regiments," they claimed. These events were significant because they represent a total revision of War Department's policy studies that recommended against the formation of all-black divisions.

This new line of reasoning reached its fullest expression during a conference held between black editors and publishers of the Associated Negro Press and various representatives of the War Department on 8 December 1941, the day after the Japanese bombing of Pearl Harbor. During the opening stages of their roundtable discussions, the conferees heard Marshall state that, although he was displeased with the progress the War Department was making toward revising its racial policies, army planners had contemplated creating a number of all-black units in all branches of the army. He then went on to astonish them by stating that among those units that the army had under consideration was an African American infantry unit of division size to be composed of black officers and enlisted men. Marshall went on to inform them that the House of Representatives had already passed a bill sponsoring the measure and that newly constructed housing would be available for the unit by the early spring.[131] By the end of January, Marshall's announcement had become a reality with the expansion of Fort Huachuca to accommodate an additional twelve thousand troops. In turn, these additional numbers of conscripts were assigned to the 369th Infantry Regiment. Combined with the men of the 25th and 368th Infantry regiments, the unit formed the first all-black triangular unit in the army and was designated the U.S. 93rd Infantry Division.[132]

African American responses to Marshall's remarks were mixed. Many black leaders had taken exception to the army chief's statement, correctly claiming it was nothing short of outright racism. For example, in a letter to Marshall immediately following the conference, NAACP executive secretary Walter White berated the army chief of staff and argued that the War Department should instead create a volunteer division that, in his words, would be "open to all irrespective of race, creed, color, or national origin." "The organization of such a division would serve as a tremendous lift to the morale of the Negro which at present is at a dangerously low ebb," he contended.[133] Some black newspapers, particularly the *Chicago Defender,* the *Baltimore Afro-American,* and the *Atlanta Daily World,* also excoriated the War Department's racial policy.[134] For example, the *Baltimore Afro-American,* in an editorial entitled "Sweet Nothings to Twenty-four Editors," claimed that the conference was a waste of time. "General Marshall," the editorial claimed, "could have made that address in less than a minute and sent the editors back home with something worthwhile to print."[135] Some black leaders and newspapers, however, embraced Marshall's idea. P. L. Prattis of the *Pittsburgh Courier,* for instance, applauded his announcement, arguing "that his present attitude, in the light of the past, represents an improvement due to greater knowledge of our problem and greater understanding." What's more, the editor also claimed that Marshall's decision was largely due in part to the campaign waged by Robert Vann, the paper's late editor, more than four years earlier.[136]

Although they represented different viewpoints, the remarks made by black press corps members reflected the extent to which African American public opinion had influenced the thinking of army officials. Because segregation was a key watchword within the War Department, army planners moved quickly to reconstitute segregated army divisions only when faced with the prospect of creating integrated units in all its branches. Yet questions among War Department officials about the input that African American society would have regarding the division's training lay on the not-so-distant horizon. Obscured from the public view with respect to the reconstruction of the unit was the impact that prospective division members would have on their training. How black troops framed, interpreted, and shaped their realities in the barracks and on the parade fields would have as much to do with the War Department's training policies as would their performances in the field. Indeed, Roosevelt administration officials and sectors of African American society had only begun to hear the voices of the young men who were swelling the ranks and whose views of military life presented fundamental challenges to the traditional army structure that they had come to know so well.

Of Sage and Sand

Fort Huachuca and the U.S. 93rd Infantry Division

> From your own experiences in the Army, you know that nothing is
> ever right with any soldier and that all complaints have to be sifted
> through in an effort to get at legitimate and just grievances of which
> there are certainly to be many.
>
> *Truman Gibson*

Without so much as an afterthought, Private Jerry Johnson shattered the uneasy truce struck by War Department officials and black press corps members in
late 1941. Two months after the U.S. 93rd Infantry Division had been mustered
into active duty, Johnson and three other division members had no sooner returned
to the 25th Infantry's Anti-Tank Company area when they received an order from
their commanding officer to join a group of soldiers in a march back to a battalion bivouac site several miles away. Although the performance of onerous tasks
like roll calls and marching were fairly typical for service personnel being put
through the rigors of army basic training, Johnson and the other trainees considered the order to be especially egregious because they had not received breakfast prior to the rigorous training session held that morning.

Each soldier had privately expressed misgivings about the order, but Johnson
was the only serviceman to actually voice his disapproval to his superior officer.
When the officer asked him why he had responded so slowly to the order, the 31-
year-old private fashioned his own critique of the army's racial policies. In response,
Johnson immediately sat down on the ground and remarked, "I ain't had no mother
fucking breakfast and I ain't going no fucking place." He went on, "I am not a
fucking kid and I am tired of you fucking with me."[1] When given an additional
order to fall in or go to the guardhouse, Johnson exclaimed, "You mother fuckers
are going to fuck me up anyway so just go on and fuck me up," and he then pro-

ceeded with an armed escort toward the Fort Huachuca post stockade, where he was subsequently charged, tried, and convicted of displaying disrespect toward a superior officer and disobeying a direct order.[2]

Although hardly unusual for citizen-soldiers unaccustomed to military discipline, Johnson's remarks and actions and the significance they held for service personnel who were stationed at the military installation did not escape the attention of the 25th Infantry cadre and enlisted men. Specifically, many white officers who were present that day believed that Johnson's critical outburst merely confirmed the unsuitability of African Americans for military duty. They argued that Johnson's insubordinate behavior simply substantiated their claims that black troops made poor soldiers. Of Johnson's comments, for instance, his commanding officer remarked during the court-martial trial, "That is the first time I have ever had a Negro soldier curse at me and I can't see any reason for him to have done so, other than his apparent contempt for authority or having anyone having authority over him."[3] In his statement to the army judge advocate general's staff, company commander Captain Edward F. Moran played up doubts about Johnson's character, arguing, "He, like so many negro troops, is a constant malingerer, is without discipline, and is the sorriest of all soldiers I have come in contact with in the last twenty years."[4]

But for the veteran black soldiers of the unit who had experienced the hard times of the pre–World War II army, Johnson's conduct elicited a different response. Johnson's outburst had violated the standards of behavior upon which their long-standing aspirations for racial equality were predicated. When queried by staff officers about Johnson's statements, for example, a veteran noncommissioned officer who had been present that morning supported the platoon commander's testimony, stating, "I have been in the army over sixteen years and I have seen poor soldiers come and go, in all this time I have never seen a poorer and more ornery soldier. Johnson is disrespectful to all of his non-commissioned officers and officers and should be eliminated from the service."[5] After deliberating less than thirty minutes, the twelve officers who served on the court-martial hearing board concurred, sentencing Johnson to a six-month sentence of hard labor in the post stockade and a dishonorable discharge with a forfeiture of pay and benefits.[6]

Johnson's actions that morning reflected a new chapter in the black experience in World War II. The verbal exchange and the subsequent trial are suggestive of the peculiar world in which Johnson and his peers found themselves. From the moment they filed through the gated entranceways of Fort Huachuca, Arizona, recruits like Johnson had their own ideas about army life and military authority and created a community based on those beliefs. However, they quickly discovered that they had entered a high-stakes poker game with all its participants engaged in a desperate struggle to win the right to represent black bodies in uniform. The policy pronouncements set forth by military officials and spokesmen gave rise to the conundrum that black division members faced whenever they tried to reconcile their pre-war ideas regarding military service with those dictated by the army and the wider African American community. Indeed, the fundamental dilemma and the political struggles over representation became just as overwhelming for the green soldiers as the arid Arizona training camp where they were initially assigned.[7]

Making the Men of the 93rd

In the spring of 1942, Pullman coaches arrived at the reception centers of Fort Huachuca carrying more than 6,000 men at a rate of 200 a day.[8] Through May and June, recruits poured in from regions all over the country. Within the first few hours of their arrival, the new division members were exposed to military authority as they began weeks of rigorous indoctrination, drill, and physical exercise. At the reception centers, black recruits formed ranks where they first responded to roll call before boarding trucks that carried them to the divisional sports arena. There they were given Army General Classification Tests and were assigned in groups to platoons and companies within one of the division's regimental components. After being driven to their regimental areas, 93rd Division recruits were separated into various battalions, companies, platoons, sections, and squads before being assigned to noncommissioned officers who guided them to their barracks, where they made up their bunks and unpacked their baggage.[9]

For many whose trip to Fort Huachuca marked the first time they had ventured far from home, the experience evoked mixed feelings of trepidation and excitement. A young draftee from Cleveland, Ohio, recalled, "I left the reception center at Columbus feeling rather low with the knowledge that we were to be so far from home when our journey ended. But when I arrived at Fort Huachuca, I remembered being pleased with the camp because it was more beautiful than anything I had ever seen."[10] Reflecting on his departure from a Maryland induction center, a former hospital attendant similarly noted: "Most of us were excited and very eager to get under way, although we all wanted to be in Baltimore just once more before leaving. But in the days after arriving at Fort Huachuca, we spent our time getting adjusted to army routine, asking questions, and looking for fellows we knew."[11]

During the first phase of the division's stateside training, recruits received instruction from seasoned black noncommissioned officers. The majority of them came from the veteran 25th Infantry Regiment, one of the original Regular Army black units that had been created after the Civil War and had served in the military for several decades prior to 1942. These NCOs spent a great deal of time training men to act like soldiers and initiating them into military life, putting the newly arrived recruits through seemingly endless close-order drill, inspections, and roll calls, as the soldiers received most of their basic training in their respective units. A typical day for the young recruits went as follows: they were awakened around five o'clock in the morning and marched to the company mess hall, where they ate breakfast. The men then proceeded to clean their living quarters before going through several hours of drill and physical exercises.

This strict regimen of mass calisthenics was both physically and emotionally exhausting. During their physical training periods, veteran noncommissioned officers made recruits march several times a week for distances ranging from 5 to 20 miles over mountains and across the arid desert, shouting words of encouragement as well as personal insults when they faltered. But most important, the veteran NCOs imparted lessons of black unity, ethnic pride, and dignity to their recruits. Cleveland resident Henry Williams recalled, "They spoke to us as if we were family members and they were the appointed heads of that family. These men really knew their business and inspired many of us."[12] According to a young recruit from Washington, D.C., who remembered the efforts made by Florida-born and veteran 25th Infantry noncommissioned officer Frank Little: "He was an old-fashioned soldier who served as a role model for us because he knew the army inside out. Little had a way of taking young draftees under his wing and this was very important for those of us who knew very little about the military."[13]

Black recruits expressed similar sentiments about the junior officers who had graduated from the ROTC programs at universities throughout the country. During this period, nearly three hundred black junior officers left their ROTC units at Howard University, Wilberforce University, and Lincoln University and received instruction at Fort Benning's Infantry School before being assigned to the 93rd Infantry Division. Others arrived from less conventional avenues. For example, St. Louis, Missouri, resident Oscar Davenport distinguished himself by earning his lieutenancy in the Citizens' Military Training Camp at Fort Riley, Kansas, in January 1942. Like other black junior officers, Davenport completed a special course at Fort Benning before heading to Arizona, where he was assigned to the division in July of that year.[14] Reuben Fraser also came to Fort Huachuca as a commissioned officer from the Citizens' Military Training Camp; he received his lieutenancy after he participated in the CMTC at Fort Riley. He reported to Jefferson Barracks, Missouri, in May 1942 and then to Fort Huachuca, at which point he received his assignment to the 369th Infantry, where he was placed in a rifle platoon.[15]

Meanwhile, many graduates of Officer Candidate School arrived at Fort Huachuca after serving in other segregated units. By the summer of 1942, the junior echelons of the division's officer corps had expanded considerably: Cecil Davis, William Jones, Robert Grant, and Ulysses R. Lee reported to the Arizona military installation after qualifying for Officer Candidate School while training at Fort Custer and Fort Devens as members of the 184th Field Artillery and the 366th Infantry, respectively.[16] By December of that year, officers with the 372nd Infantry Regiment also found themselves assigned to the unit.[17]

Among the steady stream of black officers who reported to Fort Huachuca from the infantry and field artillery Officer Candidate Schools were the large numbers of African Americans who entered the division as religious and medical officers. Most of the candidates drawn to the Chaplain and Medical corps were motivated by racial advancement, as well as their individual calling as religious leaders and medical professional men.[18] As an African Methodist Episcopal Church pastor, Springfield, Ohio, resident Charles Watkins spent much of his time addressing the many needs of his congregation, playing an active role in community activities ranging from serving as a representative on the African Methodist Episcopal Church's international council of religious education's committee for youth to working as an editor of a newspaper distributed by his church. During the months leading up to the bombing of Pearl Harbor, however, he began to develop a deeper understanding of the situation that his church members and other segments of the black community faced throughout American society and saw military service as a means of continuing his life's work. After receiving a ringing endorsement from the African Methodist Episcopal presiding elder of Wilberforce University, Watkins gained admittance to the Chaplain Corps in 1941, reporting for active duty five months later. Of his ministry to the needs and concerns of soldiers who trained at the desert installation, Watkins stated at the time, "As a Negro officer, I have tried to show by referring to concrete examples to my troops that a soldier could be sincere to his race in the quest for religious truth and that they should try to live not only as soldiers of the U.S. Army, but as soldiers of the Living God."[19]

James Whittico felt the same way. The Williamson, West Virginia–born medical doctor grew up in a family that had deep professional and race-conscious roots; his father, a physician trained at Meharry Medical College, had served as an officer in World War I, and his mother was an accomplished schoolteacher (not to mention one of the most vocal leaders in Williamson politics). By the time military planners had begun to construct plans to activate the division in 1942, the young Whittico was building a stellar reputation as a capable surgeon at Homer G. Phillips Hospital in St. Louis. He had no sooner been named as the head of surgery at the 770-bed hospital during the spring of that year when he decided to volunteer for military service. Shortly afterward, he was assigned to one of the three medical service units in the U.S. 93rd Infantry Division's 318th Medical Battalion. As Whittico arrived at the military outpost, he noted: "I feel that the only way that the Negro can be recognized is by having the best, and the more things that we can officially be acclaimed the best in, the nearer we come to winning the respect of the other races."[20]

Many young black officers who entered the unit at the time drew high praise from their subordinates for their professionalism and devotion to their duties. A recruit from Detroit described how a young 25th Infantry officer "was so competent in working with platoons and bringing them up to top shape that he was transferred in and out so many times it was comical."[21] The leadership qualities of one black officer in particular made a lasting impression on Lieutenant Edwin Lee: "It was general knowledge among the black troops that Lieutenant Clyatt McBrier, who was a regular Army soldier, was the best-trained line man in the whole division, and knew his troop and commanded them better. It finally became so obvious to everybody that he was promoted to company commander."[22]

But not all black recruits viewed the 25th Infantry noncommissioned and junior commissioned officers favorably. Friction caused by generational and class differences led a number of black GIs to question the leadership capabilities of senior NCOs and junior officers during their initial encounters. One enlisted man in the 368th claimed: "These old sergeants that have been here 25 or 30 years won't allow us any kind of chance for anything."[23] During that same period, another observer commented: "A complaint is heard so often in both the Twenty-fifth and 368th Regiments that it apparently has a solid foundation in reality. The draftees have a difficult time getting along with the old soldiers—men from the old school."[24]

Suspicion and doubt also clouded relations between the newly arrived second lieutenants and the weathered NCOs in the division. Lieutenant Elliotte Williams, who arrived at Fort Huachuca at the time, recalled some of the difficulties that he had with some of the 25th Infantry NCOs: "One problem I experienced with a few NCOs was a tendency to try to 'get over,' 'fool the man' into believing the troops were either working diligently or misappropriating government property. When challenged on this attitude, you were then accused of being an 'Uncle Tom.'"[25]

Conversely, some veteran 25th infantrymen thought that the newly commissioned officers lacked military bearing, and they resented the haughty, condescending manner they exhibited toward them. Bill Stevens, a staff sergeant in the 25th Infantry, noted: "The cadre of NCOs in the Twenty-fifth had no respect for officers, black or white, unless they were professionals, meaning from West Point or a military academy of some repute. Even officers from these academies got little respect if they didn't measure up."[26] St. Clairsville, Ohio, resident and 369th Infantry platoon sergeant John Marshall had a clear image of black officers in his unit: "At times, I didn't think their quality of leadership was all that good. They thought they were the main authorities, and some didn't know too much about anything."[27] Calvert, Texas, resident and 25th Infantry staff sergeant Marke Toles expressed similar negative views: "At Fort Huachuca, I saw some of the least prepared black officers given positions of leadership."[28]

Tempers boiled over frequently throughout the division's initial training period, and Fort Huachuca became a common site for fisticuffs, knife fights, and violent arguments between black GIs.[29] In July 1942, a skirmish took place one evening between Private James Green and Sergeant Curtis Wade after the latter instructed the soldier to turn out the lights in the barracks. After an exchange of harsh words, the noncommissioned officer attempted to force the belligerent enlisted man to carry out the order. Wade's actions failed to yield favorable results, however. After exclaiming, "I'll beat your mother fucking brains out" at the NCO, Green proceeded to pummel the sentry with his fists until he was bleeding profusely. The crisis came to a close only after a duty officer arrived and ordered them to vacate the premises.[30]

On some occasions, the altercations deteriorated into armed conflict. On one late June evening, 368th infantryman Leonard Holmes grabbed a pistol from a military policeman and fired several rounds of bullets at Private Lazarus Jones, another MP, during a scuffle at the post service club. Although the testimony of defense witnesses varied widely as to the sequence of the events, all of them stated that both Holmes and the MPs had exchanged harsh words before the MPs emptied the magazines of their weapons. When the shooting was over, several servicemen were wounded, including Holmes and two MPs. What's more, service personnel in an adjoining barracks area sustained gunshot wounds as the result of stray bullets that entered the building. Although Holmes testified in his defense that a noncommissioned officer had insulted him and that he had no idea that the weapon was loaded, the court-martial found him guilty on all counts before sentencing him to two years in the post stockade.[31]

Often beneath the surface lay regional and class differences complicated by conflicting notions of manhood. Just weeks prior to the violent exchange between Holmes and Jones, Private Joseph Shields, a 21-year-old carpenter's helper from New Babylon, New York, was attacked by 36-year-old James Rowe, a former share-cropper from De Funiak Springs, Florida, following an argument over an alleged stolen package of cigarettes in a company area of the 318th Engineer Battalion. As a number of horrified battalion members looked on, Rowe whipped out a three-bladed stiletto and stabbed the younger man in the neck. Shields did not survive the wounding; he died in the post hospital a half hour later. But for Rowe the con-sequence was historic: five months later, on 6 November 1942, he died at the gal-lows, leaving behind the ignominious legacy of being the first GI executed in the United States during the Second World War.[32]

Barracks Life, Post Life

The violent outbursts among division members during their initial encoun-ters often occurred within the living spaces that the post presented to the exhausted soldiers. Within the public spaces that the barracks provided, recruits of the 93rd Infantry Division, like men who served in other training units, organized and joined associations that served to strengthen communal bonds forged in civil-ian life. In May 1941, fifty-seven soldiers in several companies of the 368th In-fantry Regiment formed an infantry club composed of black recruits from Akron and Youngstown, Ohio. Led by Fred L. King and James Veal, the group met throughout much of their basic training to listen to radio shows and to discuss the local and national events. Furthermore, its members hosted many social events on the military post. At the same time, the men wrote letters to black newspa-pers such as the *Cleveland Call & Post* and the *Baltimore Afro-American* describ-ing their activities.[33]

Draftees from Akron, Ohio, were not the only servicemen to organize them-selves along regional lines. In a 368th's M Company barrack in May 1941, recruits from Cleveland, Ohio, created the Huachucans Association. Under the leadership of Charles Rabb, Milton Carnes, William Slade, and Henry Williams, members of the association hosted Sunday afternoon "swing sessions," cabarets, and vari-ety shows in service clubs throughout the division's initial training. Not only that, men in the Huachucans held night classes in the barracks for fellow members who wished to improve their ability to read and write.[34] By competing against one another in drill exercises, baseball games, and debates within the barracks itself, these organizations not only gave the servicemen a sense of pride but also helped to preserve friendships forged prior to the war effort as the men withstood the rigors of military training. As one young black serviceman explained in an open letter to the *Cleveland Call & Post*, "the clubs in the barracks allowed heated discussion of the war effort, local events, sociable card games, and preparation for the next day's routine."[35]

Not all aspects of this barracks-based culture relied on regional bonds, however. Others reflected the desire to compress the rank and authority structure that existed in the military. Randall Morgan, an executive officer in a company in the 368th Infantry, organized an entertainment group composed of ten privates and noncommissioned officers within his unit. Directed by Private John Stokes and regimental chaplain John De Veaux, the group held many theatrical and musical performances at the camp and participated in religious services at churches in nearby Tucson that openly advocated racial unity and international awareness. Private John McCollough was perhaps the best known of the group members. Formerly a member of a nationally renowned dance group from Cleveland, McCullough performed an interpretive routine that he called "The Life of Man" in which he conveyed the life and struggles of black laborers prior to military conscription.[36]

During the same time, in the 369th Infantry, Hanover, Virginia–born Lieutenant Benjamin Layton, Indianapolis native Simeon Ganway, and several other servicemen received commendations as well as prizes for various concerts in which they performed numbers such as "Keep Cool, Fool" and "Khaki Conga."[37] The groups organized by Cleveland resident Robert Taylor and Philadelphia-born William Kyle were probably among the most sought after organizations on post, however. In the 25th Infantry, Robert (Foots) Taylor—an established jazz trumpeter—along with Fred Smith of South Bend, Indiana; Whorley Hoff from Columbus, Ohio; Louis Hodges of Houston, Texas; and four others formed a musical ensemble. Calling themselves the "Eight Shots of Rhythm," the men performed jam sessions in many of the service clubs throughout Fort Huachuca and in nearby black communities within Fry, Bisbee, Tucson, and Phoenix. Among the popular numbers that Taylor's band performed were "Lift Every Voice and Sing," "Now the Day Is Over," and "Trade Winds."[38] Around the same time, Sergeant Fred Griffin of Clay City, Kansas, directed the twenty-eight-man 25th Infantry band, whose musicians enjoyed national reputations, including vocalist Lawrence Neely, who sang with Jimmy Lunceford, and Alton Grant, a onetime trumpet and trombone player with Les Hite.[39] In June 1942, the "Maple Leafs" under the leadership of William "Billy" Kyle—a prominent pianist who performed with the likes of Tiny Bradshaw, Buster Bailey, and John Kirby—played numbers such as "Dawn on the Desert" and "Drink to Me Only with Thine Eyes" at various dances and cabarets on the military post and throughout the region, flourishing throughout most of the division's initial training.[40]

Equally quick to volunteer their time and energies to these community-building activities were the talented black women who worked at the military installation. Although their numbers barely reached three hundred, these women played a crucial role in keeping the recruits aware of issues affecting the post community at large. For example, Winston-Salem, North Carolina–born Mary Carter, the widow of a distinguished post chaplain, served as an unofficial benefactor for black recruits, advising them on various matters such as housing, community relations, and post activities.[41] At the same time, Tuskegee Institute graduate and Texas resident Nelle Bishop Dillon left her job as the Oklahoma state supervisor of federally aided vocational schools during the summer of 1942 and traveled south to establish and operate a service club at the desert installation after her two sons were inducted into military service. In that capacity, she struggled to create a homelike environment for the soldiers and their visiting loved ones.[42] Finally, Agnes Scott, Rebecca Hill, Beatrice Gildersleeve, and Mary Brooks planned, organized, and supervised many social activities for soldiers as post dietitians and librarians.[43]

In addition to those who worked diligently on the base, a number of black women went to the military installation to help aid relief efforts as nurse practitioners, Red Cross directors, and hospital personnel. By July 1942, approximately one hundred black women had begun work at the one-thousand-bed, fifty-six-building complex, collecting medical supplies, conducting physical examinations, and visiting wards as members of the Army Nurse Corps.[44] Working alongside the nurse practitioners were the small numbers of American Red Cross field workers led by Thelma Hawes, a young social worker from Chicago's Provident Hospital. Originally hailing from Indianapolis, Indiana, Hawes reported to station hospital in early 1942 despite having graduated from the University of Chicago only a few years earlier. What's more, she had worked as a social worker for only a brief time before being assigned to the desert installation. Her lack of experience proved to be of very little consequence, however. Immediately upon her arrival, Hawes and her small team of caseworkers began to work diligently in conjunction with the army to provide counsel to servicemen on personal and family problems, financial assistance to those going home on convalescent furloughs, and guidance in convalescent recreation.[45]

Hawes also worked closely with Elizabeth Green of Pittsburgh, Pennsylvania, and New York City native Leonore Cox as they organized a series of Red Cross activities on the post, including the publication of a hospital newspaper, musical

programs, arts and crafts shows, motion picture viewings, card parties, and reading clubs for the patients.[46] By the time 93rd's stint at the military station had ended,
less than six months later, the organizing duties performed by the talented young
women were such that they earned the praise of several army and Red Cross officials.
But one caseworker held a different impression of the duties that she and other
black women and men performed at the outpost. In August of that year, she told
a fellow caseworker, "They want us out of the way. Where there would be no mix-
ing of the races. They got us out of the way. They don't care how many problems
are created by the isolation. Oh well, family-home-friends will continue to won-
der if I will get over that hill."[47]

One of the most prominent black women who encouraged black servicemen
to carve out their own separate space as well as to call attention to the bouts of
racial discrimination that black GIs faced was Shirley Graham, noted playwright,
novelist, and political activist. Originally from Cleveland, Graham had supervised
the African American division of the Chicago Federal Theater Project and had
studied at the Yale University School of Drama. Upon receiving her position as
director of the Young Women's Christian Association–United Service Organizations in 1941, she reported to Fort Huachuca, where she assumed the unenviable
task of vitalizing the post's dismal recreational activities for black soldiers head-
quartered at the base. Undaunted, Graham plunged into her project, directing many
post plays and art exhibits and creating literary societies and gatherings for soldiers to discuss various issues from military training to family concerns. She also
created a camp newspaper through which she articulated her opposition to the
racial discrimination that black servicemen of the 93rd Infantry Division faced.

On many occasions, the USO director devised her own methods to call attention to the thousands of black troops stationed at Fort Huachuca as well as the
dismal state of race relations throughout the southwestern region, reporting on
their experiences to YWCA officials, NAACP chapter members, church leaders,
and the like.[48] Furthermore, Graham's observations were conveyed in letters, stories, and editorials of the black and left press. In an article published in *Common
Sense* in February 1943, she spoke out against the racial policies of the War Department and the USO. Less than six months later, *PM Daily* carried an open letter written by Graham to President Franklin D. Roosevelt in which she took issue
with the race riots in Detroit, Michigan; Beaumont, Texas; Mobile, Alabama; and
Los Angeles, California, and also reminded the president of the sacrifices that were
being made by black service families during the period. "You must give full and
unqualified citizenship to all of your people now," she insisted.[49] Graham's "un-

precedented" efforts came to an end, however, when she was forced from her job in early 1943 after intervening in a case involving a soldier who was charged with mutiny.[50]

By the fall of 1942, 330 members of the all-black Women's Army Auxiliary Corps' (WAAC) 32nd and 33rd Post Headquarters Companies, led by Corrie Sherrard, Frances Alexander, Geraldine Bright, Vera Harrison, and Natalie Donaldson, had arrived at Fort Huachuca from Fort Des Moines, Iowa. Based on the War Department's plans formulated in May 1942, the primary duty for black WAAC members at Fort Huachuca was to release 93rd GIs from service support duties as post-exchange workers, postal clerks, stenographers, switchboard operators, drivers of light motor trucks, dispatchers, and typists, releasing them for possible combat assignments.[51] Nevertheless, WAAC officers generally believed that they played an intricate role in the struggles of black GIs for dignity within the 93rd Infantry Division. Upon her arrival at the military post, for instance, Muriel Fawcett—a Lynchburg, Virginia, native and a former West Virginia State College department head—stated, "Each WAAC is bursting with pride that she made the grade. If the men doubt that we can do the job efficiently, they will soon change their minds."[52]

Brunswick, Georgia–born staff officer Irma Jackson Cayton expressed similar views. A graduate of Atlanta and Fisk universities, Cayton had worked as a social worker and was married to noted scholar Horace Cayton before being selected as one of the first WAAC members to be trained at Fort Des Moines, Iowa, in July 1942. After gaining her commission as a second lieutenant three months later, Cayton reported to Fort Huachuca, where she, along with other members of the 32nd Post Headquarters Company, spent most of their time organizing various functions, supervising debating societies, and contributing articles to the post newspaper.[53] On many occasions, Cayton used her stature on the post to bring to the attention of black 93rd GIs that the war encompassed the political struggles of both African American women and men. In the March 1943 edition of the 93rd's *Special Service Bulletin*, for example, Cayton reminded her readers, "We must think of ourselves as brothers and sisters in arms. On our part, we are striving consciously to be courageous and reliable sisters to our brothers whom we respect and admire for their valiant hearts, for their bravery and their willingness to face death to defend the homes of America."[54]

But in many ways, black women like Irma Cayton soon found themselves both allied with and separated from the black men stationed at the army post. The strictures of race and gender affected female army personnel at almost every turn at the border installation. For instance, black WAAC members discovered that their presence at the post was also meant to support prohibitions on interracial relationships between black male soldiers and white women in the nearby towns and cities.[55] "I thought to myself," Cayton recalled years later, "so this is the Army. It was then that fully I realized that this was only the beginning of what we were to face."[56]

Creative artists and contemporary cultural figures also worked to both promote a sense of community for black 93rd GIs as well as to draw attention to their struggles along the southern Arizona border. Throughout the summer and fall months of 1942, a number of black singers, thespians, playwrights, and athletes, the most notable of whom were Ella Fitzgerald, Lena Horne, Etta Moten, Hattie McDaniel, Freddie Clark, Effert Bowman, and Joe Louis, held benefit musical performances, variety shows, and boxing exhibitions for the division.[57] On Christmas Day, radio waves of the National Broadcasting Company (NBC) carried a live performance given by World War I veteran and jazz great Noble Sissle and his orchestra at Fort Huachuca's field house.[58] Local puppeteers from small black communities in Tucson and Phoenix also entertained the soldiers, performing skits that conveyed racial consciousness and democratic principles.[59] Besides the number of prominent cultural figures who made stops in the region, a few black intellectuals and civic leaders made appearances to bolster the morale of division members. In July, William Pickens, former NAACP field secretary and director of the Treasury Department's War Bonds Division, gave a speech to the troops entitled "The Negro in the Present World Conflict" during his tour of the military base.[60] Four months later, assistant NAACP secretary and *Crisis* editor Roy Wilkins made an appearance at the army camp while visiting local branches in Arizona, Texas, New Mexico, and Colorado.[61]

Perhaps the fullest articulation of community building may be found within the 93rd Division's weeklies, *Sage and Sand,* the *Blue Helmet,* and the *Special Service Bulletin.* Appearing in the fall of 1942 under the managing editorship of Vaughn Anderson, Jack Palms, Fort Collins, Colorado–born Harold Stewart, and Minneapolis, Minnesota, resident Carroll E. Nelson, the post periodicals constituted the largest weekly newspapers in Arizona during the period and were solely supported by contributions made by black GIs. Within their eight pages and five columns, black soldiers publicized their activities in each of the three regiments; contributed biting commentary on local, national, and international news; and provided folk histories about the African past and political discourse on various aspects of military life at Fort Huachuca through verse and lyrical prose.[62] For example, a poem entitled "Brotherhood Week" written by 369th Infantry chaplain

Charles Watkins conveyed millennial images of the war and its prophetic meaning to African Americans:

Child of the boundless prairie,
Son of the Virgin soil,
Heir to the bearing of burdens
Brother to them that toil
God and Nature together
Shaped him to lead in the van,
In the stress of the wildest weather
When the Nation needed a man.[63]

The *Blue Helmet* and the *Special Service Bulletin* continued to flourish throughout the war, circulating more than twenty thousand copies before folding in January 1946. Although the commentary within these publications was uneven in quality, they reflected the vicissitudes of the everyday experiences that black division members encountered during their training at Fort Huachuca. What resulted was thus a blend of both black cultural heritage and strands of military culture—all reflective of individual ideals of manhood and middle-class respectability.

As the new military experience began to foster a unique culture among GIs, black weeklies carried feature articles about the activities of the 93rd Division at Fort Huachuca.[64] At the same time, the men in uniform who served at the military base used black weeklies to transmit news of their initial training to friends and loved ones back in their respective neighborhoods. At Fort Huachuca, Clarence Gaines, Richard Shorter, William Slade, and Gus Clark began publishing a weekly column in the *Cleveland Call & Post* describing the basic training experiences of the men in the 368th for interested readers.[65] Similarly, the *Baltimore Afro-American* received a steady stream of correspondence from James H. Pinkney reporting the tent camp activities that shaped the lives of northeasterners who found their places in the ranks of the 25th and 369th Infantry regiments at the time.[66] And as the units advanced to the critical stages of their training, Texas native and New York University journalism major George H. Fowler published a series of lengthy articles in the *Chicago Defender* reminding readers about the talented individuals who worked in the headquarters companies of the regiments and offering graphic depictions of the social conditions that servicemen encountered at the base.[67]

Two things are significant here. First, as recent scholarship suggests, African American newspapers and magazines performed functions of vital importance during the Second World War. They communicated news of the training activities of the 93rd Infantry Division to African American communities and in turn provided GIs with timely commentary on national and international events that shaped their wartime experiences. This avenue of information and protest produced considerable anxiety among Washington policymakers, army commanders, and post officials.[68] Second, the relationship between the political positions taken by black newspapers during the division's initial training and the attitudes of black servicemen as members of a Jim Crow army produced a crisis. Although the newspapers provided a forum for division members to discuss conditions in the wartime army, they also put forward ideas about how the men of the 93rd Infantry Division and other segregated units should behave as soldiers when they appeared in areas away from military bases. These images were often complimentary but sometimes clashed with the notions that the recruits held of themselves. The clash of definitions regarding appropriate recreational behavior created tension between the two parties that would soon become a major source of debate and conflict throughout the early years of the division's campaign.

Off-Post Encounters

The considerable distances between Fort Huachuca and the surrounding towns and cities and the social constraints imposed by general society also helped to reinforce the community-building efforts within the military outpost. Getting to cities and towns such as Hereford, Benson, Bisbee, and Tucson was often impossible for 93rd servicemen. What's more, surrounding towns and cities had sparse black communities and offered very little recreational outlets for black soldiers. For instance, Hereford, a small town 29 miles west of Fort Huachuca, offered only a refurbished railroad station and a combination general store and post office and had no black residents.[69]

The same can be said for Bisbee (41 miles), Douglas (63 miles), and Tucson (90 miles). Along the streets of Naco, Nogales, and Aqua Prieta, located across the Mexican border south of Fort Huachuca, black GIs found adequate amusement centers, but they rarely frequented the facilities because of the stringent gasoline rationing standards imposed by the War Department and the speed limits strictly enforced by Arizona Highway Patrol.[70] At times the strategies devised by African American soldiers from Fort Huachuca to overcome these obstacles produced moments of hilarity. During one fall evening in 1942, for instance, a serviceman was arrested by the highway patrolmen and charged with reckless driving after he was caught going 40 miles an hour over the posted speed limit and undergoing a series of circuitous routes in order to avoid arrest. Throughout his trial, the soldier asserted his innocence, attributing the moving violation to the fact that "he had borrowed an officer's car from the border fort and was simply hurrying to return it."[71]

Black 93rd Division members who managed to travel to the larger cities and towns of Tucson, Flagstaff, and Bisbee learned quickly to travel in groups, as they frequently found themselves embroiled in skirmishes against civilian police and white soldiers. On 14 June 1942, a fracas broke out at the American Legion Hall in Tucson between eight members of the 93rd Division's 368th Infantry Regiment and a detachment of police officials from nearby Davis-Monthan Field and city policemen when an MP accosted two of their companions.[72] Six weeks later, Jessie Smith, a 25-year-old army recruit from Philadelphia and member of the 368th Infantry Regiment, lay dead from bullets fired by local police in Flagstaff following claims made by several officers that he had created "a general disturbance."[73]

A few months earlier, Nogales, a small city located south of Fort Huachuca along the Mexican border, witnessed a violent clash between a group of black GIs from the division and white MPs and veterans from the 8th Air Force after two of the black GIs were physically assaulted by a group of white soldiers. The skirmish ended with black and white MPs restoring order to the city and the men of the division receiving orders from its staff headquarters never to return to the area.[74] By the end of 1942, race relations between black and white servicemen reached a new low when a pitched battle broke out between members of the U.S. 364th Infantry Regiment and MPs in nearby Phoenix. The incident was given ample space in black newspapers and generated considerable discussion among army officials about the issue of due process for black soldiers stationed at garrison posts along the Arizona-Mexico border.[75]

To make matters worse, in the neighboring, unincorporated town of Fry, prostitution, bootleg whiskey, and gambling abounded in dilapidated trailers, shacks, and shanties without running water and latrines, causing unsanitary health conditions and considerable physical danger for the servicemen.[76] Described by one newspaper pundit as an endless stream of "movable red light districts," the trailer city rested in a barbed-wire barricade complete with a military police and prophylactic station and stood approximately 200 meters from the camp gates.[77] Indeed, of the teeming commercial area, an official observed: "Fry has never even pretended to be anything but a racket town. Wine, and nearly anything else with alcoholic contents, women, prostitutes in their waning years of professional endeavor, and music of the jukebox variety are Fry's chief stocks in trade."[78]

Many 93rd Division soldiers took advantage of the physical space provided by the brothels, saloons, dance halls, and gambling dens to pursue rare moments of

intimate pleasure. Not to be outdone by one another, GIs drank, shook their heavily fatigued bodies to repetitious jukebox music, and gambled during off-duty hours.
Clubs like the Blue Moon Café and Johnnie Mae's Place offered a variety of services to soldiers from the border fort.[79] Of Fry, one 369th serviceman remembers,
"Anyone who went there was going to get caught by something—the clap, a knife
blade, or if he was lucky, a tough black fist."[80] Other 93rd Division members offered
similar assessments. Robert Johnson, a Lake Charles, Louisiana, native, recalled,
"I remember that on every pay day, soldiers would form long lines outside the village just for a half hour with women in that town."[81] As might have been expected,
however, the squalid milieu of the "Hook," as pleasurable as its experiences may
have been, unfortunately resulted in widespread cases of jaundice, yellow fever,
and venereal diseases among 93rd servicemen. The ratio of infected men per thousand in the division fluctuated between 94 and 188 during the summer months,
reaching 168 during October. By January 1943, the disease rates among 93rd servicemen began to dip below 100 a year, where it would remain throughout the
much of their stateside training.[82] This drop may have been largely due to the
men's month-long participation in unit exercises that were being held at
Charlestown, Arizona, however.

The Few army officials ignored the intolerable situation that black GIs encountered
while they trained at the southwestern outpost. During his examination of the
social conditions at Fort Huachuca and its surrounding areas, the Venereal Disease Control branch chief witnessed a dance held on post attended by a thousand soldiers and five young women. Shocked at learning about these circumstances and disturbed by their explosive consequences, James Magee, the army
surgeon general, urged the immediate removal of the 93rd from the military installation. "It cannot be too strongly emphasized that a condition exists at Fort
Huachuca which if uncorrected, will inevitably cause embarrassment to the War
Department," he warned.[83]

The army Ground Forces chief disagreed with the army surgeon general's assessment, however, and would not even consider his recommendations. After
personally inspecting the situation at Fort Huachuca in March 1943, General Lesley McNair argued that the problem could be handled satisfactorily without moving the troops. Pointing out that the venereal disease rate among men in the
93rd was lower than the national average of 200 per 1,000, McNair persuaded his
subordinates to continue the division's training at Fort Huachuca before reas-
signing the unit to Louisiana the following month. Shortly afterward, the desert
military installation would house the 93rd's counterpart, the U.S. 92nd Infantry
Division.[84] McNair and other senior army officials realized that because of the

War Department's deep adherence to a racially divided army and the racial pro-scriptions imposed by civil society, the army could ill afford to reassign the all-black unit: "The problems in connection with the placing of colored troops are continuing ones and cannot be eliminated by moving troops from one place to another." Fort Huachuca post commandant Edwin Hardy agreed, stating his be-lief that although virtually all the Arizona communities were hostile toward black GIs, "the post was the best place in the United States to train a large group of Negro soldiers."[85] However, throughout 1942 and much of 1943, the issue of troop morale and assignment dominated the policy meetings of McNair and other War Department officials.

Meanwhile, Fort Huachuca post authorities and Roosevelt administration officials, as well as several black entrepreneurs, worked diligently to regulate the prostitution and gambling in the area rather than to end it. In early June 1942, Hardy discussed the lack of entertainment facilities for black soldiers and the pos-sibility of a nightclub near Fort Huachuca with Truman Gibson Jr, a Chicago at-torney and assistant civilian aide to the secretary of war. A staunch racial segre-gationist, Hardy had hoped to turn the overcrowded housing and its hard-drinking and gambling establishments into "a 100% Negro town, to include business houses, town officials, and police department." He argued, "In view of the fact that Fort Huachuca is isolated by great distances from civilian communities, it is my opin-ion that a great benefit towards the contentment and well-being of soldiers on duty at Fort Huachuca would be accomplished if there could be provided in the nearby town of Fry, reasonable forms of amusement."[86]

Gibson concurred. Shortly afterward, the assistant civilian aide traveled to Chicago to present the idea to a group of potential investors. Among the promi-nent black Chicagoans he solicited for funding were his father, Truman Gibson Sr., president of the Supreme Liberty Life Insurance Company; Spurgeon Mor-ris, a well-known dentist; and Midian Bousfield, commander of Fort Huachuca's segregated station hospital. Although many of the businessmen expressed their skepticism over issues like land acquisition, stockholders for the project, and the availability of liquor licensing in the area, they pledged their support.[87] During the first week in July, several members of the investment group traveled to the desert post, where they discussed the project with the post commander before form-ing the Fry Amusement Company. And as a result of their subsequent meetings, the men laid the groundwork for the construction of a housing project and a large recreation center in Fry aimed specifically at quelling the racial fears of local in-habitants as well as providing black GIs with lodging and leisure during their off-duty hours.[88] Privately financed, planning for the amusement center consisted of one central building that would provide draft beer, soft drinks, and food for soldiers stationed at the base.

From the project conceived by Gibson, Hardy, and others emerged the Greentop Restaurant and Bar and a dormitory containing approximately fifty rooms. Designed by Paul Williams, a prominent Los Angeles architect, the recreation center opened in March 1943 and attracted the attention of state officials, pundits, and admirers. Yet the efforts of Hardy and his business partners to provide a recreational outlet for black soldiers bore very little fruit. By the end of 1944, the project lost thousands of dollars, and its members abandoned the project altogether when the War Department deactivated the military post.[89]

But the folding of the company and the ensuing financial difficulties experienced by Gibson and other investors were the least of their troubles. While entertaining thoughts of improving the living conditions of black Fort Huachuca soldiers with the construction of the planned facility, the assistant civilian aide and other army officials faced intense public scrutiny as a result of their association with the prostitution and gambling in the area. As the summer faded into the fall of 1942, the *Atlanta Daily World, Oklahoma Eagle, Baltimore Afro-American, California Eagle,* and local Arizona newspapers carried feature stories publicizing the building of the recreation and housing facility.[90] The business partners struggled to dispel the rumors claiming that the venture "encouraged great activity by bootleggers and dope peddlers in the area" and allowed the Chicago businessmen "to solicit life insurance within the military installation." These allegations generated so much public attention that the War Department's Inspector General's office launched an official inquiry into the matter in November 1944.[91] Although that office failed to turn up any evidence of wrongdoing, a letter written by the assistant civilian aide to Claude Barnett, the publisher of the Associated Negro Press, during the fall of 1942 provides a window into the negative images attributed to the Fry amusement project. Gibson told Barnett: "Louis Lautier yesterday talked with a Chicagoan who had come out for a conference on the poll tax. He asked Louis if he knew me—said that a man from the (Chicago) *Sun* had mentioned that the paper was planning an exposé about the center at Fort Huachuca that was set up to 'exploit' Negro soldiers. Evidently there is someone in Chicago—fairly well placed—who is out gunning for us."[92]

Whether or not Gibson's anxieties were overstated is beside the point. His observation reveals the relationship between the conduct of black troops, black middle-class notions of the behavior of black soldiers, and power. For Gibson and other company members, efforts to improve the recreational outlets for black soldiers stationed in the Arizona desert had to run a gauntlet of long-standing stereotypical images of black sexual promiscuity, hypersexuality, and miscegenation while adhering to the racially stratified hierarchies in American society of the period. In the minds of the project investors, the center preserved the reputations of black GIs stationed at the border establishment. In essence, regulating the sexual behavior of division members off base became just as important as informing the public about the unit's activities in the desert training areas.[93]

Division on Display

Publicity surrounding the desert and urban maneuvers taking place at that time overshadowed the military's efforts to regulate black sexual behavior, however. Throughout much of fall and winter months of 1942 and 1943, members of the division's 318th Engineering Battalion participated in demolition, road and bridge construction, field fortification, and tactical assault training exercises. During six days of arduous movement in late October, hundreds of men in the 593rd, 594th, 595th, and 596th Field Artillery battalions along with the 318th Quartermaster Battalion maneuvered in the northern areas of Arizona. Broken into two attacking sectors, men in these units under the leadership of Brigadier General William Spence took up offensive and defensive positions, directing barrages of artillery fire against an imaginary enemy. Around the same time, members of the 369th Infantry Regiment embarked on a four-day, 60-mile march around the Huachuca Mountains. Grim but determined, the men trudged onward, completing a 4,000-foot trek from Bear Canyon and negotiating Montezuma Pass with full knapsacks and weapons bearing down on them every step of the way. Undaunted, however, the regiment successfully negotiated the mountainous terrain, returning to the cantonment area in near record time.[94] By the end of January 1943, virtually all the elements of the division had experienced their first taste of unit training as servicemen progressed through an urban assault course in combat fighting and street infiltration staged at a nearby abandoned mining town.[95]

Almost overnight, artists and national media seized upon the promising performances of the army's first all-black division with great enthusiasm. In late December 1942, filmmaker Mervyn Freeman visited the desert installation to make a newsreel about the division.[96] Around the same time, noted journalist Earl Brown and photographer Charles Steinheimer traveled to Fort Huachuca to write a feature story on the division's training activities for *Life* magazine.[97]

Not long afterward, the training and discipline exhibited by the men of the division also captured the attention of more than a few army officials. As the men approached the end of the initial phases of their unit training, division commander

Major General Fred W. Miller proclaimed, "The men are developing into hard, efficient, resourceful, and dependable fighters and I believe they will go to town for us."[98] During a series of visits to the military installation during the latter half of 1942, Lieutenant General Walter Krueger of the 3rd Army echoed Miller's sentiments, praising the training performances of the enlisted personnel and officer corps in the division.[99] Indeed, after inspecting the division during a tour of the military post in July of that year, Brigadier General Benjamin Davis Sr., the highest-ranking African American commissioned officer in the Regular Army at the time, told the post commandant that he was pleased with the unit's progress. Witnessing elements of the division in action and smartly dressed officers and men who snapped to attention as he was being driven by in a staff car, Davis noted, "The general appearance of the enlisted personnel was above average and the Negro officers are all showing a deep interest in their work and making satisfactory progress." "Ninety-third Infantry Division is being very satisfactorily administered and trained," he stated.[100]

But in letters to his wife about his visit to Fort Huachuca, Davis also noted a great deal of unrest among the servicemen in the division, as he heard endless complaints made by 93rd servicemen of their experiences with racism within the unit. In some ways, black GIs found themselves facing situations similar to those they experienced in civil society years earlier. After taking the army's classification test, they were given assignments based on their skills and prior war occupations. Since virtually all the black 93rd recruits wanted to obtain some specialized training, those who received noncombat and heavy-labor assignments such as those in construction, engineer, ordnance, and truck maintenance units were sorely disappointed. Curtis Griffin, an unemployed worker from Cleveland, was assigned as a motor pool mechanic; 21-year-old District of Columbia resident and construction worker Tommie Pendergrass was appointed mess hall assistant; Julius Thompson, a manual laborer from Norfolk, Virginia, was assigned to the motor pool; and Robert Galley, a dishwasher from Palestine, Texas, who had hoped to earn training as a radio technician, was assigned to the mess hall.[101] The morale among the men in the division was such that Davis cryptically told his wife, "There is lots of agitation here and I shall tell you all about it when I see you."[102]

The other areas of "agitation" that Davis hinted at may have been the manner in which black division members likened the unjust racial practices in the army to the Civil War and Reconstruction. During his inspection of the division, the inspector general attaché visited the post's service club, hostess house, and guardhouse, where he heard endless stories about the treatment of black service personnel within the division. Jerry Sykes, a soldier in a company of the 369th, told the brigadier general, "I'm basically fighting against slavery down here, sir."[103] Jerry Johnson, a 25th infantryman incarcerated for insubordination, echoed Sykes's sentiments, telling the veteran officer, "The jim-crowing of our outfit down here must stop."[104]

For these African American soldiers and others, the federally sanctioned policies of racial oppression had more to do with issues of labor, manhood, and dignity than anything else. For example, in August 1942, members of the 93rd's 369th Headquarters Company staged a sit-down strike in their barracks, refusing to answer to roll call after their battalion commander had openly insulted them by referring to them as "boys." When the incident ended, the men won a small victory as the officer issued a public apology to them. As one soldier later recalled, "We knew we had won a terrific victory as incomplete as it was. A bunch of goddamned recruits defied the Jim Crow Army and won."[105]

The difficulties between African American soldiers and white officers within the 93rd Division stemmed partly from the War Department's belief that southern white officers possessed far better leadership qualifications to command black troops than did northern white and black cadres.[106] Since a large portion of the enlisted men came from the American South, its officer corps would be composed of white southerners. Within the 93rd Division's staff, commanding officer General Charles Hall hailed from Mississippi, assistant commander Edward Almond from Virginia, division field artillery commander William Spence from North Carolina, Chief of Staff Stanley Prouty from South Carolina, and another eventual division commander, Harry Johnson, from Texas.[107] In the words of Brigadier General Edward Almond, the division's assistant commander and later 92nd Infantry Division commander, "I think that General Marshall felt that General Hall, who was in command of the Ninety-third Division when I was Assistant Division Commander and was from Mississippi, understood the characteristic of the Negro and his habits and inclinations. The artilleryman at that time was General William Spence from North Carolina as I recall, who also had that understanding and I being from Virginia had an understanding of southern customs and Negro capabilities; the attitudes of Negroes in relationships thereto. I think that my selection for the Ninety-third and Ninety-second Divisions was of the same character."[108]

Many black soldiers had another image of senior army officials, however. Reporting to Fort Huachuca in late April 1942, John Howard recalled his first encounter with Captain Paul Bowen, his company commander: "As an infantry officer motivated and ready to serve my country, I reported to the company office to meet Captain Bowen, my commanding officer. After I saluted, gave my name and rank, and indicated I was reporting for duty, Bowen didn't even look up from his desk. He only said, 'I hate niggers.'"[109] Six months later, Rudolph Porter, a 26-year-old medical officer with the 368th Infantry, and his wife were driving just beyond a regimental area when a white company-grade officer stopped him for running a stop sign. Although the infraction was hardly unusual, the situation escalated dramatically when the ranking officer, in an apparent attempt to reprimand Porter, openly insulted the young physician, yelling, "Nigger, stop that damn car." After being charged, tried, and convicted of "behaving with disrespect toward a superior officer," Porter received a sentence of three months in the post guardhouse.[110]

Leavenworth, Kansas, native and 25th Infantry officer Leo Logan had a similar experience with the division commander: "The commanding general visited our company area one day and chewed me out in front of my men for not reporting properly. He ordered my company commander to court-martial me, and he held up the company commander's promotion when he wouldn't do it. I was later accused of shooting at the general, which I did not." Logan found himself transferred to the 92nd Division in September 1943, three months prior to 93rd's deployment overseas.[111] Logan's comments illuminate the circumstances under which African American GIs in the 93rd respected the authority of white officers. For them, respect for military authority was granted only when white general and staff officers affirmed the GIs' status as first-class citizen-soldiers in the U.S. Army. And in turn, black soldiers like Logan challenged that authority when they felt that their sense of dignity and manhood had been affronted.

Meanwhile, other black soldiers fashioned their own responses to these racial strictures. In late March 1943, having trained throughout much of the weekend, black troops in a mortar platoon of the 369th Infantry learned that their company commander had failed to inform their black platoon leader that his unit was scheduled to undergo tactical firing tests for the unit the following week. Led by Everett Moore, a talented young NCO from Toledo, Ohio, the men of the unit performed so well on the firing range that following Monday that they earned the praise of their young lieutenant as well as that of other black junior officers in their company and their senior inspectors from the division headquarters. Recalling the incident years later, a second lieutenant stated, "This was hardly unusual. Remember, Fort Huachuca was a desolate place, and the weekends always gave us more time to plan and prepare our strategies to cope with the following days of training. This is not to mention the fact that my platoon sergeant and the group of men under my command were fully committed to do all they could to succeed."[112] Reuben Fraser, a young black section leader in one of the division's heavy weapons companies, responded to the racial strictures in a different way. Arriving from Fort

Benning, Georgia, during this period, Fraser found unacceptable the treatment of men in his platoon and the duties to which they were assigned. In June 1943, he translated his thoughts into action when he ordered his men to bury an ammunition depot after his superiors had instructed them to unload supplies. Fraser faced immediate repercussions for this strategy when 368th Infantry commander James Urquhart learned of his act of rebellion and verbally reprimanded the young second lieutenant in front of his subordinates before deciding to fine him fifty dollars a month for a year.[113]

Such intimidating responses to everyday forms of resistance in the division produced only temporary results, however. Black soldiers in the unit slowly adjusted their strategies in order to draw the attention of the black press and African American organizations to the problem of maintaining such a large segregated force as well as to fundamental questions about the role black combat troops would play in the American war effort. Meanwhile, army officials struggled to devise training schedules for the two all-black combat divisions while maintaining the army's wartime racial policies. The longer the division trained in Arizona, however, the more glaring a problem the policy of segregation would become for the Roosevelt administration and army officials. By the end of 1942, rhetoric and reality would collide with tremendous consequences for all who were involved.

A Question of Morale

A combination of events occurred during the summer and fall months of 1942 that posed new questions among black soldiers about the division's well-being. On 4 June 1942, post adjutant general Carroll Nelson issued a memorandum establishing separate officers' clubs for all black and white cadres stationed at the base.[114] Almost overnight, black frustration boiled over. Nearly two hundred officers boycotted the service clubs and wrote numerous letters to black newspapers protesting their operation on post.[115] Even though the protest strategies failed to yield immediate results, the post commander abandoned the policy by the end of the war.[116]

Racial tensions between division soldiers and senior officials at the border fort reached a climax in late 1942 as new questions arose regarding the division's status as a viable combat unit. In October 1942, Arizona governor Sidney Osborn wrote a letter to War Department officials requesting that soldiers at Fort Huachuca be relieved of their duties in order to assist in the harvesting of the long-staple cotton crop in nearby Pima and Maricopa counties. Osborn's request was prompted largely by the war's impact on southern Arizona's languishing agricultural industry and the desperate recruiting and retention campaign made by cotton growers to meet the growing farm labor demand. In 1942, Arizona farmers had planted 122,000 of the 187,000 acres of the long-staple cotton grown in the United States. Used as a substitute for silk, the long-stemmed crop was virtually essential to the war effort, for its fibers were needed to produce parachutes, machine gun belts, naval balloons, and gliders.[117] But the incessant flow of able-bodied men to military service and local war industries like Tucson's Consolidated Aircraft Corporation spelled a smaller labor pool and "Men Wanted" signs for cotton producers throughout the region.[118]

During the summer, Arizona government, U.S. Employment Service, and Farm Security Administration officials tried to ease the impending labor shortage in cotton by employing high school students, importing migratory labor from adjacent states, and impressing into service Mexicans and Japanese Americans incarcerated at relocation centers within the state. What's more, two superior court judges from Pima County approved a proposal made by a state prison warden to use one hundred convict laborers to meet the pressing demands in Arizona's cotton fields, but the number called for by the measure was hardly sufficient. By November, seven thousand bales of the war-vital crop lay in the fields awaiting harvest as the shortage of cotton choppers reached crisis levels.[119] Insisting that the crop was necessary to the war effort, the Arizona governor claimed that, "unless drastic steps are taken to pick the crops, thousands of bales of this vital staple will be lost." Recognizing that African Americans constituted the majority of the troops stationed in the state, Osborn went on to argue that "the request for those experienced in cotton picking is no reflection upon either race when the work that they are asked to do is that which will materially aid our government in its war effort."[120]

Osborn's plea received mixed responses from the White House. Although, in a memorandum to the president in late November of the previous year, senior cabinet members had in fact mentioned the possibility of ordering soldiers into the fields during the wartime emergency, the secretary of war bridled at the idea. A onetime secretary of state in the Hoover administration and a racial conservative, Henry Stimson believed that other measures should be contemplated before utilizing the army in such a capacity. Meeting with a White House aide at the time, he stated, "I think that by getting these substitute Japs to do this labor of picking cotton, it saves us from making a bad precedent by using the army. Using the army would be impractical of efficient employment and would seriously impair its training."[121]

President Roosevelt, however, disagreed with the reservations expressed by the secretary of war and others. Unlike his administration officials, Roosevelt thought that the employment of army personnel might resolve the labor shortages in agriculture. On 19 February, Roosevelt met with Stimson, Undersecretary of War Robert P. Patterson, and War Manpower Commission head Paul V. McNutt and voiced his support for the proposal made earlier by the War Department. The president also mentioned that former South Carolina senator and Supreme Court justice James Byrnes had proposed a similar plan in which the army would assign both white and black battalions stationed in Pima County to harvest the cotton crop. Four days later, deputy army chief of staff Lieutenant General Joseph T. McNarney disclosed the army's plans to deploy black and white troops stationed at nearby military installations in the harvesting of crops in Arizona "within ten days or two weeks" while testifying before the Senate Subcommittee on Agriculture and Forestry.[122]

Why Roosevelt approved this move is not altogether clear. As scholars have noted, the president tended to display a predilection for exercising political expedience and caution by mollifying competing groups during periods of conflict.[123] In this particular case, the Arizona farm crisis and the treatment of black troops were part and parcel of the political conundrum he had faced periodically throughout his presidency: how to shore up support among southern members of the Democratic Party while reaching out (symbolically, if at all) to farm, labor, urban, and racial ethnic groups. But, in his efforts to stave off a potential policy crisis regarding the supply of labor for agriculture, the remarks made by the chief executive during a press conference on 23 February 1942 raised a more contentious question. When queried about the army's announcement in the midst of White House correspondents, Roosevelt stated:

> The Arizona case is a very special case. It's a crop that has to be got in for military reasons, if nothing else—you can't eat it—but you can use it for military—great military needs. And there were some troops—some colored and white—and I think for four or five days those troops are the kind of troops that can be used for that kind of an operation. Suppose you have a division that has had 38 weeks of training, and they need four more weeks before they are ready to go. If you start to take ten more or twenty more out of each company and put them back on the farm, you will be slowing up the readiness of that division to go into the fighting front. On the other hand, there are other troops which are not exactly in that character, they may be Services of Supply troops back home, or engineer troops, like some of these in Arizona.[124]

As accounts of the army's plans and Roosevelt's press conference hit the daily newsstands, black commentators and leaders criticized the War Department and interpreted the Arizona governor's request as a racist move to use members of the segregated division as landless farm workers or tenants. Press reports in the *Atlanta Daily World* and *People's Voice* played up the exploitative dimensions of the issue and questioned the army's intentions, suggesting that the Roosevelt administration displayed more interest in maintaining the racial status quo than in assigning black soldiers to a combat role in the war.[125] The *Chicago Defender* made this point clear in a front-page story on 6 March 1943: "Behind the curtain action, with Negro soldiers as the puppets, is being enacted between Washington and Arizona. The name of the play—Cotton Picker!"[126]

On 26 February 1943, NAACP executive secretary Walter White had advised the secretary of war that "the plan should be abandoned completely." "Our experience over a period of a good many years causes us to be certain that unless extraordinary precautions are taken, what will actually happen will be that Negro soldiers will form the bulk if not all of those so assigned to these duties," he stated.[127] The fact that members of the division were stationed in the area was very much on the minds of White and other association officials. In a letter written to the Arizona governor several days later, White also pointed out "that such an experiment in Arizona, as proposed, made it hard to avoid the conclusion that the state was selected because of the presence of a segregated division at Fort Huachuca." According to the NAACP executive secretary, the problem in the Arizona counties stemmed from large cotton planters who rebelled against Farm Security Administration regulations requiring them to provide decent wages to farm laborers. Openly expressing their defiance, some of the cotton growers had gone months without paying the minimum prescribed wage of thirty cents an hour. But White also suggested that 93rd service personnel should be used "if there were no available labor supply whatsoever."[128] Meanwhile, the plans formulated by the Roosevelt administration also prompted a flood of angry response from local association members. A black NAACP official of the Tucson chapter, Charles Douglass, wrote Walter White, "I have just written a letter to the President and the Congress protesting the proposal to have Negro troops pick cotton in Arizona. Couldn't you organize a postal campaign to protest this latest outrage? It is an insult to every one of the 13,000,000 colored folks in this country."[129]

The remarks made by White and Douglass are striking because Roosevelt administration officials had hoped to manage worker shortages in agriculture in ways that adhered to American wartime demands. In their mind, such demands were a military necessity. But Roosevelt, Stimson, and other White House officials underestimated the ways in which the social and political character of the labor duties may have tapped into the suspicions that black political leaders and pundits harbored about the army itself. The prospect of black soldiers picking cotton while wearing the nation's uniform was also an insult to the racial and gender conventions within the African American community for the appropriate masculine behavior of combat soldiers in the U.S. Army. Perhaps noted sociologist Horace Cayton may have best summed up how many African Americans viewed the issue when he commented: "I have no argument to make at the moment as to whether soldiers, white or black, should or should not help farmers whether it is picking cotton or sowing wheat. But the unfortunate thing in this instance is the Army and Arizona are starting this program of soldiers working for farmers with Negro troops and of all agricultural pursuits—picking cotton. The armed forces should bend over backwards to see that Negro soldiers are not the first soldiers to be used as farmers and that of all things they should not be assigned to pick cotton which epitomizes to many a return to slavery status."[130]

In many ways, Cayton's words proved to be prophetic. Throughout the fall and winter of 1942, division members registered their discontent over what they interpreted as the War Department's extension of the civilian racial system to military life. Throughout January 1943, black men of the 369th Infantry held a series of meetings with Chaplain Robert Smith and the 369th Infantry commander, Colonel Thomas F. Taylor, during which they railed vehemently against the cotton controversy.[131] "It is true that cotton is vital to the defense, but Negroes are not the only soldiers in the state of Arizona," a soldier stated.[132] GIs also took unauthorized sick leaves, earning stays in the post stockade for their blatant acts of insubordination. For example, a letter by Fort Huachuca station hospital commander Midian O. Bousfield to civilian aide Truman Gibson described how black GIs in the 93rd's 368th and 25th Infantry regiments had avoided being selected for the labor tasks: "These boys have played the game by 'getting sick'—they refuse to soldier, they get crippled and are subtle about it. The 368th and Twenty-fifth has had large numbers of men in the stockade and the causes are insubordination and resentment over being ordered to perform 'slave duties.'"[133]

In fact, the numbers who were incarcerated during this period bear out the assertions made by Bousfield. Out of a total of 14,775 division veterans, 492 had been sentenced to time in the stockade for insubordination between June 1942 and September of the following year—an average of 33 per month.[134] Despite numerous public denials from the War Department to the contrary, the crisis for black 93rd Division personnel was averted only when War Manpower Commission and Department of Agriculture officials deemed the movement unnecessary after agreeing to intensify efforts to import Mexican workers and Japanese evacuees into the area.[135] By April 1943, the War Department had abandoned its plans altogether.[136]

Post Departures

In late March 1943, members of the 93rd boarded Pullman coaches to journey to a maneuver area located near Camp Polk, Louisiana, but not before expressing their bitter attitudes toward the armed forces. Expelled from their barracks and ordered to turn in their supplies to the post quartermaster and to sleep outside before boarding the troop trains, forty soldiers from the 368th Infantry broke into the post exchange for blankets and warm housing. When the tense situation ended days later, all forty men were court-martialed and sentenced to sixty days of hard labor and a reduction in rank.[137] Angered by the chain of events, one black soldier recalled, "Soldiers were very resentful because the court-martials made it seem as if we soldiers, not the army, were guilty of a crime."[138] On the other hand, Midian O. Bousfield observed the destroyed building and commented, "My only hope is that these Negro troops do not receive condemnation on the basis that they just do not make good soldiers."[139]

In many ways, the incident at the train depot epitomized the early training experiences of black GIs in the division. First, army officials struggled to promote the image of a racially harmonious military while maintaining the army's discriminatory practices. However, they tended to underestimate the lengths to which black soldiers would go to create a special sense of camaraderie among them and the degree to which they would enlist sectors of African American society to aid them in their cause as they began to translate their own ideas of their roles in the war's objectives into action. Yet these notions were also often strained by the intraracial class cleavages within the army as black enlisted men and officers often felt alienated from each other. By the middle of 1943, the fractious discussions held among War Department officials and division members over the war's meaning as well as military discipline and authority began to appear in other sectors of African American society as army officials formulated plans to deploy the unit to an active theater of combat.

PART TWO

THE HAND THAT ROCKS THE CRADLE HOLDS THE SHIELD

★ ★ ★

The nation needs the brains, the energies and even the lives of every man and woman and child to make possible this supreme effort. But does this mean I must accept a synthetic unity, searing the surface of conflicts that are deep and treacherous? Am I to forget the festering sores of racial intolerance, injustice, brutality and humiliation eating at the core of my national allegiance?

Pauli Murray, 1942

There were daily and practical struggles for family and community survival that made the conflicting legacies of simultaneous collaboration and resistance to U.S. wars and the military even more complex and intricate.

Barbara Omolade, 1994

CHAPTER FOUR

Service Families on the Move

✯ ✯ ✯

We are continuing to find long delays in obtaining reports from
American Red Cross Chapters, but are finding the most of them
reasonably adequate when they finally are received. There is considerable contact with the branch chapter on the post because of
the rather large numbers of wives and other relatives residing on
or adjacent to the Post.

Thelma T. Hawes

In January 1943, Thelma Thurston Gorham stumbled upon a revelation of sorts.
After traveling to Fort Huachuca to cover the training activities of the U.S. 93rd
Infantry Division, the *Crisis* reporter was struck by the growing numbers of black
women and their families who lived at the military installation. After watching
them endure the harsh Arizona sun and the squalid, makeshift dwellings and dor-
mitories that housed them, she published an article in the NAACP house organ
in which she proclaimed:

> When it was decided to isolate Negro troops from the rest of civilization by walling
> them up, high and dry, out there in the Arizona desert, WIVES and such things were
> not taken into consideration. The WACS have their work pretty well cut out for them
> and provisions have been made for their comfort. But WIVES, and this goes for many
> posts besides Fort Huachuca, have had to clear away the underbrush along, blaze
> their own trails and learn to soldier the hard way, along with their menfolk. They
> cannot follow their husbands across, but they can follow or precede them to isolated
> posts like Fort Huachuca, Arizona, where they must adjust themselves to the other
> side of the American way of life.[1]

What fascinated and perplexed Gorham and other military officials sustained the
soldiers who trained at the desert training facility during the period. Because they

were away from most towns and cities, service family members and friends created a world for black GIs that reflected both army and home life. But their attempts to help servicemen adjust to the rigors of army life also involved collective and individual efforts to safeguard the physical and emotional well-being of GIs training in the field. As a result, a new perspective came into being, one that linked the struggles of black GIs to realize equality in the segregated army to efforts to improve social, political, and economic conditions in a racially stratified American society.

The community-building efforts made by black army dependents at Fort Huachuca and the protest politics fostered among service families during the initial training phase of the 93rd Infantry Division are the focus of this chapter.[2] During the division's training in Arizona, dependents of soldiers played prominent roles in maintaining links between the barracks and the civilian communities of America as well as in providing safe spaces for their relatives in the ranks of the segregated army. But by May 1943, as they began to pack their belongings to leave Arizona, the wartime ideals they forged at Fort Huachuca had become paradoxically fused with African American wartime politics, producing numerous uneasy moments of accord and acrimony for all the parties involved.

Relative Deployment

When the African American 93rd Division personnel began training at Fort Huachuca, hundreds of their relatives had to decide whether to accompany them to the Arizona military base. Between December 1941 and April 1943, more than nine hundred family members poured into the towns and cities near the military outpost, with the majority of the newcomers arriving from Texas, California, Louisiana, Illinois, Oklahoma, Missouri, New York, and the District of Columbia. Immediate family members—parents, wives, siblings, and children—composed more than three-quarters of the newcomers. Of these loved ones who stepped from the platforms of the train and bus depots located near the military outposts, the majority were adult females between 20 and 27 years old, and most were married. A small percentage were children under the age of 15. Although many young children traveled in small groups that included a parent and a sibling, a considerable number (63 percent of the cases examined) made the trip alone.[3] Furthermore, a small percentage of division kith and kin, like New York City resident Caroline Traynham, made the trip in stages, stopping to visit distant relatives in other towns and cities along the way before arriving at their final destination.[4]

Service family members and other loved ones migrated to the sparse Southwest for a variety of reasons. In some cases, decisions to relocate reflected the dynamic changes in their life and a yearning to maintain existing family life. In May 1941, 73-year-old Margaret Hammond faced the prospect of living in her Chattanooga, Tennessee, home alone and losing her support system when her only child, Thomas, joined the army. Too old to effectively care for herself, she elected to abandon the place where she had worked as a domestic in a white household for nearly fifty years after her husband's death to join her son at Fort Huachuca when he was assigned to the 25th Infantry Regiment. Upon her arrival, Hammonds landed employment in the post exchange, where she acquired a considerable amount of expertise in dealing with the post commander and his staff officers.[5] In a similar fashion, 57-year-old widow Mattie Walker and a small group including her daughter, daughter-in-law, and grandson made the long journey from Baltimore County, Maryland, to Cochise County, Arizona, after her son William received orders to report to the post in May 1942.[6]

Children made the move, with or without other family members, so that families could be kept together and existing family life could be maintained as much as possible. Although the move precipitated a wide range of emotions among the children, most were happy that their family was all in one place. After her mother died in 1942, 10-year-old Lillian Jones and her two sisters, Rafaela and Beatriz, had little choice but to follow their father from Nogales, Arizona, to Fort Huachuca, where he enlisted in the 93rd's 25th Infantry Regiment. While their father trained with the unit, the siblings were left in the care of an aunt who lived on the military outpost at the time. There they remained until their father returned for them in 1946 after serving in the Pacific. Lillian recalled some forty years later: "When my father left for the war, black women on post like my aunt Mrs. Crawford provided everything that we needed. They knew that my father was gone and that we really didn't like being away from him but they kept us busy every day of the week so that we wouldn't think so much about him."[7]

John A. De Veaux Jr. was 5 years old when, in May 1942, his father, a Bethel African Methodist Episcopal minister in Williamsport, Pennsylvania, reported to the 93rd as the division chaplain. During the period, John and his brother attended kindergarten and played hopscotch on the parade grounds adjacent to the barracks. He recalled one memorable occasion when he saw his first jeep: "Dad brought one home and gave me a ride in it." John and his family remained at the post until June 1943, when his father received orders to accompany former Wilberforce University president and African Methodist Episcopal bishop John A. Gregg on a six-week tour of the South Pacific to minister to the spiritual needs of black troops serving in the theater of operations. Shortly afterward, his mother took the two boys by train back to Williamsport, where they resided until their father's return from overseas duty.[8]

Some individuals decided to move in the hope of making a contribution to military post life. For instance, after her husband, Colonel Louis Carter, died in Tucson in late 1940, Mary Moss faced very few prospects other than to return to the home they had built in the affluent Blodgett Manor section of Los Angeles or to her small network of family and friends in Knoxville, Tennessee. Instead, she elected to return to Fort Huachuca, where she had worked as senior hostess of a guesthouse where her husband served as the post chaplain for the men of the 25th Infantry Regiment for more than thirty years. Shortly afterward, largely because of the shortage of civilian workers at the military outpost, Moss worked as a director of one of the base's service clubs, where she served as an unofficial benefactor for black recruits, advising them on various matters such as housing, community relations, and post activities.[9] Fifty-three-year-old Nelle Bishop Dillon made a similar life-altering decision. After her husband passed away and her sons left college to enter the army, the Tuskegee Institute graduate elected to take a leave of absence as state supervisor of federally aided vocational schools in Oklahoma to accompany them to Fort Huachuca. There Dillon lived and worked at the military post as a service club director, serving as a counselor to numerous soldiers seeking guidance on a number of issues including homesickness, training difficulties, troubled relationships, marital difficulties, and financial problems.[10]

Promises of financial assistance and temporary lodging from family members as well as the hope of securing expanded professional and economic opportunities figured prominently in the migratory impulses of more than a few who poured into the southern Arizona area during the period. In November 1942, Fort Smith, Arkansas, resident Rebecca Hill left her job as a librarian at St. Philips College to join her brother James at the military base before being appointed as the chief service club librarian.[11] Around the same time, Marie Myers moved 300 miles from Phoenix, Arizona, to Fort Huachuca to assist her cousin Elizabeth after she began her duties as a social director and library assistant at the post service club.[12] At his uncle's insistence, Morris Bowles journeyed from Chicago to live in a trailer park located near the division training area for several weeks before he landed a job as a dance instructor at the local USO.[13] In a similar vein, Mrs. J. H. Page and her husband made room in their squalid officer billets for Elizabeth Barbour after they convinced her to leave her job as a caseworker in Springhouse, Pennsylvania, to take up the position of matron of the sole women's dormitory at the military outpost. Of her experiences, Barbour recalled months later, "I was quite fortunate to find employment at the post and it wasn't much at the start. There wasn't anything in the buildings but the insides, and maybe a nail or two to hang a coat upon so to speak. But since that time, in the short span of four months, my dormitory housed approximately 300 women, all of whom were employed in various offices and post exchanges. Not a bad place for poor working women to rest in comfort."[14]

Finally, many young black women elected to join their loved ones in uniform at the Arizona military garrison after they were married. As scholars have pointed out, the two central questions of young women and men during the war were whether they should get married and whether they should have a baby.[15] But questions of when and how often to move also complicated the thoughts and actions of black women associated with the division as they pondered relocation possibilities.

The migration process and points of arrival varied widely among the servicemen's wives and families. After graduating from Howard University in May 1942, 20-year-old Virginia Quivers accompanied George Leighton to Tucson after they were married in Washington, D.C. Once arriving there, Leighton continued on to join the 93rd Infantry Division at Fort Huachuca while Quivers boarded with a woman living in the city who had five sons training at the military facility.[16] A year earlier, 23-year-old Philadelphia native Arline Bibbins spent several weeks with relatives living in Trenton, New Jersey, while her fiancé, Julius Young, was ordered to appear before an induction board at Fort Dix. After they were married and Young was shipped to Fort Benning, Georgia, in August 1942, Bibbins lived in temporary housing and worked as a waitress in nearby Columbus. There she stayed for nearly three months before moving on to Bisbee after Young was assigned to a new duty assignment in a headquarters company of the 93rd Division.[17] Indeed, so overwhelming was the wartime rush to the altar that the Tucson-based *Arizona Daily Star* reported in March 1943, "Numerous marriage licenses have been issued by the local clerk, with a large majority of them apparently going to Negroes, many of whom came long distances for the weddings. The marriage license bureau wouldn't be doing half the business it does if it weren't for the military establishments in or around Tucson."[18]

Yet the determination of black women and children to accompany their loved ones serving in the 93rd Infantry Division was hardly unique. In many cases, the migration experiences of young wives, children, and distant relatives followed a similar stepwise manner from base to base. In June 1942, Ollive Davenport and her daughter Patricia Ann left St. Louis, Missouri, to spend several weeks with relatives in Junction City, Kansas, until her companion, Oscar, received orders to travel from Fort Leavenworth to his new assignment with the 25th Infantry Regiment stationed at Fort Huachuca.[19] In a similar fashion, Jennie Smith and her daughter left their home in Everett, Massachusetts, in March 1942 to join her husband while he attended officer candidate school for chaplains at Fort Harrison, Indiana. After spending three months living in hotel rooms and boardinghouses in the area, Smith and her family traveled by train to Arizona, where her husband was assigned as a chaplain to the division.[20]

Desert Challenges

The movement of single and married black women to the desert installation raised a set of issues for state officials and white army officers with regard to the notions they held about black women's roles and acceptable female behavior. Senior army officers responded to the swelling numbers of black women and families living on the military base with attitudes that ranged from muted ambivalence to outright disdain. When Evelyn Tollette and her eight sisters moved into the area to take up residence as nurse practitioners at one of the two post hospitals in October 1942, E. B. Maynard, Fort Huachuca's chief health officer, commented, "To say that their presence is essential to well-being of everyone here would be trite, but true."[21] Other white army officials viewed the rapid influx of black women and children as an affront to long-standing military discipline and culture, however. For instance, Fort Huachuca post commander Colonel Edwin Hardy referred to service relatives as "camp leeches" and bitterly complained that the military outpost had now become "a plantation" as a result of the steady stream of black newcomers to the Arizona desert area.[22]

Senior officers also responded to the growing presence of black women at the military base with views that were tainted with stereotypical notions of sexual promiscuity, venereal disease, and moral depravity. As the division progressed through the opening stages of its stateside training during the summer of 1942, Fort Huachuca post authorities screened black women for venereal disease when they arrived in the post area. "The Negro female race is more highly sexed than the white race, thus resulting in a greater number of exposures in a given period of time," wrote a medical officer to justify the military's policies during the period.[23] Around the same time, army officials in the 9th Service Command, after investigating alleged prostitution at the military installation, concluded that they had considerable "evidence that the wives of soldiers and the wives of non-commissioned officers have been immoral," and they urged more stringent monitoring of civilian women who appeared at the military outpost.[24] By the end of the division's eleven-month training period in Arizona, such negative public myths of black womanhood, derived from mid-nineteenth-century notions of morality, only increased racial tensions at the outpost. After arriving from Chicago to meet her husband at the post in April 1943, De Loise Collins was taunted with insults by post exchange officers such as "there goes one of those nigger wives" and "cuddle bunnies," implying that she and other female relatives of the soldiers were there for the sole purpose of functioning as sexual outlets for the troops stationed at the military installation.

The tensions between black women like De Loise Collins and military post officials were deeply rooted in the military's efforts to reshape public notions of sexuality in service communities during the war. The mobilization for World War II witnessed renewed efforts by state, law enforcement, and public health officials and members of Congress to control the sexual behavior of soldiers. In early 1940, U.S. Public Health Service officials, War Department staff personnel, and members of the American Social Hygiene Association met to discuss plans to develop an anti–venereal disease program. Following their joint meetings, conferees drew up an eight-point resolution that proposed early diagnosis and detection, education, and aggressive case-finding services. Even though they struggled to adopt a comprehensive program, however, the resolution ended in failure. Yet scarcely a year later, efforts to control the sexual activity of army personnel succeeded with the passage of the May Act. Although originally designed to halt the spread of venereal disease, the legislation later allowed War Department officials to prosecute individuals, businesses, and cities that tolerated houses of prostitution and vice near military installations.[25]

But as scholars have pointed out, although the War Department invoked the act to suppress prostitution in areas surrounding Camp Forrest, Tennessee, and Fort Bragg, North Carolina, the legislation actually allowed army officials at military bases like Fort Huachuca, Arizona, and authorities in nearby cities and towns to link public health efforts to "protect" soldiers on leave from prostitution to distorted images of black women.[26] Commentary by an observer visiting a segregated military base during the period provides a window into the beliefs that many white senior officers held with respect to the images of black women who appeared at the training areas: "I was seated next to the colonel in command of the camp. There were colonels to the left of me, colonels to the right of me, all over forty. They were officially glad I was interested in the troops, etc. The next topic revolved about the case of a soldier who had been accused of raping a colored girl. This to the present company being an impossibility on the face of it, the accusation got some ordinary laughter and the soldier was freed by both present and past juries."[27]

Black service family members and friends who ventured to Fort Huachuca that summer resisted these demeaning perceptions and fought to preserve their integrity. In May 1942, 24-year-old Hazel Craig found herself barred from entering the military base when she refused to subject herself to venereal disease screening by army examiners.[28] Three months later, Izola Wilder followed a similar course of action while traveling with her fiancé, William Jones, an officer with the division's engineering battalion. Wilder had no sooner arrived at the military installation when she nearly came to blows with a military policeman after he made remarks alleging that she had slept with every GI on post and suggesting that she check into a nearby clinic for possible treatment for "bad blood."[29]

At the same time, the determined efforts made by Izola Wilder and other 93rd Division family members to join loved ones in uniform stationed at Fort Huachuca aroused equally impassioned responses from African Americans living on the military post. Many black division cadre members went to great lengths to lend material and emotional support to the vast numbers of black women and children arriving at the post. One officer who was particularly concerned with the on-base conduct of African American women was Colonel Midian Bousfield, the station hospital commander. A prominent Chicago physician and longtime consultant to the American Public Health Association, Bousfield issued a series of memorandums to women who arrived at the military camp, urging them to adhere to conventional notions of respectability and counseling them on the need to maintain the highest degree of moral rectitude while visiting the base. In addition, he crafted an elaborate list of dos and don'ts regarding appropriate language, clothing, areas of visitation, and social activities. Pressing his point even further, Bousfield stressed that racial uplift depended on the conduct of women at the post. "With a view of avoiding trouble, embarrassment, and adverse reflection on the military establishment and the race in particular, it must be kept in mind that where there are large groups of men removed from the restraining influences of home, many things are liable to occur that would not occur under the usual and normal conditions," he warned.[30]

Yet even though black camp officers like Midian Bousfield made efforts to counter the negative sexual stereotypes of black women traveling to the area, they expressed mixed feelings about women who lived at the military installation. The ambivalent attitudes expressed by Bousfield and other post members were derived from gender notions voiced within the black community that were themselves a product of centuries of racial oppression, class antagonism, and sexual exploitation. For Bousfield and other black cadre members stationed at the base, the prospect of large numbers of female service relatives migrating to restricted areas clashed with the patriarchal notions that they, along with other segments of the African American community, held regarding a black woman's place in wartime. Between 1941 and 1943, for example, black weekly newspapers ran articles and political cartoons with titles such "A Wife's Place at Home" or "The Soldier's Wife" which described the war-related movement of black women to military areas as "traffic in romance."[31] Similarly, newspapers instructed women in the ways of dignified womanhood and proper etiquette at military camps. And instructions on how to behave were often followed by warnings of the dangers that awaited those women who did not possess the qualities of true womanhood. In a February 1943 article in the *Baltimore Afro-American,* a writer advised young female service relatives, "Let your soldier know you're coming to see him," and went on to issue the following warning: "If you're inclined to be flirtatious, bury those inclinations when going to see your soldier. You'll find he's twice as jealous now that he is a soldier as when he was a civilian. Your inclinations may get him in the guardhouse and they'll surely get you nowhere."[32]

Service Family Relations

More often than not, moralistic messages of the importance of black female respectability were also laced with Victorian notions of home and family and presented in language similar to that which circulated throughout society at large during that era. In late 1942, for example, Columbus, Georgia, native and division medical officer William Allen described his wife's migration experiences to the Southwest in the following manner: "My wife visited me at Fort Devens when I received my transfer orders; we were able to make a most pleasant, leisurely trip from Boston via St. Louis to Fort Huachuca. She has since moved to nearby Tucson where she is keeping the home fires burning. Hanging new curtains, planting flowers, buying new furniture, and doing the thousand and one things women like to do in preparatory to the end of the war."[33]

Despite the prevalence of such notions, however, some of the women who eventually moved to Fort Huachuca struggled with the decision about whether to follow their loved ones in uniform or to stay behind and pursue their professional ambitions. A longtime resident of Maxwell, California, Mildred Monroe faced tremendous pressure when her fiancé demanded that she give up her promising career as an actress to join him at Fort Huachuca after he proposed to her in June 1942. At the time of his proposal, Monroe had just signed a contract for a role in a new MGM film after having doubled for actress Lena Horne in the 1942 musical production of *Cabin in the Sky.* Of the offer, Monroe recalled: "I really wanted to act . . . when I started auditioning for parts, Bob would come up to me and say that he didn't see why I had to be so far away when he was in the middle of preparing for the biggest job that he would ever face." Unable to prevail upon her fiancé to accept her expanded opportunities, however, Monroe bade farewell to Hollywood and left acting behind altogether: she moved to Arizona and married Bennett in December of that year.[34]

But not all family members chose to relocate to areas near the military installation. Some decided to live apart from their loved ones in uniform and adopted a strategy of periodic visits as a means of rekindling and stabilizing kith and kin relationships. Some black professionals traveled back and forth between Fort Huachuca and places as far away as Michigan, North Carolina, Illinois, New York, Indiana, Louisiana, and Florida. Ora Wesley took time away from her Kannapolis, North Carolina, public school teaching position to make several trips to Fort Huachuca throughout 1942 and 1943 to visit her husband, John, a chaplain in the 93rd Division during the early months of the unit's training.[35] Likewise, throughout the spring and summer months of 1942, Dorothy Ferebee, a prominent physician in the District of Columbia, left her private medical practice and her extensive community activities as chairperson of the Family Planning Committee of the National Council of Negro Women to take periodic trips to Fort Huachuca, where her husband, Claude, trained as a dentist with the division's Medical Corps.[36] Meanwhile, others visited the post and then returned home to their professional jobs in nearby cities and towns like Tucson, Phoenix, and Bisbee, Arizona.[37]

For some black family members, visiting their loved ones in uniform was even more difficult. Desperately wanting to be near her husband as he and other division members began their training, newly married Eliza Hollis traveled periodically to Fort Huachuca despite suffering from advanced tuberculosis. Eliza became even more determined to stay connected with her husband as her chronic health problems became more acute. During one of her bus trips in early May, the 30-year-old woman became so violently ill that station hospital personnel had to provide her with medical assistance immediately upon her arrival. After post medical authorities determined that she was too weak to return to her point of origin, Eliza yielded to the suggestions of the authorities and her husband that she be placed under the care of tuberculosis specialists in nearby Tucson. After she arrived at the sanitarium on 7 June 1942, her condition deteriorated dramatically, however, and she died less than a month later.[38]

In October, Edna McCoy traveled to Fort Huachuca from Cameron, Texas, to care for her son Jeremiah, who sustained a fractured skull while training at the base. After entering the post a day later than planned, McCoy was overwhelmed by a series of emotions ranging from the excitement of taking the trip to the shock of seeing her son's weakened physical state. But her struggles to maintain contact with her son were compounded by her difficulties in locating adequate lodging in the American Red Cross headquarters during her stay and by the obstacles that the expired seventy-two-hour base pass presented to her plan of staying as close as possible to her offspring. Not only that, but the elderly woman also learned that military regulations forbade her from traveling with the soldier after he received orders transferring him to a general hospital in his hometown. Carrying a letter of identification from her home American Red Cross chapter, McCoy forced her way into the Red Cross headquarters and demanded that she be allowed to accompany the departing soldier. After consulting with the commanding officer of the post hospital, Red Cross staff workers managed to secure an additional ticket, thus paving the way for McCoy and her young son to travel back home together.[39]

It is important to note that, regardless of the reasons for deciding to make the trek to the Southwest, the actions of these service family members represented much more than an ad hoc response to a wartime situation. As John Byng-Hall and other scholars remind us, the complex interplay of kin-related roles, collective ideologies, and expected norms and behaviors shaped the efforts of families to meet the needs of their loved ones throughout much of the twentieth century.[40] In ways similar to the Great Migration, black families shouldered the burden of moving to the defense areas where loved ones struggled to make the life-altering transition from civilian to soldier. Soon, however, the everyday living conditions in southern Arizona would provide a significant part of the equation that shaped the relationship between African American division members, American society, and the state during the war.

Housing and Discrimination in Southern Arizona

As service families began to appear in towns near Fort Huachuca during the division's stateside training, many of them found themselves in dire need of adequate accommodations, since the wartime expansion of the aircraft manufacturing industry had resulted in housing shortages and cramped housing facilities in the area. Although, on the eve of the United States' entry into World War II, War Department planners had determined that housing for black troops would be allocated on a proportional basis, post construction moved slowly. In March 1941, the Public Buildings Administration of the Federal Works Administration announced the construction of 30 additional one-story, single-family dwelling units at Fort Huachuca for the dependents of the approximately 150 noncommissioned officers who were serving with the 368th and the 25th Infantry regiments.[41] Nine months later, a Phoenix-based engineering firm held a series of meetings with army officials whereupon it received a contract from the War Department to construct 1,400 additional buildings on the military post. Of the post quarters, approximately 450 were designated as temporary housing accommodations for black enlisted personnel, but only a few of the buildings were completed, hardly enough to meet the demands of GIs once they reported to duty.[42] And as the winter faded into the spring of 1942, only 150 completed buildings were available for occupancy to black enlisted men and families at the post.[43]

Even if resourceful dependents managed to secure suitable accommodations on the military reservation, they soon faced exorbitant rental rates that vastly exceeded the housing allotments servicemen received for living there.[44] What's more, the War Department's policy of 1942 compounded their woes by discouraging noncommissioned and commissioned officers from bringing their families to army posts.[45] After spending several weeks investigating the housing situation at Fort Huachuca during the spring of 1942, assistant civilian aide Truman K. Gibson recommended the immediate construction of suitable quarters for soldiers and civilians at the military installation. "Resolution of this perplexing problem will do much toward maintaining a high morale on the post and in the division," he argued.[46] However, the problems of housing for dependents at Fort Huachuca would continue unabated well into war and long after the War Department had reassigned the division to Fort Polk, Louisiana.

Not only did black newcomers face the problem of locating adequate housing on the outpost, but they also encountered blatant acts of racial discrimination from white residents, civilian law authorities, and civic leaders when they sought accommodations in surrounding communities. Throughout the division's initial training, the reactions of people in Arizona cities like Bisbee, Tucson, and Douglas to the massive influx of African Americans were based on long-held attitudes influenced by vicious racial stereotypes. At the same time, many townspeople expressed fears about the impact that black servicemen and their families might have on prevailing class and gender relationships. In response, residents created various obstacles to limit the presence of the newcomers in their areas. During the spring of 1942, white inhabitants of nearby Tucson, along with city government officials and the chamber of commerce, openly opposed the presence of African American families searching for lodging and recreational facilities in the vicinity, claiming that to have Negro troops and their families in the city "would injure its reputation as a resort city because Negro soldiers and their families would over-run the city and cheapen its real estate values."[47]

To make matters worse, when most black service families arrived in the city, they learned of a decision by local housing authority officials to abandon existing plans to build a low-cost housing center for service families and war workers. Responding to their constituents, Tucson officials decided that the need for housing was not immediate and could await the end of the war.[48] Meanwhile, Bisbee Merchants' Association and Chamber of Commerce officials, neighborhood real estate brokers, and utility companies refused to even provide black service dependents with a list of possible housing vacancies in surrounding city neighborhoods.[49] "It is the general feeling among Arizona communities that the lodging and sexual outlets of Negro soldiers and the dependent population of Fort Huachuca should be maintained within their own communities and not depend upon these old-established white communities to absorb such outlets," claimed one official.[50]

But the statements made by city officials belie the fact that Arizona cities like Bisbee, Douglas, and Tucson were in the midst of unprecedented economic and social dislocations that were punctuated by the wartime boom in industry and a rising tide of racial and ethnic tension. With the American defense buildup and the attack on Pearl Harbor, congressional leaders became very interested in Arizona, believing that the state's mild climate, sparse desert spaces, and ample mineral deposits made it an ideal site for aircraft production facilities, mining activities, and military bases. Throughout the early 1940s, the southern Arizona region became a destination for black people hoping to secure skilled positions in the copper mines of the Phelps-Dodge Corporation in Bisbee and at the air base in Douglas. Although the region's population fluctuated wildly as a result of the constant turnover of military personnel, statistics from the 1947 County Data Book indicate that the number of African Americans in Bisbee and Douglas increased modestly between 1940 and 1943, growing from 1,942 to 2,300.[51] Of the total number of migrants, approximately 200 claimed to have been relatives of 93rd Infantry Division members stationed at nearby Fort Huachuca.[52]

African American newcomers to these urban areas received a hostile reception from townspeople and mine workers, who worked diligently to maintain the color line at all costs. Upon their arrival, many black migrants found themselves restricted to menial unskilled jobs and low pay in the mines and ostracized by white miners who decided to simply quit rather than work alongside them. As they made their way home from work, more than a few young black laborers were harassed and beaten by transplanted white southern workers while local law enforcement officers looked on nearby, and African Americans were refused service in nearby restaurants, saloons, and stores.[53]

Black newcomers also encountered limited housing options in these cities. Although the number of African Americans in the residential areas increased, the number of housing units remained constant throughout the 1940s, hardly approaching the increasing demand for lodging. Finally, many property owners and landlords refused to register their living accommodations with the Federal Rent Control Program officials, thus allowing them to charge exorbitant rental rates (amounting to as high as $75 a month in some cases) and to evict, with very little compunction, newcomers who were unable to pay them.[54]

But perhaps Tucson was more affected by these changes than were any other urban centers in the region. Surrounded by scenic mountain ranges and dotted with rocky patches of greasewood bushes and cacti, Pima County's largest urban center had long enjoyed a well-earned reputation as a renowned tourist resort. Its winter temperatures averaged 66 degrees Fahrenheit, and the city's downtown commercial district annually received as many as 11,500 visitors who frequented its hotels, inns, and motels and the guest ranches and houses of prostitution on the outskirts of the city. But by 1942, the incipient stages of the American mobilization also witnessed the arrival of the Consolidated-Vultee Aircraft Corporation and the establishment of the Ryan School of Aeronautics and the Davis-Monthan air base in 1942, bringing to the city an abundance of federal defense contracts, a massive inflow of money, and thousands of newcomers in search of greater job opportunities.[55] Correspondingly, from 1940 to 1943, more than 70,000 people moved to Arizona, and Tucson's population soared from 35,000 to nearly 45,000 residents, reflecting a substantial increase in residents over the census figures recorded two years earlier.[56] African Americans constituted nearly 1,500 of the new arrivals, of which 441 had ties to military personnel in the region.[57] By the war's end, black newcomers peaked at 3,000, representing approximately 3.5 percent of the city's total population.[58]

As with Bisbee and Douglas, the wartime prosperity also strained Tucson's meager resources. Throughout the spring and summer of 1942, home construction and apartments and rooms for rent lagged far behind public demand. As black migrants expanded Tucson's population between 1940 and 1945, available single-dwelling lodging in the city increased by only 4 percent during the same period. As a result, the city offered very few options for incoming workers, service personnel, and their families.[59] Meanwhile, blocks of city-owned tracts of land located on the city's North Main Street lay undeveloped.[60]

Determined to avert the impending crisis, Federal Housing Authority officials elected to eliminate the National Housing Agency's income ceiling for occupancy in the La Reforma Housing Project and contracted with private developers to construct 150 dwellings to house the city's swelling military and defense population in September 1941.[61] By August 1942, however, the volume of requests had surpassed the number of available facilities, and the construction permits issued to private housing contractors had reached an alarming rate. Tucson's chamber of commerce reported "that unfurnished houses are practically non-existent and the number of furnished houses is too small to accommodate the anticipated demand this fall and winter."[62]

Compounding the housing-shortage problem for black newcomers was the geography of race—Tucson's segregated housing patterns restricted black newcomers' options even further. Many division family members arrived in the city only to find themselves completely shut out of the decent, single-dwelling rental areas and channeled into substandard public housing projects located along South Meyer and South Main streets, areas that were heavily populated by defense workers who had migrated from the South. More often than not, living conditions in the rooming houses, hotels, and apartments in these areas, despite their high rents, were unhealthy and overcrowded; these areas also had no street lighting, deplorable city services, and inadequate transportation. Indeed, the conditions in the neighborhoods were so bad that one newcomer recalled, "In one specific area, seventeen families used the same outdoor toilet. In addition to this, it was found that one woman was using it who was quarantined with smallpox."[63] When faced with such wretched conditions, some newcomers placed themselves on waiting lists for indefinite periods or simply gave up hope of locating a place to live and returned home.[64]

Adding insult to injury, the discrimination that African American families and friends of 93rd personnel faced in the private and public housing market corresponded with the problems they confronted in the area's public accommodations. In Bisbee, Douglas, and Tucson, many civilian merchants placed signs in their shop windows that read "No Service to Negroes" and "We Reserve the Right to Refuse Service to Any-one." City police officers patrolled the streets, seeking to tighten their control over the local segregation etiquette, practices, and customs with nightsticks and guns.[65] As the foot traffic of black service dependents increased, the rapidly changing economic conditions, the housing shortages, and the heightened racial tensions that existed in the city created a cauldron of hostility that more than a few observers feared could boil over at a moment's notice.

Black reporters visiting the desert resort area throughout the wartime period predicted that a crisis was looming. After touring Tucson, for example, *Baltimore*

Afro-American correspondent Henry Jethro wrote in August 1944, "Citizens here are tiptoeing around town on top of racial dynamite. The next gale that sweeps from this western city will doubtless bring the clash of whites, colored citizens, and Mexicans."[66] Hazel Daniels, a white Tucson resident, had earlier voiced the same sentiments. In an *Arizona Daily Star* editorial published in January 1942, Daniels noted the ways that the war intensified social relations in the city and warned, "It is problems such as the ones at issue now in the city which will create unrest, antagonism, and hate on the part of Negroes causing them to commit anti-social acts."[67]

The resentment, suspicion, and fear that white Arizona residents like Daniels expressed toward African American service families boiled over into acts of violence that summer. In June, after spending most of the day searching for housing in Tucson, Addie Alexander and Jeannette Kinchion decided to go to a nearby American Legion Hall to order dinner. Not long after the two women had settled into a booth for an evening free from their frustrations of searching for a place to live, they were informed by a military police officer that the restaurant was "off-limits to prostitutes and that they had to leave." Refusing to simply endure the verbal assault, Alexander and Kinchion decided to remain seated. After a bitter exchange of words and blows, they, along with a group of servicemen also visiting from Fort Huachuca, were arrested, charged, and sentenced to sixty days in jail for "inciting a riot."[68]

Throughout that summer, most of the skirmishes that broke out between service relatives and city law enforcement officials tended to reflect conflicting notions of personal dignity. In the early morning hours of 1 July, for example, bystanders watched in awe as Maxine Willie Welch and Ples Elsworth Russell were taken away by Tucson law enforcement officials and charged with assault and battery after they challenged two men who had insulted them. The heated exchange of words quickly escalated into blows as the two black women proceeded to pummel the men's heads with their fists, shoes, handbags, and bottles. Less than twenty-four hours later, a justice of the peace ruled that the two women were guilty and ordered them to leave the city after they completed a sixty-day stint in the county jail.[69]

Often the clashes between service relatives and townspeople produced deadly results. On 11 November 1942 a group of people in Bisbee looked on in horror as Clay H. Moore—a white mining employee—whipped out a pocketknife and stabbed 25-year-old Willie Diggs, a Chicago native, in front of a saloon, killing him instantly. Stationed at nearby Fort Huachuca, Diggs had obtained a twenty-four-hour leave from the desert installation and had just arrived in the Arizona-Mexican border town to help his ailing grandmother find housing when he was violently attacked. Immediately after the murder, one of the onlookers contacted civilian aide William H. Hastie, who then requested that the War Department investigate the events leading up to Diggs's death.[70] Furthermore, the civilian aide dispatched his assistant, Truman Gibson, to look into the matter. Their investigation into the violent attacks did not result in a single prosecution. Although Moore was arrested and War Department officials assured Hastie that the mining employee would be prosecuted for the crime, he was later absolved of all wrongdoing in the matter.[71] At the same time, the assistant civilian aide expressed some skepticism regarding the eyewitness accounts of the incident, claiming that the investigators "were not fully advised of the circumstances."[72]

Throughout the entire ordeal, the killing of Diggs and the refusal of the Bisbee police department to investigate the crime astonished many black migrants who lived and labored in the mining town. "I asked the Chief of Police when the trial would be held," one observer noted; "he said that he didn't think there'd be one. How in the name of Blackstone can a man be indicted for murder in any degree if a formal inquest *is* not held?"[73] Shortly afterward, the concerns voiced by the bystander may have been brought to the attention of army officials, who feared further deterioration of race relations in the area. In December 1942, Colonel Hardy, the Fort Huachuca post commander, placed military police personnel permanently in the town when Bisbee officials asked him to head off future skirmishes between miners and black GIs and families.[74] This measure yielded very little success, however. By the spring of 1943, the small mining hamlet experienced a considerable degree of out-migration after Bisbee town officials declared that the city was "out of bounds" to members of the 93rd Infantry Division and requested that Fort Huachuca post officials discourage service personnel and their dependents, friends, and neighbors from moving to the area.[75]

Quite often racial strife revolved around the clothing and hairstyles worn by young black service relatives as they worked to create their own unique identities. During the period, three young black men, Elzie Smith, Leonard Parker, and Earlie Pierce, were shoved to the ground and arrested in Tucson for allegedly crossing the street against traffic. The incident had occurred days after the young men had arrived in the city from Fort Huachuca, where had they visited their Mississippi relatives serving in the 93rd's 368th Infantry Regiment. Although the men were cleared of all charges and released, press reports labeled the men as vagrants, and local police paid more attention to the conk hairstyles and highly stylized baggy attire sported by the young newcomers than to anything else.[76] Describing them as a "band of young, bushy-haired hoodlums," Harold Wheeler, the city's police chief, directed his officers to stop such colorfully dressed migrants for questioning and to have them present induction classification cards that indicated their draft status. "If they are guilty of any infraction, however small, of any city ordinance, pick 'em up," Wheeler told his subordinates.[77]

Police surveillance of black newcomers mirrored the brackish waters that swirled around Tucson's racial and sexual politics. The problem that law authorities and white citizens in Tucson had with the large influx of soldiers and their relatives had more to do with the threat that they allegedly posed to the region's fragile racial and ethnic boundaries more than anything else. And more often than not, as in many areas across the country, the racial etiquette, customs, and traditions of the city's residents reflected their fearful images of consensual sexual relations between black men and white women. Since its inception, Arizona state law included measures aimed at controlling the social activities of African Americans and Mexicans, including premarital sex, prostitution, and juvenile delinquency, as well as policies banning interethnic marriage and cohabitation. Throughout the city streets of Tucson and Nogales, police officers patrolled the dance halls, cinemas, and amusement resorts of the Mexican–African American neighborhood to enforce the separate-but-equal legislation. Over time, tensions increased as police officers rounded up many transplanted black migrants and Mexican women with loved ones in uniform, arresting them on trumped-up charges of solicitation and contributing to juvenile delinquency. "My duty is to not ask persons whether or not they are juveniles or adults," asserted Maude Howard, a prominent city policewoman at the time, "but to see if they are white, Mexican, or colored." "Colored persons should have their little affairs to themselves so that they don't have to bother with white persons," Howard claimed.[78]

On countless occasions, black servicemen and their Mexican-born family members and friends found themselves face to face with the discriminatory actions taken by the local police force. On one August evening in 1942, a Mexican woman and a black division officer arrived in Nogales from Fort Huachuca in search of temporary housing. For the recently married young pair, a one-bedroom apartment in a town located near the United States–Mexico border would be better than the scarce housing projects they faced at the nearby military installation. Their hopes were dashed, however, when a police officer approached them at the entrance of a rental development and asked them to provide racial and marital identification. After carefully scrutinizing the documents, the policeman informed the couple that the development was for whites and Mexicans only and ordered them to leave the premises. Around the same period, the words conveyed by a 21-year-old married Mexican immigrant woman from Agua Prieta describing her experience while returning home from a long day's work at a Tucson drug store serve as a vivid reminder of what might happen to individuals who violated the city's racial and gender etiquette: "I was going home from work one evening when I met a soldier that I recognized. We stopped on the street to chat a few minutes and as we were about to leave, a cop came up and arrested us. I don't know what they did with the soldier but they took me to jail and told me that if I were ever caught talking with another colored person they would keep me in jail."[79]

Throughout the division's training at Fort Huachuca, the housing situation and the patterns of Jim Crow social order affected the relationships between black 93rd service relatives and the friends they made in southern Arizona. For new arrivals, their experiences in the Arizona-Mexico border region were to have profound ramifications on how the soldiers defined their service to the country and obligation to their families. As the servicemen began to settle their families in areas adjacent to Fort Huachuca, they began to reconfigure their identities to meet the challenges of the defense buildup and military training. By the time black service families departed the region, its poor housing conditions and borderland racial practices had caused them to develop a new political outlook that allowed them to conform to the national wartime objectives but which remained flexible enough to retain its grassroots character.

Close Quarters

In response to the housing shortages and the antagonism they encountered in many neighborhoods in cities such as Tucson and Bisbee, many black service families sought refuge in the small black communities surrounding Fort Huachuca. Throughout the fall months of 1942, Fry, Arizona, resident Lelia Moore's 160-acre ranch, which lay just beyond the north gate entrance of the outpost, served as the central site of a small trailer park that housed more than twenty family members and friends of division soldiers.[80] Near Moore's ranch stood a church that had been hastily converted into a boardinghouse to accommodate the influx of military dependents.[81] In the surrounding cities of Benson and Douglas, Olivia Booker, Gladys Wells, and sixteen other service families lived in a converted grocery store and garage.[82] In the fringe areas of Tucson, Althea Young, Geraldine Dubisson, Louise Hairston, Jennive Johnson, and Sara Hardy lived in a former grocery store that had been converted into an apartment building.[83] Many family members recalled the makeshift housing arrangements with great detail. "You have to remember, sir, that many army wives like myself who came to places like Fort Huachuca, came without having made arrangements for housing," insisted Jean

Cooper. She went on to explain, "You can't even imagine how I must have felt after traveling for hundreds of miles to Tucson, Arizona, and having to search everywhere for a room only to have the USO find a boarding house where six women had to share two rooms. It was not at all what I thought life as the wife of an army officer was going to be like at all . . . but we hung in there, all right."[84]

As if attempting to settle in southern Arizona weren't difficult enough, many 93rd service families who sought housing near Fort Huachuca also discovered that they had to undergo an elaborate interviewing process by the people who owned boardinghouses, hotels, and rooms in the vicinity. A successful interview largely depended on the traveler's ability to present an acceptable persona to the host; the interviewee not only had to demonstrate a familial connection to the soldiers in training but also had to agree, verbally, to uphold the social customs, traditions, and practices of the community at large. In addition, more often than not, it was also necessary to have some connection with the lodger's distant family members or friends in the place of origin. As her husband, Walter, trained with the division, Michigan native Freida Bailey spent great deal of time moving by train between Detroit and various areas of the American South and trans-Mississippi West. Bailey recalled one incident that occurred when she was trying to find housing adjacent to the military bases:

> I went into the colored section of town. Many times, I went down and to tell you the truth, I was scared to death. Sometimes, when I got there, no one was there to meet me and my husband couldn't get away from camp. I would go to hotels and sit in the lobbies where I was quite conspicuous. On many occasions, however, a USO hostess, usually a black woman, would come into these places and after exchanging introductions, would tell me that she lived nearby and liked to greet the relatives of soldiers who were away from home. What's remarkable about this is that because her mother was from Ecorse and I was coming from Detroit, she took a liking to me. And when I told her that my husband was stationed nearby and I had no place to stay, she said, "Oh, my dear! . . . You are coming to my house to stay with me."[85]

When Pauline Redmond joined her fiancé, Theodore Coggs, at Camp Swift, Texas, in March 1942, the 30-year-old Chicago native found that her visits required calling cards and letters of introduction from people who had lived in the towns from which she had moved. "The hosts were very nice to me," Redmond recalled, "but they just wanted to know who was coming into their communities." This practice continued in Arizona after the couple was married and Theodore had reported to Fort Huachuca seven months later.[86]

As the 93rd servicemen continued to train in Arizona, family members and friends rarely ventured beyond the immediate Fort Huachuca area because of the considerable distances between cities and towns in the American West and opposition to their presence by the whites who lived in them. As a result, the boardinghouses, hotels, and trailers in which service families lived became spaces in which they resurrected African American social, political, religious, and civic forms to reestablish family and community networks. And because of their own relocation experiences, service families often provided a support network for other women, children, and men who wound up in cities and towns located near military outposts.[87]

In the fall of 1942, ten women traveled from Cleveland, Ohio, to join their relatives in uniform at Fort Huachuca. After arriving in Tucson and spending countless days in search of adequate housing in the city, they found rooms at the boarding home of Mrs. Ada T. Washington—a prominent member of the Young Women's Christian Association and a National Association of Colored Women member. After meeting groups of women who shared their predicament, the ten Ohio women resolved to organize a social club. Composed solely of women from Cleveland, the group called themselves the Military Aid Club and hosted fund-raising events such as cabarets, raffles, and dinner matinees to finance round-trip train and bus tickets for those women who wished to make periodic visits back to the Cleveland area. At the same time, club members held numerous public gatherings and lectures during which they discussed events affecting their families in their hometown communities and the lodging needs of black family members of servicemen arriving in the city.[88]

Not all such organizations were regionally affiliated. Throughout December 1942, black women formed associations based on mutual interests. Douglas, Arizona's G Avenue USO served as the gathering place for members of the Spelman Club during the period. Composed largely of public school teachers who had graduated from Atlanta's Spelman College and whose husbands served as officers in the division, the group met periodically to discuss the issues of the day affecting African Americans as well as editorials and essays that appeared in the black press.[89] At the same time, approximately 250 wives and family members of 93rd officer personnel participated in such gatherings as the "Literature and Poetry Hour" and joined the "Dramatics," the "Beauticians," and the "Camera" clubs at the Hanna Hall Recreation Building in Fry, Arizona. During the weekly luncheons held throughout the period, club members munched on baked chicken, green beans, and potato salad while listening to lectures and speeches delivered by noted African American leaders including Mabel Staupers, the executive secretary of the National Nurses' Association; Lieutenant Susan Freeman, chief nurse at Fort

Huachuca's station hospital; and Jane Hinton, a Harvard Medical School graduate and chief researcher at the station hospital.[90]

As many scholars have observed, black women's organization leaders like Mary McLeod Bethune expanded their long-standing approaches to self-help, racial uplift, and community development to offset the harsh realities that black women, men, and children encountered during Great Depression and World War II America.[91] But noted historian Deborah Gray White may have put it best when she wrote, "Clearly the Depression and the war forced new ways of thinking about black women, the black masses, and gender relationships. Did black women need separate organizations to speak for them, or could race associations do as good a job? If African American women did have their own representation, who should speak for them, and what kinds of programs did they need to pursue?"[92]

In many ways, White's invocation and line of inquiry might be extended to the models of organizing that took place among black service family members living near military bases in Arizona at the time. Like members of the National Council of Negro Women during the period, the women in these service-related organizations forged strong friendship and family networks that provided support with regard to both their immediate concerns for their loved ones in the U.S. military and their everyday experiences with discrimination in the area. The social experiences of service family members and the material conditions they encountered in southern Arizona shaped and transformed their identities as black citizens, voters, and service club members. Thus, these women's service-related organizations represented much more than a vehicle of self-help or community improvement. Rather, they gave rise to a particular brand of group activity that combined grassroots networking and national politics.[93]

As the members of the division began to train in earnest, a series of incidents occurred in nearby Tucson that brought this perspective sharply into focus for all to see. Throughout the war, the lack of adequate recreational facilities along Tucson's Twelfth Avenue posed a serious problem for soldiers and their families who poured into the desert resort. Prior to Pearl Harbor, white GIs frequented the American Legion Hall Dugout located in the downtown section of town. Built in 1922, this facility was equipped with a bowling alley, pool tables, a drinking saloon, a spacious dance floor, vacant rooms, and an ample supply of volunteers.[94] Yet black soldiers stationed at the military installations in the area were barred from the recreational facility and were forced to attend activities held at the local armory. The dilapidated building was located on the outskirts of town and was hardly an adequate site for black GIs who flowed into the city, and it served as a vivid reminder of their role in the war and second-class status in the southwestern city.

As one serviceman put it years later, "Tucson residents resented all of us from Fort Huachuca who came into town. But they especially hated when we entered their bars and taverns. Tempers were short, tensions ran high, and there was constant fear of a race riot."[95]

But the early months of the American entry into the war had adumbrated a new dismal chapter in the history of Tucson's attitudes toward African American military personnel, causing black morale to spiral even further downward. In early January 1942, Federal Security Administration regional representative Howard Beresford met with the city's chamber of commerce to consider a grant from the administration to be earmarked for the construction of a USO for black enlisted men. He told those present that "the job of our agency is to see that boys, no matter what their race or creed, are given fair treatment. We are crusading for the American soldier and to see that he is well taken care of. If I were a Negro soldier at Fort Huachuca, I would want to come to Tucson. You can't deny an American soldier the right to go into any community."[96] However, after encountering a great deal of resistance from prominent townspeople and various city government officials to the initiative, Beresford decided to withdraw his support for the idea, arguing that "it was not advisable to establish the proposed center at this time."[97]

Shortly after Beresford's announcement, outraged service family members established the Twelfth Avenue Club and launched a series of activities to improve the inadequate USO quarters in January 1942. Led by Hazel Merrill, Margaret Knight, Rose Barnes, Mary Euell, and Ada Washington, organization members spearheaded a lobbying campaign calling for USO recreational programs for loved ones in uniform who spent their weekend furloughs in the city. At the same time, they sponsored public-speaking campaigns to push the city council to build adequate day nurseries, elementary schools, and housing for the families of black GIs.[98] Meanwhile, Lucille Kelly and other members of the Mothers Club held chitterling and tamale dinners at a nearby Elks lodge in order to raise funds for a day nursery.[99] Then, later that month, the efforts made by black service relatives received a boost from a rather unexpected source when an open letter was published in the *Arizona Daily Star*. Spurred on by the city's failure to provide adequate recreational facilities for Fort Huachuca military personnel, Ada P. McCormick, a prominent publisher of a local magazine, issued a bitter and passionate statement that framed the issue for everyone involved:

> The USO raised money from all the people all over the country for the recreation of all the soldiers. It didn't raise money from the white people and refuse it from the colored people. The colored man and woman contributed to the fund just as you and

I did. However, the question that is clear to me is that a soldier from Fort Huachuca doesn't walk a hundred miles on a six-hour leave. But whether they do not come because they know it is impossible from a military shortage of time and tires to get here or whether they feel that they are despised and rejected of men, that is what will make the difference in the hearts of every one of those soldiers and of their relatives and friends. If we betray our colored soldiers, we will be doing what Hitler wants so much for us to do, dividing ourselves.[100]

The Twelfth Avenue Club's campaign and McCormick's plea produced a deluge of responses. Between January and April, the city's largest newspaper, the *Arizona Daily Star,* was flooded with letters from Tucson residents. Quite often, many of the campaign's most vocal supporters turned out to be white women and men, producing rare moments of interracial cooperation in the otherwise segregated southwestern setting. Ellen Stuart Russell, a longtime white resident and schoolteacher at Russell Ranch Elementary School, wrote a rejoinder that supported the building of a recreation center in the city. Russell declared, "My personal opinion is that now is not a time, if ever, for people of the intelligentsia of our democratic nation to vocalize prejudice against any who share in protecting and precipitating the interests and ideals of their country."[101]

Yet while many white Tucson residents conceded that recreational facilities for black enlisted men should be improved, most couched their arguments for a new USO center in patriotic language that also reflected the notion of white supremacy and Jim Crow sentiments. In the pages of the city's largest weekly, a white Tucson resident argued, "As a native Virginian, I speak from experience. No race responds more readily to fair and decent treatment; or goes bad in the wrong environment, as does the Negro, if uneducated. Certainly, these colored boys, often away from home for the first time, deserve a clean, respectable recreation center among their own people, whose culture is the white man's culture."[102] "What I have seen of the Negro soldier," another writer asserted, "is that he is respectful, well-behaved, and a credit to the uniform he wears. I have noticed particularly because I am a Southerner. Give the Negroes a center where they can feel welcome among their own kind."[103]

Between January and March, the local YWCA served as a frequent site of intense debate as members of Tucson's League of Women Voters invited Twelfth Avenue group leaders to discuss the pros and cons of building a community center for black enlisted personnel in the city. There women in the audience heard arguments presented by Estelle Nobles and Doris, Marjorie, and Mildred Hudson advising them to press the city council for the construction of a new USO facility. But the positions advanced by the organization members fell on deaf ears. The members of the League of Women Voters were more interested in having them allay their fears over the possibility of large numbers of soldiers using the new facility and its location rather than in discussing the dismal state of the facilities that existed for black GIs in the region.[104]

Many longtime black residents who raised their voices in support of the club's initiative saw the issue quite differently. Lenore Kelley, a black woman who had lived on West Third Street since 1922, wrote a missive exhorting Tucson citizens to support the Twelfth Avenue Club's initiatives and asked, "Are we to sit idly by and have our democratic rights taken from us without a fight?"[105] Some residents interpreted the city council's indifference toward building the USO center as a class issue. Several weeks after McCormick made her appeal, Henry McClaine, a black man originally from South Carolina, placed the matter squarely in the context of notions of racial uplift and respectability:

> Speaking of Negro soldiers, here in Tucson, the only recreation outside of Fort Huachuca afforded him are saloons, dives, and gambling joints. While other soldiers have the YMCA, clubs and other wholesome entertainment, Negro soldiers have no other places to go. Wake up America and learn a lesson from the Pearl Harbor Incident! The ones that dealt your navy the deathblow were foreigners given the hospitality of your homes, schools, and vital industries. On the other hand, we only ask to mingle with the best class of our people in a Recreation center run and operated by us. Wake up Tucson before it is too late.[106]

Still others, like the Reverend Holton H. Collins, pastor of the Colored Methodist Episcopal Church, castigated the city council for its stance regarding the proposed center and called attention to the conundrum that African Americans faced periodically in the large-scale wars that occurred throughout United States history. Shortly after Beresford withdrew his proposal, Collins wrote an editorial that was published in the *Arizona Daily Star.* "Ever since the dark days of savage slavery, the Negro has cried for justice," Collins declared. "Today he is still pleading because justice has not been given. Now the 'hue and cry' is on for a small drop-in center for the Negro soldier. Someone seems to have forgotten that democracy means equal opportunities for all people. Is the Negro, even in giving service to our country not 'worth' a small 'drop-in center?'"[107]

As the mild winter season faded into the spring of 1942, the Twelfth Avenue Club's campaign expanded to include other prominent groups in the city. At the Mount Calvary Colored Baptist Church in April, church members gathered to hear Twelfth Avenue's Margaret Whittaker discuss topics such as "How the Soldier and the Community Can Help One Another in This Crisis."[108] A month later, Elizabeth Morris and other auxiliary members of the city's American Legion chapter voiced their support for the group's cause after Eleanor Coleman appeared at their Charles Young post to discuss the club's organizing activities.[109] Through the campaign, many black city dwellers used pen and paper to register their displeasure with the city's policies. Finally, as the Tucson USO and activities of the club moved closer to becoming a headline story, leaders of the Tucson chapter of the National Association for the Advancement of Colored People were not to be outdone. In late July, chapter officials called a special meeting to discuss the issue. Among those in attendance was Hazel Merrill, one of the charter members of the service-related group.[110]

By the first few weeks of the following year, the Twelfth Avenue Club had realized a substantial victory when members of the city council voted unanimously to create separate USO facilities for black soldiers as well as to provide substantial funding for the construction of a day nursery, kindergarten, and elementary school. City officials also agreed to issue construction permits for thirty additional housing units for the families of black enlisted men in the area.[111] Shortly afterward, Eleanor Coleman and other service relatives established a USO center in a remodeled store building in the southwestern portion of the city. The center soon became the locus for entertainment, rooms, employment, and debates about the issues affecting black GIs stationed at Fort Huachuca.[112] As Goldie Carter, a member of the YWCA's National Board, observed at the time, "The club became a center where soldiers could meet their mothers or fathers; sisters or brothers, and enjoy an educational and recreational program with them."[113] But the significance of the two-pronged approach devised by the women to address the needs of their families and its infinite possibilities for realizing social change during the national emergency did not escape the attention of the people who were directly involved in the campaign. For example, Hazel Merrill later recalled, "To me this proved to be an interesting experiment but such a thing had proven effective in a great many cases."[114]

Around the same time, division relatives also challenged the discrimination that black soldiers faced while riding on public transportation in the Southwest. On 16 July 1942, Houston native Lillian Knox and her son Alfred had just entered the train station to board a passenger car returning to Fort Huachuca when the GI discovered that he had misplaced their tickets. After being advised to go to the nearest Western Union telegram office to report the loss of the ticket to his commanding officer, the Houston native promptly walked into a waiting room and entered a nearby telephone booth—at which point three white MPs emerged from an adjacent area and ordered him to hang up. At that moment, Alfred learned that he had violated the sanctity of southern segregation customs: he had just broken the color bar by entering a "whites-only" waiting area. Joined by Houston policemen, the MPs twice told him to leave the room, but Knox ignored their commands. Shortly afterward, the police began to beat the infantryman with their clubs. As the 25-year-old lay helpless on the ground, Lillian came to her son's aid after hearing the commotion, screaming, "Don't kill my son—I'd rather that you kill me!" but to little relief. By the time the confrontation had ended, the 52-year-old woman had received a severe beating, and her son was placed under arrest on charges of breach of the peace. He was then placed in a patrol wagon and driven to a nearby hospital, where he learned that he had sustained considerable loss of eyesight. To make matters worse, when Lillian asked about her son's whereabouts, law enforcement officials denied that the young man was in their custody. The elder woman's fears were alleviated only several hours later after she spoke with her daughter-in-law, who informed her that the battered serviceman had been transferred to a military hospital.

In the three or four weeks following the ordeal, the actions of the military police had attracted a firestorm of attention from the black press. Between 18 July and 3 August, the *New York Amsterdam Star-News, Kansas City Call, Pittsburgh Courier, Atlanta Daily World,* and *Houston Negro Labor News* carried headlines titled "Soldier on Leave Beaten Badly by MPs," "Race Soldier Beaten for Using Telephone," "Wanted to Send Telegram," "Soldier Beaten by MPs in Railroad Station," and "White Military Police Beat Race Soldier Tuesday."[115] At the NAACP's thirty-third annual convention, held in Los Angeles in July, delegates attacked the War Department's policy on segregation and called for Washington policymakers to focus their attention on the racial discrimination that black soldiers faced throughout the country.[116]

Knox's mother, however, decided to take matters into her own hands. Demanding that legal action be taken in her son's defense, Lillian Knox dispatched a letter of protest to army officials, stating, "If I hadn't been there, the police would have killed my son." "But how many Negroes are to be beaten in the Southwest without any record being made of these incidents?" she asked. Lillian Knox's question was left unanswered. While the War Department and the mayor's office moved to quell further criticism, army and city officials had barely gone through the motions of investigation before blaming the beleaguered soldier for the incident. Not only that, members of the interracial committee appointed by the mayor to study civilian-military relations in the city absolved the MPs of any wrongdoing in the matter. "The MPs had to use strong measures to get good discipline," a military representative commented.[117]

Throughout the war, however, the actions taken by Lillian Knox resonated in the thoughts of thousands of 93rd GIs whose voices were being blunted by the realities of military discipline. As illuminated above, the efforts made by black family dependents on behalf of soldiers training at Fort Huachuca inaugurated a new strategy that collapsed the public and private spaces that the larger society used to describe protest politics during the war. At the same time, black service families and 93rd Division members opened multifaceted lines of communication with spokespeople within the African American community that would remain open as the war progressed. Yet the relationships they shared with black civilian organizations and leaders often became tenuous when they were filtered through the prism shaped by soldier, family, and service community concerns. All the while, the system of racial discrimination practiced by the army and society at large continued to shape the perspectives of black service households and communities regarding the purposes of the war and military service. To understand where these factors would stand in relation to the evolving ideas held by African American families and division personnel regarding the war, we must now explore the policies of official Washington and the impact they had on black GIs and their families as division members began to face the distinct possibility of fighting and dying overseas.

CHAPTER FIVE

War Maneuvers and Black Division Personnel

✯ ✯ ✯

We pledge allegiance to the United States of America . . . to its
all-out victory over the forces of our enemies on the battlefront
in every section of the world. We pledge allegiance to the principles
embodied in the Constitution of the United States and in the Bill
of Rights. To full participation in the fruits of victory. . . . Victory
both at home and abroad . . . we pledge our all.

Editorial, Pittsburgh Courier, *1942*

The Double V Campaign, if anything, may have pushed black
troops overseas prematurely. I recall sharing with others negative
feelings about imminent combat when we could see so little being
done for us at home. Now that I think of it, the campaign waged by
black newspaper editors may have worked wonders at the national
political level in Washington but did little for black troops who were
training in the field.

Elliotte Williams

In 1943, Ralph Ellison observed that the attitudes of African Americans toward
their wartime experiences fell into three categories: acceptance of the limited nature of their participation in the armed forces and defense industries; rejection
of the Allied war effort altogether on the basis that they should be accorded the
same opportunities as all other American citizens; and a combination of some
aspects of both attitudes with the goal of transforming the nation's struggle against
fascism into one of total freedom and equality for all people. Of the three perspectives, Ellison warned:

These attitudes must be watched, whether displayed by individuals or organizations. They take many forms; the first being exploited by those who like the Negro best when he is unthinking or passive. The second will help only Fascism. Third contains the hope of the Negro people and is spreading; but these hopes can be used by the charlatan and agent provocateur as well as by the true leader. In this time of confusion many wild and aggressive-sounding programs will be expounded by Negroes who, seeking personal power, would lead the people along paths away from any creative action. Thus all programs must be measured coldly against reality. Both leaders and organizations must be measured not by their words, but by their actions.[1]

Ellison's admonitions resonated with division members who entered the latter stages of their training in 1943. When the soldiers departed Fort Huachuca for the maneuvers areas of Louisiana and California during the spring of 1943, most of them had subordinated the Allied war aims to their own struggles in the U.S. Army and to issues affecting African American society. In addition, they discovered to their dismay that the political programs and rhetoric espoused by African American leaders bore very little resemblance to the realities they encountered in the Jim Crow army. Facing a seemingly perplexing situation, 93rd Division members would give consideration to only some of the political stances taken by black middle-class spokespeople and organizations, totally disregarding their rhetoric when it failed to coincide with the GIs' immediate circumstances.

As the soldiers began to express a sense of bewilderment regarding the wartime positions taken by black community leaders, black military families and communities were encountering their own conundrum. They, too, framed their perspectives in ways that drew upon the pro-democratic impulses of the war effort. As their relatives in the division negotiated the Louisiana and California landscape, service relatives began to link the antiracist politics of the war to service-related issues in ways that asserted power and authority over the material conditions of black military life. Indeed, in the ensuing months of 1943, service family members, War Department officials, African American spokespeople, and members of Congress intensely debated the essence of American citizenship itself. However, the efforts of division families bore little fruit. Just as the service families' perspectives of race and the war had begun to resonate with sectors of the African American community, their voices were muffled by the War Department's plans to deploy the division overseas and the ambitions of prominent black organizations and leaders to realize their own objectives of gaining first-class citizenship. Little did the division members realize it, but as they began boarding the transport ships heading for the South Pacific later that year, the intense discussion surrounding their training and deployment sounded the opening salvos of a multi-ple-front war that would challenge the most creative energies of everyone asso-ciated with the unit for the rest of the unit's campaign.

Southern Field Maneuvers

Immediately after arriving in Louisiana in April 1943, division members be-gan to prepare for combined tactical operations against the U.S. 85th Division, a unit composed of Mississippi National Guardsmen. During the weeks that fol-lowed, they trudged through the wild, sparsely populated eastern Louisiana coun-tryside while carrying 80-pound packs. During the period, they dug and prepared cleverly concealed foxholes while contending with dangerous climatic conditions, chiggers, and poisonous snakes. Under the watchful eyes of 3rd Army commander Courtney Hodges, 93rd Infantry Division commander Fred Miller, Brigadier Gen-eral Benjamin Davis Sr., civilian aide to the secretary of war Truman Gibson Jr., and black press corps members, troops executed a series of combat operations that War Department officials expected them to perform on the battlefield. The men climbed into foxholes, inspected machine gun nests, and threaded their way through barbed wire entanglements while withstanding a barrage of indirect fire from the division's three field artillery battalions.

During one particular exercise, the men effectively defended a railroad center from enemy artillery fire by using advance posts to prevent 85th Infantry Divi-sion members from reaching their main line of resistance until reinforcements appeared nearly two days later. During the second phase of the training, division members distinguished themselves during a night retreat under live ammuni-tion fire. As powerful windstorms and horizontal rain swept over the scantily veg-etated terrain, division members repaired to a defensive perimeter replete with carefully constructed barbed wire, foxholes, trenches, and well-concealed machine guns.[2] Not long afterward, the division's senior officers allowed the men a rest period to check their equipment and to pursue leisurely activities in nearby towns and cities.[3]

The division's response to the simulated battlefield conditions bolstered the con-fidence of senior army officers in attendance. After observing the division mem-bers go through the motions of firing at attacking enemy forces, 93rd Division commander Fred W. Miller spoke highly of the fighting quality of the men. After watching the men in the 318th Engineering Battalion negotiate a river-crossing problem during the second phase of the exercises, 15th Corps commander Major General Wade Haislip expressed his belief that "this last exercise showed the best troop leading on both sides that we have seen in these maneuvers." "There is no question about who is in command. I am particularly pleased to feel that the last maneuver is the best," he claimed.[4] An official who recently arrived in the area from the War Department's Inspector General's Office in Washington concurred. During a tour of the black unit in action, Brigadier General Benjamin Davis Sr. noted, "The conduct of the division in this maneuver was generally satisfactory. All of the officers and men seemed to be very enthusiastic about their work in connection with the maneuvers. The officers expressed great confidence in the ability of their units to carry out orders and withstand the hardships incident to the maneuvers. They reported that the non-commissioned officers are developing an appreciation of command and leadership responsibilities."[5]

Ironically, the efficient manner in which the soldiers carried out their operations and the familiarity and ease with which they handled their weapons undermined the army's long-standing negative views of black behavior on the battlefield and emphasized what black soldiers could do if given the opportunity. Almost overnight, the need to point up the contradiction between the exemplary conduct of the division under fire and the army's racial views fired the imagination of those individuals who attended the field training exercise. News of the division's performance and the morale of the servicemen flowed from the communiqués, editorials, and feature articles filed by the *Chicago Defender*'s Ben Burns, *Baltimore Afro-American*'s Carl Murphy, *Atlanta Daily World*'s Robert Ratcliffe, *Cleveland Call & Post*'s William Walker, *Pittsburgh Courier*'s William Nunn, and *Michigan Chronicle*'s Paul Keen, to name a few.[6] During his visit with soldiers at the "front," the NAACP's *Crisis* editor, Roy Wilkins, proclaimed, "The 93rd has every weapon needed by a combat division and the men are very proud of their outfits, especially the tank men."[7] So moved was *People's Voice* correspondent Oliver Harrington by the division personnel that the cartoonist decided to turn to sketch pad and pencil to immortalize their activities in Louisiana for all to see.[8] And upon his inspection of the division's activities, Ben Burns, *Chicago Defender* staff correspondent, echoed these sentiments. After witnessing the men's performance firsthand, he remarked, "There is a healthy race consciousness among the men of the Ninety-third. They know well the histories of their units and are determined to uphold their prestige in World War II."[9]

For their part, division members used space within the daily newspapers to publicize their own impressions of the 3rd Army exercises. As the maneuvers moved into full swing, the *Baltimore Afro-American* published a poem titled "Maneuver Lament" by Christo Waller and Ernest Davenport describing their activities along the Louisiana-Texas border area:

Thinking, thinking, thinking
Of the things I left behind
Here is where I put in writing
What is heavy on my mind.
We had dug a million ditches
And cleared ten square miles of ground
We have drunk our beer and whiskey
In the "honky tonky" towns.
But there's just one consolation,
Gather round me while I tell,
"When we die, we'll go to heaven
For we have done our stretch in hell."[10]

Around the same period, the *Pittsburgh Courier* received the "93rd Division Psalms" by 369th Infantry enlisted man Thyr Byrd, whose verses depicted the Roosevelt administration's prosecution of the war and black life in the 3rd Army maneuver area in a lighthearted manner:

Mr. Roosevelt is my shepherd, and I am not in want (for anything).
He maketh me lie down in foxholes and slit-trenches.
He leadth me across rivers of running water.
He restoreth my pay by allotment.
He leadeth me in the path of tall pine trees, with my namesake.
Yea, though I walk through muddy and "reptile"-infested forests,
I do feel evil, because snakes, mosquitoes and ticks are after me.
The cook preparest my chow in sanitary and field kitchens
In the presence of my enemy (snakes, mosquitoes, and ticks).
The Supply Sergeant anointest my head with a steel helmet;
The helmet runneth over the head (my head).
But after spending 13 years and 8 months with the armed forces,
I will happily dwell on the field for the "duration."[11]

The division's maneuvering activities that spring, however, elicited a mixed response from Louisiana's newspapers and elected officials. For example, while the *New Orleans Times Picayune* allocated only a small portion of space to the Associated Press's coverage of the exercises, the *Louisiana Weekly,* one of the oldest black newspapers in the state, ran only one brief article on the training experiences of black 93rd GIs.[12]

But this reticence was not confined solely to African American newspapers across the state. The whispers of apprehension over the division's activities also could be heard among white politicians and pundits in the region. In the months leading up to the exercises, southern whites living and working throughout the 4th Corps area expressed alarm over the prospect of thousands of armed African Americans descending on the state. The widespread fear stemmed from the fact that the war had accelerated the structural changes that had begun in the South during the 1930s. As a result of the massive flow of men to the armed forces and defense industries and the growth of New Deal programs in the region, many southern whites suspected that life below the Mason-Dixon Line, which had been historically shaped by the power of white privilege and characterized by a fear of miscegenation, would slowly change. And no group roused the anxieties shared by white supremacists across the South more than the hundreds of African American soldiers stationed at the training camps scattered throughout the region. In his *To Stem This Tide: A Survey of Racial Tension Areas in the United States,* published at the time, sociologist Charles S. Johnson noted that in states like South Carolina, Louisiana, Mississippi, Georgia, and Texas, "resentment develops against Negroes whose army orders give them duties and responsibilities which take them out of roles which are customary for Negroes in the community." According to Johnson, much of the anxiety that white southerners felt toward black GIs sprang from the untenable situation in which residents across the segregation-era South found themselves in the war against fascism. "A general contradiction," he believed, "is to be seen between the Negro status and the soldier status when the attempt is made to preserve the color line in the communities near army camps and in the camps themselves."[13]

As black troops began to pour into the corps area, the gap between professed democratic principles and Jim Crow reality became ever more apparent as southern white fears of black militancy found expression among the region's political elite. During the 1942 U.S. Senate race, members of Louisiana civic organizations and business establishments attended gatherings held across the state throughout that summer to hear racial diatribes issued by candidate E. A. Stephens. Running against incumbent Allen Ellender, Stephens claimed that "colored organizations were sitting around midnight candles planning to remove segregation from the South" and warned, "Unless we do something about this menace, social equality will be forced down the throats of white people in the South."[14] Later that year, Louisiana congressman Newt Mills also warned that grave danger awaited white women in the state if "the colored boys remain at home while the white boys, the best blood of America, are taken and sent off to the battlefields to die."[15]

Around the same time, rumors of impending race riots and insurrection reached new heights in nearby Alabama when the War Department announced that the 93rd Division's sister unit—the U.S. 92nd Infantry Division—would be mustered into service and stationed at Fort McClellan. Alarmed by the possible challenge that the segregated troops presented to the state's racial and political order, Senator John Bankhead wrote to army chief of staff General George Marshall suggesting that the War Department reassign black troops stationed in the South to northern areas. "Our people feel that by locating Negro troops in the South in immediate contact with white troops, at a time when race feeling among the Negroes has been aroused, will result in conflict," Bankhead declared. "If race soldiers must be stationed in the South as a result of social or political pressure, can't you place Southern Negro soldiers there and place the Northern Negro soldiers in the North where their presence is not likely to lead to race wars?"[16] The army chief of staff rejected Bankhead's request, however. Claiming that the resolution of social problems was not one of the army's responsibilities, Marshall told the Alabama senator, "While our policy in general is, when practicable, to station Northern troops in Northern states and Southern troops in the South, and also to station colored troops in localities where a commensurate Negro civilian population exists, the implementation of the policy must be second to military requirements."[17]

Ironically, Marshall's adherence to the army's policy regarding the stationing of racially segregated units like the 93rd Infantry Division in southern backcountry areas precipitated the very social and political situation that the War Department had wished to avoid. As they progressed through their training, many division members could not help but notice the poverty-stricken world of the rural South. Scattered throughout the countryside, thousands of landless tenants, largely black, continued to labor on farms cultivating cotton, a situation that perpetuated endless debt and intolerable living conditions. And in the surrounding towns of Leesville and Many, Louisiana, black inhabitants worked on farms and in the sawmills and kitchens for as low as $1.50 to $3.00 a week while living in squalid conditions.[18]

For the polyglot mixture of GIs in the unit—northerners and southerners, self-employed and unemployed workers, college graduates and self-educated men—these conditions made them place their new struggles in the racially segregated army in a broader context. As Indianola, Mississippi, native Edwin Lee, a medical officer with the division, noticed when he arrived in Louisiana, "It was during the division's maneuvers training that I became fully familiar with all the prejudicial practice in the Army, the difference in the way the whites and blacks were treated, and that's where I saw the greatest amount of poverty that I'd ever observed. Western Louisiana is absolutely, I believe, the most poverty-stricken place I've seen in the United States. I lived and grew up in Mississippi, but I don't think I ever saw anyplace quite as poverty-stricken as Western Louisiana."[19] In a similar vein, an infantryman from North Carolina reflected: "In training in this area, I couldn't help but be impressed with the poverty of the land. The people and race made no difference in the poverty. How some of these people lived in those houses was a mystery. They didn't seem to grow enough of anything to live on for two weeks."[20] In contrast, 22-year-old Nelson Peery remarked, "I tried to understand this grinding poverty and the inability of the South to combat it. I had seen enough evidence that the southern white farmers and workers were not any different from people anywhere else. Somehow so many of them had bought the idea that the road out of their poverty lay in pushing the blacks farther down it. I knew one thing for certain: the blacks had to defend themselves until the whites learned better."[21]

In many ways, the responses of division troops to their immediate surroundings corresponded with their reactions to the racist violence and discrimination that black GIs encountered throughout the South during the period. In what historian Ulysses Lee has termed "the harvest of disorder," racial tensions exploded between black soldiers and white GIs throughout the spring of 1943 at Camp Van Dorn, Mississippi; Camp Stewart, Georgia; March Field and Camp San Luis Obispo, California; Fort Bliss, Texas; Camp Philips, Kansas; Camp Breckinridge, Kentucky; and other stateside training areas.[22] In Louisiana, Camp Livingston and Camp Claiborne were also sites of numerous verbal jousts, fistfights, and shootings that took place between black GIs and white civilians, as well as military and civilian policemen, as black servicemen found themselves being subjected to discriminatory insult and injury at almost every turn.[23] And as recent scholars have pointed out, these racial disturbances largely centered upon battles over public transportation and the racial customs, mores, and traditions of the South.[24] A report filed by an FBI agent in Louisiana at the time provides an example. After observing a skirmish between soldiers and a white bus driver in nearby Alexandria, the bureau agent noted that much of the racial antagonism between white citizens and black GIs rested upon the fact that "Northern Negro soldiers were not aware of the custom of segregation in public conveyances" and that "the Southern Negro soldier is not as retiring and subservient as would be expected, possibly due to the change occurring from better income in the Army than he previously had under the Southern system."[25]

For black soldiers in the division, however, the color lines drawn on the buses carried a different meaning. Black GIs who attended the segregated USO clubs in Many and Leesville faced the prospect of going elsewhere to board an Interurban bus heading back to Camp Polk or spending hours waiting for the next conveyance to arrive owing to overcrowded buses filled with white passengers. As a result, many soldiers received negative marks for being absent without leave when they reported to their company areas.[26] Such was the case of Private Isaiah Johnson while training in the Camp Polk maneuvers area. After his company had received a weekend pass at the end of three long weeks of field training, Johnson and several companions went to Many, where they spent the evening imbibing the riffs and sounds of music and strong drink at the "Bucket of Blood"—the sole honky-tonk available to black soldiers in the town. Hours later, the men prepared to board a public bus heading back to the bivouac area only to be told that there were no seats available to them. As Johnson recalled of that night, "The white soldiers were permitted to load on the public bus first to return to camp; then members of the all-Japanese 100th Battalion; and then, since all of the seats were filled by then, left us colored soldiers with no way to get back to camp." Despite feeling completely frustrated, however, Johnson and his mates simply waited for the next bus to arrive the following morning, upon which they promptly departed.[27]

On many occasions, fights broke out between black servicemen and bus drivers as soldiers struck back against perceived and actual injustices. Returning to Camp Polk after spending a short time in Many, Warrant Officer James Randolph accompanied his wife, Walta, to a local bus station where she was scheduled to board a bus bound for Birmingham, Alabama. As they boarded, however, a violent verbal exchange took place between the young couple and Orval Pritt—a local white bus driver—after Randolph refused to answer questions with "sir." The situation escalated when Pritt refused to pick up Walta's garment bag and yelled, "Boy, didn't I tell you to stop telling me what to do." Not to be outdone, the young officer retorted, "I may be a Negro, but I'm no boy. Just hand me my wife's bags." After turning away from Pritt, Randolph went on to assist his wife only to receive a rain of blows from a blackjack wielded by the driver. The soldier emerged from the beating moments later with severe neck and back injuries and his head bloodied and swollen. Shortly afterward, the couple found themselves evicted from the bus and placed under arrest by town deputies for disorderly conduct and breach of the peace.[28]

Often, the issue of conflict between black servicemen and white civilians and military police revolved around the terrain of dignity and masculinity, namely, a conscious rejection of their "place" as "boys" in the Jim Crow South. In the words of one soldier writing home to his mother in Newport News, Virginia, during this period: "As you know, I've never had any hate in my heart against one race. But these poor whites and their attitudes toward the Negro are abominable. They think we're primative [*sic*] . . . children. The officers have warned us against going into town . . . , so we can hardly get around. Pray for me Ma, for I've forgotten how."[29]

Draftee Cyril Ralph Powell learned that going into town, especially by oneself, was dangerous. The former Chicago resident had completed his basic training at Camp Wheeler, Georgia, before being assigned as a replacement in the 369th's D Company in June 1943. After enduring two weeks of strenuous training, Powell had obtained an overnight pass to nearby De Ridder, where he spent the entire evening at the segregated USO club. While walking alone to the bus station, which was some distance from the USO, hours later, Powell was approached by four white civilians in a car who asked him if he wanted a ride back to camp. Upon entering the car, Powell was seized by two of the men and, in the heat of the struggle, was branded by a hot iron that they had in the front seat of the car. He managed to escape only by leaping out of the speeding car and hiding in a nearby field. However, even though Powell received twenty-nine days of medical treatment at the post hospital, his face was scarred beyond relief. Writing to the *Chicago Defender* months later, he tried to explain how he might have avoided being hurt that evening: "I am convinced more than ever that if I had been accompanied by other members of my company, this misfortune would not have happened. The problem itself stemmed from a lack of respect and that lack of respect comes from a lack of power. If I had the numbers that night, the problem would have been solved."[30]

Conflict also revolved around the issue of the dignity of black women. When traveling to see loved ones in uniform who participated in the war games, female service relatives, like the soldiers, found themselves facing the realities of southern racial politics and, especially in the case of the women, sexual stereotypes. During the training in Louisiana, black women related to division members were viewed as promiscuous, disease-carrying camp followers. As black women, children, and men began to appear in nearby Leesville, a town official remarked, "Dozens of diseased Negro women infest the town. Fifty percent are prostitutes and ninety-nine percent of them are diseased." The presence of service relatives produced an equally inspired, but different, response from black Louisiana residents. For instance, a resident living in Leesville at the time blamed the increased numbers of black service wives, daughters, and sisters for the deplorable housing conditions, the bartering of bodies, and the high levels of venereal disease that existed in the town. "The moral situation is bad," he claimed.[31]

By May 1943, several events had gripped the attention of African American troops who trained in Louisiana and demonstrated how race, sex, and dignity converged in the thinking of division members and their families. State troopers and black military policemen seized a group of seven female service relatives from their rooms in a local Leesville boardinghouse after they arrived in the area. After being charged with vagrancy, the women were placed in a patrol car and carted off to the downtown jail, where they were subjected to physical and emotional abuse, including numerous blood tests for venereal diseases by local physicians and assaults from law enforcement officials. While describing the incident to NAACP executive secretary Walter White at the time, one soldier in the division warned, "This is destined to lead to some serious trouble." Two days later, division members were awakened at dawn and ordered to line up before a local bus driver and white soldier after the two men alleged that they had been beaten by a serviceman claiming to vindicate the honor of the women involved in the incident. However, neither man could identify their assailants. Six hundred division members responded to the incident, however, by filing a joint petition with the national office of the NAACP in which they denounced the action taken by the division's senior officers. They argued, "Wives, sisters, mothers, and daughters of soldiers from all parts of the 'United States,' whose Constitution stands for democracy, have suffered the greatest embarrassments that could be thrown upon any form of womanhood." "Is that the kind of 'Democracy' we are supposed to be fighting for?"[32]

On the other hand, the willingness of the division members to confront the racial mores of the Louisiana hinterland through collective effort also drew a response from high-ranking army officials. For example, the G-2 of the division's intelligence headquarters described the individual and collective actions taken by the division soldiers as "communistic or un-American activity that seems to concentrate solely on the 'Race' problem."[33] Similarly, during his inspection of the division in late April, Benjamin O. Davis Sr. met with black company and platoon officers and enlisted men and exhorted them to be ambassadors of good will, to adopt the "correct mental attitude," as well to warn them to steer clear of possible trouble with local townspeople.[34] Interestingly, Davis, a career army officer, had had encounters with several black junior officers in the division over the past year and doubted their leadership abilities. For example, he wrote in a letter to his wife during that period about a black second lieutenant with whom he "was not so impressed" and expressed his hope that "the men will not run into anything because thus far, the townspeople think well of them."[35]

Although he knew about the problems that black soldiers faced in the area, the general underestimated the devastating impact that his comments had on the morale of the division members who trained in the area. Private Clenon Briggs recalled, "Davis spent a great deal of time running around inspecting the areas where he knew he would find the least trouble. He was a handkerchief head nigger pure and simple."[36] Julius Thompson echoed Briggs's sentiments: "We looked at General Davis as if he was a house nigger . . . because he had never commanded troops in the field and was merely in administration all of his career. He had the attitude that seemed to state to us that he was with us but he was not for us."[37] Some, however, expressed different attitudes about the general's visit. New York resident Elliotte Williams had vivid images of Davis that day:

> The word was quickly passed around the division headquarters of his impending arrival and the need for white officers to display the usual military courtesies. After listening to a deluge of complaints, he made a short speech covering all he had heard and then told us that our primary concern should be training ourselves and our men for combat for it would enable us to stay alive and demonstrate our ability to perform as well as any other soldiers. The Army was not ready for social integration nor should we devote our attention to such matters in the short time we had available to do our job. Since we had so many men who were lacking in formal education who had scored in categories 4 or 5 on the Army General Classification Test, I was inclined to agree with him but it still hurt.[38]

And still others tended to agree with the general's comments and cited the attitudes of black officers as the main cause of concern. St. Louis, Missouri–born Reuben Fraser Jr., who had been on special assignment with the division headquarters, recorded in his diary at time that "although Davis had carefully tried to explain to these men a few important things, he was unable to reach all of them for some were void of any intelligent reasoning and felt that the general was a Negro working against them. In my opinion, General Davis was interested solely in helping the Negro in the army. However, neither he nor any other Negro could solve our many problems overnight."[39]

Black army officials were not the only ones who frustrated the aspirations of division personnel. Most black soldiers expressed ambivalent attitudes toward the black press corps members and black public officials who covered their activities during the maneuvers. On the one hand, they counted on the black press to publicize the racism and discrimination they encountered in the Jim Crow army as well as to provide a link between the training areas and their hometowns. Throughout the field training exercises, division troops met with members of the black press and various black leaders to bring the inequalities of army life to their attention as well as to point up the racism and poverty they encountered in the area. While visiting the area, *Cleveland Call & Post* correspondent William O. Walker met with Cleveland natives Herbert Lowry, William Derr, Alfred Lee, S. Clarence Stinger, and Robert Ward, and the five men remarked on the army's promotion policies and their relations with local townspeople.[40] Around the same time, when

Michigan Chronicle newspaperman Louis Martin visited the division bivouac site, he interviewed fellow Detroiters Tony Watson, James Bryson, James Johnson, Robert Bennett, and Chester Mallory and listened to comments they made regarding army life; he also provided them with information about the well-being of their loved ones.[41] As Nelson Peery, a GI with the division at the time, later recalled, "We needed the protection that the black press, Gibson, and Davis gave us . . . because whatever happened, they were going to expose it."[42]

On the other hand, the black press's lackluster attention to the poverty that black servicemen witnessed in Louisiana and the racism they faced in the armed forces repelled many GIs. For example, despite listening to soldiers formerly from Chicago reel off endless stories about their experiences with racism within their own ranks as well as the struggles of local Louisiana townspeople, *Chicago Defender* correspondent Ben Burns reported that the division had a promotion problem, but he dismissed the stark conditions that the men saw in outlying areas.[43] Black public officials also failed to address all the issues. While visiting the maneuver area at the time, civilian aide Truman Gibson told New York City native Monroe Dowling, a black junior officer in the division's Adjutant General Corps, "Do not get too discouraged at what the men tell you and try to disregard some of the external manifestations of prejudice in Louisiana." Expressing more interest in the division's performance during maneuvers than in the well-being of the men themselves, Gibson went on to state, "I am seriously concerned about the Negro officers lest their attitudes will injure themselves and the entire division."[44]

Despite acknowledging the harsh realities and frustrated aspirations that black GIs and their families encountered in the Black Belt, the recently appointed civilian aide also feared that the heightened tensions in the region would derail his plans to get the War Department to soften its discriminatory racial policies. Echoing the gradualist approach adopted by his predecessor twenty-five years earlier, Gibson stated during a July 1943 interview with a reporter from the *Baltimore Afro-American,* "I think the army is as much opposed to injustice as anyone else. I know what they are doing against brutality. But until we change our laws, colored soldiers are amenable to state law." In a remark that revealed the contradictory nature of black wartime politics, Gibson also went on to deflect public criticism of the army's efforts to defend the rights of African Americans in uniform. When asked about the army's role in investigating complaints made by black soldiers at various military bases and towns across the region, Gibson stated, "There is no easy way out. The power to punish offenders of the colored soldiers is in the hands of the FBI. In bad situations, the army's only course is to declare the place out of bounds."[45]

But there is another explanation for Gibson's position as reflected in this state-ment. The Chicago native's response reflected the conservative politics that he embraced. A self-styled moderate on questions of race, Gibson adopted a cau-tious political style that allowed him to negotiate racial tensions between black army personnel and civilian communities with minimal fanfare during the wartime period.[46] The civilian aide elaborated on his low-key approach several years later in a late 1944 memorandum to Assistant Secretary of War John Mc-Cloy. "Though I know it is not necessary," Gibson observed, "I want to assure you that I have no political interests one way or another. If I had a major inter-est at the moment, it would be to get out of my present position as rapidly as possible, having just about reached the limit of my ability to serve as a *middle man* (his emphasis), absorbing gripes and complaints in person by mail and tele-phone all day and most of the night."[47]

It is important to distinguish between the approach adopted by Gibson and others in the civilian aide's office, which viewed the morale of black soldiers sim-ply as a bureaucratic matter, and the discussions taking place among black com-munities and neighborhoods about the plight of black GIs stationed in the South. For example, noted writer Ann Petry observed the frustration expressed by black residents of the Mid-Atlantic coast—sentiments that were also voiced by segments of the African American community nationwide—regarding the stationing of black troops across the South during the wartime period. In a famous 1947 novella ti-tled "In Darkness and Confusion," Petry gave expression to this distress through the story of a transplanted black southerner who learned that his son had recently been transferred from nearby Fort Dix, New Jersey, to a military base in Georgia. "Sam's being in the army wasn't so bad," the central character in Petry's essay mused; "it was his being in Georgia that was bad. They didn't treat colored people right down there."[48]

As the summer of 1943 approached, the cautious views expressed by Gibson and the black press corps strained their relationships with division personnel. In the middle of the extensive newspaper coverage of their activities, soldiers felt compelled to contest the accounts of their performances filed by black corre-spondents. In June, a GI stationed at Camp Polk, Louisiana, wrote a letter to the *Chicago Defender* in which he announced that "a series of recent articles on the Ninety-third division maneuvers in Louisiana have been acclaimed with unani-mous disapproval by the men of the division." The news articles, he argued bit-terly, "deal more with what your correspondents think rather than what is actu-ally happening. The folks back home aren't interested in what someone THINKS we're doing, they want to KNOW. Why don't you print what we're really doing?"[49]

Many division members agreed with this sentiment. In the words of 595th artilleryman Robert Galley, a native of Palestine, Texas: "My comrades and I did not like it. They'd rather claim that everything was going well for us instead of reporting what was really going on down in Louisiana."[50] Houston native Asberry McGriff expressed similar sentiments: "We were tired of the army race relations and grew even more tired of the Southern way of life surrounding most of the training camps. But we complained even louder of the lack of concern shown by Truman Gibson, B. O. Davis, and the black newspaper reporters because we thought they shoulda known better."[51] A soldier in the division who wrote Gibson at the time chose to use stronger language to describe his view of the civilian aide's efforts during the period: "Mr. Gibson, if you have to pay for the sins of not reporting the sins against Negroes, well you would burn the rest of your life for we are being treated as if we are enemies."[52]

On the surface, statements made by division members about their frustrations over talking with War Department officials and members of the black press about the army's racial practices appear to have been knee-jerk reactions to life in the American South. But events unfolded later in 1943 that forced 93rd Infantry Division personnel and their loved ones to adjust their attitudes toward military service altogether. This altered sense of consciousness would, in turn, compel them to formulate new strategies that both complemented and diverged from the larger overall objectives of the black community and the army.

Seeds of a New Perspective

A series of events concerning the War Department's promotion and troop employment policies cultivated the service-related politics practiced by 93rd Infantry Division personnel and their loved ones. In the early 1940s, black officers in the division received promotions more slowly than did their white counterparts because of troop overstrength and the limited number of position vacancies within the division. At the beginning of the unit's training, more than 640 officers headed its ranks, and the special task positions and operations duties that had been created to accommodate this large number of officers had an adverse effect on the division cadre.[53] For example, in the opinion of War Department officials, the unit had more than 150 excess black junior officers (out of a total of 499). Left unabated, the condition worsened over time as large numbers of second lieutenants continued to report to the unit.[54] As a result, by August 1943, only 26 percent (126) of the black officers assigned to the division had received promotions through the ranks as the average time in grade rose from 5.7 months to well over 10 months.

Of these advancements, 63 percent occurred in the infantry. Although some of the unit's excess officers were later assigned to the other black infantry division, the 92nd, so many junior black officers arrived daily that one officer who was on special assignment at the time recalled years later, "Any officer who spent most of his time in special service duties [non–Table of Organization positions] was used but seldom promoted."[55]

The staffing flaws within the division frustrated the advancement opportunities of those who worked as special service officers, USO liaisons, and special duty officers. Denver resident Charles J. Blackwood, the highest-ranking black officer in the division, supervised the cadre in the Special Service Office before being mustered out of the service one day after reaching retirement age in 1944.[56] Philadelphia-born Second Lieutenant George Nicholas worked as a mess supervisor and served in other capacities as an excess officer in his company for nearly nine months before being transferred to the 92nd Infantry Division in August 1943. Recalling his difficulties advancing in his unit, he stated, "With the surplus of officers in the division, there was very little hope of ever being promoted."[57]

The overstrength problems largely stemmed from the War Department's dim view of black cadres and its practice of barring black officers from outranking or commanding white personnel.[58] In January 1943, for instance, army planners stipulated that "except for medical officers and chaplains, senior Negro officers will not be assigned to a unit having white officers of other arms and services in junior grades." The policy also went on to state that "no white officer be placed under the immediate command of a Negro officer and that, when white officers of a unit became subordinate to a Negro officer through promotion of such Negro officer in the unit, the white officers would be transferred."[59] And the division's command structure strictly adhered to this policy during the opening stages of unit's training. As one black officer assigned to the 93rd's Medical Corps during the period recalled, "Leadership positions were occupied by white officers, . . . this included of course, the colonel, the lieutenant colonel and all of the majors."[60]

In some cases, black junior officers performed for months duties that ordinarily would have been done by higher-ranking officers. For example, despite graduating second in his class from Fort Benning's Officer Candidate School and first from Communications School, Martin Winfield, a former postal clerk from Chicago who was gifted with what an observer described later as "a photographic memory," remained a second lieutenant for two years before he received his promotion. Yet a white second lieutenant assigned to the division was promoted to captain and assigned to the division headquarters within the same amount of time despite being court-martialed and found guilty of embezzling government property.[61] In another case in point, whereas Robert Blair, a white second lieutenant in the Quartermaster Corps, received a recommendation for promotion days after he was transferred to the division's Inspector General's Department, Robert Grant, a black field artillery officer, worked as the assistant battalion motor officer for months before receiving an advancement in rank.[62] Recalling his bitter experience, Grant stated, "During my assignment with the Ninety-third Infantry Division, I have found that Negro officers have had to hold positions for periods of months before being recommended for promotion, in other words he had to prove his ability first. On the other hand, white officers were recommended as soon as they accepted the assignment which has helped to destroy the eagerness, efficiency, and interest of Negro officers."[63]

The policy, which further inhibited promotions to deserving and able black officers, confirmed their already dim view of military life. When in February 1943 division commander Major General Fred W. Miller assembled the men and informed them about the War Department's policy barring the promotion of black officers above the grade of first lieutenant, many openly expressed their anger at the War Department's racial policies.[64] For instance, blaming the War Department, Elliotte Williams recalled, "Their prophecies of failure were self-fulfilling, designed to demonstrate the expected inferiority of black troops and black leadership."[65] For 25th infantryman and Leavenworth, Kansas, native Leo Logan, the army's promotion system left a lot to be desired. He recalled, "I was passed over several times while white officers, whom I considered not as qualified as I was, were always promoted."[66]

The limiting of promotions for the unit's black officers also attracted considerable attention from the African American press corps. Upon learning of Miller's declaration on 28 February, staff reporters from the *Chicago Bee* immediately contacted the War Department's Public Relations Office about the issue only to be disingenuously told that policymakers intended to launch an investigation into the matter to determine the authenticity of the order. And as the debate over the status of black officers in the unit deepened, a *Bee* editorial asked, "If Negroes can't advance beyond first lieutenant in a unit where the entire division is composed of Negroes, does it seem logical that the army has a place for them in units where the personnel is composed mainly of whites—or where white soldiers, even if officers, are of a rank lower?"[67]

Press corps members also began to question the role that the unit would play on the battlefield. Around the same time, the *Baltimore Afro-American* attacked the reasoning that army officials used to defend the army's employment policies for black officers in the division. In an article titled "Is the 93rd a Token Unit?"

reporters contended: "The explanation was made that the order would not prevent officers from being recommended for promotion beyond the rank of first lieutenant but if they are so promoted the officer in question could no longer serve there. The War Department should realize that a commander would not dare recommend a good officer if he is going to be lost to the division." From the NAACP's national office, *Crisis* editor Roy Wilkins remarked that if Miller's announcement was true, then "the War Department has tossed away, in one stroke, all the gains it has made in Negro public opinion, through the operation of the non-segregated officer's training schools." With regard to the promotion ceiling imposed on black junior officers, Wilkins concluded, "Now the hopes of our men, and of our people, are dashed by the old, old, pronouncement: 'thus far shall you go and no further, because you are black.'" Others were similarly direct about the War Department's policy. Around the same period, the comments of the 93rd Division commander elicited a sarcastic note of criticism from "Charley Cherokee," a syndicated columnist for the *Chicago Defender*. But, unlike the others, the editorialist placed the issue squarely in the context of unit morale. In a column titled "The Ahmed Forces, Suh," he declared, "In Huachuca, the Ninety-third Division has had ample time to ponder and brood in the Arizona desert. Stories come from there—the men don't like the way that Negro officers are being treated. Colored non-coms beg the Negro papers to send someone out and get the real story and pretty damned quick. Yes sir; hell's a-brewing."[68]

Soon afterward, the black press's scrutiny of Miller's statement regarding the promotion of black 93rd officers triggered a response from military planners. During a 4 March 1943 press conference, *Chicago Defender* correspondent Harry McAlpin asked Secretary of War Henry Stimson "if it was true that Negro soldiers in the division had been informed by their commander that they would not rise above the rank of First Lieutenant." Stimson vehemently denied the story, labeling Miller's comments as "mere gossip." The secretary of war then proceeded to defend the army's policies, stating, "You know I have promoted many Negro officers, making one of them a brigadier general."[69] Meanwhile, Washington policymakers had decided to investigate individual complaints of promotion practices in the division firsthand. Having very little information about the division's morale, Undersecretary of War Robert P. Patterson dispatched Colonel Edward S. Greenbaum to observe troop morale in the division later that month. As an executive officer in Patterson's office, Greenbaum had established a well-deserved reputation among the General Staff for tackling tough administrative issues.[70] And as public dissatisfaction with the army's policies began to increase steadily over the next few months, the Inspector General's Office also ordered Brigadier General Benjamin O. Davis to the area to study the unit's promotion policies.

Unaware of each other's presence, both men arrived at the division headquarters around the same time. But by the time they had departed, their impressions of the morale of black officers and enlisted personnel in the unit couldn't have been more different. After slipping into the division area without attracting attention from its staff, Greenbaum discovered that "among the colored officers there are a few who are doing fine work. . . . The balance of them, however, exhibit a total lack of responsibility; are disinterested in their work, are inefficient, lazy and unable to learn some of the most elementary things." Of the morale of white officers who were assigned to the all-black unit, Greenbaum noted, "Practically all of these men came to camp with the usual Southern feeling in reference to negroes and were resentful of the fact that an effort was being made to train negroes as combat troops."[71] Davis presented a different picture, however. After visiting all the regimental and battalion units that made up the division, Davis reported, "All officers and men seemed to be very enthusiastic about their work in connection with the maneuvers." And he went on to add that the troop's "morale is excellent" and that the "commanders expressed a desire to lead their units into any theater of operations assigned to the division."[72]

As Greenbaum, Davis, and other army officials worked to deflect public criticism of the army's policies toward black officers, a coterie of white officers within the unit moved behind the scenes to create promotion opportunities for its own black officers. Perhaps two of the most outspoken members of the division's senior officer corps were Fred Miller and Thomas Fenton Taylor. Miller, a 52-year-old officer from Manchester, Iowa, had no sooner arrived at Fort Huachuca to assume command of the division at the end of 1942 when he learned of the backlog of black officers awaiting promotion. Over the next six months, Miller transferred black personnel to vacant cadre positions created by the departure of higher-ranking white officers from the division. In some cases, the division commander assigned qualified black junior officers to service support units where they held supervisory positions above the white cadre without holding the appropriate rank. All the while, he wrote diligently to the army high command in the hope of obtaining clarification about the status of black officers who were to be promoted within the unit, but to no avail. Although Army Ground Forces Headquarters granted the division commander the latitude of exercising his own judgment in the matter, his efforts to establish an effective promotion policy in the division produced very little results.[73] By the beginning of the summer of 1943, the promotion practices and the indifferent attitudes exhibited by the War Department toward the segregated unit left Miller frustrated and dispirited. In June, he left the division for El Paso, Texas, where he retired from the army a year later.[74]

Thomas Fenton Taylor adopted a similar strategy. Born in Tennessee in 1889, Taylor graduated from the U.S. Military Academy in 1915. After a steady stream of promotions with the U.S. 5th Infantry Division and study at the Infantry School Advanced Course and the Army War College, he was appointed as the regimental commander to the 93rd's 369th Infantry in June 1942.[75] There he soon developed a reputation among the men of the regiment as being fair and impartial. According to Elliotte Williams, "Colonel Taylor was an old field soldier who vowed he would bring his command through on time despite the fact that other commanders were complaining in division staff meetings of their inability to meet their training goals and were weeks behind schedule. As sure as his word, on the last day of field exercises, he led his regiment back to the division area, looking proud and sharp, counting cadence and singing."[76] Likewise, John Howard recalled, "Colonel Taylor was considered a renegade because he would always challenge the status quo. When he became regimental commander of the 369th Infantry Regiment, he made an extremely unpopular decision."[77]

The decision to which Howard alluded was Taylor's successful drive to create the first battalion primarily staffed by black officers in U.S. history.[78] Like Fred Miller and a few other senior white officers in the 93rd, Taylor felt that black officers would perform and succeed if given the opportunity, but he immediately saw that they had been placed in almost impossible situations and that white superior officers used their shortcomings to justify racist beliefs in black mental inferiority and cowardice under fire. So committed was the 369th Infantry commander to equal performance standards that he decided that he would rectify the situation when given the chance. That opportunity came in June 1942, when Charles Blackwood reported to the division as the unit's special services officer.[79]

In Taylor's view, Blackwood was uniquely suited to fulfill his aspirations. A career officer, Blackwood had fought on the battlefields of France during the First World War as a member of the all-black 92nd Infantry Division. In 1918, after returning home, he worked as an engineer with the Burlington Railroad and received additional training at the Chicago School of Engineering while advancing in the U.S. Army Reserves from captain in 1926 to the grade of major in 1938. In March 1942, Blackwood reported to active duty and was immediately assigned to Fort Benning's Infantry School before being appointed to the 93rd Infantry Division three months later.[80]

Encouraged by Blackwood's credentials, Taylor persuaded Charles Hall, the previous division commander, to assign Blackwood to the 369th Infantry Regiment in June 1942. There, Blackwood, along with several talented junior officers, helped organize a special training element within the unit. Within a matter of months, these officers had transformed nearly six hundred illiterate and semi-illiterate draftees into efficient soldiers.[81] Impressed with Blackwood's organizational abilities, Taylor then managed to have the special service chief placed in command of a battalion within the 369th, realizing that War Department policy wouldn't allow white company commanders to serve under a black field-grade officer.[82]

Not long afterward, Taylor's strategy resulted in a directive by division commander Major General Raymond Lehman designating the 369th Infantry's 1st Battalion, commanded by Blackwood, as the first all-black organization in the division.[83] Based on Lehman's plans, white officers in the unit were replaced by black officers who were transferred to the battalion after receiving recommendations from the regimental commanders of the 25th, 368th, and 369th Infantry units. Operating under the intense public and official scrutiny, the men in the battalion performed so well in their training that visitors couldn't help but be impressed. For Taylor, however, the experiment had a bittersweet ending. In August 1943 he was transferred to the Infantry School at Fort Benning, Georgia, where he remained until he was retired a year later.[84] But after hearing that Taylor had been transferred, Monroe Dowling, a black junior officer in the division's Adjutant General Corps, commented, "That was the greatest loss that could have happened to us just at this time. He was a fine man and he was trying to do right by colored officers. In fact, while none of the other colonels wanted the black battalion as a part of their command, Taylor said he would take it and that he would make it work . . . , and he did just that."[85]

For division troops, the faith that staff officers like Thomas Fenton Taylor expressed in their junior officers if given an opportunity diverged widely from the War Department's dim view of black cadres. Clarence Ross, a native of Little Rock, Arkansas, remarked, "We knew that black officers in the division had it hard because they had to reassure us that they would look out for us while at the same time, uphold the training principles of the Army."[86] In a similar vein, Louisiana native Private Clenon Briggs stated, "As enlisted men, we saw that black officers were treated as second-class citizens . . . , very much like we were being treated."[87] Another soldier commented, "Most of the black junior officers were from the ranks. We had known some of them as enlisted men and soldiered for them, making them look good in front of the commanding officers."[88]

And as the days folded into weeks, the voices of private citizens, community leaders, and organizations connected to the division grew louder, asserting that the War Department's promotion polices had flown in the face of President Roosevelt's stated goals for a war for democracy. Shortly after the division arrived in Louisiana, servicemen and USO club workers packed an auditorium at Fort Bragg, North Carolina, for a three-day conference devoted to issues regarding the war. During the gathering, they heard Civilian Defense Office administrator and 93rd Division relative Pauline Redmond Coggs deliver a series of speeches on the topic "The Role of Negro Women in the War" during which Coggs mentioned her husband Theodore's stint of duty and roundly criticized the army's promotion policies.[89] In Atlanta, Georgia, members of a club composed of mothers with sons serving as officers in the division filed a petition with the War Department, demanding that the army reverse its discriminatory racial policies. "It is still true that the hand that rocks the cradle rules the world," they declared.[90] Then in Illinois, concerns expressed over the plight of fellow comrades and division officers Orion Page, Castine Davis, and Martin Winfield prompted members of the Chicago branch of the National Alliance of Postal Employees to create a war service committee to wage a public campaign on their behalf. A few weeks after the division left the Bayou State, the organization had gained such prominence that when members of the Alliance of Postal Employees gathered in St. Louis, Missouri, for its biennial convention later that year, alliance officials adopted a militant platform, demanding that its branch affiliates create similar organizations and that the army abandon its racial practices.[91]

Responding to public criticism of its policies, army officials, ever mindful of bad publicity, made a series of moves. After witnessing the division's activities in Louisiana swamps on 26 April, officers from the Inspector General's Office and General Davis promoted seventy-six infantry and field artillery second lieutenants who had distinguished themselves during the field exercises.[92] Less than two days later, the Inspector General's Office promoted approximately forty additional officers and specifically mentioned eight black officers for their tireless devotion to duty.[93] At the same time, however, many white officers were promoted as well, reflecting the War Department's adherence to a policy of not allowing black officers to outrank their white counterparts.

Meanwhile, division personnel used the War Department's policies as a strategy to carve out spaces of dignity within the armed forces. Many black officers attached to the division openly sought assistance from various leaders and newspapers, requesting special appointments as a way of avoiding being mustered out of the army or placed in black units stationed in the Jim Crow South.[94] Specifically, GIs felt that black War Department officials like General Benjamin O. Davis and civilian aide Truman Gibson would act to safeguard their collective interests.

"You can facilitate favorable consideration through all these damn places in the District of Columbia beginning with Army Ground Forces, the Adjutant General and the Provost Marshal General's Office and I believe with the necessary publicity, it can be done," one officer reminded the acting civilian aide.[95] George W. McKinney wrote Gibson, stating, "I learned from another officer that if I ever applied to the School of Civil Affairs to let you know and maybe you could encourage the application through the Provost Marshal's Office." These ventures faced tremendous odds owing in part to an unwritten policy among War Department officials and the division high command to keep the General Staff and special staff sections limited exclusively to white officers. For example, working as the assistant to the chief of staff in the division's intelligence and adjutant general's department, Tampa, Florida, native John Armwood and San Bernardino, California, resident James N. Reese were the only black officers assigned to the General Staff headquarters.[96] Gibson's failure to push more forcefully for the inclusion of black officers in the schools also may have contributed to the problem, however. While Gibson responded to these inquiries by stating that he would relay their suggestions to the Provost Marshal General's Office, many of their requests were largely disapproved, ignored, or not supported by the civilian aide.[97] More than a few officers, for instance, requested Gibson's assistance only to be told by the civilian aide, "I do not know that I can be of any assistance to you in this transfer."[98]

But even as Davis and Gibson scrambled to provide aid for the disgruntled soldiers, it had become clear to black GIs that the traditional avenues for seeking redress would no longer be adequate. As the division's stateside training moved into a new phase, they increasingly sought out new strategies through which their problems would capture the full attention of army officials, civil rights organizations, and black leaders. And before long, the ground upon which public debate over the army racial practices and troop morale had rested began to shift into unrecognizable territory as new voices on the democratic principles of the war entered the fray.

New Voices in the Struggle

In July 1943, the first echelon of U.S. 93rd Infantry Division troops left Louisiana for the Desert Training Center in California.[99] As the unit departed, the division's ranks were expanded to include an influx of officers who arrived from Tuskegee, Alabama, and Fort Benning, Georgia.[100] There the incoming officers, along with some four hundred enlisted men who arrived from other replacement centers, participated in refresher courses in basic training and physical conditioning and played a major role in the 4th Corps maneuvers. As the men soon discovered, the 120-degree days posed a challenge to the fittest of physical constitutions. For weeks on end, division members had withstood 25-mile hikes out of "Camp Clipper" into jagged mountain areas and snake-infested hills to maneuver against armored infantry divisions slated for duty in the North African campaign.[101] As if withstanding the climactic conditions were not enough, 93rd GIs had to complete a series of division-size combat exercises before enduring a strenuous infiltration course in which ball ammunition and exploding dynamite charges were hurled close to their prone positions. By the end of the summer, the troops had barely rested before the division received orders to move against the all-white U.S. 90th Infantry Division.[102]

As the troops negotiated the harsh California climatic conditions, family relatives from black communities across the country began to stream into areas adjacent to the training center where they could provide a sense of home to the soldiers in training. In Pasadena, Needles, Ludlow, and San Bernardino, groups that included Wilamina Biddiex, Freida Greene, Ethylin Jordan Rice, and Ruby Royston could be seen departing Pullman trains from Washington, D.C., Detroit, Chicago, and Alexandria, Louisiana, to join their loved ones in the desert.[103] In Los Angeles, Mildred Monroe, Penelope Smith, De Loise Collins, Muriel Farmer, and Gloria Evans arrived around the same period.[104] There, they lodged with families that had recently relocated to the metropolitan area. Those who came to the desert area alone traveled with other service relatives; some migrated with friends. Along with Thelma Watson—a friend from Chicago—Thelma Thomas and Jessie Clinton left the Windy City for San Bernardino, where they boarded with Izelle Posey, a longtime resident of the city.[105] Despite the strict training schedule of the unit, division members reciprocated the moves of their relatives by spending their Friday evenings negotiating the arduous trips to the Pacific coastal towns only to make the trips back to the maneuver area less than thirty-six hours later. As one soldier who made the weekly trips recalled, "We would slip out every Friday, drive one hundred miles and get up on Sunday in order to make to reveille the next day."[106]

As the soldiers and families related to the unit moved to reconnect their households, the Mojave Desert served as a critical turning point in their lives, since the GIs now began to contemplate the certainty of being assigned overseas. Many soldiers linked the imaginary battles they waged against an unforeseen enemy in the desert to the individual and collective struggles they waged on the American social, political, and economic landscape and within African American society itself. Often these discussions took place in the homes of relatives or friends in the outlying communities. Rubye Shipley opened her Los Angeles home to her brother-in-law Samuel Tyree and a group of soldiers arriving from Camp Clipper, where they discussed the racial politics of the war.[107] Nearby, Octavia Green opened the door to her Los Angeles home to Christo and Laura Waller as well as the families of division GIs originally from Baltimore, Maryland. Throughout the period, news about the army and their hometown dominated their conversations.[108] Around the same time, the residence of Lawrence Raibon provided the setting for Richard Cook, Alberta Dawson, and seven other division members to discuss the war and military service.[109] The interaction proved to be useful to both parties. The exchanges offered service family members and contemporaries invaluable insight into the events that were shaping the well-being of GIs training in the maneuver area while the soldiers gained a better understanding of the issues that were affecting their loved ones in their former hometowns.

Meanwhile, a combination of events intensified the grassroots discussions that were taking place among black division members and civilian communities about military service and hometown events. Begun in early 1942, the Double Victory initiative waged largely by the *Pittsburgh Courier* proposed that victory had to be achieved over enemies both abroad and at home, and it had a tremendous effect on African American communities across the country.[110] Throughout the pages of the *Courier,* huge banners carrying the "VV" emblem appeared during the period, and almost overnight Double V clubs were formed from Los Angeles to New York, embracing the concept and adopting its cause as their own.[111] Many prominent black religious and political leaders supported the concept and urged their clubs, lodges, churches, fraternities, and civic groups to support the campaign for various reasons. In St. Louis, Missouri; Florence, South Carolina; and Fort Worth, Texas, for example, local NAACP branch chapters used the slogan to recruit hundreds of new members, and some ten thousand members were mobilized in Evansville, Indiana, during the period.[112] In June of that year, YMCA executive Dr. Channing Tobias urged a packed audience at the Morehouse College commencement exercises to "continue to fight on two fronts."[113] Dr. D. V. Jemison, president of the National Baptist Convention and chairman of the National Negro Council, pledged his support and urged his followers to endorse the campaign, and the Reverend Dr. Thomas Harten, pastor of Brooklyn's Holy Trinity Baptist Church, told his congregation, "I want a 'Double Victory' even if it takes five or ten years for it to become a reality."[114]

In essays, poems, and stories supporting the Double Victory strategy, many individuals measured African American patriotic support for the war effort by the yardstick of racial progress. Witness, for instance, Los Angeles writer and lecturer Irene West's poem entitled "The Double V Crusaders":

> The Sun-tanned Yanks are on the march.
> They're building their own "Triumphant Arch."
> All the races will pass, I'm proud to say
> Thru the "Arc De Triumph," they're building today.
> The long suffering South will burst in bloom
> As they march, march, march, o'er defeat and doom.
>
> Not a white man's puppet, but a child of God!
> Granted his share of this sacred sod;
> Won by martyrs who challenged this age,
> By your own intellectuals, leaders, and sage.
> The "VV" Crusaders are fated to win,
> And wipe out a three hundred year old sir.[115]

Much of this poem linked the willingness of black soldiers to die in battle to the African American struggle for full equality. Similarly, J. C. Rowlett's poem entitled "Strong upon a "Double V" connected the outcome of the war to freedom to conditions endured by southern slaves during the American Civil War:

> Play your harps, ye black musicians,
> Strong Upon a "Double V,"
> Play regardless of conditions
> We're fighting for Democracy.
> Play your harps, ye black musicians
> Make the echoes ring afar.
> Break the bonds of human slavery
> Till the gates of freedom swing ajar.[116]

From the spring of 1943 to the beginning of the following year, black political and religious leaders and organizations began a massive campaign to have the division committed to an active theater of operation. Moved by the unit's progress shown to them by army officials in Louisiana, black newspapers such as the *Chicago Defender,* the *Pittsburgh Courier,* the *Cleveland Call & Post,* and the *Baltimore Afro-American* had adopted the cause as their own, publishing numerous editorials excoriating the War Department's reluctance to use the all-black unit against enemy forces. While covering American troops in Egypt and the Mediterranean theater of operations, for instance, *Pittsburgh Courier* correspondent Edgar T. Rouzeau openly questioned why the War Department refused to commit black ground forces and warned that "the Negro Press should realize that something has to be done."[117] In late November, NAACP executive secretary Walter White wrote a letter to Stimson, requesting that the secretary of war comment on the status of the 93rd after the NAACP had learned of a rumor that elements of the division reportedly had been slated for guard duty on the Pacific coast after the unit had been broken up. "Inasmuch as the Ninety-third was the first Negro combat division to be activated in this war and inasmuch as Negro Americans have entertained high hopes of the contributions these men would make in combat areas, you can appreciate the effect of the reported action upon the Negro civilian population," White told him.[118] The adjutant general replied to the NAACP executive secretary that rumors regarding the 93rd were unfounded and that the unit was conducting tactical exercises at the California-Arizona maneuver area.[119] What he omitted was that the men of the 93rd had received alert orders for overseas service from U.S. Army Ground Forces ten days earlier.[120]

Historian Joyce Thomas points out that black GIs registered their displeasure with the racial discrimination practiced in the army by writing letters and asserts that the black campaign for equality within the military closely resembled the struggles in the civilian sphere. "The most frequently used form of protest or 'agitation' for 'racial rights' among the articulate was letter writing," she argues.[121] But while Thomas points out the flurry of correspondence between the parties, she pulls back from considering how the lines of private conversations and public action were reflective of the face-to-face meetings of the participants involved. Nor is it clear what happened when both parties agreed or disagreed on a particular issue.

If African American soldiers resorted to letter writing and other literary strategies to register their discontent, it was because they understood that they had an accessible constituency whose views of the war's meaning spoke for them as citizen-soldiers, namely, their immediate families and communities. In black newspapers and left-wing periodicals, service families and communities sought to raise their voices to advance their own interests, which at times coalesced and clashed with those of the very communities in which they lived and worked. And quite often, they had to camouflage their identity to avoid persecution. While her husband, Theodore, trained with the 93rd Infantry Division in 1942, for instance, Pauline Coggs and noted civil rights activist Pauli Murray published an article titled "Negro Youth's Dilemma" in *Threshold,* an organ of the United States Committee of International Student Service. While castigating the apparent clash between the country's professed commitment to extending democratic principles abroad and its system of racial discrimination in the armed forces, the former Chicago resident, however, omitted her name from the author's byline in order to evade public scrutiny.[122]

To some of her contemporaries, Coggs's reasoning for anonymity reflected a deep concern to protect her professional career. As Pauli Murray later recalled, "The two of us collaborated on the article, but because of Pauline's vulnerable position as a federal employee, it appeared under my name only in the April issue."[123] But the young woman's decision to avoid the public spotlight also may have reflected her recognition of the potential threat that her words carried for her husband's well-being. "Tee and I were followed by FBI agents during his entire stint of duty in the division, and we knew that any racial stuff would adversely affect him," Coggs recalls of this period.[124]

On other occasions, articles published in black periodicals during the division's training reflected discussions that were taking place within military households over the war's meaning and the impact it had on the direction of African American politics during the period. Such was the case of Edward Smith-Green. The Brooklyn, New York, resident had no sooner graduated from Officer Candidate School in 1942 when he received orders to report to Arizona, where the division was stationed. However, the 24-year-old City College of New York graduate was unclear about the war's meaning and its larger implications for the African American struggle for equal rights. Prompted by these uneasy feelings, Smith-Green used the pages of the *Pittsburgh Courier* in October that year to publish a letter to his father—pioneering UNIA member Edward Smith-Green Sr.—entitled "Dear Dad: What Am I to Adopt as My Philosophy of the War?"[125] The Smith-Green family was not alone on this score. About two years later, the *Washington Tribune* published a letter written by former District of Columbia resident Walter Sanderson, an officer assigned to division, to his father that read, "Things are looking dicey for me down here in the world's backyard. Tell everyone there that moral victories and race politics don't count for us. Believe me when I say, the world is a lot bigger and more real when you face the immediate prospect of being shot at."[126]

Still others expressed their ambivalence in the unpublished correspondence they exchanged with family members from afar. For example, one soldier in the 369th wrote in a letter penned to his mother during the period, "You know, just eighteen months ago, Uncle Sam sent a mob of 16,000 men to Fort Huachuca. A lot has happened since. Thru the storm of war, that mob has been molded into a force that will be terrible to face in battle." On the surface, the soldier was describing the training of the 369th Infantry and how his company was being molded into a combat-ready outfit, emphasizing his willingness to engage enemy forces. Yet his letter carried a double meaning, reflecting not only his commitment to fighting racism in American society but also an implicit negation of black middle-class notions of how African American soldiers conducted themselves in the army.[127] The soldier went on to describe a racial incident during that period between black 93rd Division members and white soldiers in the 90th Infantry Division over a roadblock. He concluded his letter by stating, "I'm sure that we will keep this aggressiveness and will be hard to mess with in civil life." When asked about the letter years later, the veteran recalled, "I wanted my mother to know that I was doing okay but I did not want to die for a system that upheld lynch laws, mob violence, segregation, and daily humiliations."[128]

For many division servicemen, the *Pittsburgh Courier's* Double Victory Campaign and the push by black leaders to commit them to an overseas theater of operations epitomized the distance between the views they held of themselves as soldiers and the role that segments of African American society envisioned for them to play in the long-term goals of the black freedom struggle. In September 1943, correspondents from the *Chicago Defender, Chicago Bee,* and the *Pittsburgh Courier* traveled to California to survey division personnel about the impact they thought their wartime contribution would have on the postwar world. The responses of the GIs were mixed. On the one hand, soldiers attached to the division felt that their stint of duty under fire would provide justifiable evidence in a case for racial justice. And quite a few expressed the hope of returning to a better life after the war. For example, a Cleveland, Ohio, resident commented, "Life after the war will be different and my participation in battle has to be taken in consideration. I hope to be fortunate enough to return to my previous way of life, but I expect to make a change." Similarly, a former schoolteacher from Trenton, New Jersey, remarked, "The Army has opened many new fields of endeavor to men who otherwise would have never had the opportunities. It will provide men with new contacts and new experiences which have made a deep impression on their mode of livelihood and thinking." And still another serviceman, from Morristown, New Jersey, stated, "I feel that jobs will be scarce after the war, but I also feel that my wartime service will help me in my climb toward success."[129]

But on the other hand, the hopes that many division servicemen expressed regarding the potential benefits that their wartime contributions would bring to them were tempered by the resentment they felt toward the actions taken by black middle-class leaders, newspapers, and organizations on their behalf. Responding anonymously, soldiers in the division castigated *Chicago Bee* reporter J. Robert Smith and other journalists, accusing them of falsely reporting the status of the division and calling for the unit's deployment before it was adequately prepared for action. "It will be tantamount to wholesale murder if we are sent into combat service," the men claimed. The soldiers implored the reporters to "acquaint the Negro editors with the plight of the division so that they may publish the entire story."[130] Even more revealing were the reactions of óne Mississippi-born soldier upon hearing about the campaign: "I deeply resented the campaign for they (black newspaper editors) were intent on us going off and maybe getting shot for rights that we didn't have ourselves."[131]

Decades later, division members continued to take the men who covered their activities in the desert to task over the paradoxical position in which the *Courier's* pro-democratic rhetoric had placed them. "The Double Victory Campaign," recalled Reuben Fraser, "was of no value to the men in the 93rd whatsoever."[132] Remembering the efforts of the black press during that period, Nelson Peery wrote, "We did not trust them (the newspapers). We knew that their strategy to gain equality for black people (and leadership for themselves) was having the black soldier make greater sacrifices and show greater patriotism than the whites. The black press did not understand that we were a part of the new struggle of the colored nine-tenths of humanity to gain dignity."[133] And Asheville, North Carolina, native Bismark Williams commented on the black newspapers during the period when he wrote home, "So, they think we're anxious to fight, do they? Well, we're not, not by a damned sight. The people we want are the crackers. Not only was World War I left unfinished, but the Civil War needs some more attention too."[134]

As the division trained in the desert, many GIs translated their mixed feelings regarding their possible overseas deployment into unorganized acts of resistance. Some absented themselves from the maneuvers area only to reappear days later. Such was the case of Private Adam Hutton. In late September 1943, Hutton decided to leave Camp Clipper for nearby Needles without approval from his superior during the maneuvers. To make matters worse, he had stolen a jeep from the battalion motor pool. Not long after his departure, several officers driving from the camp area spotted Hutton on the two-lane highway, traveling at speeds exceeding 60 miles an hour. After a lengthy chase, they managed to intercept the vehicle and placed him under arrest. However, Hutton remained unflappable. Before entering the military police station in Needles, the 21-year-old serviceman told the arresting officers that he was "going out to look for a dog" and disappeared into the desert; he didn't show up at the military post until weeks later. Hutton was subsequently court-martialed and sentenced to six months' hard labor in the division stockade.[135]

Around the same time, Cornelius Compton also used flight, though for a some-what different reason. An officer with the division's field artillery battalion, Compton left for Needles one Friday evening in early November 1943 despite receiving an assignment from his superior officer to be duty officer at the military post that weekend. Shortly after returning to the camp, the 26-year-old former National Guardsman was summoned to appear before a court-martial trial board and was found guilty of committing an act of insubordination and stripped of his commission.[136] When asked later why he had decided to leave the area, Compton explained, "My wife had an ailing heart so I left camp to take care of her. But the executive officer of my battalion had it in for me ever since I told him that this war was not my war. It was a White Folk's War."[137] Still others feigned illnesses and committed acts of self-mutilation in order to obtain honorable discharges and transfers out of the unit. As Helena, Montana, resident Edward Soulds, an officer with the division, later recalled, "I saw one young soldier use a razor blade to slash between his toes, then rubbed GI soap therein causing his feet to swell to such proportions that he was unable to wear foot gear or walk."[138]

Meanwhile, the actions taken by service dependents and communities to express their frustration with and resistance to the army's policies closely paralleled the strategies of their loved ones in uniform. In October 1943, several dozen families related to the division joined together to pen an open letter to the editors of the *Los Angeles Tribune* excoriating the practices of the War Department; it read: "We hereby charge the army with practicing discrimination and segregation; we maintain it is an un-American organization because it is undemocratic. Why do you practice discrimination and segregation thereby furthering a national evil?" But the editorial went on to warn members of the black press corps of the dire consequences of uncritically accepting lofty rhetoric without receiving any assurances of future changes: "We regret the necessity of having to make this accusation against a national organizations like the Negro press. But we not only honor our boys for their sacrifice; we recognize our responsibility for their well-being and the world that they have left behind and, to which, God grant, they will return. We will not sit idly by and watch discrimination flourish while our brothers, sons, fathers, husbands, and sweethearts are fighting to their last breath for the preservation of their country, families and communities they all love so well."[139]

So, for many 93rd Division GIs and their families, neither patriotism nor the desire to fight for the four freedoms enunciated by Franklin Roosevelt guided their wartime struggles; rather, their struggles reflected the complex linkage of military service and war to the racial indignities they encountered in civil society. They also point toward the relationship that existed between black soldiers, service communities, and various segments of African American society. Many black middle-class leaders based their support for the war effort on self-styled calculations for their own racial advancement, and they didn't feel the need to fully explore the criticisms aired by black servicemen and their loved ones regarding the Double Victory Campaign because it would have required actions that violated their future interests. And although many black 93rd servicemen and military communities offered grudging words of praise and admiration for traditional black leaders and organizations in newspapers, magazines, and other arenas, they also articulated feelings of alienation from them in the barracks and maneuvering areas of the army and its surrounding communities. In rare instances, the tensions between black 93rd Division personnel and the black elite boiled over, causing numerous moments of frustration.

Eyefuls of Home on the Pacific Ocean

At the beginning of December 1943, Deputy Inspector General Roger Williams and General Benjamin Davis Sr. inspected the combat readiness of the division at the California-Arizona maneuver area and declared that the unit was fit for overseas movement provided that the artillery section of an ordnance light maintenance company completed its training. After observing the men negotiate a series of maneuvering problems during the six-day period, both men stated, "The discipline and morale are very satisfactory. The men have confidence in their officers, in their training, and in their ability to defeat the enemy."[140]

Shortly afterward, the servicemen at Camp Clipper spent the remainder of December preparing for their movement overseas. While the soldiers prepared to make their way to San Francisco, where they would board transport ships bound for the South Pacific, many of them received furloughs to meet with their families and friends. During these meetings, family members and friends shared deep feelings of pessimism and foreboding, for they did not know whether their loved ones would be returning home. Washington, D.C., resident Marguerite Summers recalled seeing her fiancé, John Howard, for the last time: "I didn't want to say good-bye because I felt that he would not come back. To make matters worse, he persuaded me not to come to the train station to see him off."[141] For a Chicago native, the ordeal was so unbearable that she decided to express the following to her betrothed on paper, "You're going off to a far off strange land where you will see many wonderful things probably both beautiful and horrid, and I won't be there to share them all with you. Stephen, why are you fighting? It all boils down to the fact that you are on a foreign soil to free the enslaved peoples of a foreign land while at home they step on the faces of your brothers."[142] And as Pauline Coggs recalls, "I knew that he had to go like everyone else, but I did not want to see him used as a symbol of something."[143]

To be sure, black division wives, other family members, and friends did not want to see loved ones in uniform going into combat, as more than a few balked at the idea of having African American soldiers fight and die for professed democratic principles that they enjoyed neither at home or in the army. As a press correspondent who witnessed many of the bittersweet farewells observed, "One lad spoke with his mother as tears rolled down their cheeks which touched that final moment when 'goodbye' was uttered among them for the last time. Another spoke of the baby he wouldn't get to see as he or she would be born in his absence. Solemn vows of faithfulness were expressed by young men to their sweethearts. And husbands chatted to their wives of immortality and then set those thoughts aside as blessed. 'Goodbye, home, Goodbye America, until we meet again' could be heard among all."[144]

Days later, the servicemen made their way to the staging areas of Pittsburg, California, where they boarded the USS *West Point*, the USS *General John Pope*, the SS *Lurline*, the USS *Holbrook*, and the USAT *Torrens*. As *Courier* reporter William "Billy" Rowe, who covered the division's departure, observed, "All the men took to the rails, in one emotional surge, all with but one idea in mind, to get an eyeful of home embraced by the outlets of the Pacific Ocean."[145] But as the soldiers leaned over the railings of the huge liners, many felt the same pessimism and foreboding that their family and friends had expressed during their farewells. Los Angeles native Arnett Hartsfield recalled "looking at the Golden Gate Bridge as my troop transport ship sailed by wondering if I'd ever see home again."[146] Indianola, Mississippi, native Edwin Lee, who had been married just seven months earlier, recounted, "I remember how sad my wife seemed when I went home and told her that I was going to leave with the cadre going overseas. Unless you have lived under that threat of going away from home and not coming back, it's very difficult to imagine the sad feeling that one undergoes."[147] And in a letter home, Nelson Peery articulated the gut-wrenching anxieties that many 93rd Division personnel felt about possibly being assigned to combat duty and ways in which they drew upon scripture to inspire them for the struggle that lay ahead: "I went to Brad's bunk and I was surprised to see that instead of a bottle between them, there was a Bible . . . they were reading about Job and his suffering and comparing it to our own. We then had a few drinks of bathtub wiskey [sic] to toast the New Year in. Tyson said, 'I know what you all are thinking, and I'll toast it . . . , "Lord, if somebody gotta die 'fore next Christmas, don't let it be me."'"[148]

The responses of black division GIs to leaving California marked a fundamental shift in the relationship they shared with the larger African American community and the federal government. No longer would they be treated as individuals; rather, they would now be upheld as representatives of the race by the black press and viewed by War Department officials as experiments in battlefield conduct and combat efficiency. And for black 93rd Division personnel and their families, the new challenges prompted a new set of priorities as the physical terrain of struggle shifted from stateside training to the South Pacific.

The 93rd Division barracks at Fort Huachuca, Arizona, in 1942. Once the soldiers arrived in Arizona, barracks life fostered a host of associations among division members. Courtesy of Fort Huachuca Museum Archives

On 8 August 1942, 93rd Division family members including Geraldine Dubisson, Mae Bridgeforth, Leonora Glenn, Alvirita Turman, Vanorian Schell, and Edith Melendez were photographed by the *Pittsburgh Courier* as they visited loved ones who had just graduated from the Medical Field Service School held at Carlisle Barracks, Pennsylvania. Courtesy of the *Pittsburgh Courier*

Is THIS the Army, Mr. Jones?

This political cartoon, which appeared in the 6 March 1943 edition of the *New York Amsterdam Star-News*, brilliantly reflects the ways in which the African American press scrutinized the duties assigned to black soldiers of the U.S. 93rd Infantry Division during the war. Courtesy of the *New York Amsterdam Star-News*

Soldiers posing with Joe Louis at Camp Clipper, California, in November 1943. Entertainers like Louis, Hattie McDaniel, and Lena Horne worked diligently to keep the physical well-being of black 93rd Division members in the public spotlight. Courtesy of Record Group 407, Records of the Adjutant General's Office, the National Archives and Records Administration

Not only did division relatives, such as the Greene family pictured here in 1943, provide a sense of community and fellowship to black servicemen training in the Deep South and Southwest, but they also empowered the GIs long after they left the shores of the continental United States. Courtesy of Walter R. Greene III

Division members who had trained in California contemplate the sobering possibilities of war and death aboard the SS *Lurline,* bound for Guadalcanal, in January 1944. Courtesy of Record Group 407, Records of the Adjutant General's Office, the National Archives and Records Administration

Opposite: In the spring of 1944, the Russell, Treasury, and New Georgia groups of islands served as the areas in which elements of the 93rd Infantry Division conducted their combat missions. Like many GIs who stepped ashore at the time, division members found the terrain to be as treacherous as the enemy forces they faced.

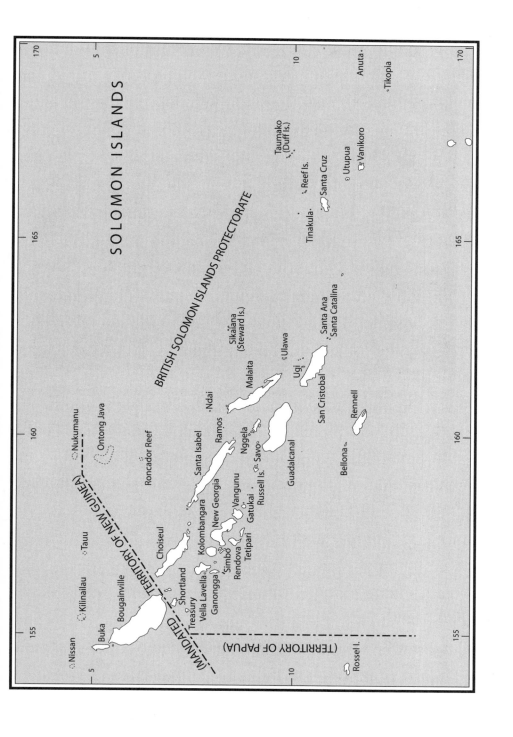

Division members evacuating wounded soldiers of the 25th Infantry Regimental Combat Team during a patrol on Bougainville in 1944. Courtesy of Record Group 407, Records of the Adjutant General's Office, the National Archives and Records Administration

Opposite: Allied landings in the New Guinea area between 1943 and 1945. As Allied forces advanced up the chain of Pacific islands toward Japan in late 1944, troops assigned to most of the battalions and companies of the 93rd Division had entered a new phase in fighting, carrying out dangerous operations to subdue Japanese forces that were still active in the area.

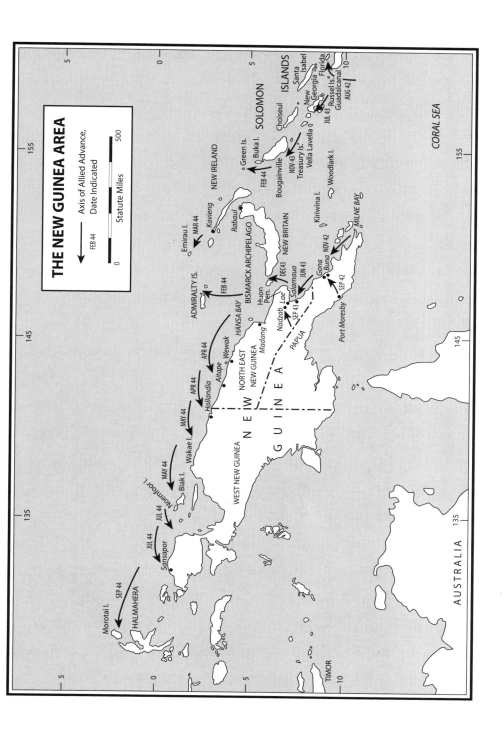

THE NEW GUINEA AREA

→ Axis of Allied Advance,
   Date Indicated
FEB 44 Date Indicated

Statute Miles
0 _____ 500

SOLOMON ISLANDS

Santa Isabel
Florida
New Georgia
Russel Is.
Guadalcanal AUG 42
JUL 43

Choiseul
Vella Lavella
Treasury Is. NOV 43
Bougainville
Buka I.
Green Is. FEB 44
Woodlark I.
Kiriwina I.

NEW IRELAND
Kavieng MAR 44
Emirau I. MAR 44
Rabaul
ADMIRALTY IS. FEB 44
BISMARCK ARCHIPELAGO
NEW BRITAIN
Huon Pen. DEC 43
HANSA BAY
Lae SEP 43
Nadzab
Gona NOV 42
Salamaua JUN 43
Buna NOV 42
Milne Bay
Port Moresby SEP 42
PAPUA

Wewak APR 44
Aitape APR 44
Hansa Bay
Hollandia APR 44
Wakde I. MAY 44
Biak I. MAY 44
Noemfoor I. JUL 44
Sansapor JUL 44
WEST NEW GUINEA
NORTH EAST NEW GUINEA
Madang

N E W   G U I N E A

Morotai I. SEP 44
HALMAHERA

TIMOR
AUSTRALIA

CORAL SEA

The Reverend William H. Jernagin and members of the U.S. 93rd Division, southern Philippines, November 1945. Clergymen and other visiting dignitaries served as a conduit of information about issues affecting loved ones at home as well as a sounding board as the servicemen voiced their frustrations of dealing with racism in the Pacific. Courtesy of Record Group 407, Records of the Adjutant General's Office, the National Archives and Records Administration

Alvirita and Frank Little at a ceremony marking the 200th anniversary of the army held at Fort Huachuca, Arizona, in July 1975. Former 93rd GIs and their families used reunions and other gatherings to give new meaning to their World War II experiences. The division insignia—the Blue Helmet—is prominently displayed on the wall behind them. Courtesy of the Fort Huachuca Museum Archives

PART THREE

RACE AND SEX MATTER
IN THE PACIFIC

✶ ✶ ✶

In Leyte, I first ran into the oft-repeated and completely un-justified canard about the cowardice shown by Negroes of the Ninety-third Division. A public relations officer who believed that I was just another white newspaper correspon-dent went out of his way to tell me that Negroes were no good in combat and that in the invasion of Bougainville, the Ninety-third had been given an easy beachhead to take, but that the division had broken and run under fire, "causing death to many officers and men in the white division on either side of them."

Walter White, 1948

We knew how to order. Just the dash
Necessary. The length of gayety in good taste. . . .
But nothing ever taught us to be islands.

Gwendolyn Brooks, "Gay Chaps at the Bar," 1945

CHAPTER SIX

War, Race, and Rumor under the Southern Cross

> Rumor travels when events have importance in the lives of individuals and when the news received about them is either lacking or subjectively ambiguous. The ambiguity may arise from the fact that the news is not clearly reported, or from the fact that conflicting versions of the news have reached the individual, or from his incapacity to comprehend the news he receives.
>
> *Gordon Allport and Leo Postman, 1947*

One early April morning in 1944, Lieutenant Oscar Davenport and his platoon found themselves negotiating the dense undergrowth of the Bougainville jungle. The 30-year-old officer from Tucson, Arizona, and other members of the 93rd Infantry Division's 25th Infantry Regimental Combat Team had no sooner entered the Allied defensive perimeter in the Solomon Islands group than they received orders to occupy a reserve position for an element of the Americal Division. For Davenport and his platoon, the patrolling missions carried out in the sector were simple: to establish a trail block some 3,000 yards in front of the main perimeter. As one GI serving with the unit at time remembered, "Most of the activity on the island consisted of patrols. We—when I say we, I mean our outfit—went out on routine patrols and occasionally they got into fights with some remnants of the Japanese army that had been left there."[1]

But what ordinarily should have been one in a series of routine missions gave way to personal tragedy and public spectacle. After wading their way through the turgid waters of the Torokina River, Davenport and his men had traveled along a path when they encountered enemy fire. Nearly forty-five minutes after the firing began, the young lieutenant, along with seventeen enlisted men, lay dead, and seven others were wounded. Interestingly, several eyewitnesses later claimed that, just minutes before the burst of enemy fire, Davenport had held up a newspaper clipping he had recently received from his wife, Ollive, reporting him as "missing in action."[2]

The rumor that Davenport had been missing in action was just one of many rumors circulating at this time, some of them suggesting that the 93rd Infantry Division was unsuitable for combat duty. During the weeks and months that followed the incident, army officials used such rumors as a way to reinforce the low expectations they had of the battlefield conduct of segregated black units like the 93rd in the South Pacific. By the time the division had left the Solomon Islands, the rumors had spread to such an extent that they reached the White House and beyond. Black spokespeople, pundits, and service-related communities worked diligently to counteract their chain-letter-like speed and force by devising their own independent communication networks. Yet often the zealous efforts made by the black press to publicize racism in the South Pacific as well to affirm the actions and identities of Davenport and his comrades on the field of battle carried their own ambiguous messages. Throughout 1944 and early 1945, Bougainville served as vivid reminders to black and white observers alike of how war, race, and rumor would structure the South Pacific experiences of those who served in the unit.

Negotiating Military Life under the Southern Cross

After enduring nearly a month at sea, the 93rd Infantry Division's regiments and their attached field units disembarked at several points in the South Pacific before being assigned mainly to the Russells (Banika), Vella Lavella, Guadalcanal, and New Georgia.[3] There, under the leadership of Major General Raymond Lehman, they spent the first three weeks setting up camp before participating in training exercises in jungle patrolling, perimeter defense, and first aid. These activities were a far cry from the desert maneuvers they had practiced less than six months earlier.[4] As they proceeded through this seasoning process, newly arrived 93rd servicemen encountered unfamiliar sights, smells, and noises in the dense terrain. Edwin Lee, a 25th Infantry medical officer assigned to Guadalcanal during the period, recalled, "It was a disturbing experience for me to be on this island; nothing but trees, the smell of dead animals and sometimes human beings. I think the thing that stands out in my mind most is the rain every day at two o'clock and the lonely nights in which you could hear all sorts of sounds."[5] Private Bismark Williams, a native of Asheville, North Carolina, echoed these sentiments: "The weather was damp and muggy, so it was necessary to keep your boots dry to avoid jungle rot."[6] Houston resident Asberry McGriff, an enlisted man who trained with a platoon in the 368th Infantry on the Russells, claimed, "Unless you took care of your things properly, your clothes became rotted and mildewed and your weapon rusted."[7]

Many African American soldiers in the 93rd Infantry Division responded to the unfamiliar conditions by reestablishing prior semiformal and formal organizations. For example, Kansas City, Kansas, native Andrew Isaacs; Lake Charles, Louisiana, native Robert Johnson; and twenty other black enlisted men in the 93rd Infantry Division Signal Company formed an organization based on their affiliation with the company and called themselves the 93rd Signal Club. Composed predominantly of Los Angeles natives, the group met periodically as the unit moved throughout the Pacific theater.[8] In a similar fashion, members in several companies of the 93rd's 318th Engineering Battalion held parties throughout the spring months of 1944 during which they decorated the recreational building and rearranged tables to resemble a cabaret. As the men enjoyed a down-home cuisine of steak with brown gravy, barbecued pig, mashed potatoes, buttered rolls, and greens provided by Jesse Barnes and Thomas Grace, they listened to selections played by 368th Regimental Band, watched impersonations performed by Richard Bethel and Joseph Edwards, and heard speeches given by Lieutenant William Collins and regimental chaplain Thomas Diggs.[9] As a member of the 368th's Antitank Company, 25-year-old New York native Cesly Peterson edited the regiment's weekly publications, the *Clarion* and the *Daily Mail,* making them the most requested sources of information within the division. By the end of the war, Peterson's efforts had earned him the Bronze Star Medal.[10]

Popular aesthetic forms also constituted a critical element in the transplantation of African American culture. More than twenty-five hundred enthusiastic soldiers attended USO performances led by *Cabin in the Sky* movie star Kenneth Spencer and Julie Gardner, a soloist prominently featured in Earl "Fatha" Hines's orchestra, as well as vaudeville acts staged by Flo Brown and Ferdie Robinson.[11] Many soldiers gathered together in company headquarters and the regimental amphitheaters to listen to "Tan America on the Air," a radio show directed and produced by 369th infantryman Ted Clarke, and jazz recordings played by the radio show entitled "The Voice of the Valley."[12]

The selection of favorite pinups also served as a medium through which black division members created a sense of camaraderie in an unfamiliar environment; it also bound them together in a form of male solidarity. In late 1944, for instance, black GIs in the 93rd unanimously elected *Stormy Weather* motion picture star Lena Horne as their pinup girl, and copies of her photograph could be found on display in hundreds of tents, recreation halls, jeeps, and trucks scattered through-out the division's regimental and company bivouac sites. Taking a distant second were Hazel Scott and Katherine Dunham.[13] Around the same time, 368th Infantry soldiers from Pittsburgh wrote letters to black newspapers, requesting autographed photos of noted pianist and arranger Mary Lou Williams.[14]

On the surface, this practice appears to support the idea that the collection and circulation of pinup photographs by soldiers and military officials in World War II reflected their view of women as sexual property or prized possessions as well as inspirations for fighting for their country. Indeed, as recent scholars have noted, for white GIs and military officials in a war that was racialized, pinups and the women who posed for them functioned not only as an inspiration for fighting—"protecting the girl next door"—but also as symbols of "white supremacy."[15] But pinups also seem to have served as substitutes for actual physical contact with women. The army's semiofficial publication, *Yank* magazine, received hundreds of letters from GIs stationed in the Pacific theater which defended the value of pinup photos. One writer suggested, "Maybe if some of those 'panty-waists' had to be stuck some place where there are no white women and few native women for a year and a half, as we were, they would appreciate even a picture of our gals back home."[16] And around the same period, one psychiatrist who studied GIs in the war maintained that pinups served as "a social affirmation of virility by virtue of the public display and approval they were invariably accorded."[17]

But for black troops stationed throughout the South Pacific, the circulation of pinup photographs reflected their different experience of the Pacific war—and their somewhat different needs. Pinups of black women not only boosted the spir-its of black servicemen but also brought a sense of home and their own culture to their immediate surroundings. While stationed on Bougainville, men in the 369th Infantry's Coral Reef Club held a contest during which they selected Los Ange-les native Alice Jones as "Pinup Girl of the Week," and soldiers in the 25th Infan-try's D Company chose Columbus, Ohio–born Jean Parks as their favorite, while black Ohio GIs in the 368th Infantry expressed their preference for Cincinnati native Lillian Lemons.[18] Perhaps the words of an army private serving with the division's quartermaster company on Guadalcanal at the time may have voiced what was on the mind of many black GIs when he stated in a letter to the *Balti-more Afro-American*: "We boys in this theater of war are feeling somewhat slighted. Every magazine and paper we get has pictures of pin-up girls in Hollywood, but why can't we have pictures of colored pin-ups from our neighborhoods for our tents? We would appreciate it if you'd send us some."[19] In response, black news publications like the *Chicago Defender, New York Amsterdam Star News, Atlanta Daily*

World, and *Pittsburgh Courier* published numerous photographs of actresses, star-lets, and service dependents in bathing suits with captions reminding the soldiers serving in the Pacific of their obligations to home, hearth, and the race.[20]

Meanwhile, the first few weeks of the division's campaign consisted of endless hours of unloading supplies, building tents, clearing brush, and building roads in stifling heat and suffocating humidity. And to make matters worse, once GIs attached to the division had arrived in the Solomons, they discovered that, like so many soldiers of time immemorial, they faced the minor objectionable features of life in a rear sector of an active theater of operations: namely, monotonous food, sleepless nights, and army overmanagement. During the spring months of 1944, platoons and companies within the 369th led by junior officers such as John Howard, Arnett Hartsfield, Anthony Paul, Frank Christmas, and Julius Young were assigned to unloading supplies onto the docks of Guadalcanal.[21] But men with the 369th Infantry were not the only troops to perform such duties. Members of the 368th Infantry Regiment, including Raymond Jenkins, Randall Morgan, and Julius Thompson, carried out port battalion duties on Banika in the Russells.[22] Meanwhile, Luther Williams, Charles Cleveland, Albert Lott, William Upshaw, and other members of the 25th Infantry Regimental Combat Team and the 318th Engineering Battalion toiled for hours at a makeshift sawmill on nearby Bougainville Island.[23] Edward Soulds, an officer with the 368th Infantry Regiment, described the garrison duties performed by his unit after arriving on one of the atolls in the Russells: "We disembarked on Banika and this real estate became our home for awhile. Unloading was fatiguing as hell; we had to clear jungles to set up tents to house the troops, the headquarters and tons of equipment."[24]

Such mundane duties were hardly unusual for rear echelon troops passing through an Allied area of operation during the war. During the Allied campaign to extend the perimeter inland in late 1943, white enlisted men and officers of the army's 37th Infantry Division arrived on Bougainville. Before taking their place along the front lines, troops had unloaded nearly 3,200 tons of supplies while enduring numerous strafing attacks from enemy torpedo bombers and fighters.[25] After the Bougainville campaign passed to the command of the 14th Corps in December 1943, elements of the Americal Division received orders to report to Bougainville. There the men of the unit's 164th Regiment spent much of their time constructing earthworks and other defensive positions while performing reconnaissance patrols throughout the area. Indeed, as historians have noted, although "many of the duties were invaluable for the divisional staffs and the artillery, the men involved considered it foul duty, repeated over and over again seemingly without purpose."[26]

But in a setting where racial prejudice and discrimination had as much to do with the black World War II experience as did the violence meted out against the Japanese enemy, dignity and manhood formed the prism through which division members perceived their duties in the South Pacific.[27] It was not long after they had landed in the Solomon Islands that many 93rd Division GIs learned that the military personnel with the 24th Infantry Regiment had spent more than twenty months toiling as stevedores and security forces, loading and unloading ships and performing patrolling missions in the theater of operations.[28] And for most of the men in the division, the noncombatant duties diminished the stature of soldiers who had previously trained for action at the front. For example, in the words of Muskogee, Oklahoma, native Theodore Coggs, a Howard University graduate who was assigned to the 368th Infantry during the period, "The regiment then went to Munda and Hollandia where the men are building roads and unloading ships. I don't know the future mission of the division or the regiment and it is a little confusing to all of the officers."[29] And as Lieutenant John Howard remembered, "Unloading ships was an unnerving experience when we first started because stevedoring was totally alien to us. We deeply resented this because we were basically being used as labor troops, and it was just another example of how the army didn't want us to lead. When the time came for rest and relaxation, we were constantly being ordered back to jungle training areas."[30]

Others likened the duties to those performed by slaves in the antebellum South. After he and other enlisted men in the 369th's Service Company spent days unloading 2½-ton trucks and other heavy equipment, Little Rock, Arkansas, native Clarence Ross recalled feeling "mad as hell. It was as if we were the slaves and the white officers in our outfit were the overseers. They would get us up each morning and place us in designated spots on the docks, where we would unload tons of equipment sometimes on one meal a day."[31] Asheville, North Carolina–born Bismark Williams voiced similar sentiments: "Instead of treating us like men, the white commissioned officers saw us as their servants who need only a little encouragement to 'tote that barge and lift that bale.' The whole situation was based on race, and we were very disappointed with the duties they imposed on us."[32] These duties greatly hampered the already low morale of many 93rd servicemen and served to increase their skepticism of military life. Walter Greene, a Detroit native and 25th infantryman, stated, "One of the most disappointing things to us was as soon as we arrived in Guadalcanal we were put to work loading and unloading ships."[33] And an observer remarked, "We walked into this place and came face to face with heart break. This thing is so drastic I can't believe it. From the way it looks, we are heading for the labor line."[34]

Of course, not all black GIs felt this way. For example, Louisiana-born share-cropper and 25th infantryman Clenon Briggs viewed the assignment of black sol-diers to service duties as a way of protecting their physical well-being: "I person-ally had no problems with unloading ships because I didn't like the jungle training and the front line."[35] But the fact that the men perceived the service sup-port work as inappropriate for trained combat troops captured the attention of the senior members of the 93rd high command. During a tour of the 93rd veterans in action less than a year later, the commanding general commented, "The fail-ure to send Negro troops into combat is very bad for their morale and causes them to be resentful."[36]

The resentment that black 93rd servicemen felt regarding these duties mani-fested itself in many ways. Some division members engaged in various forms of workplace resistance analogous to those developed in the urban industrial envi-ronment. For example, men within various elements of the 25th Infantry refused to adhere to uniformed military standards. During an inspection of 25th in-fantrymen laboring in rear areas of Bougainville Island in late April, the 93rd Di-vision commander, Leonard Boyd, reported that many soldiers failed to salute white officers and displayed their uniforms in a disheveled manner.[37] Less than two weeks later, the 93rd Division commander visited soldiers in the 25th Infantry's 3rd Bat-talion and noted that many of them refused to shave and wear shoes.[38]

Other soldiers took more drastic action. In June 1944, Raymond Abernathy, James Hill, and William Wright of the 93rd Special Medical Detachment received a reduction in rank and transfers to the 368th Infantry after they refused to un-load ships by staging a makeshift sit-down strike along the docks of Stirling Is-land.[39] On Guadalcanal, Reuben Fraser openly expressed his disagreement with the work assignments. In March 1944, Fraser, a second lieutenant in a heavy weapons company of the 368th Infantry, was ordered to build a stockade for him-self after he wrote an unofficial letter to the War Department protesting against the dirty, labor-intensive duties that his unit performed as port battalions. After Fraser added board tents, screen wire, running water, and electricity, the regimen-tal staff headquarters, led by 368th Infantry commander James Urquhart, requi-sitioned the building, claiming that the building was too good for him. "I figured that if I was going to be in there," Fraser recalled, "then I was going to fix it up perfectly. You know . . . , I was very adept at turning various adversities to my ad-vantage." Fraser's struggles for dignity were short lived, however, as his acts of re-bellion were spontaneous responses to seemingly impossible situations. His mil-itary career came to an end when he was mustered out of the army two months later.[40] Sickness also functioned as a form of resistance. Throughout the months of May and June, an officer in the 93rd Division's Medical Detachment duly reported large numbers of 93rd servicemen placed on sick leave and declared, "The assignment of troops to punitive (labor) duties is one of the factors tending to lower their morale."[41]

The attitudes and responses of black 93rd GIs to these noncombatant tasks stemmed largely from the War Department's racist reliance on exaggerated stereotypes regarding black capabilities under fire accompanied by its difficulties in finding a theater commander who would place the division at the fighting front. In early March, the director of the operations division commented extensively on the employment of black personnel: "Since the Army cannot afford the luxury of organizing tactical units which will remain in the United States for the duration of the war . . . the Army intends that colored units shall eventually be employed overseas to the greatest extent that their capabilities permit. As the end of the war draws nearer, 'people,' both white and colored of lower classification grades will gravitate toward less complicated tasks and conversions must be made. It is likewise inevitable that units with the most advanced training will continue to be the first employed in battle." As a division composed largely of draftees who had obtained scores in the fourth and fifth categories, the 93rd would be placed in service support functions. Left unchanged, this policy was followed by theater commanders throughout the Pacific.

Questions of Deployment

Throughout the winter and spring of 1944, a peculiar set of circumstances fueled public speculation regarding the deployment of African American troops in the Pacific. In late January, officers with the 930th and 931st Field Artillery battalions learned that they had been transferred to the U.S. 92nd Infantry Division. Shortly afterward, the artillery units, which made up the core of the 184th Field Artillery Regiment, were converted into engineer combat battalions to construct roads and bridges. For the men with the 930th and 931st and their respective communities, the conversion of these units was significant. As former National Guard cadres, they had spent nearly two years training at Fort Custer, Michigan, after the historic 8th Illinois had been mustered into federal service and reorganized into separate elements.[42] Meanwhile, the activities of the troops with the 2nd Cavalry Division and their whereabouts raised questions of mounting intensity. Activated at Fort Clark, Texas, in 1943, elements of the 2nd Cavalry, which also contained the old 9th and 10th Cavalry regiments, had been assigned to North Africa. But, at the time, the status of the cavalry unit remained shrouded in secrecy.

The official silence regarding these units didn't last long, however. On 1 February, New York congressman Hamilton Fish wrote a letter to Secretary of War Henry Stimson inquiring whether the War Department planned to deploy black troops in front-line action in Europe and Asia. Fish asked the secretary of war whether there was any truth to the rumor that the personnel in several black tank destroyer outfits that had undergone training at Fort Hood, Texas, had been transferred to quartermaster companies after the units had been inactivated.[43] As a former officer with New York's famous 369th "Harlem Hell-fighters" regiment during the last war, the Republican congressman believed that he had more than a passing interest in the well-being of African American units in the present conflict. "I don't understand how it is that four separate colored regiments made such gallant fighting records in the last war, which was won in approximately nineteen months and yet no colored infantry troops have been ordered into combat in this war," Fish exclaimed.

Less than two and a half weeks later, Stimson replied to Fish's inquiry, directly addressing the fate of black troops and where they would stand in relation to the battlefronts of the Second World War. The secretary of war confirmed the reports that elements of the 184th had been converted into service support troops. According to Stimson, the 930th and 931st, as well as other antiaircraft, tank destroyer, and coast artillery units, had been trained originally to counter a possible enemy attack upon the continental United States, but they were now being reassigned because the danger had since passed. But before Stimson completed his remarks, the logic of his statement followed an all too familiar course. Specifically pointing out the 930th and the 931st, he claimed that their conversion was absolutely necessary because, owing to their lower educational backgrounds, "many of the Negro units have been unable to master efficiently the techniques of modern weapons."[44]

Within a matter of days, Stimson's remarks had exploded into a cause célèbre. Banner headlines carrying his statement appeared on the front page of black weeklies throughout the country. On 4 March, the *Pittsburgh Courier* carried a story headlined "Stimson Should Quit," claiming that by questioning the competency of black combat units, the secretary of war had "stirred up a hornet's nest here." In a similar fashion, the *Chicago Defender, Atlanta Daily World, Houston Informer, Columbus Ohio State News, Oklahoma City Black Dispatch,* and *Michigan Chronicle* carried the secretary's statements on their front page.[45]

At the same time, Stimson's comments impugning the intelligence of black combat units attracted considerable criticism from black congressional leaders as well as from other sectors of the African American community. Responding to the secretary's remarks, Illinois congressman William L. Dawson angrily stated, "He is either woefully ignorant on the matter of Negro troops or purposely carrying out the pattern of fascist elements within the military establishment whose purpose is to discredit the Negro fighting men of this nation."[46] Roy Wilkins and other members within the NAACP national office also responded angrily to Stimson's comments. In an editorial in the *Crisis* titled "Army Labor Battalions," Wilkins bitterly denounced the War Department's decision, declaring that the statement "has infuriated Negro Americans as has no other single incident since Pearl Harbor." Referring to the persistent rumors surrounding the 2nd Cavalry Division, he went on to ask, "If combat units are so badly needed, why are Negro units being broken up into service troops?"[47] The targets of the secretary's attack also raised their voices in a chorus of reproach. Major Ovid Harris, a former commander of the 184th Field Artillery Regiment, wrote a letter to President Roosevelt, arguing that the regiment's high IQ rating repudiated Stimson's claim that "many Negro units have been unable to master efficiently the techniques of modern weapons."[48] Not long afterward, the responses escalated from printed words to actions. On 5 March, hundreds of people assembled in Chicago to protest against Stimson's remarks. Sponsored by the National Negro Council and the Chicago Committee of One Thousand, conferees adopted a resolution demanding the resignation of the War Department head. "The ouster of Stimson would speed victory over the Axis nations," they proclaimed.[49]

Hoping to stem the growing controversy over the War Department's racial policies, the secretary promptly held a press conference to clarify his remarks. Meeting with a group of black press representatives, he categorically denied that he and other War Department officials assessed the combat efficiency of the 930th and 931st Field Artillery battalions on the basis of their intellectual capacities. "The fundamental principle involved that has been overlooked in my letter is that changing conditions necessitates the organization of more units to service duties and fewer of those for combat than was required a year ago," he claimed.[50] Within several weeks, however, reports on the deactivation of the 2nd Cavalry Division and its conversion into service troops in North Africa reached the press, and telegrams, letters of protests, and editorials poured into the White House from across the country excoriating the War Department's employment of black troops.[51]

As the controversy heated up that spring, Stimson and members of the Advisory Committee on Negro Troop Policies, including Assistant Secretary of War John J. McCloy and representatives of each major agency within the General Staff, met and agreed to recommend the 93rd Infantry Division for front-line duty. However, many of the committee members present that day expressed very little faith in the fighting abilities of black soldiers. Harboring definite reservations about using blacks in combat, Stimson stated, "The Army has been drifting in regard to putting the colored troops into combat action. Of course this comes primarily from their former bad record as combat troops and the fear of putting them into any of the important positions in this critical war."[52] Echoing Stimson's apprehensions, Theater Operations Division deputy chief (G-3) Carl Russell commented that it would be disastrous to impose black troops on the theater commanders but also stated his belief that the War Department would be forced to recommend the 93rd's conversion if it was not used in combat. Civilian aide Truman Gibson, Ray Porter, also from the Operations Division, and Personnel Section representative Miller White, however, disagreed with Stimson and Russell and recommended that the War Department organize the 93rd's regiments into combat teams and order the theater commanders to use them as a matter of "national policy." After agreeing on the measure, the committee submitted the recommendation to the secretary of war, who relented and signed it.[53]

Complying with their recommendation, General Marshall radioed Lieutenant General Millard Harmon in the South Pacific less than a week later, asking the theater's chief commander to place the 93rd's 25th Regimental Combat Team in action as soon as possible.[54] Although Harmon assured Marshall that he had taken steps to adequately train the division, he told Marshall that he had not planned any amphibious operations for the unit in his theater of operations. The commander earlier was very critical of the idea to place such a large number of black troops in his area.[55] Indeed, as scholars have noted, the general view in Washington and throughout the Pacific during this period was that the troops of the 93rd should be assigned to areas as far away from front-line duty as possible.[56] But Harmon recognized the dilemma that Marshall and other War Department officials faced, and this may have contributed to his ultimate acquiescence in the matter.

By the end of the month, however, events had occurred on Bougainville that forced the War Department and the South Pacific high command to reconsider their previous contingency plans. In early March 1944, troops of the American 15th Corps had largely broken the last large-scale Japanese offensive against the main defense perimeter on Bougainville Island. Numbering more than fifteen hundred men, enemy forces led by Isashi Magata had suffered tremendous casualties. Under the shadow of darkness, Japanese troops used the Numa-Numa Trail to repair toward the northernmost portion of the island while contingents of Major General Iwasa Shun's forces retreated to its southern region. However, numerous American patrols traveled beyond the American defense perimeter only to encounter considerable enemy fire from well-placed, camouflaged positions along the trails. In addition, army officials, notably 14th Corps commander Oscar Griswold, felt that the retreating Japanese forces posed a real threat to the airstrips in the area if they made a concerted effort.

Given the gravity of the situation, black GIs figured prominently in the 14th Corps' offensive strategy. On a clear night in mid-March, 1st Battalion members of the all-black 24th Infantry Regiment, led by Henry McAllister of Hamburg, New York, successfully assaulted Japanese troops attempting to infiltrate Allied communications and supply lines at Empress Augusta Bay. By the end of the combat patrol, the men had moved several thousand yards beyond the defense sector and had come relatively close to the Japanese lines, killing one enemy soldier and evading ambush attempts during the fighting. Shortly afterward, they relieved the beleaguered men of the 148th Infantry's 2nd Battalion at Hill 700, otherwise known as "Cannon Hill." The performance of the soldiers in the battalion was striking because, until that point, the unit had been originally assigned to service functions loading and unloading ships and building roads at Efate in New Caledonia. Therefore, many military observers who expressed skepticism regarding the fighting abilities of black troops were pleasantly surprised. For example, Griswold reported that the unit "was given a sector of the perimeter and did an excellent job in organizing and preparing its defensive position."[57] During his weekly press conference held on 6 April, Stimson reported on the 24th Infantry's role in repulsing the Japanese attack against the Allied perimeter at Empress Augusta Bay and ended much public speculation by stating that the 93rd Infantry Division had arrived at advanced bases in the South Pacific.[58]

Once the exploits of the 24th Infantry Regiment hit the newspapers, army officials renewed their interest in committing the men of the 93rd to combat.[59] On 18 March, General Marshall radioed General Harmon again requesting that the unit be used in action after it received adequate preparation. The army chief of staff stated his belief that the men of the 93rd Division should be placed in the most advantageous position possible because the War Department was under intense scrutiny not only from the black press for failing to place the unit in combat but also from critics of the employment of black troops in the Pacific theater in general who would watch the army's use of the all-black division closely. Regarding the extent of public attention to the division's initial performance, Marshall reminded the South Pacific commander that "the first reports of its conduct in action undoubtedly will be headlined in this country." "It is therefore important that news releases and reports from the theater on the conduct of these troops be strictly factual," he ordered.[60] Four days later, Marshall again contacted Harmon, inquiring about the extent of the 24th Infantry's operations on Bougainville and future assignments that he had contemplated for the unit.[61] On 23 March, Harmon complied with Marshall's directives when he instructed the 14th Corps commander to take the following actions:

> Harass and deny to the enemy his line of supply from the southern Bougainville area by the use of artillery and such air and naval surface forces as may be available to you, with particular attention to that area in the vicinity of the Reini River. . . . At the earliest practicable moment . . . conduct limited offensive operations against the west (right) flank and rear of hostile forces in your front with a view to interrupting or cutting their line of communications with Northern and Western Bougainville and destroying the maximum possible number of the enemy and his material. As a corollary an opportunity will be afforded for the seasoning and employment of Negro combat forces. To assist in the accomplishment of the foregoing you will be reinforced in the immediate future with the Twenty-fifth Infantry combat team reinforced.[62]

As the men of the 25th Regimental Combat Team advanced toward Bougainville Island in March 1944, little did they realize the precarious situation they faced. First, officials within the War Department had taken a far greater political interest in the employment and the use of their division than they had for any other unit assigned to the Pacific theater. This interest and the events that followed held long-term implications for many black 93rd Division personnel, army officials, and various segments of African American society. Second, although Harmon and other officers within the South Pacific high command had followed Marshall's directive to commit the division to front-line action, their execution of those orders was overshadowed by their deeply felt resentment over what they viewed as Washington's intrusion into their theater of operations. Their efforts to deploy the division were also affected by their belief in racist myths of black cowardice and questions about the leadership capabilities of African American cadre. In addition, Harmon and the other officials misread the new perceptions that division servicemen expressed about themselves as they now became soldiers with a new sense of purpose, namely, the protection of their very being while struggling to wage war against American race relations in an international context. The newly discovered perspectives espoused by most division troops sometimes would overlap with but at other times fly in the face of the political stances taken by African American leaders and spokespeople. It is to the circumstances that led to the clash of visions between black division troops, army officials, and African American society and the strategies that the men devised to negotiate these dilemmas that we must now turn.

Baptism under Fire in the South Pacific

The first contingent of the 25th Regimental Combat troops, along with the 593rd Field Artillery Battalion and an assortment of the 93rd's medical and engineering elements, left Guadalcanal for Bougainville Island's Empress Augusta Bay perimeter on 26 March. Among those in this group of 4,234 enlisted men and officers were Lonnie Goodley of Halletville, Texas; Nehemiah Hodges of Chicago; Oscar Davenport of Tucson, Arizona; James Reese of Cotton Plant, Arkansas; and Walter Sanderson, Lemuel Penn, and Conway Jones of the District of Columbia.[63] For Hodges, Goodley, and Davenport, this journey would be their last, for they would die in the Bougainville jungles less than three weeks later.[64] The thought of not returning safely weighed heavily on the mind of many of the men during this period. For example, Edwin Lee remembered, "We lived every day on those transport ships for what it was worth because everybody figured that some of us would not come back from Bougainville."[65] Within days, the men of the 25th Regimental Combat Team had established a bivouac area and prepared local security positions after they were assigned to the 14th Corps. Shortly thereafter, they received additional training in patrolling and jungle operations as corresponding units of the American Division. Less than a month later, troop transport ships carrying men of the division's headquarters and detachments of medical, quartermaster, and ordnance companies arrived at the Torokina Strip.[66]

Very shortly after arriving on Bougainville, many of the black servicemen discovered that the Pacific War was much more than just a struggle against fascism; it was a racial war fought on multiple fronts. For example, as the hours dragged into days, many division soldiers couldn't help but recognize the disheartening irony of fighting troops of darker hue who were fighting on behalf of fascism while, at the same time, the division soldiers were fighting white racism within their own army. As Nelson Peery in the 369th Infantry recalled, "It wasn't right. It didn't sound real. We were out there killing people to protect something we hated."[67] Calvert, Texas, native Marke Toles of the 25th Infantry remembered: "Many of the Japanese soldiers were starving and wouldn't attack us unless we attempted to ambush them."[68]

But these sentiments changed somewhat after many black GIs witnessed the savagery of war and the jungle fighting encouraged soldiers on both sides to dehumanize each other. On many occasions, soldiers went out on daily patrols and faced endless hours of peril. Wilmington, Delaware, native Julius Young and Indianola, Mississippi, native Edwin Lee probably understood this sort of abstraction of the enemy better than anyone else. Young and Lee recalled going out on one of the first patrols on the island and not knowing whether their next actions would be their last. "To go out in the jungle and establish a perimeter while searching for Japanese stragglers created a certain edginess in the men," recalled Young.[69] Lee recounted one patrol: "As we were walking along in single file, I heard someone making noise and we looked, and by that time the shooting seemed to break out everywhere. It was a Japanese soldier up in the tree. This was a habit that the Japanese troops had. If a Japanese soldier was wounded, if they were of a nature of being suicidal or a volunteer, they'd leave him behind. And often times they would be up in trees. This was about the closest call that I had that I knew about."[70]

The Japanese, in turn, had negative opinions of the character of black U.S. soldiers. In October 1944, American army intelligence officers stumbled upon a report filed by the Japanese Grand Imperial Headquarters that contained information about the strength and disposition of black service personnel serving in the South Pacific area and their performance in the field. The contents and the assessments made in the report are quite revealing. According to Japanese intelligence, there were approximately twenty-five thousand black troops in the region, many of them serving with the U.S. 93rd Infantry Division. With regard to the capabilities of the division's enlisted personnel and its junior officer corps, the message echoed some of the beliefs held by many white officers and observers in the American army. For example, the report noted, "The abilities of the American Negroes are relatively outstanding but they generally are indolent, have little willpower and are inclined to be cruel, and lack spirit of unity." But the intelligence dispatch also revised previous reports filed with the imperial headquarters which claimed, "Negroes are unsuitable officers," and it contended that the reports were not only erroneous but "unjustified." "Since the founding of America, the Negro has been maltreated, and therefore there is a deep feeling of hate toward the Caucasians on the part of the Negro," the communication pointed out. On the racial situation in the South Pacific theater of operations, the report concluded that, despite the stellar battlefield performances of black soldiers in the Solomon Islands, "there is still an ever present conflict of feeling between the Caucasians and the Negroes."[71]

Many of the perceptions that Japanese intelligence held of the tensions between white soldiers and black GIs in the South Pacific and of American race relations in general made their way into the nightly radio shows broadcast by "Tokyo Rose"— a name used to refer to several English-speaking women broadcasting Japanese propaganda.[72] Working directly from the Japanese mainland, these propagandists frequently made black GIs serving throughout the Pacific the targets of their invectives against American units. Many of their broadcasts sought to cause fric-

tion between Allied soldiers and to lessen African American morale by reminding them of the futility of fighting for democracy abroad while being denied first-
class citizenship in the United States at the time. For example, a propaganda story
that GIs heard during a shortwave broadcast in the South Pacific in March 1944
provides a window into the lengths to which Radio Tokyo had gone to raise questions of doubt in the minds of black soldiers serving in the area: "A captured Negro soldier revealed that Negro troops are demanding that American troops should
share the same risks, and not leave them to face the Japanese alone. He added
that Negro troops are fed up with the discrimination meted out to them by the
Americans, and Australian soldiers feel the same way about the Americans as the
Negroes do."[73] Although U.S. soldiers recognized the propaganda broadcasts for
what they were, they still produced a myriad of emotions among the division troops.
As Technical Sergeant Bennie Etters of Marygrove, Mississippi, recalled, "The Japanese let you know who you were, and what a hard time you were having back in
America. This was propaganda that could divide units because it was hitting home
on a lot of things that were true. But our main concern at the time was how they
got their information."[74]

Not long after arriving in the area, the battalions of the 25th Infantry Regimental
Combat Team and their attached field organizations underwent a baptism by fire,
and most of the troops acquitted themselves quite well. Given orders to pursue
and destroy withdrawing enemy forces east and north along the Laruma River as
a part of the U.S. 37th Infantry Division, the 25th Infantry's 2nd Battalion, led by
West Point graduate Arthur Amos, departed from the Numa-Numa Trail and de-
scended by rope down a 60-foot bluff overlooking the river. No sooner had the
men in one of the battalion's companies, led by LaGrange, Texas, native Dewitt
Cook, covered the crossing of the river than they drew enemy fire. By the end of
the firefight, several Japanese snipers lay dead. Several hours before the 2nd Battalion's operations, Brooklyn, New York, native and battery man Isaac Moore of
the 593rd Field Artillery Battalion pulled the lanyard on the first firing piece, ex-
pelling the first round of ammunition against enemy forces by the division in World
War II.[75] The work done by the men in the 593rd Field Battalion in constructing,
occupying, and firing from their gun positions at enemy targets was so impressive that it received special commendation from Americal Division artillery commander W. C. Dunckel.[76] The performances of Wade Foggie, from Anderson, South
Carolina, and Will Morey, from Greenville, Mississippi—who on 3 April had set
up and fired eight rounds from their rocket launchers into three heavily armed
enemy pillboxes, rendering them inoperable—earned them the Bronze Star.[77]

Lesser known were the actions of Isaac Sermon of F Company, St. Petersburg,

Florida–born Frank Little of G Company, and Ewel Polk of Los Angeles. When his company encountered an ambush by opposing forces during a patrolling assignment, Sermon fired his Browning automatic rifle into a well-concealed area until enemy guns were silenced. Afterward, he managed to keep his position in the advancing patrol until he dropped from exhaustion and the loss of blood resulting from multiple gunshot wounds. For his efforts, Sermon later earned the Silver Star.[78] Little, a native of Philadelphia, distinguished himself under fire when he directed his company in ground combat against the enemy, knocking out several machine gun nests during the fighting.[79] And Ewel Polk's performance garnered him a battlefield commission after he assisted his company commander in bringing his company through a Japanese ambush without serious casualties.[80]

Meanwhile, the other battalions of the regiment took part in the action. Men in the 1st Battalion's C Company, under the command of Wilson Kispert, fought the elements of Hill 500 as much as the enemy until they were forced to retreat to the main perimeter.[81] Throughout much of May, a reinforced platoon of the 93rd Reconnaissance Troop, led by Charles Collins, operated along the East-West Trail mapping the paths between the Saua and Reini rivers where they had to endure stiff resistance from opposing forces on various occasions. During one firefight, the patrol was ambushed by a large Japanese contingent, and large numbers of men (including Collins himself) suffered serious injuries and several were reported missing in action.[82] But not before James Owens, from Cleveland; Walter Jeffress, from Waterbury, Connecticut; and Clarence Reese, from Cotton Plant, Arkansas, knocked out a Japanese mortar squad despite being surrounded by enemy forces. For their efforts, these men received the Bronze Star Medal.[83] By the summer of 1944, the 25th Regimental Combat Team and adjoining personnel had performed numerous tactical operations throughout much of the area, often encountering natural obstacles such as jungle growth and rushing streams. As 25th infantryman and patrol leader Walter Greene recalled, "We went on patrol every day, at least the lieutenants went out every day with different men and we were in a combat situation for two months, every day, seven days a week."[84]

Black 93rd GIs also paid a heavy price for their role in the operations along the Numa-Numa Trail. During a patrolling mission, an ammunition and pioneer platoon, led by John Trice, had fallen prey to an enemy ambush while trying to evacuate troops of the American Division's 132nd Infantry. By the end of the fighting, Hugh Carroll, Oginal Ryan, William Ash, and Joseph Mallory lay dead, and the platoon was forced to retreat to the perimeter. But Stephen H. Simpson singlehandedly destroyed a Japanese machine gun nest during the fighting before helping a patient back to the American Division outpost, receiving special commendation.[85] During this opening stage of fighting, nearly thirty soldiers were killed, and nearly sixty were wounded.[86] The efforts of the men of the 25th Combat Team were reinforced by the evacuation of casualties by medical officers and men in a medical detachment under the direction of Meharry Medical College and Howard University–educated surgeons George Porter and Philip Williams. Carrying wounded men over a very steep saddle between Hills 250 and 600 to field ambulances posted nearly 6 miles away, most of the men performed extraordinary duties as ward attendants, litter bearers, and surgical technicians, often under intense enemy fire.[87]

Porter and Williams were not the only African American surgeons who worked to reduce the high rate of casualties in the Solomon Islands that summer. A medical detachment of the men formed litter bearer squads that greatly assisted the 25th Infantry's 2nd Battalion during its operations along the Numa-Numa Trail, sometimes carrying men nearly 3,000–4,000 yards back to the company perimeter. When men in the platoons, led by District of Columbia residents Conway Jones and Walter Sanderson, sustained shrapnel injuries moving against Japanese troops along the East-West Trail east of the Torokina River, medical officers Dunbar Gibson and Ernest Williams and their aides crawled from one foxhole to another cutting and bandaging their wounds.[88] What's more, clearing stations, commanded by Washington, D.C., natives and Howard University Medical School graduates Harold Whitted and Lincoln Shumate, received special commendations for their efficient treatment of wounded 25th Infantry soldiers during the first weeks of the fighting.[89] And on nearby Stirling Island in the Treasury Group, Claude Ferebee—a Norfolk, Virginia, native and a graduate of Columbia University Dental School—established and operated a dental clinic that paid special attention to the needs of the men in the 369th Infantry.[90] The extent to which 93rd medical officers won a hard-earned acceptance from their superior officers was reflected in the praise of the division psychiatrist written after he witnessed their deft handling of the combat team's casualties despite the lack of manpower and supplies in early April 1944. "In view of the foregoing conditions," he wrote, "I consider the progress made by the officers and men of the 318th Medical Battalion in handling the entire situation a good job."[91]

During this period, African American soldiers in the division encountered many situations in which they found themselves compelled to combat racism in the military at the same time that they waged war against the enemy and the treacherous climate. First, many soldiers attached to the unit sensed the reluctance expressed by some 14th Corps officers to accept them as combat troops. Throughout the operations on Bougainville Island in April and May, division members constantly complained of unclear field orders, insufficient patrol preparation time, and the indifferent attitudes that 14th Corps officers expressed toward their actions. In several instances, their suspicions were warranted. For example, in requesting Fiji scouts for a late April attack, 93rd Division commander Leonard Boyd was told by the G-3 that "the Corps Commander [Griswold] had refused to let the Fijis go, stating that we had to stand on our own sometime and we could start now."[92] Boyd interpreted Griswold's denial as evidence of the corps commander's willingness to prove the division's unsuitability for combat. Less than a month later, he wrote to his superiors, "The implication was not flattering to our troops and was another instance of the lack of concern in the Ninety-third Division as to their success in battle. I feel that the higher officers in Fourteenth Corps are perfectly willing to see this division relegated to service troop status and that they do not want relatively untried colored troops, with their racial problems, under their command. Our campaign here is a shotgun marriage to the Fourteenth Corps and it is apparent that we have two strikes on us and no balls."[93]

Other officers in the area also sensed the attitudes detected by Boyd and other 93rd servicemen. When sociologist Edward Hall visited black troops in the Pacific theater during the summer of 1944, he noted, "White commanders of higher echelons did not know what to do with Negro units because if nothing else, they were a subject of embarrassment."[94] And in February 1945, Harry Johnson, who had just been appointed as the division commanding general, made a similar observation when he stated: "No white officer likes to be assigned to a Negro outfit because of the present attitude of those high up towards Negroes. He regards such an assignment as partaking of the nature of punishment and as reflection on his capacity."[95]

The attitudes expressed by Boyd and Johnson did not escape the attention of many black 93rd soldiers, who deeply resented the condescending attitudes of senior white officers toward them within their own ranks. Many black officers felt that some white officers in command of segregated outfits considered their assignments as a punishment and worked desperately to obtain transfers to other units. In an intelligence report written at the time, the 369th Infantry S-2 commented, "The fact that morale of the white officers within this organization is low is definitely shown by their private conversations. Most of the white officers are discontented because they say they were not rotated to white units as was originally planned during the activation of the regiment."[96]

Detroit resident and division medical officer Robert Bennett observed this resentment firsthand. At the end of the 25th's campaign on Bougainville, Bennett wrote, "It is known among the troops that many of the white officers who were in command positions do not care to serve with Negro troops. Evidence for this sentiment includes the numerous statements and requests for transfer or reassignment with white troops made by these officers when it was learned that the unit was definitely moving overseas."[97] James Whittico, who commanded the division's clearing station during most of its combat activities on Bougainville, echoed Bennett's sentiments when he wrote during the same period: "It's a known fact that many white officers serving with the Ninety-third Division had no desire to serve with Negro troops." Whittico also claimed that many white officers interpreted patrolling with black troops in the Bougainville jungles as a form of punishment: "White officers seldom went out with patrols on Bougainville and saw patrol assignments as punitive measures for those junior officers against whom there existed grievances or prejudices."[98]

White officers were not the only soldiers associated with the division who expressed apprehension about receiving such assignments. George Little, the division's chief psychiatry officer, noted in late April 1944, "Some junior officers believed that patrol duty is used as a punitive measure. Patrol duty should be limited to the best soldiers and should carry with it a certain amount of distinction . . . the attitude to be attained should be 'you are selected to go on patrol because you are a good soldier' rather than 'if you do not behave, you will be sent on patrol' and the soldier thinks he may be killed."[99] Another 93rd serviceman, who was assigned to the 593rd Field Artillery Battalion during this period, echoed Little's sentiments: "There was an unwritten rule expressed among enlisted men at this time . . . you screw up and the company commander will get a transfer for you to the infantry and that eventually led to patrolling assignments. For this reason alone, no one in my unit wanted to be transferred."[100] And Julius Young, a 22-year-old second lieutenant who had openly protested the army's promotion policies in 1943, witnessed this practice firsthand. "As a result of the statement that I made, I received a lot of assignments that I shouldn't have been getting, and I probably did more patrolling than any other junior officer in the outfit . . . sometimes staying weeks longer than the next officer."[101]

On numerous occasions, black 93rd GIs alluded to these sentiments in communiqués, letters, and speeches conveyed to loved ones, prominent Afro-American leaders, black press corps members, and government officials. Nelson Peery wrote home to his mother while convalescing in a Bougainville clearing station hospital from gunshot wounds sustained during a patrolling mission, "Something must be ready to come off pretty soon. Yesterday my company commander came up to see the men and then the top kick [first sergeant] and my battalion commander comes around to console me. I'll bet they try to send me back on patrol when I get back."[102] Likewise, George Leighton, an officer with the 25th Infantry, wrote to First Lady Eleanor Roosevelt from the front: "Not far from my bomb-proof shelter are Negro soldiers who are shedding their blood in a way that made sad reading for race relations in our country."[103]

Some conveyances of these sentiments were less oblique than others. In an early July 1945 letter, civilian aide Truman Gibson was told by a high-ranking black officer in the division's 318th Medical Battalion about "a definite, but unofficial attempt being fostered out here, to forever keep the unit in obscurity and to discredit anything that they might do, which would place them in a favorable light as combat troops." The officer went on to describe the racial indignities that black GIs faced in the Pacific and warned Gibson that "the present policy of temporizing the public back home as to what we are doing should be stopped . . . I cannot understand how and why newspapers continue to print false statements about us."[104] Later that month, several officers in the division wrote *Norfolk Journal and Guide*'s publisher, P. B. Young, complaining of the lack of promotions in the Medical Staff Headquarters even though there were a number of vacant positions. They told Young:

> We must exert more and constant pressure through existing and future contacts and channels to correct the practices going on here-now . . . because there is a increased fervor to depress, discredit and criticize the Negro officer. The enlisted personnel also feel these acts keenly. We cannot stand idle; we need outside help. We therefore solicit your good offices and unbiased opinion on the matter. Request that if you find our problem sufficiently important to the race as a whole, that segment of service we represent, then contact the War Department with all the fervor of that race through all available channels now open or to be opened.[105]

K Company and the Rumor Mill

The uneasy feelings that black division members had regarding army life and senior cadres in the corps area became specific concerns during the spring of 1944. On the morning of 7 April, 180 soldiers in a reinforced company of the 25th Infantry's 3rd Battalion made their way down the north side of Hill 250 and crossed the east and west juncture of the Torokina River. Led by K Company commander Captain James Curran, 164th infantryman Ralph Brodin, and Lieutenant Oscar Davenport, the men then proceeded to hack their way along a prominent enemy trail nearly 2,000 yards into thick undergrowth. Led by K Company commander Captain James J. Curran, 164th infantryman Ralph Brodin, and Lieutenant Oscar

Davenport, their mission was to set up an ambush on the Japanese path approximately 3,000 miles from the river. Armed with nine additional Browning automatic rifles, two light machine guns, and only one 60-millimeter mortar, the men were a part of the intensive patrolling conducted by the 25th Infantry's 3rd Battalion north and east of Hill 250. But the men were not told that, just two days earlier, a reconnaissance patrol from Company K had reported that, although enemy resistance was slight, the trail had been heavily traveled by nearly a hundred Japanese foot soldiers who had evacuated the area five days earlier.[106]

As the company traveled along the trail, the platoon leaders relayed the company commander's order of movement to their subordinates. But what followed afterward has been subject to conjecture. According to verbal instructions given by Curran, the first platoon had the mission of providing security to the front and breaking the trail; the second platoon had been ordered to provide flank security, and the third platoon had received instructions to provide rear security. All had gone well until the patrol discovered an old Japanese hospital area surrounded by five bamboo shelters just a few miles from the trail block. Sending out finger patrols to the right, left, and rear as previously ordered, the black enlisted men and officers of the first platoon, led by Abner Jackson, Clarence Adams, and Nathan Love, among others, drew fire from several Japanese soldiers about 15 yards away. When Curran attempted to regroup by instructing the men to fan out to the left and right in order to report what they saw, intense fire from Japanese forces broke out from the immediate front.

Meanwhile, the men in the first platoon made the best out of a bad situation until enemy fire forced them to retreat to the rear of the company. Left exposed to enemy fire, most of the black soldiers in the second and third platoons heard orders given by Curran to form a retreating line—but bedlam resulted as indiscriminate firing took place all around them. Only after forward observer William Crutcher ordered the 593rd, the division's field artillery unit, to fire nearly twenty-five rounds on the area did the unit manage to regain control of the situation. However, by the time the members of K Company regrouped at the company command post on Hill 250, twenty enlisted men were wounded, and the body of Oscar Davenport lay among those killed in action as a result of his efforts to maintain control over his men during the skirmish. Among the missing were Edward Dennis, James Graham, Hue Morrow, and five other men; also missing were a radio, a light machine gun, the 60-millimeter mortar, and valuable combat equipment. Days later, a detail of men led by Abner Jackson returned to the area, where they found the bodies of the dead men and the equipment lost from the previous day. Shortly afterward, the bodies of Oscar Davenport and the seventeen men killed in action were laid to rest in a makeshift cemetery on Bougainville Island, and the army notified their next of kin.[107]

K Company's difficulties that fateful day spurred controversy as Americal Division investigators struggled during April and May to piece together the unit's actions. After interviewing the enlisted men and officers who participated in the patrol, the inspector general found that the initial shooting of the finger patrols directed by Curran caused the men to open fire in the direction of units next to them, and he charged Edward Dennis, who had returned to the battalion command post just hours after the incident, with "misconduct" in the face of enemy fire. He remarked, "The failure of the mission of Company 'K,' Twenty-fifth Infantry Regiment, 93rd Division, rested with the actions of a number of enlisted men who lost control of themselves to the extent that they did not obey repeated orders to keep their positions and to hold their fire and this influenced others by their actions. The actions of these men in a large measure may be attributed to their being under fire for the first time and it is not possible to fix specific responsibility."[108]

But the soldiers who testified told a different story. Will Jones, a squad leader in the first platoon, recalled, "The formation the Japanese were in was of a horse-shoe shape, men on both sides of the trail. They probably saw us before we entered the bivouac area and we were more or less surrounded." Jones went on to explain that his platoon had to endure a very difficult withdrawal under fire, commenting, "We did everything we could to get out of the situation."[109] When asked where his platoon was located, Edward Dennis told a colonel, "Platoon, sir, I had trouble just getting myself out." Eventually cleared of all charges, Dennis was evacuated to a nearby medical facility for physical exhaustion a week later.[110] Eyewitnesses to the firing that occurred during the incident suggested that the heavy undergrowth greatly exacerbated the mobility and communication problems of the unit. For example, when told by Captain Curran to have his platoon hold the line with machine gun fire, first-platoon leader Abner Jackson replied, "I don't see how I can"—with no support on his platoon's right flank, Jackson was concerned about incurring numerous casualties. Yet while obeying the direct order and proceeding to rejoin his unit at the front, he heard a messenger state that Curran had wanted the platoon to get the wounded to the rear and set up security for them.

Confusion as to the manner in which the men received the order also may have led to the platoon's retreat, thus exposing the second and third platoons to greater danger. Some GIs pointed out that the Japanese shouting commands to them in English only added to the confusion. John Marshall, a sergeant in the second platoon, recalled, "The Japanese in front shouted in English, 'cease-fire' and 'hold your fire.'" Forward observer William Crutcher remembered that he heard four or five Japanese speaking to the men from their right and the left. In the words of Hilary Moore of the second platoon, "The men seem to become excited by the 'yelling' of the Japanese." James Graham, an enlisted man in the first platoon, stated, "I shot one Jap right in the chest and the Jap yelled, 'you got me' in plain English. This led me to believe that it was one of my own men." Isaiah Adams also recounted that "their voices sounded funny but you could hear them repeating everything we said. When we said, 'hold your fire,' they mimicked the order in their high pitched voices."[111]

However, more than a few enlisted men and officers in K Company blamed the unit's difficulties on the actions taken by their company commander. Twenty soldiers interviewed by the inspector general pointed out that Captain Curran, who had remained largely in the company rear area, had little grasp of the situation they faced at the front. For example, John Marshall testified that the men in third platoon demanded to withdraw and reorganize only to be told to stay on the line and fight. Likewise, Clarence Adams of the first platoon stated, "After the fighting started, I said to a sergeant, we need someone on the right side of the trail. The sergeant then told me that Captain Curran said that the second platoon was coming but the platoon did not come."[112] Nevertheless, the 93rd headquarters' investigation of June 1944 absolved Curran of responsibility in the matter, and members of the 25th Infantry high command recommended disciplinary proceedings and the reclassification or "weeding out" of lieutenants Moore and Jackson from the unit.[113] During the same period, Isaiah Adams and Leroy Morgan were court-martialed and reclassified for stateside duty.[114]

What the men of K Company failed to realize at the time was that the patrol incident had rekindled the rumors about the performance of black troops in the field and the assumptions that army planners held regarding the fighting capabilities of black enlisted men and officers. Written at the end of the 25th Infantry's campaign on Bougainville Island, 14th Corps commander Oscar Griswold's conclusions provide a window into the eagerness with which the army high command wanted to confirm their negative attitudes regarding black troops and how K Company's ordeal tended to overshadow the overall contributions made by the division:

(1) It is apparent that the unit had had little "jungle training"; consequently, as individuals or as a unit, there were not prepared to handle adequately problems encountered in jungle operations. Most individuals showed willingness to learn from white troops; however, their ability to learn, and to retain what has been taught, is generally inferior to that of white troops.

(2) In general, discipline seems satisfactory; however, there is a tendency on the part of junior colored officers to make the minimum effort to carry out instructions. This same tendency exists among the enlisted men when they received instructions from these junior officers. As a rule colored officers do not have control of the enlisted men. On the other hand, those units having a large proportion of white officers appear to be better controlled, trained and disciplined.

(3) Initiative is generally lacking, especially among platoon commanders and lower grades. The presence of higher-ranking officers, especially whites, is necessary to assure the tackling and accomplishment of any task.

(4) To date, the Twenty-fifth Infantry, though better trained than the 1st Battalion of the 24th Infantry, has not progressively improved to the extent of the later unit.

On the basis of his negative assessment of K Company's difficulties, Griswold had initially rated the performance of the men in 25th Infantry Regimental Combat Team as "poor" compared with that of other infantry units in the theater, but his staff persuaded him to raise his estimation to "fair" for political reasons.[115]

Griswold's harsh assessment, however, did not escape the attention of the division's senior cadre. For example, 93rd Brigade commander Leonard Boyd noted in early May 1944, "This critical attitude has been manifested in General Griswold's criticism of individual acts as indicative of all troops in the division. Informal conversation with American Division and Corps officials leaves no doubt in my mind that most of them have a basic distrust of the Negro officer and his ability to lead Negro soldiers in combat."[116] Greencastle, Indiana, native Richard Hurst, who furnished radios and field artillery support for the 25th Regimental Combat Team, commented years later, "The officers under the Fourteenth Corp Command seem to have a disdainful view of our outfit because I know that the Twenty-fifth Infantry did their part in the patrolling and reconnaissance mission. . . . I was there. I never had anyone tell me of any cowardly acts by the Infantry; if anything, the comments were the opposite."[117] Yet many of the officers within the division repeated rumors of cowardice among black soldiers in K Company. In June 1944, 25th Infantry Regimental Combat Team commander Edwin Yon commented, "There were many instances of excellent leadership that produced aggressive action and successful results. Unfortunately there are others that were rather sordid and showed a lack of leadership in its entirety. For instance, helmets of a friendly patrol were seen through the bushes in the distance. A few minutes later some guns of its own battalion far to its rear were test fired. The patrol stampeded back to the company perimeter."[118]

For black GIs who served in division-size units within the segregated army else-where during World War II, the distorted information provided by rumor often carried deep racial overtones. For example, groups of men from the all-black U.S. 92nd Infantry Division disembarked in Naples, Italy, in August 1944 after spend-ing nearly two and a half years training in Alabama, Kentucky, Indiana, and Ari-zona. Three regiments and an assortment of special combat teams, tank destroyers, and field artillery battalions of the 92nd Division participated in the Arno River seizing and crossing as the 5th Army advanced toward the Gothic Line of the north-ern Apennines while attached to the 4th Corps's 1st Armored Division. While in the area, its regimental combat teams successfully engaged German forces, ex-tending the front more than 20 miles. However, the conduct of some of the troops on the battlefield attracted controversy. During the fall of 1944, an element of the 92nd Infantry Division sustained heavy casualties when it encountered fierce en-emy fire in its attempt to gain and hold Mount Cauala. By the time the unit left Italy, the officers and enlisted men with the division were reorganized and reas-signed, with many of them subjected to summary court-martial trials and reduc-tions in rank. To make matters worse, vicious rumors about their conduct under fire circulated widely throughout the European theater, even reaching the Senate floor.[119] Terms like "mass hysteria," "lack of pride of accomplishment," and "melt-ing away" filled the numerous reports filed by army officers and observers blam-ing the difficulties of the division on its black officers and enlisted personnel.[120] But many black soldiers with the division and black reporters covering the divi-sion contested the negative judgments of their performance in the field of battle. As one former black officer with the unit recalled years later, "The Ninety-second Division was permitted (or caused) to fail in certain combat operations; and those failures were documented for the specific purpose of discrediting blacks as efficient officers and combat soldiers. Therefore, the Army used the division as a convenient scapegoat to maintain the status quo in the military establishment and in society."[121]

This was also the case for the men who served with the 93rd Infantry Division in the Pacific war. The unit, it was suggested over and over again, was a poor in-fantry organization commanded by inefficient black junior officers, but it was bet-ter than average in housekeeping duties. For example, while touring various areas of the Southwest Pacific during February of the following year, a public relations officer in a forward area told NAACP executive secretary Walter White that the 93rd Infantry Division, which had been assigned to beachhead in Bougainville, had broken under fire and run, causing a large number of white officers and en-listed men to lose their lives. Some of the rumors were even circulated by 93rd

Division officers themselves. During the fall of 1944, 93rd Division chief of staff Stanley Prouty, who had just returned from the South Pacific theater, met with John J. McCloy and told him that the 93rd Division had failed to take a beachhead at Bougainville Island.[122] A month later, Southwest Pacific theater commander Douglas MacArthur quoted Griswold's assessment of the 93rd, rating the work of the division's infantrymen as poor, the performance of the artillery men as good, and its vehicle maintenance "of high order." "The general level of leadership was poor, particularly in the companies and platoons," MacArthur stated.[123] Around the same time, 8th Army commander Robert Eichelberger inspected the men in the 93rd Division and claimed, "I have never seen so much snap in my life. They had every vehicle polished, the engines were cleaned up fine, and every colored boy saluted as far as he could see you."[124]

To make matters worse, the disparaging view of the unit reached the Roosevelt White House. After receiving news about the performance of the 25th Infantry in May 1944 from Undersecretary of War John McCloy, Henry Stimson observed, "I do not believe they can be turned into really effective combat troops without all officers being white. This is indicated by many of the incidents herein."[125] By the end of the war, the racist misperceptions regarding the actions of the men in K Company had reached such a level that army chief of staff George Marshall echoed Stimson's view that the 25th Infantry's performance "is a very clear demonstration of the unreliability of Negro troops unless they are at least supported by white commissioned and non-commissioned officers."[126] Four years later, he told a reporter, "The men of the Ninety-third wouldn't fight . . . , couldn't get them out of the caves to fight."[127] Although Marshall should have known better than to have made such an erroneous statement, the fact that he and Stimson held such strong viewpoints illustrated the readiness on the part of some War Department officials to use the flimsy evidence collected by 14th Corps investigators both to denigrate the fighting abilities of black soldiers and to demonstrate white supremacy.

But not every senior official in Washington accepted Griswold's negative view of the 25th Infantry's performance. Upon learning of the 25th Infantry's action under fire at Bougainville, John McCloy stated: "Although they show some important limitations, on the whole I feel that the report is not so bad as to discourage us. The general tone of these reports reminds me of the first reports we got of the 99th Squadron. You remember that they were not very good, but that the Squadron has now taken its place in the line and has performed very well. It will take more time and effort to make good combat units out of them, but in the end, I think they can be brought over to the asset side."[128]

Home Front Perceptions

Around the same time, as the speculation surrounding the ordeal of K Company began to heat up, black 93rd servicemen and sectors of the black community worked to counter the distorted information relating to their conduct on the field of battle. Largely revolving around a discourse of racial democracy and home, formal and informal networks of communication sprang forward in order to challenge the biased accounts and to serve as reservoirs of resistance. Throughout the spring months of 1944, the *Cleveland Call & Post*, the *Baltimore Afro-American*, the *Pittsburgh Courier*, the *Chicago Defender*, and the *Chicago Bee* were filled with front-page stories filed by war correspondents and soldiers alike about black courage and heroism in the Pacific. Banner headlines such as "93rd Pushes On in Drive against Japs" and "93rd in South Pacific" hailed the activities of division members at every turn.[129]

And the informal communication networks forged between division members and correspondents circulated news about other black units in the Pacific as well as for loved ones at home. Of his coverage of the 93rd Division's activities in the Pacific, for instance, *Chicago Defender* correspondent Enoch Waters remembered, "My job was quite simple. I followed the same procedure as the unit moved from each island, getting the names and hometowns of as many men as possible who were engaged in different types of assignments. Interestingly, many of the men were as hungry for the news of the Pacific War as the people back home. And I tried to answer the questions that I thought were in the minds of people back home for every black family was concerned about the fate of its young men in the military. I believed their primary concern was not how the war was progressing but how the GIs were doing."[130]

But nowhere were these formal and informal networks of communication made more evident than in the campaign waged by NAACP national secretary Walter White to draw the attention of federal authorities and African American society to the army's employment of the division in the Pacific. In the early months of 1945, White was traveling extensively throughout the region visiting black GIs on the battlefield when he heard rumors regarding K Company's difficulties on Bougainville Island and countless stories from black press correspondents that the 93rd Division had been reconstituted for labor duties.[131] Inquiring further into the matter, White appeared at the 93rd Division headquarters at Hollandia, Dutch New Guinea, where he heard reports given by Brigadier General Leonard Boyd, 368th Infantry commander James Urquhart, 318th Medical Battalion commander

Robert Bennett, and other officers of the unit's activities on Bougainville. Boyd told White that "the story was a lie out of the whole cloth" and explained to him that the Bougainville assault had been made and the defensive perimeter established four months prior to the arrival of the 25th Regimental Combat Team. According to the division brigade commander, "The Twenty-fifth Infantry had accomplished its mission in a manner that was commendable for a veteran outfit, outstanding for a unit in its first combat action." And White heard other officers claim that the 93rd Division had performed the very limited combat duties assigned to the unit in a creditable fashion and that the stories that surrounded the division's participation in the taking of a beachhead on the island were absolutely false. Several officers in the U.S. 37th Division who witnessed the 25th Infantry in action echoed the observations of Boyd and other division cadres and told the NAACP secretary that the unit "conducted itself well at Bougainville."

After learning the events surrounding the reported Company K episode, however, White met with several 93rd Division GIs, who informed him that Harry H. Johnson, the newly appointed division commander, had greatly bolstered the unit's morale by relieving incompetent white officers and those who attempted to use their affiliation with the division to obtain promotions and transfers out of the unit. But White also learned, to his dismay, that many of the unit's capable and fair-minded West Point–educated officers, such as Arthur Amos, George Coleman, Carl McFerren, and Federick Bendtson, had been transferred out of the division to the Americal Division. The soldiers then went on to express their resentment over the transferring of black officers out of the division who disagreed with unit policies regarding promotion and assignment, and they conveyed their fears that the division would be converted into service units similar to those that had replaced the 2nd Cavalry Division in North Africa.

Hoping to focus the War Department's attention on what he perceived as a demoralizing situation for the division troops, White adopted the cause as his own and dispatched a detailed report of the unit's travails to President Franklin Delano Roosevelt on 12 February 1945. Protesting against the unit's unloading ships and rudimentary drilling during the past nine months, White recommended that the division be reconstituted as an integral unit, relieved of its garrison duties, and retrained for front-line action. The NAACP secretary also demanded that the War Department bring to an end its assignment of reclassified white and black officers to the division, the transferring of all white officers out of the unit who objected to serving with black troops, and the placement of black officers in the division headquarters. Finally, White demanded that the army investigate Southwest Pacific theater commander Douglas MacArthur's policies regarding black troops, noting, "Statements have been made to me by responsible persons that MacArthur is at least partly responsible for the failure to train properly and utilize the Ninety-third Division in combat." White's suspicion of the lack of action taken by MacArthur and high-ranking members within the Southwest Pacific command may have been heightened by the fact that when he requested an interview with the general regarding the use of black troops in his theater of operations, he was denied a meeting on several occasions on the grounds that the general was in the midst of planning the recapture of the Philippine Islands.[132]

Yet when asked by the War Department two weeks later to respond to White's accusations of a deliberate campaign to disparage the 93rd's front-line activities and the Southwest Pacific's inefficient employment policies regarding the unit, MacArthur presented another view. The Southwest Pacific commander referred to the comments made by the 14th Corps about the unit's performance seven months earlier as a way of justifying the duties he assigned to the division. "The First Cavalry, Seventh, Seventy-Seventh, Forty-First and Thirty-Eighth Divisions were all superior to the Ninety-Third except in the matter of motor maintenance," MacArthur claimed. With regard to White's argument that the 93rd had been broken up, he contended that few divisions within the Southwest Pacific area sustained their initial makeup. According to MacArthur, the 93rd Division's duties in the Southwest Pacific theater centered upon holding the defensive perimeters of occupied areas, performing labor details in port areas, and training for combat patrols. With this, he informed the War Department that the division had been alerted for movement from Hollandia, New Guinea, to Morotai, where it would be employed against enemy forces in the area. Referring to the assignment and transfer of white officers both in and outside the division, the Southwest Pacific theater commander also argued that while every unit assigned to the area found itself compelled to follow this policy because of the limited number of replacements, many of the 93rd Infantry Division's capable field-grade officers had been requested by other units. On White's claims of racial discrimination toward the unit, MacArthur finally remarked, "The violent opinions and unfounded statements of Mister White would seem to mark him as a troublemaker and a menace to the war effort."[133]

The Southwest Pacific area commander, nevertheless, recognized the adverse publicity surrounding his handling of black troops in his theater of operations and agreed to meet with the NAACP executive secretary to discuss the 93rd at the division headquarters at Hollandia in early March 1945. During their high-profile meetings, MacArthur repeated his claim that "race had nothing whatsoever to do with the Ninety-third's ability to fight." Recalling his service as a junior officer who commanded Filipino troops decades earlier, the general argued, "Any man who says that another man's fighting ability can be measured by color is wrong." MacArthur based his reasoning for not utilizing the division on the lack of shipping and his inspectors' reports on the division advising him that the unit's morale was low.[134]

MacArthur's remarks seem to have allayed White's apprehensions somewhat because after learning that the 93rd had been reassigned to Morotai, the NAACP secretary wrote the general less than a week later: "You certainly acted promptly after our talk of March 1. Your action in bringing the division together in one island for the first time since the Ninety-third left the States will undoubtedly have immediate effect in improvement of efficiency and a sense of unity."[135] What White failed to realize at the time, however, was that MacArthur had no intentions of employing the division in front-line duty and had planned to use the unit only as rear-echelon forces in his plans to reenter the Philippine Islands. In fact, according to the plans of 26 February adopted by Southwest Pacific theater commander, the 93rd would perform "garrison duties on occupied islands and on Morotai" and would be used only in the later stages of the operation as mopping up forces.[136]

MacArthur's encounters with the NAACP executive secretary and his attitudes toward black soldiers in the military may have been as paradoxical as the responses among 93rd Division members to their overseas experiences. For example, division officer Francis Ellis, a native of Chandler, Oklahoma, who was present during the general's meetings with the NAACP executive secretary, described an incident that occurred on the last day:

> When Walter White came to Hollandia, Dutch New Guinea, after the *Pittsburgh Courier* and the *Baltimore Afro-American* made a lot of noise about the 93rd being changed over from infantry troops to labor troops, General MacArthur wondered why this white man was so concerned about black troops. On the last day when the general, White, and their aides were ending their discussions and were bidding each other good-bye, MacArthur asked him why he was so interested in these niggers anyway. When White told him that he too was black, the general turned and left the division headquarters without saying another word.[137]

White's efforts, however, also had their limits, as not all black 93rd GIs favored the stance that he taken on their behalf. No sooner had the NAACP leader arrived stateside than he received a letter from sixteen division servicemen withdrawing their membership and criticizing the organization's efforts to redeploy them to front-line duty:

Your organization has failed to confine your work to the home front. This was substantiated by a recent visit to our organization by one of your representatives. The
only person that he contacted was an officer, whose name cannot be mention [*sic*]
hereon for various reasons. The only thing that he seems to be interested in, was the
engaging of our organization in more combat. He didn't bother to ask nor inquire
why we have been overseas for approximately fifteen months and haven't seen nor
been near any signs of civilization for recreational purposes or otherwise. Person-
ally, we feel that he didn't give a darn as he hasn't experienced the separation as we
have from our loved ones. In other words, take care of the home front, we'll handle
things from this end.[138]

And still other GIs with the unit expressed a jaded view altogether of the war
correspondents who covered their activities. Specifically, although many division
members felt that the correspondents had worked diligently to circulate news of
their contributions to the war effort, they sometimes resented their zealous efforts
to cast them as symbols in the struggle for equality. The tension between black
journalists and troops serving on the battlefield manifested at many levels. While
traveling with the division throughout the Solomon Islands in 1944, *Chicago Defender* correspondent Enoch Waters was approached by several angry GIs and
roundly criticized. Waving a clipping taken from the *Defender* that clamored for
their deployment to battle, the soldiers told Waters, "I don't know whom you folks
think you're speaking for, but it certainly ain't us. You folks are sitting back at home
and too old or too beat up to be drafted. It's easy to say let them fight and die."
When the *Defender* correspondent reiterated the position taken by the press and
the NAACP that their placement in combat units served as an indication of fairer
treatment in the army, GIs jeered him derisively and asked, "Why should we volunteer to sacrifice our lives for a Jim Crow country?"[139] In a similar vein, when
asked by a member of Howard University's administration to reflect on his wartime
experiences, officer George Leighton wrote home from the Pacific during the period:
"I can tell you that here among our troops the average colored soldier is becoming more and more disgusted with the pitifully asinine reports that are printed
each week in the *Afro-American*, the *Pittsburgh Courier*, and the *Chicago Defender*.
Not only are those articles inaccurate. They go so far as to print blatant falsehoods
that make the colored troops the laughing stock of the white soldiers who know
the true facts."[140]

Little did Leighton and other black 93rd GIs realize it at the time, but many
service dependents and friends had reached a similar conclusion. After receiving
word of her husband's passing, Ollive Davenport was putting her life back together

and caring for her daughter Patricia Ann when she was invited to Fort Huachuca to accept her husband's Bronze Star as a tribute to his self-sacrificing deeds in the Bougainville campaign. Although no record survives of what she said on the day of the ceremony, in its coverage of the event, the *California Eagle* published photographs of the Tucson, Arizona, resident standing proud and resolute before members of the post high command.[141] But *Eagle* correspondents failed to realize that with her attendance at the ceremony and the countless statements made by service family members and friends around the same time, Ollive Davenport and other service relatives had emerged as the chief custodians of the physical and emotional well-being of their loved ones in uniform. And in the process, they became important leaders in efforts to effect social and political change on a number of levels. For army planners, government officials, and black leaders and institutions, their voices in support of black servicemen would rumble loudly, resonating across the country as well as throughout the Southwest Pacific theater.

CHAPTER SEVEN

Relative Security in the Southwest Pacific

*　*　*

Perhaps nothing perplexes the outside observer more than the popular term and the popular theory of "social equality." The term is kept vague and elusive and the theory loose and ambiguous. One moment it will be stretched to cover and justify every form of social segregation and discrimination. The next moment it will be narrowed to express only the denial of close personal intimacies and intermarriage. The very lack of precision allows the notion to rationalize the rather illogical and wavering system of color caste in America.

Gunnar Myrdal, 1944

"I am writing about a matter concerning my brother, Sergeant Samuel Hill," began Grace Davis in a letter written to the judge advocate general in November 1945.[1] On the surface, Davis's missive appears to be quite simple: a letter expressing concern for the physical well-being of a service family member in time of war. But the nature of Davis's inquiry and the sequence of events that it referenced carried a political subtext. On 9 January 1945, while serving with an echelon of the U.S. 93rd Infantry Division, Samuel Hill and one other soldier were arrested and charged with raping a Papuan woman in the Netherlands East Indies.[2] Despite conflicting testimony rendered by prosecution witnesses during the court-martial proceedings, members of the hearing board dismissed the charges against the other GI. The 28-year-old Detroit, Michigan, resident was found guilty, however, and faced a penalty of being dishonorably discharged and the forfeiture of his benefits in addition to serving a lifetime of hard labor.[3] Shortly afterward, Hill was transferred to the United States and confined to the U.S. Penitentiary in Washington State.[4]

Given the relationship that existed between black GIs and the American military justice system in the early twentieth century, the swiftness of the legal process should not be surprising. As recent scholars have noted, disproportionate numbers of African American soldiers in the European and Pacific theaters of operations had been tried and executed for such capital crimes prior to and during the Second World War.[5] However, Samuel Hill's case and its immediate aftermath are significant for several reasons. First, the case highlighted the degree to which the army's relationship with black GIs in an international setting intersected with American domestic racial and sexual politics. By the time the division stepped ashore at Dutch New Guinea in the fall of 1944, the army's employment of African Americans in the Pacific had been reconfigured to encompass notions of patriarchy and white male privilege. While dispersed throughout the Pacific, black division members faced overwhelming obstacles, working as service and support troops loading and discharging ships and providing local security for radar installations while drawing enemy fire. Southwest Pacific theater commanders also drew upon sexualized racial stereotypes of African American men as rapists to justify policies limiting the social interaction between black GIs and indigenous populations in the area. In addition, in the weeks following the Japanese surrender, most African American service personnel experienced tremendous difficulties in securing passage home owing to a demobilization system that favored front-line troops.

The case reflected the bold leadership of African American grassroots institutions that rallied to the cause of black 93rd GIs. Within weeks after news of Hill's trial reached the United States, for instance, service relatives like Grace Davis sprang into action, firing off numerous telegrams and letters of protest to military officials, the White House, and congressional leaders, as well as to high officials within the NAACP. In the process, the drama surrounding Hill's case graced the front pages of newspapers around the world and unveiled the sexual dimensions of the army's racial politics for all to see. Indeed, by the time Samuel Hill had arrived in Washington to begin his laboring ordeal, the edifice of race and sex would provide a stage upon which the contradictions of American domestic reality and wartime rhetoric would be showcased.

Discipline in the Southwest Pacific

As the summer faded into the fall of 1944, the Bougainville campaign had drawn to a close, and the battle-tested echelons of the 93rd Infantry Division began to make their way northwestward toward the southern Philippine Islands. After boarding transports at Empress Augusta Bay, the division's regimental combat teams and headquarters company arrived at the Green and Russell Islands group, where they established base security against enemy attack while undergoing refresher training programs. At the same time, men of 368th Infantry's 2nd Battalion moved from the Russells to Vella Lavella in the New Georgia group, where they continued to perform labor details unloading ships at the port while providing security patrols on the island. Among those who participated in the intensive operations were Raymond Jenkins of Memphis; Randall Morgan of Chicago; Edgar Davis of Montclair, New Jersey; Malcolm Brown of Seattle; Julius Thompson of Norfolk, Virginia; and William "Billy" Kyle of Philadelphia. There they remained until the unit was ordered to accompany the remainder of the regiment to nearby Munda before heading to Morotai Island in April 1945.[6]

Other contingents of the division seem to have had the same duties as the 368th Infantry's 2nd Battalion. Members of the 369th Infantry Regiment assumed command of the Emirau Island after arriving from Guadalcanal during the late summer months of 1944. Encountering very little opposition, the troops bolstered the island's defenses while undergoing a strict regimen of combat training. From Munda to the Finschafen to the St. Mathias Islands group, African American servicemen with the 93rd spent endless days loading and unloading supplies at ports while providing island and base security.

The division's defensive preparations were part and parcel of a larger Allied Pacific drive in the making. To the northwest of the New Guinea and Bismarck Archipelago, where most of the division's units were concentrated, lay the coastal islands of Wakde and Biak, two prime airfield sites that the Southwest Pacific headquarters hoped to secure for future Allied bomber operations in the Philippines. According to historian Ronald Spector, "An added incentive to these plans was the fear that these fine airfield sites might soon be utilized by the Japanese in a counterattack unless the Allies moved quickly."[7] In a similar fashion, the Dutch New Guinea anchorage and other bases in the region were to serve as strategic supply points and staging areas from which to launch a concerted land-based aircraft attack on Japanese forces between New Guinea and Mindanao. The patrolling operations performed by the 93rd Infantry Division and other units in the Hollandia region were important because refortification of the vital airfields by the enemy would create a setback in the Allied plan to advance into the Philippines and beyond.[8]

But as the soldiers advanced from island to island, few failed to notice the precarious predicament of black servicemen in the Southwest Pacific theater. Albert Evans, a soldier in the 369th Infantry, recalled, "Upon leaving Munda our battalion was sent to the Admiralties. This is where we were used as stevedores completely."[9] At the same time, Julius Young, a former resident of Wilmington, Delaware, also experienced the situation firsthand when he received an order from the division headquarters to evacuate an airstrip on New Guinea. Young recalled, "I told General Eichelberger's adjutant general that this must be a mistake to send me down here to do this because I don't know how to do this. But when he radioed back to division headquarters, they told him that I was the man." Undaunted, Young and his men worked day and night until they completed the task—seven days earlier than scheduled. For his distinguished performance, the young lieutenant received a commendation from 8th Army headquarters but failed to receive the Bronze Star because of a statement he had made criticizing the army's deployment policies.[10] Describing the division's activities during the period, Claude Ferebee told a contemporary, "We are no longer under the Army you were acquainted with or mentioned. Just like a one-horse freight train—always side tracked. We are and have been as I used the term in a discussion the other day: racial prisoners of war."[11] And as Edward Soulds, a soldier assigned to the unit, put it, "We struck our blows against the enemy by throwing, stacking, un-stacking, loading and unloading supplies in warehouses. The black officers and troops began to accept their fate, knowing full well that "Mac" (MacArthur) had no intention of giving our outfit a crack at the big time. Not only that, but even if you wanted to go home and you had enough points, you were stuck."[12]

What Claude Ferebee, Edward Soulds, and other 93rd GIs failed to realize, however, was that the army's deployment policies had much more to do with the logistical problems that the Southwest Pacific area was experiencing at the time than anything else. From the fall of 1944 well into the spring and summer of 1945, the excessive retention and slow turnaround of ships and the shortage of service troops in the theater had greatly hampered the lines of communication, supplies, and equipment required for the day-to-day operations of divisions and supporting troops bound for duty in the Philippines. Because the Southwest Pacific area commander had habitually used ships in his theater as floating warehouses, the number of ships retained in the Southwest Pacific rose from seventy-one in January 1944 to well over two hundred eleven months later.[13] Conversely, the ratio of combat to service troops in the Southwest Pacific area was nine to one.[14] As a result, the American invasion of Luzon slated for December 1944 year was not launched until mid-January 1945.

In an attempt to alleviate the logistical situation, army chief of staff George Marshall ordered MacArthur to reduce the number of ships retained in his theater to under a hundred by mid-January. Furthermore, Marshall tried to get MacArthur to close down some of his rear bases in the theater and demanded that the commander adjust the number of operations he planned to undertake based on the shipping already available in his area. "Our global commitments cannot sustain this extraordinary tax against shipping effectiveness. Your future operations and those in other theaters are already penalized by shipping shortages," Marshall warned, but to no avail. In February 1945, the War Department reported that of the 446 vessels within the theater, 102 were idle, waiting to load or discharge, 62 were docked for repairs, and 165 were setting sail for forwarding ports.[15] By the time the first echelon of the 93rd, along with the 25th, 37th, 40th, 43rd, and Americal divisions, arrived in the Southwest Pacific area, at least 33 of the 86 noncombatant ships anchored in the Hollandia harbor needed unloading, with 33 held awaiting discharge and 24 others awaiting deployment to Leyte.[16] Indeed, by the time soldiers of the 93rd Division arrived in the area, the service troop and shipping crisis that had been brewing for nearly two years in the Pacific had become an urgent issue.

Back-Channel Strategies of Resistance

While stationed on the nearby Treasury Islands, thirty-three black officers, including Walter Greene, Lorenzo Blount, Julian Dawson, George Looney, and Edward Strawther, received refresher courses in officer basic training during the summer and fall months of 1944.[17] Where the reorientation course stood in the priorities of the Southwest Pacific campaign is unclear, but the purpose of the instruction remains vivid in the memory of the officers who participated in it. Once the junior officers arrived at the training facility, they realized that the return of their units to the fighting fronts of the Pacific War was not part of their superiors' plan. Charles Lynn, a native of Peoria, Illinois, and other members of the 25th Infantry Regiment had no sooner arrived on Green Island from combat operations on Bougainville that September than he received word that he had been assigned to Stirling Island to attend a special school for division officers. When Lynn and fifteen other junior officers arrived at the isolated military outpost, they encountered endless roll calls, calisthenics sessions, and command and control problems. As Lynn recalled, "There we were to prove our efficiency and better our attitudes or be reclassified." Shortly afterward, Lynn boarded a plane that took him to Ora Bay, New Guinea, where he stood before members of a reclassification board and was promptly discharged from the army "for conditions other than honorable."[18]

For Walter Greene, a fellow 25th Infantry officer from Detroit, the retraining of black officers in the division had more to do with their standing in the army than with deficiencies exhibited on the field of battle. "The black enlisted man did not get this kind of pressure from white officers," Greene remembers. "As a matter of fact, he could be almost decent to the dog-foot soldier, but their hostility to the black officer bordered on paranoia. A black man as their peer they could not stand and they did their damnedest to break you through humiliation and frustration." He recalled that his troubles with his superior officers at the officer retraining facility began when he discovered that the school was operating outside the purview of the War Department—and thus illegally. "To keep it hidden from Washington, the general did not maintain a morning report. We were being carried on the morning reports of the outfits to which we belonged, like all was well."[19]

When Greene realized that he could not be court-martialed for refusing direct orders at the school, he and eight other officers refused to report to formation and ignored commands to return to their previous units. By the time word of their resistive acts reached the division headquarters and before a course of disciplinary action could be carried out against them, the school ceased operations, and he and the other black officers who remained at the camp received orders transferring them to the Molucca Islands, near Morotai. Throughout the process, Greene and his fellow GIs remained undaunted. While awaiting transfer, the 25-year-old GI and other soldiers wrote letters to loved ones and friends in an attempt to draw national attention to their travails in the Southwest Pacific.

While undergoing the officer retraining program, Julian Dawson and a group of officers also penned several round-robin letters to family members and associates, informing them of the daily indignities they encountered at the hands of the senior division staff officers charged with running the facility. "We are catching hell," the soldiers wrote, but their efforts produced little results. Much of the correspondence never made it out of the Southwest Pacific area. And for Julian Dawson, the son of a well-known surgeon, his problems were only just beginning. Within months after he was discharged from the army for "conduct unbecoming an officer," the Chicago resident returned home only to receive a letter from his local draft board, ordering him to report for reinduction as a private.[20]

Throughout World War II, army intelligence personnel tended to scan such powerfully written letters by black GIs for sensitive information relating to battlefront conditions in the Southwest Pacific. Most of the time they dismissed the exchanges as typical complaints of army life in rear echelon areas. Indeed, as Samuel Stouffer and other members of the Research Branch of the army during the period and recent scholars have attested, vast numbers of soldiers spent their leisure time writing such letters during World War II.[21] Black GIs were no exception. As students of the African American experience in the war have also recently documented, however, army censors often screened black soldiers' letters for derogatory comments relating to their treatment in the segregated army.[22] In the Southwest Pacific theater, censors engaged in a concerted effort to deflect public criticism away from the army's treatment of black troops. For military intelligence officials in the 14th Corps, the slightest reference to racial injustice in black soldiers' letters raised fears of the detrimental consequences that soldiers' discontent with racial conditions would have for Allied forces waging war in the Pacific.[23]

During the month of September 1944 alone, base authorities sifted through approximately two million pieces of mail, from which they extracted large amounts of correspondence by military personnel citing the state of race relations in the army. "Many of these comments are written by colored troops," one base censor wrote at the time. "And the majority of them are expressions of discontent with existing conditions."[24] As the division headquarters assumed control of base operations on islands scattered throughout the theater, the commanding general of the 93rd Infantry Division worked tirelessly to suppress outgoing material relating to racial attitudes within the unit, often instructing base censors to sanitize or detain all correspondence that contained derogatory statements.[25]

Around the same time, counterintelligence and S-2 officers also lectured division personnel endlessly about the need to abstain from divulging to their loved ones details about their situation overseas that might jeopardize security.[26] And as if this were not enough, G-2 officials cracked down on what they considered to be breaches of vital military security, meting out heavy fines and punitive measures against those soldiers who violated censorship regulations. Unsurprisingly, such stringent measures clashed with the perceptions of many black GIs attached to the unit, as they perceived the regulations as yet another weapon in the arsenal of military racism. For instance, like so many other servicemen stationed overseas at the time, a black GI from Minneapolis experienced the sanctioning power of the division's intelligence apparatus firsthand. During the period, he wrote a letter to his mother railing against the indignities that he and other soldiers encountered while serving in the area and announcing his intention to desert the army. A few days after base censors intercepted his letter, both he and his mother were visited by G-2 staff officers. The former soldier explained, "You have to remember that such repression was necessary in their eyes because they [army officials] wanted to make sure that ideas like those that I was expressing didn't get out to the public."[27]

However, many letters containing incisive commentary on the treatment of blacks both abroad and at home escaped the attention of army officials. Hoping to get their letters past the censor and avoid official persecution, black 93rd GIs and loved ones at home described race relations in the army as well as in society at large using coded language that seemed virtually indecipherable to army counterintelligence officers. Employing various neighborhood and household-specific symbols and cues, public and private correspondence often carried cryptic messages that could only be interpreted as ironic expressions of everyday life in the face of power. As his unit moved from Bougainville to Green Island in October 1944, for instance, Cleveland resident Thomas White wrote a letter to his wife in which he included a short poem titled "Somewhere in the South Pacific" that parodied the vicissitudes of black life at the front:

> Somewhere in the South Pacific where the sun is like a curse,
> And each long day is followed by Another . . . slightly worse
> And the men dream and wish for greener, fairer lands.
>
> Somewhere in the South Pacific where a girl is never seen,
> Where the sky is never cloudy and the grass is always green.
> Where the bat's mighty howl robs a man of blessed sleep,
> Where there isn't any whiskey, and the beer is never cheap.
>
> Somewhere in the South Pacific where the mail is always late
> And a Christmas card in April is considered up to date.
> Where we never have a payday and we never get a cent,
> But we never miss the money because we'd never get it spent.
>
> Somewhere in the South Pacific where the ants and buzzards play,
> And a hundred fresh mosquitoes replace each one you slay,
> So take me back to Frisco; let me hear the mission bell,
> For this godforsaken outpost is a substitute for HELL.[28]

On the surface, White was describing the dense, wet, and impenetrable jungles of Guadalcanal and other islands in the South Pacific and the daily bouts of "chicken shit" tyranny that he and others encountered while in military service overseas. Yet on another level, his verses conveyed to his wife the deep sense of foreboding that he and other black soldiers felt while living and laboring in a zone of combat.

White's missive also alluded to their trials and tribulations in the South Pacific. At the time, he and other members of a service company of the 25th Infantry Regiment had been assigned to an atoll near Green Island, one of the central staging points for the segregated unit. Every day during a six-month period, he and his company alternated between unloading ships and conducting patrol missions before Australian forces finally relieved them. During his stint of duty on the island, heightened racial tensions strained relations between black GIs and their commanding officers. Of his experiences on Green Island, White recalls: "We had some of the worst white officers I had seen in my life. I don't know where the hell they came from. To make matters worse, on the Green Islands, we didn't get any mail; we didn't get any food. The only reason we didn't starve to death was because of them Australians when they came to those islands." In August 1944, White enjoyed a small victory of sorts when he and another associate pilfered a case of whiskey from the tent of his commanding officer and distributed it to men in their company. He reflected years later, "I saw all this whiskey piled up there, and it was just me. I figured that I had as much right to it as my CO did, so I just took it."[29]

Like Thomas White, other GIs translated their concerns of war into lyrical prose. In other instances, servicemen used apocalyptic images to convey to people at home the violent aspects of Pacific War and their meaning for soldiers and civilians alike. For example, in September 1944, Chicago resident William Couch penned the following poem, titled "To a Soldier," in which he described the savagery of war for his fellow South-siders:

Here where the cock sounds his synchronized song
in a sunless morning
and the caravans of young move towards the
battlefronts, leaving behinded the degraded
cities wild-eyed and dim-lit like an old man
fallen . . .
where flowers and time accumulate to dust
and the barbarous weed grows in the night
night taller than a child's reach

(O, brother say!)

The planted cannon replies to the
last word, living urge of flesh
that aimlessly scratched the ground with
bayonet point
or, valiant, alert, steathly [sic] moved into HELL.[30]

Scottsboro in the Pacific

More often than not, the oblique messages relayed by division members carried news of racial incidents that were steeped in sexual tension. On 2 June 1944, George Murphy, a field artillery officer stationed in New Guinea, wrote home to his boyhood friend and *Chicago Bee* columnist Abe Noel, and his words appeared in the black newspaper a few weeks later in the following manner: "Take notice, my friend, that I'm in a new location, trying to duck malaria and dengue fever. Please let my folks in Chicago know my new A.P.O. so that they can be of service to myself and other soldiers." Murphy then went on to provide commentary on events that shaped the lives of black GIs stationed throughout the Southwest Pacific at the time. He stated, "I see that the NAACP has hold of our Scottsboro case. Remember two of the five boys condemned to die for a trollop instead of for freedom were from my old outfit? . . . We spent much time explaining to the young Australian lawyer hired to defend the men that although the men were charged with rape on the blotter, they committed an even worse crime according to the unwritten code of the American social system."[31]

The cause célèbre to which George Murphy cryptically alluded had occurred in early 1944. On 15 March six black soldiers in a quartermaster amphibious truck company were accused of raping and having carnal knowledge of two white army nurses in the South Pacific. In many ways, the incident encompassed themes of sexuality, the protection of white womanhood, and political and social arrangements, issues that had historically shaped African American life in the United States. While stationed at Milne Bay, New Guinea, two white GIs, Thomas Havers and James Flanagan, along with two U.S. Army Nurse Corps officers, Ruth Irvine and Marie Weaver, were parked in a restricted shore area when six black men reportedly approached them and forced the women into a wooded area, where they were allegedly assaulted and then raped.

Accounts differed widely, however. The accused men emphatically proclaimed their innocence, insisting that the alleged victims had solicited them for sex but that they had turned them down. However, both Flanagan and Havers claimed that five members of the group threatened to kill them if the women refused to have intercourse with them. Furthermore, when questioned during the initial judge advocate general's query into the matter, the two nurses appeared confused when asked to identify their attackers during a company formation held at the time, accusing up to nine soldiers who stood in the ranks. But when pressed further by army investigators, the two women conjured up long-standing images that cast their alleged assailants as black rapists.

As Walter Luszki, an officer who served in New Guinea at the time, points out, the evidence introduced in the court proceeding should have been treated with caution because of the disparity in the accusers' testimonies, the poor visibility that evening, and the statements of the accused denying that they had had intercourse with the two women.[32] Nonetheless, shortly afterward, military authorities arrested the six men and charged them with violating the Twenty-fourth Article of War. At their trial a few months later, court members listened to only three days of testimony before finding all six men guilty, and the judge sentenced each man to die by hanging.[33] And with the approval of General Douglas MacArthur, commander in chief of the Southwest Pacific area, the men were promptly transferred 175 miles north from Milne Bay to the New Guinea Detention and Rehabilitation Center, where they awaited summary execution.[34] Less than a month later, a small group of the center's military staff watched as the soldiers' bodies swung from the gallows.[35]

The motivations behind the Southwest Pacific commander's order to execute the soldiers are unclear. In his memoirs, MacArthur failed to mention the Milne Bay case and other capital-offense cases tried in his theater of operation.[36] And as his biographers have pointed out, it is difficult to determine where the Southwest Pacific theater commander stood on the subject of race and military justice.[37] But it is possible that the general's juridical policies reflected southern mores of race, place, and custom. The general kept quiet about the army's long-standing system of racial segregation and offered virtually no leadership on issues affecting black servicemen in the theater. In fact, he adopted a laissez-faire approach toward civil-military affairs, deferring the administration and adjudication of civic issues to territorial, municipal, and colonial authorities as well as to members of his staff. As Joseph Rauh, an officer who served in MacArthur's headquarters at the time, recalls, "You know, the military commander in the area can bar people and the general barred any Military Government troops from the States. He wanted to do it out of his own people."[38]

In addition, MacArthur worked diligently with civilian authorities to impose policies restricting relations between black GIs and local women, stationing black units in isolated territories and confining them to racially segregated locales in major urban centers. After black troops arrived in Australia during the early stages of the war, for instance, MacArthur wrote to George Marshall, "I will do everything possible to prevent friction or resentment on the part of the Australian government and people with regard to the presence of colored troops . . . their policy of 'White Australia' is universally accepted here . . . however, by utilizing these troops in the front lines away from the great centres of population . . . I can minimize the difficulties involved."[39] And as the war continued, the general's efforts to maintain the color line in the Pacific also dominated the thinking of white officers and enlisted men throughout the theater. Quite often, efforts made by the Southwest Pacific theater command to regulate interaction between black army personnel and civilian female populations tended to be wrapped up in stereotypical portrayals of black male bestiality and a patriarchal discourse of the protection of white womanhood. As one officer assigned to the 14th Corps at the time commented: "One must go armed on dates or MPs will send girls home because of the danger of attack by Negroes."[40]

Throughout the war, cases or incidents involving black GIs accused of rape rarely appeared in major American daily newspapers. But almost a year before the Milne Bay incident, news of a rape case involving two black soldiers stationed in the South Pacific alerted African American service relatives both at home and abroad of the intense battles that black GIs faced. While serving on New Caledonia in May 1943, 19-year-old Frank Fisher and 20-year-old Edward Loury traveled from their encampment to nearby Noumea to enjoy the sights and sounds of a carnival. A few kilometers beyond their base camp, the GIs hailed a ride from two other soldiers who were also planning to attend the event. When the party reached an area described by residents as "Prostitute Hill," Fisher and Loury alighted from the vehicle and continued their journey to the social function on foot. However, after advancing several hundred yards toward their destination, they encountered a white officer and a New Caledonian woman walking from a wooded area to a jeep parked along the side of the road.

After stopping and exchanging pleasantries, the officer asked the two GIs if they were interested in purchasing sexual favors from the local woman. The officer then addressed the woman in French, and the woman responded in kind, leaving the two black servicemen confused as to what the pair had discussed in their presence. The couple invited the two GIs to a secluded spot in the area where they were induced to engage in sexual relations with the woman, but it is unclear whether the men paid the woman. When Fisher and Loury later reappeared at their bivouac area, the two Port Company members were arrested for the alleged rape of the New Caledonian woman. Less than a month later, the two soldiers appeared before a court-martial trial board, where they were found guilty, sentenced to a dishonorable discharge and life imprisonment at the U.S. Penitentiary, and forced to forfeit their pay and benefits—even though the French penal code in New Caledonia called for a lesser sentence. In addition, the two soldiers were not allowed to appeal their convictions, and they were subjected to the "third degree" tactics of military police while confined to the stockade.

In the months that followed, William Hastie, chairman of the NAACP National Legal Committee, and Vito Marcantonio, president of the Communist Party–led International Labor Defense, launched a spirited campaign on their behalf, filing petitions with the secretary of war to overturn the original convictions and bringing public attention to the plight of black soldiers in the Pacific theater. Not long afterward, their efforts bore fruit. On 31 March 1944, the assistant secretary of war intervened, reducing the sentences of the two young men from life imprisonment to ten and eight years, respectively. But the overwhelming number of court-martial cases of rape brought against black GIs serving in the Pacific produced an avalanche of criticism of the army's racial practices from stateside observers. "The petitioners are innocent of the crime of rape," Marcantonio and Hastie complained, arguing that "there is no room in the United States Army for Scottsboro Cases."[41]

Thus, by the time black servicemen arrived at their newly assigned island posts at the end of 1944, they had discovered that the racial and sexual arrangements of the Deep South intersected with the rank prerogatives of the American military throughout the Pacific theater.[42] From Australia to Dutch New Guinea to the Philippine Islands, rumors of rampant interracial sexual activity and the paranoid efforts made by white officers and enlisted personnel to impose a racial color line in the Pacific sowed seeds of discontent among African American GIs stationed throughout the theater. As Philadelphia native Clifford Bell, a 23-year-old soldier serving in the Southwest Pacific, put it in a letter he wrote to his mother at the time, "I can understand the treatment that is received by us in the Southern States because it has been going on for years. But it seems just as bad over here. The white soldiers have told the Philippinos [sic] that we are no good and that we are slaves who will rape their women. As far as I can see my service in this man's army over here has been for white supremacy."[43]

Samuel Hill and the Transpacific Court of Public Opinion

Clifford Bell was not the only GI in the Southwest Pacific to experience the ways in which sexual politics underlined race relations in the theater. While serving in Dutch New Guinea during the winter of 1945, Samuel Hill witnessed its extraordinary power firsthand. After reverting to divisional control, Hill and his company had moved from Stirling Island to Hollandia, New Guinea, where they received orders to establish a security perimeter covering the supply routes along

Tanahmerah Bay. On 7 January 1945, the 28-year-old noncommissioned officer and another 93rd Division member found themselves embroiled in a politically charged incident when they decided to venture beyond the base headquarters. After searching for souvenirs along the shoreline during that afternoon, the two GIs had no sooner returned to the company area than they were ordered to report to a special company formation where they were identified and charged with sexually assaulting a woman who lived in a nearby village. Although military authorities dropped the charges against the other soldier, the division provost marshal, Major Hugo Goetz, brought charges against Hill for allegedly "forcing and feloniously, against her will, having carnal knowledge" of the native woman. Hill, who insisted on his innocence, faced a sentence of death if convicted.[44]

The court-martial convened on 7 March 1945 at Hollandia. Samuel Jarisetou, a Depapre villager, testified that, on the day of the incident, he had encountered Hill and three other GIs in two villages located near the bay while visiting his adoptive father and his family who lived in the area. Then Jarisetou pointed out that while two of the men left the village, Hill and another soldier stayed behind, claiming that they "were looking for a woman." He went on to contend that when his father resisted their demands, Hill drew a firearm and placed it near his head while the other serviceman forced one of the women to the ground and raped her. Meanwhile, the prosecution sought to bolster its case by producing a map depicting the trails in the area as a way of firmly establishing a link between the whereabouts of the two soldiers and the time that it would have taken them to negotiate the distance between the two villages. Finally, the prosecution produced Baroe Banondi, the alleged victim, who had pointed to ten men present at the hearing earlier as accessories to the crime. Under cross-examination, however, Banondi confessed to members of the court-martial hearing board that she could not recall ever meeting Hill even though she had identified him as the culprit two months earlier.

Banondi's conflicting testimony reflected the precarious notions that African American GIs in the division and South Pacific Islanders held vis-à-vis each other and how their understandings of each other informed their initial encounters throughout the theater. On the one hand, the views that black GIs held of South Pacific natives were shaped by discourse on South Pacific civilization that was prominent in black newspapers during the period.[45] During the early stages of the war, the African American press tended to describe Fijians, New Guineans, and other Pacific islanders as "Fussy-Wuzzies" and "headhunters."[46] And more often than not, these stereotypical images were linked to the popular images of South Seas women depicted in Hollywood films like *South of Tahiti* that were released just prior to the division's arrival in the area.[47] While stationed in New Guinea, the division personnel couldn't help but draw upon these images while meeting the island women in the area. For example, after making contact with the native population that spring, Cecil Davis, an officer with a company in the 368th Infantry, wrote home to a distant relative, "As we walked through the streets of the village, I first saw the female of the species—not one, but many of them, peeping at us from doors, windows, and from behind huts." Davis went on to add, "The women who had gone back to their jobs, were clad only in a red cloth made to resemble a skirt and worn very low on the hips. They were not as handsome as the men."[48] On the other hand, while it is difficult to pinpoint with precision the images that Pacific islanders held of American GIs, the scant evidence of their impressions of the black American GIs they encountered during this period reflects deep-seated feelings of alienation and cultural misunderstanding. For example, Peter Lait, who was 8 years old when he lived in the nearby village of Tadis, New Guinea, during the war, recalled years later, "There were some black American soldiers, probably not Papua New Guineans. They were with the white Americans. And when the Americans came, they caused confusion among us."[49]

Witnesses called to the stand during Samuel Hill's court-martial hearing presented contradictory versions of the incident. As doubts about Hill's guilt mounted, eyewitnesses for the defense focused on two main issues: Hill's whereabouts and the time frame in which the incident had taken place. Private Alford Edwards, a member of the company's second squad, testified that he had accompanied Hill to an oil dump near Tanamerah Bay that morning and that the young sergeant had been with him when the alleged incident had taken place. Sergeant Jackson Meadows, the second squad commander, added that he saw the Detroit, Michigan, native that morning but did not see him again until one-thirty that afternoon. Private Sammie Oglesby told the board that he had seen Hill and Edwards standing along the waterfront at the very moment the shots rang out and that Hill was unarmed. Shortly afterward, he recalled, he was approached by Samuel Jarisetou and asked for the names of the two soldiers, to which he responded "Frankenstein" and "Count Basil." But most important, Oglesby, along with other servicemen called to the witness stand, recalled seeing Hill in the company area between one and two-thirty that afternoon, refuting the prosecution's contention that he had returned to the encampment much later.[50]

Hill's senior officers, serving as witnesses for the defense, also refuted the evidence presented by the prosecution. For instance, the prosecution had used tire tracks from a jeep to claim that Hill was present at the village during the incident. However, Lieutenant Everett M. Porter, Company L's executive officer, testified that both of the vehicles that were assigned to the unit were present and accounted for throughout the day in question. In addition, Captain William P. Hurd, his superior officer, took the stand on behalf of his NCO, pointing up the efficiency ratings that showed Hill to be an exemplary soldier. The lack of evidence in the case and Hill's distinguished service record made very little difference, however. On a secret written ballot, three-fourths of the all-white court-martial board found the noncommissioned officer guilty and sentenced him to death within two days.[51]

The controversy surrounding Hill's trial and the speedy conviction reached by top-ranking officers in New Guinea gripped the attention of division members stationed throughout the Southwest Pacific area. While attending the proceedings, Captain Matthew Lowe, the regiment's ranking chaplain, and Captain S. McMaster Kerr, the base stockade chaplain, both noted the fault-ridden process that resulted in Hill's conviction. Prior to the hearing, the black and white men of the cloth met the defendant and began raising objections about the racial constitution of officers appointed to the board. In early February, Lowe wrote a letter to 93rd Infantry Division commander, Major General Harry Johnson, requesting that he appoint black officers to the General Court. "There are many known instances in the history of American Civil Courts in which decisions involving Negroes have been revoked and new trials ordered by higher courts on the grounds that possible prejudice existed since no Negroes were chosen to sit on the jury trying the case," Lowe argued. And although Kerr did not "personally question the integrity of any White Officer who might be chosen to constitute the court," he informed the commanding general that "Sergeant Hill feels there is a strong possibility of prejudice."[52] Nevertheless, the requests made by the religious leaders were greeted with silence from the division's highest-ranking officer.

Why the division high command elected to take such a noncommittal stance remains unclear. A career officer with the Texas National Guard, Johnson had been selected by 6th Army commander Lieutenant General Walter Krueger to assume command of the division in August 1944 after leaving North Africa, where he led the recently disbanded 2nd Cavalry Division.[53] For the Southwest Pacific field commander, Johnson's assignment to the segregated unit was ideal, for the Houston native had long enjoyed a reputation as a highly professional officer who stressed moderation on questions of race. But more important, Johnson had ably displayed the ability to lead African American troops, a talent that made him uniquely qualified in the eyes of his superiors for service in the Southwest Pacific theater area. "I've served with colored troops for many years and I think I know them as well as any white man ever could," Johnson once claimed.[54] Press correspondent Charles Loeb of the National Negro Press Association also admired the general and observed while touring Hollandia that "the men are crazy about the general. They'd go to hell for him."[55] However, critics argued that Johnson's reluctance to use his influence to eliminate racial prejudice in the units he led only aggravated the plight of the men who served under him.

After Hill's conviction and throughout his appeal of the case, Chaplains Kerr and Lowe conducted their own investigation into the case, upon which they discovered the patchwork aspects of the evidence presented by the prosecution, casting further doubt on the legitimacy of the whole trial. In the weeks following the trial, the two clergymen again wrote a joint letter to the 93rd commander, raising questions regarding the victim and the eyewitnesses who failed to identify Hill as the assailant during the trial. They also charged that while one of the prosecution's main witnesses claimed that he had seen Hill in the village that day, he was not present when the alleged act had taken place. They also pointed to the fact that a medical report, completed prior to the trial, found no physical evidence of rape in the case. Moreover, when the priests visited the stockade during the trial, two GIs approached them and confessed to committing all the actions attributed to Hill in the case except the actual rape.

After they failed to elicit an adequate response from the division high command, Lowe and Kerr sought assistance from the area Judge Advocate General's Office in Australia to plead their case. Pointing up the pervasive nature of racial prejudice in the military's prosecution of the case, the religious ministers told the assistant judge advocate general, "The hostility of the court was in evidence throughout the trial and the law members displayed a bias attitude toward the accused by frequently restricting the counsel in question and explanations." "The facts of the this case and trial will undoubtedly be brought to the attention of the American public and especially those organizations (White, Negro, and mixed) and individuals who are manifesting a deep interest in Negroes in the armed forces and particularly in the Ninety-third Infantry division," they warned.[56]

Even as the two chaplains spoke, word of Hill's case and the plight of the 93rd Infantry Division members serving in the Netherlands East Indies area raced across the Pacific Ocean into the homes of black service families and neighborhoods, producing a rippling effect throughout the African American community. While confined to the area stockade, Hill dispatched a letter through Chaplain Lowe to his brother Theodore and sister Grace Davis, informing them of his predicament. He then went on to ask them to request a transcript of his court-martial hearing from the Judge Advocate General's Office in Washington, D.C., and upon receiving the copies, to forward them on to the NAACP national headquarters. "I'm writing this letter so that you know that I'm still overseas and in a great deal of trouble," Hill told his siblings.[57] As an active member in the local Detroit branch, Theodore turned first to the NAACP national office to seek his brother's release. The 36-year-old Detroit machinist ended his letter by stating emphatically, "I am a member of the NAACP. Can you help us?"[58]

As the controversy surrounding Hill's arrest, trial, and incarceration began to surface, local NAACP branches in towns and cities across the United States mobilized into action. In Hill's hometown of Detroit, branch members launched a vigorous campaign on his behalf, staging rallies and speaking engagements at the Exhor Temple.[59] In the District of Columbia, more than three hundred members representing the local NAACP branch and an array of local church, civic, political, and fraternal organizations held a series of discussions before drafting a resolution calling for an army inquiry into the number of court-martial proceedings brought against black soldiers in the Pacific. In addition, conferees drafted a petition demanding that Congress pass permanent fair employment practices legislation. Among the 93rd Infantry Division relatives and friends who attended the meetings were Thomasina Johnson, Pauline Redmond Coggs, Minnie Wrenn, and Mordecai Johnson.[60] And in Philadelphia, more than two hundred people packed St. Matthews Church, where they listened to Walter White and other NAACP officials discuss Hill's case and the Pacific theater activities of soldiers who were members of their congregation. After the two-hour session, they adopted a resolution demanding that the War Department investigate the merits of the case.[61]

Once the local calls for Hill's clemency quickened, members of the national office of the NAACP and the black press followed suit. Immediately upon returning from the Pacific in early April, NAACP executive secretary Walter White met with Undersecretary of War Robert P. Patterson. Among the items the two men discussed were Samuel Hill and the disproportionate numbers of cases brought against black servicemen stationed in the Southwest Pacific.[62] And former 93rd Division serviceman and assistant special counsel Franklin H. Williams and other officials at the national NAACP headquarters in New York collected sworn statements from Chaplains Lowe and Kerr that they attached to a brief filed with the secretary of war, demanding clemency on Hill's behalf. "It is our belief that Samuel Hill is innocent of the crime of which he has been convicted and we hope that the enclosed material will be given full and favorable consideration by the Clemency board when his case comes before that board for review," Williams stated.[63]

Hill's case combined with the public's growing awareness of African American contribution in the Southwest Pacific may have bolstered the number of NAACP memberships among division servicemen. Within the unit, memberships grew slowly. In February 1944, only 93 troops joined the NAACP.[64] But between November of that year and March 1945, the number of membership applications filed by black division soldiers and officers stationed throughout the Southwest Pacific jumped from 3,600 to well over 5,000.[65] Primary recruiters during the membership drives included African American clergy led by Oscar Holder, Andrew Johnson, Everett Hewlett, John Bowman, and Harlee Little, most of whom ministered to the men at the regimental level.[66] Of the growing number of division personnel flocking to the organization, executive secretary Walter White remarked after returning from the Pacific, "We are going to have a great reservoir of support in the postwar years from the men out there who seem to be deeply grateful for our interest in their welfare."[67]

As Samuel Hill's case attests, the actions taken by spokespeople and organizations within the African American community to safeguard the interests of black division servicemen stationed throughout the Southwest Pacific were prompted by the GIs' abilities to resist and transcend the racial prejudice of and mistreatment by the military authorities in the theater and their close relationships with their families and communities. Once African Americans stateside learned of the travails faced by black uniformed personnel in the Pacific, they often decided to take active roles, demanding that army authorities remedy the abuses that black soldiers faced in the region. The potential for a relationship between black military families and the black elite was partly based on the ability of prominent organizations and leaders to mobilize their resources in ways that assisted the families' efforts. Although both parties expressed grave concern over the well-being of black division members, the events in the Southwest Pacific would present new challenges to that relationship. Indeed, as the division progressed toward the Philippines, the fluid conditions of the Asian-Pacific war and the continuous physical and psychological strain of fighting in the island jungles would soon precipitate strategies and tactics to which traditional modes of protest would hardly apply.

Race across the Southwest Pacific

In April 1945, the 93rd Infantry Division reassembled at Morotai Island. After arriving on the island's forward area, the unit relieved the U.S. 31st Infantry Division as the principal force in the area. The division's mission was to operate the supply points as the chief administrative army organization in the area. Yet as soon as 93rd servicemen reported to the area, they found themselves working feverishly alongside the Australian dock crews, most of whom had been overwhelmed by the backlogged supplies and equipment waiting to be shipped to Allied troops staging for the Australian invasion of Borneo. Within a two-month period, the men in the division had unloaded nearly 320,000 tons of supplies and equipment and had managed to obtain an average tonnage output per hatch per man higher than that of any other organization in the theater.[68] For their efforts, members of the division received a special commendation from 8th Army Headquarters in July 1945.[69]

In the minds of most 93rd Division soldiers, their survival strategies and job performances were inextricably tied together. As he inspected the unit in May 1945, medical officer Captain Robert Bennett noted: "Despite their adversities, they are doing their utmost by their accomplishments to continue to prove that they are the best outfit from every point in this theater. Despite the types of missions assigned to them, they have performed each time in a superior manner, as evidenced by the commendations that have piled high upon them. Yet they continue to be by-passed and unnoticed."[70] Likewise, Captain George Leighton witnessed the important duties carried out by black servicemen in the Moluccas. While visiting bases where division members were stationed, he remarked, "I have seen Negro engineers building roads over which important supplies have gone from depot to ships. I have seen Negro quartermaster battalions organize and operate depots that supplied frontline troops in contact with the enemy thousand miles away. But I have also seen Negro stevedores with units in Finschafen with sweat on their faces and their rifles nearby to fight off the Japs. With numerous Negro troops performing work in this manner, that would make any group proud."[71]

As they served in these administrative functions, many black 93rd GIs encountered racism in the Southwest Pacific theater. Some of the incidents occurred between black and white GIs, and they often nearly came to blows. For example, upon landing at the southernmost tip of Morotai in April 1945, several members of the 369th Infantry clashed with military policemen of the 31st Infantry Division after they were physically and verbally assaulted while visiting a nearby hospital. Only after the 93rd Division's commanding officer replaced the all-white military policemen with those from his unit and the 31st Division departed for the invasion of the Philippines was the deadly situation diffused.[72]

This was not the last time that the two organizations would exchange unpleasantries, however. Later that year, a shootout nearly occurred between soldiers in the 93rd's 368th Infantry Regiment and members of the 31st Division after twenty black GIs had attempted to employ several Filipino women as domestic servants. When it was all over, the commanding generals of both divisions reprimanded the officers and NCOs who were involved, but they issued a directive restricting only the black soldiers from using the recreation areas.[73] John Howard had vivid memories of the 31st Division: "Many of these soldiers were from the Deep South and brought to their experience their built-in feelings about black people. They tried to avoid our unit as much as possible."[74] Julius Becton expressed a somewhat different view: "The fact that the 93rd Division and the 31st Division shared several islands showed a lack of sensitivity to the racial issue by General MacArthur and his commanders."[75] Conversely, theater censors quoted an unnamed officer with the 31st Division who wrote home describing the roles that the National Guard outfit had envisioned for themselves and where they stood in relation to all-black units stationed throughout the area at the time: "This division is more or less famed for its ability to 'handle' the niggers. Race hatred is actually encouraged by both Battalion and Regimental Commanders."[76]

Even so, some black 93rd GIs and their white comrades developed a better appreciation of each other after making close contact on occasion. For example, while guarding two Japanese officers in June 1945, Edward Quinn, a white U.S. 7th Division infantryman from Rome, New York, and John Simpson, a soldier from Birmingham, Alabama, flew to Tacloban, Leyte, where they spent three days with members of the 369th Infantry. Quinn recalled, "We were hosted by 369th Infantry Regiment that was based north of Puerto Princess. Our prisoners were also guarded by a squad from the U.S. 93rd Infantry Division. We shared the tents, food, and lives of the men of the 93rd and were treated royally. I remember they even shared their beer rations with us. The soldier who accompanied me was out of his element, however, because he later told me that he only thought of colored people as 'niggers.' Although this experience only lasted three or four days, it left me with a favorable, lasting impression about the men of the Ninety-third Division."[77]

The hopes of interracial cooperation that some black division members and white servicemen shared while serving together in the Pacific were soon dashed by racial hatred spewed by policymakers back in Washington, D.C., however. On 29 June 1945, Mississippi congressman James O. Eastland stood on the Senate floor and delivered a blistering speech, disparaging the performance of black troops in Europe. Questioning the suitability of permanent fair employment practices legislation, the junior senator from the Magnolia State argued that the agency granted an unfair advantage to returning black soldiers, who in his estimation were "an utter and dismal failure in combat in Europe." Citing the activities of troops serving with the U.S. 92nd Infantry Division in Italy, Eastland claimed, "The soldiers had no initiative, no sense of responsibility, very low intelligence, and were a failure. . . . It was a mistake to send them to Europe, they should be returned from Europe and sent to the Pacific, where there are races of color. . . . Why are we being asked to set an unfair preference against the white soldier for the benefit of the returning Negro veteran, solely because he is a member of a minority group which sells its votes to the highest bidder in political campaigns?" Eastland queried.[78]

The Mississippi statesman soon had an answer to his question. Two weeks later, Undersecretary of War Robert Patterson vehemently denied Eastland's charges against the 92nd Infantry Division during a press conference and claimed that the senator had misrepresented the views of the American commanders in Europe. Pointing to remarks made by generals Dwight D. Eisenhower, Douglas MacArthur, and Ira Eaker, Patterson went on to chronicle the favorable reports that the Inspector General's Office had received regarding the performance of black troops in European and Pacific theaters. "The statements of the commanders in the field do not support the conclusions drawn by Senator Eastland," he argued.[79]

In the Southwest Pacific, officers of the 93rd Division fashioned their own collective response to the Mississippi congressman. A few weeks after Eastland made his remarks, Lieutenant Edward D. Smith-Green and other officers were flabbergasted when they received a copy of the *Pittsburgh Courier* and read the senator's diatribe against black servicemen. Angry and embittered, the 25-year-old Brooklyn, New York, native and fifteen other officers dashed off an open letter to the *Courier*, arguing that, "as appointed leaders of men, the plight and embarrassment of our soldier, all soldiers, who read such speeches, concerns us. Out here we have learned to work together, play together, fight and suffer together—not as white or Negro soldiers—just soldiers. White soldiers, Negro soldiers, soldiers of Jewish, Italian, German, and Japanese extraction, soldiers of every race, color, and creed who are real Americans will make their combined will quite evident to all concerned when they can once more speak and act for themselves." "With the exception of our families, no one who has not been in this inferno is qualified to speak a word against us," they insisted.[80]

Meanwhile, service families in the United States translated Green's call into action. About three weeks after Eastland's speech, 93rd Division officer Judson Williams's mother, Marie, decided to act on behalf of her son and others who wore the nation's uniform. In late July, the Philadelphia native wrote the Mississippi senator, demanding that he apologize for his impugning statements regarding the performance of black servicemen in the war. A few days later, the elderly black woman, along with twenty-five hundred division relatives from the New Jersey cities of Patterson, Princeton, and Newark, spearheaded a letter-writing campaign, demanding that the army chief of staff publicly repudiate Senator Eastland's attack on the integrity of African Americans serving in Europe and Asia. "The senator's unwarranted attacks hit colored soldiers fighting at the battlefront below the belt," she argued. When later asked about her actions, Williams replied, "I keep up with the news and follow important commentators. What I don't agree with, I try to take in stride but I could not take Senator Eastland's unfair, untruthful, and hateful attack."[81]

By the end of July, division troops had barely reported to duty in the Southwest Pacific when they discovered that the danger of serving on Morotai was heightened considerably by the threat that the remaining 500 Japanese troops on the island and 35,000 enemy forces on nearby Halmahera posed to its main perimeter. To counter the possibility of enemy reinforcement, 93rd Division patrols were sent out daily to stop all Japanese island movement during the spring and summer months of 1945. Negotiating the lush green jungle in the Libano and Tijoe areas, squad patrols led by Glen Allen, Arnett Hartsfield, John Sarazen, and George Shuffer engaged in extensive operations between the Radja and Bobo rivers.

In early August, a nine-man patrol led by Stanley Nakanishi and Alfonzia Dillon maneuvered along the Tijoe River, where they encountered and captured Colonel Muisu Ouchi, commander of all Japanese troops on Morotai and the highest-ranking Japanese officer captured during the war. Around the same time, elements of 369th Infantry Regiment's Company L advanced along the tributaries of the Libano River, where they drew fierce gunfire from a large enemy command post. After subduing the threat, they captured several members of Ouchi's high command.[82] After the elements of the division moved on to the Jolo area of the Philippine Islands during the closing phases of the war, troops of the 368th Infantry under the command of Alamanca Williams of Crawfordville, Indiana, and Ricardo Santioga of New York City endured numerous enemy attacks as they conducted steady reconnaissance of Japanese positions. Negotiating the nearly impenetrable jungles and mountainous terrain, division troops worked diligently to drive out and destroy enemy forces commanded by Major General Tetsuzo Suzuki. Among those who participated in the action were William Ray, Dunbar Gibson, Robert McDaniel, John Blalark, John Coghlan, Raymond Jenkins, and James Whittico.[83]

Meanwhile, Lieutenant Wallace Gant and GIs attached to the 25th Infantry and the 369th Infantry had just completed their patrolling missions on Morotai and Jolo when they learned that hostilities had ceased on 10 August.[84] Expressing a deep sense of relief, Nelson Peery may have voiced what was on the mind of many of the men when he wrote from the front at end of the war: "Our job has been to hold the island, theirs to retake it. It's really nasty business hunting them down like dogs and killing them but of course they have also killed some of us. But most of all we paid an exceedingly small price of our victory."[85] According to Edwin Lee, "It was sort of like a cops and robbers comedy because there must have been fifteen thousand men in our division and we were holding the perimeter, so to speak."[86] Julius Becton, a young lieutenant from Pennsylvania, remembered: "For me, the hardest part about patrolling was during the clean up operations when we tried to convince the Japanese in the hills that the war was over."[87] By the end of the fall of 1945, the men who had survived the jungle patrols of Bougainville and Morotai began to process and evacuate all Japanese prisoners of war while division members in the 368th were held responsible for supply points at Agusan, Davao, and Zamboanga.[88]

Yet while division troops began to cast their eyes homeward, they found themselves at the heart of several demobilization issues. As the war began to wind down in Europe in September 1944, the War Department issued a statement outlining the army's plan for the redeployment and demobilization of military personnel after the defeat of Germany. Under its plan, service forces were to be promptly transported from Europe to the Pacific, and enlisted personnel received credit for the number of months served since 1940, the number of months served overseas, battle participation record, and number of dependent children. Each GI with an initial adjusted service rating score of at least 85 was eligible for discharge.[89] One's eligibility for discharge, however, was contingent upon whether replacements from Europe could be obtained and the availability of shipping in the theater of operations. These factors had a tremendous impact on the War Department's demobilization plans, for the discharge rate of African American servicemen in the segregated units failed approach that in white outfits owing to the overwhelming number of troops in noncombatant roles and the army's difficulties in procuring replacements for them. After the German collapse in Europe five months later, for instance, less than 1 percent of the three hundred thousand troops qualified to return home from the Pacific theater came from all-black outfits.[90]

As the contradictions in the army's discharge policies became more apparent, prominent black leaders quickly pointed out the discriminatory aspects of the point system as they railed against the War Department's demobilization policies. In May 1945, Edgar Brown, director of the National Negro Council, argued that the "point system represented the rankest kind of discrimination against Negro troops because most were segregated in work and non-combat units and could not receive points for combat work." "Negroes in overseas armies will be last to return home," Brown predicted.[91] A month later, Walter White wrote a letter to the War Department proposing that a special point system be installed for the discharge of black service troops. Criticizing the army's partial demobilization plans, the NAACP executive secretary declared that "a grave injustice is being inflicted on these men who, in most instances, have absolutely no control over their being assigned to service duty which deprives them opportunities for combat. As a result, they will return to the United States or be discharged from the army at a much later date than white soldiers," White claimed. Throughout much of the spring and summer of 1945, black newspapers, notably the *Michigan Chronicle,* the *Houston Informer and Texas Freeman,* the *Philadelphia Tribune,* the *Pittsburgh Courier,* and the *New York Amsterdam News* carried editorials castigating the army's plan for partial demobilization, and their reporters penned feature articles discussing the fairness and logic of the point system.[92]

While the debate over the demobilization of black troops heated up in the United States, the soldiers of the U.S. 93rd Division expressed their own thoughts about returning stateside. In the words of one division soldier, "We seemed stuck in the Pacific theater. The seesaw effect of preparing to unload and stack shipments of supplies and clear jungles with no possible chance of going home had a negative effect on us. Our morale, which was already low, was disintegrating into anger and resentment."[93] After learning of the army's readjustment policy while stationed in the Pacific, 24-year-old Private Robert Johnson wrote home to his mother in Louisiana, "It is unfair to us that we are not able to earn discharge credits with combat stars—five points each—because we are non-combat duty. I tell you mother, there shall be no world peace until the white man sees the fact that Negroes and all darker races are human beings too. Why don't they send us home or treat us like human beings?"[94] In a similar vein, Houston native Charles C. Qualls, an officer with the division, offered the following remarks in a letter home at the time: "In an officers' meeting today, the die was cast. The white officers of the division have been transferred to the Thirty-first (Dixie Division) manned by men from Alabama, Mississippi, and Georgia, in order to get them home. Colored officers will be left behind, even though many of us have 90 or more points because if we travel with a white outfit there may be friction."[95]

The friction that Qualls mentioned in his correspondence reflected the pressures of the Asia-Pacific war. In late 1945, the southern Philippine Islands had become a racial pressure cooker. Black and white servicemen quarreled over money, liquor, and—above all else—women. As *Baltimore Afro-American* correspondent Julius Merritt noted in early 1946, sexual tension lay at the heart of the fracases between black and white servicemen in Manila. Merritt wrote that "not infrequently frictions and fistic brawls over women have occurred in the streets and quite often they have marred town social functions where white and colored soldiers have come together for a good time."[96]

The color line existed throughout the area. Along the pathways and sidewalks of southern Philippine island towns and cities, the men encountered USO clubs and YMCA buildings signs designating "colored" and "white" patrons and segregated swimming pools. American Red Cross installations located near the work and lodging areas were segregated.[97] The situation that black division members faced in Manila elicited the following response from a GI: "There was a dance to which we were all invited, white and Negro alike. However, when we asked Filipino girls to dance, a white captain was standing nearby and said in a very loud voice, 'you niggers are not going to dance with the Filipino girls.' This is one of the causes of constant friction between white and Negro men in the armed forces. We are all fighting together for the preservation of all that we know and love, but behind the scenes, the Negro is still the goat so far as white America is concerned."[98]

To make matters worse, as division troops moved through the remote areas of the southern Philippine Islands, they learned that they were the subjects of vicious racist notions perpetuated by white enlisted men and officers. Black men, it was suggested over and over again, were poor fighters, exhibited apelike qualities, and possessed tails.[99] As one soldier recalled, "Stories like that were told by white soldiers to render us in the sight of others as an inferior group. We had to remember, of course, that many of the innocent believers had never seen a Negro unit until we arrived in the area. Instead of being discouraged, I, myself, and other soldiers in the unit became strongly filled with the ambition to prove to the white race that it took more than consistent tales to block our fight against racial prejudice and discrimination."[100] Likewise, in a letter to his minister back home, Roosevelt Jones, a soldier assigned to the division, lamented the way race and rumor structured relations between black servicemen and Leyte populations living in the battle zone areas: "We are not allowed to even the leave the area. The white soldiers are permitted to do anything. We have to do all of the dirty work, and our food is different from that served to white troops. And worst of all, the white officers and soldiers are teaching the people in the Philippines that the Negro soldier has a tail like a dog that comes out at night and goes back in during the day." "I hope that you will publish this letter so our families can see how much trouble we are catching over here," the Washington, D.C., resident exclaimed.[101]

At the receiving end of Jones's plea was a clergyman of tremendous consequence. A minister at Washington, D.C.'s Mount Carmel Baptist Church, the Reverend William Jernagin received an invitation from Secretary of War Henry Stimson through the chief of chaplains in November 1944 to visit servicemen fighting on the battle fronts of the Pacific area as a representative of the Fraternal Council of Negro Churches in America. After accepting Stimson's request and overcoming bureaucratic red tape, the venerable 76-year-old church leader, along with an army chaplain, left the United States on 1 October aboard a commercial airplane bound for Honolulu. After stopping briefly in the Hawaiian Islands, the two men continued on to Manila, where Jernagin met with port battalion troops and chaplains ministering to the needs of servicemen stationed in the area.

During his visit in the Southwest Pacific, the pastor traveled to Tacloban, Leyte, and DelMonte, Mindanao, where he met with the enlisted men and officers of the 93rd Infantry Division. During his brief stay, Jernagin was struck by the low morale of the division and the frustrations that servicemen expressed over the discriminatory practices they encountered as well as the promotion and transfer policies within the unit. Observing the differences between the men of the all-black unit and troops of the 31st Division, which was also stationed on the island, he noted, "On this island there was a division of white troops for which there was a distinct command operating differently from that of the 93rd Division. This white division had had no more overseas duty than the 93rd but at the time of my visit they were loading for the return trip home while the Negro outfit was waiting for the shipping pressure to be relieved so that they could come home." When Jernagin later asked division commander General Leonard Boyd about the division's predicament, he responded, "The Thirty-first was a Dixie Division and it was not possible to send Negro officers back in command of White troops." Witnessing the dispirited attitudes expressed by division members, Jernagin tried to placate the GIs by arguing that "their country has been proud of their work as soldiers during this war" and that the nation "must likewise be proud of them as citizens during the peace." But upon leaving the division command post the next day, the church leader recalled "feeling a sense of sadness for the Negro division seemingly so defeated." "I knew that there was and is only one answer. This world must become a Brotherhood."[102]

Jernagin's remarks to the troops rang hollow for division troops who listened to him that day, however. Of Jernagin's experiences in the Philippines, Sergeant Lee Merriwether noted, "It appears that in a large measure our present leadership has failed. I'm sure that they can be replaced with new and young blood; individuals who are more qualified who will sacrifice themselves to reach the goal that we all so desire."[103] However, a Houston native was more caustic in his assessment of the religious sage. In a letter to the editor of his hometown newspaper in November 1945, he observed, "Now I see that we can not beat army Jim Crow. Dr. Jernajan [*sic*] spoke to the men of the regiment yesterday and to sum up his speech in a few words you get this statement: 'Remember you are Negroes and stay in your place when you return home.'" Reflecting on the public clamor for the repatriation of troops from the Pacific, the soldier went on to state, "We, too, are soldiers and we feel that our plight should be a matter for the attention of the people of our race. Our wives, sweethearts, parents and friends can aid us by writing the War Department, NAACP, Urban League, congressmen, CIO and other organizations."[104]

Soon the potentially explosive situation gave way to a season of violence. In the suburbs of Manila, soldiers with the 369th Infantry exchanged blows with white MPs when a black soldier was shot and killed by a white guard at the quartermaster depot after he was accused of stealing a bundle of clothing. The incident ended with black MPs restoring order in the city and the troops receiving orders from division staff headquarters to return to their company compound.[105] While laboring along the docks of Tacloban, Leyte, division members clashed with white MPs on 11 August after ten soldiers were physically assaulted by groups of white GIs.[106]

On 1 September *Pittsburgh Courier* war correspondent William "Billy" Rowe and Philippines Red Cross director James Smith were touring a section of Manila where a series of clashes had just taken place between black and white servicemen when three MPs approached them and demanded that they produce identification. After they protested against the officers' requests, the military policemen drew their firearms and pointed them toward the pair before firing a round of shots in their direction. Luckily, Rowe and Smith escaped unharmed, but the incident left an indelible impression in the minds of the two men. "The acts committed against us were done solely because some members of our race and military police had indulged in a melee, causing one or more persons to lose their lives. All attempts to settle our differences were lost with the heated desire of those we encountered attempting to solve a situation outside of the law," Smith observed.[107] Indeed, the situation between black division troops and white soldiers in the area was so volatile that the 93rd Division commander commented, "[The] recent instances of racial disorders give me grave concern as to the adequacy of preparations which have been made to prevent such incidents." "The commanding officer of the staging area must maintain adequate supervision over all troop units at all times," he stated.[108]

Meanwhile, the near riots sparked renewed calls for the shipment of black troops from the Pacific to the United States. In Washington, reports on the Tacloban incident were filtered through the chief of the War Department's Intelligence and Security Division to General Marshall, Assistant Secretary of War John McCloy, transportation chief Major General Charles Gross, and civilian aide Truman Gibson.[109] After receiving the report, Gibson warned Secretary McCloy, "The priority of return for colored troops to the United States has to be greatly advanced."[110] Shortly afterward, assistant personnel chief of staff Major General S. G. Henry and assistant operations chief of staff Major General I. H. Edwards appeared before the Military Affairs Committee; they discussed a range of issues, from the Intelligence and Security Division's findings regarding the racial situation among black troops stationed in the Pacific to various aspects of the War Department's partial demobilization plan. During the opening stages of their discussion, congressmen heard the two men state that there had been a change in War Department policy in that the critical scores of enlisted personnel and officers in the Pacific would be reduced from 85 to 80. "These scores will be further reduced as fast as practicable," they advised.[111]

Around the same time, the Office of the Chief of Transportation made plans for the repatriation of black troops. In early September, representatives of the chief of transportation met with sixty army port commanders in San Francisco. Among the chief topics discussed was the racial situation among black troops in the Philippines, the problem of shipping capacity, and the scheduling, reporting, and employment of troop transports. After two days of discussions, conferees resolved to convert 210 Liberty ships into troop transport fleets, of which 27 were to be used to repatriate army personnel stationed at bases throughout the Pacific. Among those converted to make the trip to the Southwest Pacific were the USAT *David Shanks* and the USS *Tailfair Stockton,* whose hulls would be used to transport members of the U.S. 93rd Infantry Division home.[112]

The Journey Home

In January 1946, many of the 93rd servicemen with enough points to be discharged from the service prepared to board ships heading to redeployment camps located at Agusan, Mindanao, and Tacloban, Leyte, where they were processed for the final trip home. As they trudged along the various gangplanks to their debarkation points where they boarded the USAT *David Shanks* and the USS *Tailfair Stockton,* one can only imagine what must have occupied their thoughts. Many of them who had entered the army at Fort Huachuca as teenagers from all parts of the country now returned home as seasoned war veterans with a better sense of themselves and American society. Although all were relieved that the ordeal of war was finally over and yearned for the comfort of home, some pondered the ways in which their lives were altered. "For four years I had been molded by the army and the war. Socially disoriented, and as unsure of civilian life as I had been of army life four years before, I was going back to try and weave 1946 to 1942," Nelson Peery recalled.[113] Edwin Lee expressed similar sentiments: "When I boarded that troop transport ship, I experienced a number of emotions; exhilaration that we were going home but a sense of bewilderment because I didn't know how my family was going to receive me after all that time."[114] Frank Little noted, "I tried to adjust myself to be comfortable anywhere without being a foreigner, but going home was perhaps the strangest feeling of all because we had been through so much."[115]

But many of them realized that, despite the war, Jim Crow racism and discrimination in American society remained unchanged and a new battle would soon begin. One soldier wrote home while aboard the *David Shanks,* "Ma, I have been through a lot with this war for freedom and all and I am ready to claim what's mine. There are some things that I will see stopped when I get home."[116] Perhaps Chaplain Charles Watkins summed up what was on the minds of many of the soldiers when he told the men of the 369th Infantry, "Men, we have finished our course. The men of the 369th lived and fought like soldiers but the fight is not over. Don't be satisfied with the way things were. Don't ever let anyone ever again tell you that you are inferior because you are black. We fought on the side of the Lord. Don't desert Him when you get home."[117]

Meanwhile, back in the United States, one division soldier was beginning to realize that the battles that black GIs had waged to secure freedom had taken a new turn. After leaving the U.S. Disciplinary Barracks in Kentucky, Samuel Hill reentered the army as an enlisted man reduced in rank. Assigned to the U.S. 24th Infantry Regiment, he served a short stint of duty in Japan before receiving a discharge in 1949. Shortly afterward, he returned to the United States and settled in Denver, Colorado, where he hoped to find work and resume his life. When Hill reported to his local Veterans Administration office, however, the former Detroit native was told that the in-between nature of his discharge made him ineligible for educational funding, employment preferences, unemployment compensation, and housing and small business loans under the GI Bill of Rights. After several fruitless months of appealing the Veterans Administration ruling in his case and searching for employment, he left Colorado and traveled to New York City, where he worked a series of temporary jobs until the late 1950s. It is at this point that Hill and his whereabouts disappear completely from the historical record. But just as Hill was negotiating his postwar travails, relatives associated with the division gave new meaning to his military service by requesting copies of his service record and petitioning the Veterans Administration to reexamine the nature of the discharge given to the former GI. In 1961, Hill's brother-in-law, William Hurd, wrote a letter to the judge advocate general in which he stated, "It is my firm belief that I have a legitimate interest in the general court-martial of Samuel Hill because the charge against him has had an adverse influence upon my family." Thus, for Hurd and other service family members, the reclamation and revision of the institutional memory surrounding Hill's wartime record served as a means to carve out a new sense of dignity and self-determination as well as to articulate aspirations for postwar freedoms that were now both immediate and non-negotiable.[118]

And it was from this collective sense of awkwardness and determined hope to realize real progress in American society that black 93rd GIs and their families began to prepare for the soldiers' journey home. While many of them were leaving the jurisdiction of the armed forces, the relationship between themselves, sectors of the African American community, and the federal government would now take a different turn, from one of wartime consent and conflict to one of postwar struggle and estrangement.

Epilogue

Black 93rd Division Veterans and Former Service Families after World War II

> It's a pity that he could live through World War II and not be able to return home to live within the boundaries of his own country with safety and security.
>
> *Georgia Penn, 1964*

> Our task is to refocus the attention of Negroes who have attained middle-class status on the problems of the impoverished and to develop a sense of responsibility toward creating better conditions for everyone.
>
> *Walter Greene, 1970*

In the 1956 major motion picture *High Society,* legendary Louis Armstrong and his orchestra perform at a wedding attended by characters played by Bing Crosby, Grace Kelly, and Frank Sinatra. At the beginning of the film, Armstrong and his fellow band members narrate the premise of the movie while traveling aboard a bus bound for Newport, Rhode Island. Later in the movie, at a dinner party for patrons of the wedding, host Bing Crosby introduces several members of Armstrong's band before settling on the prominent pianist, loudly proclaiming to the audience, "That is Mister Billy Kyle."[1]

William "Billy" Kyle's postwar story was as noteworthy as the melodic sounds that emanated from his piano. After returning to the United States at the end of the war as a veteran of the U.S. 93rd Infantry Division, the West Philadelphia classically trained pianist rejoined John Kirby's "Flow Gently Sweet Rhythm" sextet and worked with Sy Oliver before striking out on his own in 1952.[2] Along the way, Kyle worked with jazz luminaries such as Billie Holiday, Rex Stewart, Lionel Hamp-

ton, and Buck Clayton and performed in the Broadway musical *Guys and Dolls*.
After Kyle joined Louis Armstrong's All-Stars in 1952, his piano playing became
more unorthodox. In his keyboard progressions, he struck an uncanny balance
between short single-note solos and finely textured ensemble passages. And not
long afterward, Kyle's piano playing became a prominent part of Armstrong's band.[3]

In many ways, Kyle's piano playing in the MGM production paralleled the postwar experiences of former GIs who served in the all-black unit. Like Kyle, former
93rd Division members sought the solace of familiar surroundings, family members, and friends after the war. After enduring nearly two years of negotiating the
ports and jungles of the Pacific, they wished to reap the benefits of winning the
"War for Democracy." However, this was not to be. No sooner had they begun to
reappear in their old neighborhoods and communities than 93rd veterans and their
families found themselves fighting the vestiges of Jim Crow racism while being
swept up in the anticommunist hysteria and the civil rights urgency of the 1950s
and 1960s. Soon, the racial tenor of the times impelled many black World War II
veterans to fashion their own creative approaches to meet the vast political, economic, and social challenges present on the American domestic landscape.
Indeed, the dialectical themes of ensemble and dissonance structured the lives
of former servicemen like William "Billy" Kyle from the moment their troop transport ships docked at the ports of Camp Stoneman, California.

Home Front Receptions

In early February 1946, 649 black veterans of the 93rd Infantry Division who
sailed aboard the troop transport ship USAT *David Shanks* tramped down the gangplanks of the San Francisco Port of Embarkation, where they were greeted by a
crowd of excited relatives and friends.[4] The men were the last elements of the division to return home from the Pacific theater before the unit was inactivated later
that month.[5] Upon their arrival, the servicemen received orders to proceed to various disposition centers scattered throughout the country where most of them
turned in surplus clothing and equipment before being discharged from the army.
For many of these men, the return home produced a myriad of emotions as they
reminisced about how far they had come since their training at Fort Huachuca,
Arizona, and maneuvering exercises in the swamps of Louisiana and the desert
sands of California, not to mention their stint of duty on various islands throughout the Pacific. Yet as the soldiers ambled along the pier toward the musical sounds
and cheers emanating from well-wishing admirers, they couldn't help but contemplate their reentry into American civil society.

Most of the black division veterans returning home probably had an immediate experience similar to that of John Maupin. The 27-year-old dentist stepped down from the *David Shanks* into the loving arms of his wife, Elizabeth, whom he married just before being deployed overseas. Sharing precious moments of prayer, jubilation, and out-processing, the pair struck out eastward aboard a train steaming toward New York City, where they met with family members and friends to renew old acquaintances. Shortly afterward, John and Elizabeth bade their relatives farewell before arriving at their family home in White Plains.[6] Elsewhere, Everett Hewlett followed a similar pattern. When he arrived in the San Francisco Bay Area, the Pennsylvania church minister simply gathered up his meager belongings, collected his discharge papers, and rushed home to Harrisburg, where he was reunited with his wife, Mary, and their two children. A few days later, he journeyed to Richmond, Virginia, where he received handshakes, hugs, and kisses from his parishioners, whom he had left four years earlier.[7]

Meanwhile, in Washington, D.C., members of the 25th Infantry Regiment who saw action in the Southwest Pacific received an emotional welcome from district residents. The unit traveled en masse from California to the nation's capital, where they marched through the streets, basking in the outpouring of applause from the throng of onlookers who gathered along the city sidewalks.[8] And describing the heart-tugging reception he received when he appeared in doorway of his family home, a Minneapolis native recalled, "Mom, smiling with tears in her eyes, wiping her hands on the apron, came toward me. I embraced her. She seemed so small, weeping silently, her graying head against my shoulder. Her sailor was home from the seas. Her soldiers were home from the war. All her sons were home. It was a time for weeping. I was really home."[9]

Anxious to cement bonds established prior to their military service, quite a few former GIs rushed to the altar during the immediate postwar months. Washington, D.C., resident John D. Howard remembered, "As soon as I got home, I grabbed my future wife, Marguerite, and left for New York and married her."[10] Likewise, former division member William Fentress wasted no time in meeting Cynthia Milford for a wedding ceremony at St. Mary's Church in her hometown of Taylorville, Illinois. Immediately embarking on married life, the couple moved to Dallas, where he landed work as a machinist.[11] And former division chaplain Harlee Little walked out of a separation center in Columbia, South Carolina, onto a bus heading to Wadesboro, North Carolina. After spending some time in the sleepy little town, the 28-year-old minister married his longtime fiancée, Merriam Sanders, before a small group of family and friends. Shortly afterward, the pair moved to Charlotte, where he obtained employment as an instructor at Hood

Theological Seminary of Livingstone College and she taught in the public school system.[12]

Some former GIs, like Joseph Chretien, migrated across the country after making a commitment to marriage. Originally hailing from San Angelo, Texas, the former signal corps officer left the army in February for Los Angeles, where he met and married Lorain, Ohio, resident Margaret Julian. When faced with the life-altering decision of whether to return to the southwestern or midwestern region of the country, the two young adults elected to strike out in an entirely different direction, settling in the Pacific northwestern city of Seattle, Washington. Like others of their generation, the Chretiens hoped to build a lasting union in new surroundings.[13] The same could be said for Reuben Fraser. Shortly after leaving the army, he traveled to Fort Sheridan, Illinois, where he was reunited with Chicago resident Zola Lang, who had just recently arrived in the states after spending two years overseas as an Army Nurse Corps officer with the 168th Station Hospital in Liberia. Immediately upon entering wedlock, the pair moved to St. Louis, Missouri, before heading to Minneapolis, Minnesota, where he became a machinist in the local Dodge plant and she landed work as the head nurse practitioner in one of the city's largest hospital facilities.[14]

In some cases, however, the changes brought about by the war disrupted existing relationships. As historian Elaine Tyler May has noted, the war-induced restructuring of social relations in households and communities gave way to postwar friction between returning GIs and their wives.[15] Often behind the tensions in the partnerships lurked disappointment and deep-seated resentment. This was the case for former division physician and Los Angeles native Lincoln Shumate and his wife, Hazel. Before they were married in 1939, Hazel had aspired to become a newspaper columnist. But after the war, Lincoln complained that she was spending too much time away from home and that she was too "career minded." Unable to reconcile their differences, she sued for divorce, accusing the X-ray specialist of "extreme mental cruelty" in 1946. After the divorce was finalized, Hazel continued to pursue her career, becoming a freelance photographer while studying fashion design in Paris.[16]

After returning from the Pacific, Claude Ferebee expressed similar complaints about his wife Dorothy's pursuit of a career. Before the war, the former Howard University College of Dentistry instructor and his wife, a prominent instructor of obstetrics in the university's medical school, had planned to continue their joint work in the small health clinic that they had opened in the northwest section of Washington, D.C. But after his first few months at home, their relationship soured as Dorothy's practice expanded to meet the demands of her growing numbers of patients while his office visits declined. Of the tension-filled moments that shaped their postwar relationship, she later recalled, "He was becoming more and more resentful of everything I was doing as a woman. The fact that I became busier and had perhaps a larger group of patients didn't set too well with him. And for that reason, he became very unhappy and insisted that I give up my work. Of course, I wasn't going to do that."[17] After four years of trying to mend their differences, the estranged couple decided to go their separate ways in 1950, ending a nearly twenty-five-year marriage.[18]

After the disbandment of the division, the unit's veterans began to make the slow transition to civilian life. Quite a few moved quickly to take advantage of the benefits under the Servicemen's Readjustment Act. After being mustered out of the service in 1946, George Leighton returned to Harvard University and resumed his studies in civil and criminal law.[19] Likewise, Samuel Allen returned home and studied at New York's New School for Social Research for several years before heading to Paris to take courses at the Alliance Française and at the Sorbonne.[20] Others went into business for themselves. Upon his discharge from the army, for example, William Ray returned to Indianapolis, Indiana, where he opened a real estate office.[21] After being hospitalized for four months, Julius Thompson left the army to live with his family in North Carolina before moving on to Newark, New Jersey, to work in a General Motors plant. Shortly afterward, he left the plant and became a correctional officer at the Jamesburg Training School for Boys before opening a small tavern in East Orange, New Jersey.[22]

Yet some found the adjustment to civilian society to be quite difficult as they tried make some sense of their wartime activities. Much to their chagrin, many black 93rd veterans found that the social fabric of American society had changed very little from what it had been before they left. Some were put through a series of humiliations and assaults on their dignity from the moment they left their separation centers. For example, after being discharged from the army at Fort Dix, New Jersey, in March 1946, Julius Young returned to Wilmington, Delaware, where he resumed work in the Coca-Cola Company. There, Young soon discovered that even though he had fought for democratic principles in the army, racism in American society still persisted. He recalled: "I knew that things were not quite right out here, but I thought my boss (a comptroller from Georgia) and I were on pretty good terms when I was drafted into the service. But when I came home wearing an officer's uniform, he seemed to want to change and told me that I had gotten to be such a big guy in the army that he didn't think that I was going to come back to them. After several run-ins with him, I realized that things were never going to be the same, and I had to accept it." Disillusioned with the labor practices of the company, he promptly quit his job and attended an auto mechanics school while receiving benefits under the GI Bill before opening an auto body shop in 1948.[23]

Young's experience was not that unusual. Immediately upon their return stateside, black former GIs were harassed, beaten, and murdered with impunity by white civilians and police authorities. Isaac Woodward had been blinded by a South Carolina police chief while still in uniform; brothers and former GIs Charles and Alonzo Ferguson were shot to death by a local law enforcement official in Freeport, Long Island; and James Stephenson, a World War II veteran, was arrested and beaten mercilessly by police officers in Columbia, Tennessee. Massive unemployment in the auto, steel, and electronics industries and the defeat of permanent fair employment practice legislation left many civilians and former black servicemen jobless and embittered as the country began to demobilize the armed forces and accelerate its reconversion from wartime to peacetime production. Despite the passage of the Servicemen's Readjustment Act (GI Bill), thousands of black GIs had yet to realize its benefits. Existing veterans' organizations such as the American Legion and the Veterans of Foreign Wars refused memberships to black veterans in states like South Carolina, Georgia, Mississippi, and Louisiana, while segregating them in other states. Although returning African American war veterans and mainstream black political leaders became more militant, they faced numerous obstacles throughout much of the South as racist reactionaries employed numerous tactics to maintain the color line as well as to prevent African Americans from registering to vote. Internationally, the growing chasm between the Soviet Union and the United States and the mounting anticommunist hysteria by the end of 1946 spelled months of increasing government harassment and persecution and union expulsion for many black progressive organizations and leaders.

To make matters worse, white residents and law officials in cities like Chicago, Detroit, and Los Angeles rioted against black former GIs when they sought entry into previously all-white housing areas.[24] Indeed, the problems and inadequacies of the post–World War II world were so severe for black former servicemen that one Berkeley, California, native and former soldier made the following comment to his wife after he returned home in early 1946: "I just fought one war and now I face another. I'm not going to back down and I'll fight this one until the last."[25]

These words were spoken by DeWitt Buckingham, a former medical officer with the division. After leaving the army in early 1946, the Mississippi native and his wife, Mamie, elected to remain in the East Bay Area after he was appointed to the staff of the Kaiser Permanente and Herrick hospitals in Oakland. In Berkeley, the couple thought they had found the ideal setting when they discovered a house owned by a white optometrist in a maturing neighborhood. The pair had no sooner moved into their new home, however, than members of the Claremont Improvement Club, a local homeowners association, moved to evict them from the property they owned. Requesting that the doctor and his family relinquish their rights to the property, association officials brought legal action against the married couple, claiming that the agreement that they reached with the previous owner had violated an existing restrictive covenant that "forbade residence in the area of persons not of pure Caucasian blood." In the weeks and months that followed, tensions mounted as the Buckinghams had to endure die-hard white resistance in the form of both the legal challenges filed by lawyers representing the homeowners association and harassment from local residents who were active members of the organization.

Not all the residents approved of the discriminatory measures, however. White community members who were sympathetic to the plight of the young couple rallied to their cause. And on the roles played by white residents in the dispute, Buckingham commented at the time, "Many of my neighbors visited me and volunteered help to fight the suit. I was surprised yet gratified by their response and welcomed the organized effort they offered."[26] Two years later, the Buckinghams and their supporters realized an enormous victory when the district court of appeals overthrew a previous decision rendered by an Alameda County Superior Court judge that had permanently enjoined the family from occupying their home.[27]

Many servicemen, however, elected not to leave the army; after discovering that military life was so much to their liking, they made it a career. After the war, George Shuffer entered the U.S. Army Reserves and served with such distinction that he was rapidly promoted through the ranks to brigadier general; he received various assignments for the next thirty-five years before being appointed to the Pentagon staff office in 1967.[28] In a similar fashion, Oscar Holder remained active in military service and served as an instructor at the U.S. Army Chaplain School at Carlisle Barracks, Pennsylvania, for four years before entering the Army Reserves with the rank of colonel.[29] John Q. T. King left active duty in 1946 and spent the remainder of his military service in the Army Reserves, eventually earning the rank of major general before retiring in 1983.[30] Benjamin Hunton served as an instructor at Fort Benning's Infantry School in Georgia for three years before moving on to train cadets at Howard University. Shortly afterward, he was released from active duty and served in the U.S. Army Reserves until he was recalled to active duty and appointed the commander of the U.S. 80th Infantry Division's 317th Infantry Regiment. Hunton advanced through the ranks until he reached the rank of major general and assumed the duties of commander of the U.S. 97th Reserve Command at Fort Meade in Maryland.[31]

Others extended their military service as enlisted personnel. After he returned stateside in November 1945, Asberry McGriff promptly reenlisted and remained in the army for nearly thirty-five years before retiring in 1967 at the enlisted grade of master sergeant.[32] Likewise, Frank Little returned stateside and reported to a training regiment at Camp Stoneman, California. There he handled and processed troops departing for overseas duty until he received orders assigning him to a quartermaster depot in Tokyo during the spring of 1948. During his stay in Japan, Little earned the Bronze Star Medal and a promotion to first sergeant for his distinguished service and witnessed the disbandment of the 25th Infantry Regiment as a result of President Harry S. Truman's 1948 executive order desegregating the armed forces. In 1952, he was transferred to Fort Lawton, Washington, where he served out the remainder of his military career before retiring and moving to nearby Seattle twelve years later.[33]

The Fighting Resumes

Meanwhile, the public debate over the 93rd Division's contribution to the worldwide conflict had begun. During the early months of 1945, Washington officials, led by Assistant Secretary of War John J. McCloy and civilian aide to the secretary of war Truman Gibson, held a series of conferences and meetings with members of the Advisory Committee on Special Troop Policies to discuss the employment of African Americans in the postwar military establishment. Among the chief topics that generated much discussion among committee members was the effectiveness of black officers and enlisted personnel in front-line combat. Following several months of exploring possible changes in army racial policies, members of the committee resolved to dispatch questionnaires to senior army commanders in Europe and Pacific, soliciting their views regarding the performances of the all-black 92nd and 93rd Infantry divisions serving in their respective theaters of operations.[34]

The negative responses presented by senior officers were hardly surprising, as many of them were rooted in racist notions of white supremacy and couched in stereotypical language stressing black cowardice and incompetence under fire. In fact, some officers, such as the 5th Army commander in Italy, Lieutenant General Lucian Truscott, and 92nd Infantry Division commander Major General Edward M. Almond, tried to link the division's perceived shortcomings to "the lack of dependability in Negro officers and enlisted men; especially is this the case in infantry combat." "My experience of three and one-half years in an attempt to create a combat infantry division comprised of only Negro units convinces me that it is a failure," General Almond concluded.[35] The statements made by Almond were echoed among the unit's staff and junior officers. For example, Major Thomas Saint John Arnold, the 92nd Infantry division's operations section chief, expressed his contempt for the fighting abilities of black troops, stating, "I don't trust Negroes. White officers who work with them have to work harder than with white troops." Perhaps even more revealing were the views expressed by the intelligence section commander when he employed the following baseball analogy to describe the successes and failures of black soldiers in the field at the time: "The Ninety-third Division was one out. The Second Cavalry Division was the second out; and now the Ninety-second Division is at bat with one strike already over on us."[36]

Not all the army's senior officers shared this view however. On the question of whether African Americans were good soldiers, Lieutenant Colonel John Sherman commented, "It was remarkable that would-be critics of the Negro soldier regularly ignore our other Negro division, the Ninety-third, which had done extraordinarily fine fighting in the Pacific islands, and whose record in World War I, is described in an official Army publication as 'one of the noblest of American arms.' From every continent and sea are returning the thousands of white officers who have developed a solid respect for their Negro troops and are determined that they receive in our country the rights, privileges, and opportunities which they have helped to preserve for the rest of us."

Throughout the spring of 1946 and well into the winter of the following year, popular, professional, and service newspapers, journals, and magazines were filled with stories that assessed the battlefield performances of the U.S. 93rd Division and other all-black units. Publications such as *Annals of the American Academy of Political and Social Science*, *Journal of Clinical Psychopathology*, *American Journal of Psychiatry*, *Survey Graphic*, and the *American Journal of Sociology* offered articles describing the shortcomings of black troops in the Pacific theater of operations.[37] In April 1946, *Harper's Magazine* carried a story by Warman Welliver, a company commander who served with the 92nd Infantry Division during the war, who argued that the "policy for colored troops has been an almost absolute failure." In addition to casting doubt on the fighting capabilities of his own infantry unit during the Fifth Army Offensive of 1945, Welliver blamed the black press for playing up the activities of the 93rd Infantry Division in the Pacific when the unit was "actually doing little more than mopping up in the wake of other divisions' conquest."[38] To the critics of black divisions in the war, Welliver's observations about the 92nd and 93rd Infantry divisions provided further confirmation of the ineptitude of black infantrymen and their questionable fighting abilities on the battlefield. Agreeing with Welliver's assessment of the conduct of soldiers in the field, *Harper's Magazine* carried an editorial penned by former 93rd artillery officer Oliver Allen, who claimed, "In the Bougainville campaign, the infantry of the Ninety-third suffered from many of the same difficulties experienced by the Ninety-second." "I do not see any reason to doubt the essential fact that the Army has had any more success using colored troops in the artillery and reconnaissance and armored units than in the infantry."[39]

Later that year, the *Infantry Journal* published a story by Robert Cocklin, a former artillery staff officer who served with the 93rd Division in the Southwest Pacific. In this article, titled "Report on the Negro Soldier," Cocklin downplayed racial discrimination and prejudice as the underlying reasons for the problems that black 93rd Division members faced in the Jim Crow army, stating that they had been an everyday reality for most of them prior to their entrance into the military. Like Welliver, he laid much of blame for the controversy surrounding the combat record of all-black units like the 93rd Infantry Division at the feet of the black press. But at the same time, Cocklin expressed a great deal of contempt for black soldiers, arguing, "Full success and maximum efficiency cannot be insured by the War Department alone. A grave responsibility rests with the colored soldier himself. By exemplary demeanor and a determined effort to do his level best, he can go a long way toward breaking down the prejudices that now exist."[40]

Quickly recognizing the threat posed by the denigrating remarks made by senior army commanders about African American service personnel and outraged by remarks made by policymakers and senior white officers, black political leaders, reporters, and sympathetic white supporters told another story of black soldiers who served in the field. Throughout 1946 and 1947, black newspapers, notably the *Pittsburgh Courier,* the *Baltimore Afro-American,* the *Chicago Defender,* and the *Michigan Chronicle,* sided with the soldiers in uniform and were filled with a number of feature articles, reports, and editorials complaining about the negative assessments of the fighting capabilities of black soldiers in Europe and Asia.[41] Meanwhile, on the floors of Congress, New York senator Robert Wagner and California representative Helen Gahagan Douglas rebutted the negative views by citing the endless acts of heroism performed by black soldiers in Europe and Asia.[42] And scores of veterans' organizations, former GIs, and service families initiated letter-writing campaigns to army chief of staff George Marshall, protesting the injustices that black GIs faced in Europe and Asia.[43]

In a 1947 letter to the editor of the *American Journal of Sociology* titled "Race

Relations in the Army," Lawrence Reddick, a University of Chicago–trained historian and curator of the Schomburg Collection of the New York Public Library, clearly pointed out the stakes in the public debate. Noting the aspersions cast by social scientists on the character of black troops under fire, Reddick commented, "It is worth while to watch the fabrication of the social myth of the Negro's role in World War II. Not only are the news stories that came back from the war fronts, outbursts of oratory of certain members of Congress, and the 'official' releases of the War and Navy departments worthy of analysis, but the studies of scholars deserve to be examined with some attention to orientation and attitude content. Their conclusions do not vary too much from the basic thesis of more crudely stated observations that (1) the Negro was not much good as a fighting man and (2) little could be done about racial discrimination and segregation because American society is as it is." The seething curator went on to stress the importance of getting all sides of the story, stating, "It is as important to get impressions and opinions about Negro servicemen as held by white officers and administrators of the military as it is to get comparable sets of impressions of and opinions about white officers and others held by Negro servicemen." Not long afterward, Reddick elaborated on his remarks during a speech before members of the Society for Ethical Culture in New York. Before concluding his address, he issued a stern warning to members of the audience: "If this campaign is not nipped in the bud, many more anti-Negro officers will write their memoirs, anti-Negro congressmen will quote the memoirs for the *Congressional Record*. Textbook writers will then quote the *Congressional Record* and we will have a generation growing up believing that Negroes are inferior fighters and therefore deserve inferior citizenship rights."[44]

Little did the venerable historian realize it, but the challenge he posed to audience found expression in the thoughts and actions taken by black former division members around the country. Throughout 1946 and 1947, former servicemen formed veterans groups in Ohio, California, the District of Columbia, and New York in ways reminiscent of their self-organizing experiences while serving in Arizona, Louisiana, California, and the South Pacific during the war. But whereas the affiliations between black GIs and their families worked to protect their physical well-being during the early 1940s, these organizations served to reclaim their images as African American soldiers who had served honorably on the battlefields of World War II. In Cleveland, for instance, a group of veterans under the leadership of former division members Henry Williams, Clarence Gaines, Fred Ezelle, and Thomas White resurrected the Huachucans' Veterans Association.[45] In December 1947, the Blue Helmet Association was formed in Stockton, California, with Clarence Ross as its national director.[46] Elsewhere, other former 93rd GIs organized groups on a state- and citywide basis. In September 1946, African Americans in Jackson, Tennessee, established the Tennessee Veterans Association.[47] In Los Angeles, division veterans created Club Thirty-four at the Trinity Baptist Church. The organization aimed to educate the metropolitan community about the experiences of World War II veterans and to assist black newcomers to the city.[48] And in New York City, division chaplain Oscar Holder and two hundred other former soldiers gathered at the Elks auditorium and formed the Negro Council of Allied Veterans.[49]

Meanwhile, more prominent veterans organizations followed a different course. Throughout the period, veterans linked their campaigns to reclaim their presence in World War II to vital postwar issues of concern, including the right to vote, jobs, education, housing, health care, civil rights, and antilynching legislation. In large groups like the American Veterans Committee, several former 93rd Division GIs and their family members including William Nunelly and Vasco Hale mobilized hundreds of veterans in Illinois; Washington, D.C.; Milwaukee, Wisconsin; New York City; and Hartford, Connecticut.[50] As an organization that was explicitly progressive and integrated in its makeup, the AVC pushed for antidiscrimination, permanent fair employment practices, housing, minimum wage, and anti-poll-tax legislation. And many division veterans, buoyed by the antiracist and prodemocratic tenor of the AVC program, rushed to fill its ranks. For example, former 93rd Division officer Edward Smith-Green Jr., founder of the Flatbush chapter of the American Veterans' Committee in September 1946, remarked, "No one has more contempt for Senators Bilbo and Eastland than I do. But let's face it. We Negroes are going to have to tell our story and no one can do it for us. We can fight, we will fight, and we must fight."[51] Meanwhile, members of the national planning committee wrote a letter to the secretary of war, demanding that the army reopen its investigation of the employment and performance of black troops in Europe and Asia. Citing the black soldiers' double burden of fighting both the enemy and racism within their own ranks, committee members argued, "The armed forces, in their segregation of white and Negro troops and its report on the Negro soldier, have perpetuated an un-American prejudice."[52]

Throughout much of the early postwar period, among those who held national planning positions within the AVC was Franklin Williams, a Flushing, New York, attorney and former member of the 93rd Infantry Division. Williams, a Fordham University Law School graduate, had worked on a wide array of military issues affecting African Americans as assistant special counsel with the NAACP's legal staff and expressed his belief that "Negroes have been so oppressed and exploited under our current system but it has not made us desire any change in the fundamental principles of our government. We like the Constitution. It's good. The only trouble is that it isn't enforced."[53] In July 1946, he was elected to head the AVC's New York Area Council and helped to write the organization's platform statement on civil rights that was adopted by national planning committee leaders at their quarterly meeting held in Chicago in early 1947.[54] Williams continued to work with the AVC on securing benefits for African American veterans for the next four years until he left for California, where he became the West Coast regional director for the NAACP in 1950.[55]

The AVC was not the only organization that seemed attractive to the former 93rd personnel during the period. In April 1946, more than three hundred former servicemen convened in Chicago's DuSable High School to form the United Negro and Allied Veterans of America. Within the year, the organization had grown to well over ten thousand members with forty-one chapters in twenty-one states and had attracted many former GIs, including 93rd Division chaplain Charles T. Watkins.[56] Interracial in its makeup and espousing a Marxist-Leninist perspective, the UNAVA directed its energies to addressing the special problems encountered by returning African American soldiers and pursued their agenda on multiple fronts between 1946 and 1948. In Michigan, for instance, the Detroit chapter of UNAVA, led by Fletcher Routt, traveled throughout the summer of 1946, staging open demonstrations in Lansing and Detroit in order to call attention to the problem of inadequate housing facilities for black veterans.[57] In September, fifty veterans from the New York State chapter of the organization participated in a national pilgrimage to Washington, D.C., protesting against the wave of lynching across the country. Among those who gathered in the nation's capital was Oscar Holder, a former division member.[58] And two months later, UNAVA members in Chicago gathered outside the city's Airport Homes to demonstrate their support for black former servicemen and their families whose attempts to move into the housing project were met with hostility.[59]

Other 93rd veterans continued their fight at home through previously established public health organizations. In June 1946, fifteen of the sixty black former physicians who were originally assigned to the division attended a conference sponsored by the National Medical Association to pledge their support for the proposed Wagner-Murray-Dingell Health legislation that was being debated by congressional members on Capitol Hill. Specialists and physicians who attended the three-day program included Cervera Little, Harold Whitted, Edmond Noel, William Smith, and Arthur Thomas.[60] Around the same time, Washington, D.C., physicians Charles Adams and Claude Walker joined the district's Medico-Chirurgical Society's Veteran's Affairs Committee and were joined by Roger Thurston and Hildrus Poindexter, all outspoken medical corps personnel with the division during its South Pacific campaign years earlier. Together, they worked tirelessly for a ten-year health program for veterans who had returned from the Second World War.[61] Three years later, former 93rd Division medical officer and San Francisco resident William Thomas and his wife, Hortense, served as members of the San Francisco Medical Society, establishing a mental health advisory group to treat veterans dealing with psychiatric disorders. Broadening their efforts, the pair also joined forces with the California State Medical Society and the American Red Cross, playing key roles in tackling public health issues affecting black and white veterans living in the state.[62]

And still other former 93rd Division personnel and former service family members pursued veterans' concerns through benevolent societies and civic organizations. During the postwar period, the number of lodge memberships held by black World War II veterans exploded, and the leadership of these organizations focused on ways to ease the movement of former GIs from the battlefield to civilian life. After returning to Cleveland, Ohio, after the war, Fred Mabra joined the Sutterville Heights Optimist Club.[63] He and other members developed programs to assist the former GIs who were beginning to trickle into the Cleveland area. James Whittico, a former physician with the unit, was elected medical director of the Prince Hall Shriners in 1955 and raised money for hospitals and medical clinics treating former servicemen living in the greater New Orleans metropolitan area.[64] When lodge members of San Francisco's Masons launched their campaign to instruct Bay Area veterans how to use the ballot to gain representation on the city's redevelopment agency in 1947, San Francisco native Herbert Henderson stood among them.[65] And John and Marguerite Howard, whose parents were prominent members of the organization, joined the District of Columbia's Masons after returning home in 1946. Howard, Marguerite, and other members played central roles in providing social, cultural, and entertainment activities for city newcomers as well as working to improve housing and employment conditions in the area. Of the order, Howard later recalled, "Masons, like us, really took care of their own in those days. We had a tightly knit group, and the grand matrons organized most of the community activities in our Northeast neighborhood."[66]

Replete with ritualistic passwords, parade dress, and social status ranking, veteran and professional organizations and benevolent societies provided former 93rd GIs and their families with a chance to make the transition from a military environment to a peacetime setting. Most important, the organizations allowed veterans and service communities to retain and reinvigorate the institutions they had created during the wartime emergency. Indeed, for former servicemen and their loved ones, aspects of wartime and peacetime American life were so tightly bound together that they felt compelled to rely on the military-induced calculus that had served them so well during the early 1940s. By the early 1950s, however, a sequence of events would require them to alter their previous strategies of empowerment in order to meet new social, political, and economic challenges.

Veiled Changes

Other former 93rd GIs joined the struggle for civil rights. In 1951, George Leighton stood before a Cook County judge facing a charge of dubious merit. After arriving in Chicago in 1946, the 37-year-old former serviceman and fledgling defense attorney had joined the prominent law office of Loring Moore and William Ming, where he quickly established a reputation among his legal peers as a talented and fearless barrister. At the same time, he joined the legal arm of Chicago's NAACP branch and played a key role in the association's campaign against the education and housing discrimination encountered by black residents in the city.[67]

Shortly after being elected chairman of the association's legal redress committee, Leighton found himself propelled into the national spotlight when he agreed to represent fellow World War II veteran Harvey Clark and his family in July 1951. The Clarks had encountered scores of angry white protesters and law enforcement officials when they attempted to occupy an apartment in the predominantly white neighborhood of Cicero. But less than two months after filing an injunction with a federal judge barring the Cicero Police Department and other town officials from interfering with the Clarks' entry into the home, the NAACP official learned that he, too, had become the subject of legal prosecution. On 22 September a Cook County grand jury brought charges against the attorney and several others, alleging that they had engaged in a "conspiracy to incite a riot and to injure property . . . by causing a depreciation in the real estate price by renting to Negroes."[68]

As soon as word of the indictment against Leighton reached major black newspapers, numerous civic, church, and labor organizations staged rallies, protesting against the riots. Within days after a verdict had been reached in the Cicero case, the *Pittsburgh Courier*, in an editorial titled "This Must Be Fought!" issued a call to the cause which few could ignore. "These indictments," the writer explained, "must be fought with all of the energy we can command because they will, if they stand, establish a precedent which will serve for the prosecution of every Negro everywhere who seeks to defend the persecuted; and every citizen who tries to

rent property to Negroes where certain vicious elements do not want them to move."
On 2 October members of the interracial Chicago Civil Liberties Committee assembled at the Metropolitan Community Church and demanded a federal grand
jury probe to determine whether the civil rights of Leighton and Harvey Clark had
been violated.[69]

After reviewing the case, Judge Wilbert Crowley in the Criminal Court of Cook
County dismissed the indictment in October and declared, "There is no sufficient
charge of conspiracy to injure property and it seems contradictory that unknown
persons can suffer financial loss."[70] Meanwhile, the Cicero case had worked its
way into the attorney general's office of the Justice Department, where a grand
jury was impaneled to determine the cause of the disturbance. After several weeks
of reviewing the case, the jury members indicted four town officials and three police officers for conspiring to prevent the army veteran and his family from entering the suburban neighborhood.[71] The victory won by Leighton and his NAACP
officials was short lived, however. A few years later, the U.S. attorney persuaded
the federal judge presiding over the case to drop the indictments brought against
law enforcement.[72] But as Leighton's activities on behalf of a fellow veteran and
his family suggest, black World War II veterans had recalibrated their wartime political struggles to fight for postwar civil rights. Caught up in the vortex of Cold
War racism and social restructuring, George Leighton and other former World
War II GIs fell back on the familiar terrain of community concerns and grassroots activism that served them so well during the war.

George Leighton's actions were not isolated. After leaving military service in
1945, Theodore and Pauline Coggs relocated to Wisconsin, where they plunged
into community affairs. After Theodore earned a law degree from the University
of Wisconsin at Madison, the couple headed for nearby Milwaukee, where they
quickly became active in various neighborhood causes. In 1950, the pair helped
to revitalize the local branch of the National Association for the Advancement of
Colored People and worked diligently to coordinate several community groups
that studied housing discrimination and police brutality cases as well as the rise
of racial tensions between black and white residents in the city.[73]

Similar were the efforts of Clarence Gaines. Appointed director of health and
welfare services in Cleveland, Ohio, during the late 1960s, Gaines campaigned
openly for many social causes and helped integrate birth control services within
the African American community despite objections raised by the city's Roman
Catholic Church officials.[74] In a similar vein, James Whittico was elected president of the National Medical Association in 1968 and worked tirelessly to end the
policies of hospitals that openly discriminated in their staff appointments and pa-

tient admissions.[75] Elder B. Hicks became a staunch leader for social and political change within the American Baptist Church in the United States and used the organization as a vehicle to promote a policy of racial inclusiveness in Baptist churches scattered throughout the South in the 1960s.[76] Still others translated their household and community concerns into action through electoral politics. Detroit's deputy mayor Walter Greene worked hard during the 1970s to improve the lot of the city's working poor through favorable legislation.[77] And throughout the 1950s and 1960s, William Thomas, Edwin Lee, and John De Veaux struggled to achieve political and civil rights measures through local Republican and Democratic committees.[78]

Some former division GIs addressed their local concerns by way of alternative politics. While laboring as a bricklayer in Detroit and Cleveland by day, Nelson Peery retained his radical convictions and maintained his close ties with the American Communist Party during the immediate postwar period. By the late 1950s, however, he had had serious disagreements with party leaders over issues of race and class ideology and decided to leave the party. Of his problems with the party officials during this period, Peery recalled, "The justice department had basically broken the revolutionary cultural workers within the party in the North, and the CP had capitulated to the demands of the government and agreed to dissolve the National Negro Labor Councils and end the party's influence in the steel, timber, and mining industries in the South. It was at that time that I believed that the Communist Party leadership had betrayed the black masses, and I wanted nothing else to do with it."[79] Peery eventually went on to become the general secretary of the Communist Labor Party during the late 1960s and continued his struggle against racism and injustice.[80]

In a similar fashion, Michigan resident Raymond Jenkins embraced black nationalist politics to call attention to the ills of his community. After leaving the army, Jenkins returned to his family home for a brief period before heading back to Michigan. After arriving in the Motor City, he quickly established himself as a central figure in the city, working as a real estate broker while serving as a member of the city council for a number of years. But in 1958, Jenkins had experienced an epiphany of sorts when he learned that his grandfather Will Mobley, a former slave who lived to age 104, had passed away from natural causes. At his funeral, he recalled, "As a sharecropper, my grandfather had to give so much of what he earned to the plantation owner that he never could escape debt. And when he died, the relatives had to pass the hat to bury him. That kind of shook me up."

Not long afterward Jenkins discovered a cause through which he could channel his growing frustration. In March 1967, he guided through the Detroit City

Council a bill calling for the U.S. government to place forty billion dollars into an education fund for black colleges and trade schools. A year later, he launched his own national protest movement aptly called Slave Labor Annuity Pay (SLAP), demanding that the U.S. government pay reparations to the descendants of slaves for centuries of forced labor by their ancestors and its lingering effects. With virtually no staff and meager resources, Jenkins worked furiously to make his cause known by bombarding like-minded groups with leaflets, delivering speeches, and sending letters to prominent black spokespeople. Less than fifteen years later, his efforts were rewarded. In September 1987, members of the National Conference of Black Lawyers, the New Afrikan Peoples Organization, and the Republic of New Africa convened in Washington, D.C., where they decided to take up the issue. By the summer of 1989, news of Jenkins's efforts had even reached Capitol Hill as Michigan congressman John Conyers introduced a resolution in a legislative session of the House Judiciary Committee demanding that his colleagues set aside eight million dollars to study the effects of slavery as well to create a formula for reparations. And as determined young reparations advocates and support groups stood facing a new millennium at the end of the next decade, more than a few would refer to the stalwart figure of the thirty-five-year campaign affectionately as "Reparations Ray."[81]

As the experiences of Raymond Jenkins and other former 93rd Infantry Division members demonstrate, they were neither the most visible spokespeople nor prominent representatives of the emerging civil rights movement of the period. But they knew that the issues of concern that people expressed in their neighborhoods and communities about their economic and social conditions were just as important to them in postwar America as the issues of war and death they faced in their youth during World War II. As Jenkins and his cohort approached middle age, issues relating to housing discrimination, police brutality, underemployment, and reparations provided them with rare opportunities to put into practice the lessons of organization, strategy, and politics they had learned years earlier. With this, black veterans and their communities stood resolute in the cause of economic and social justice. However, as the lessons of grassroots activism and local unity tended to bind black former 93rd GIs and their neighborhoods more tightly together, the racial strife and structural changes brought about by postindustrialism fractured the power and direction of their relationship. It was in this context that the well-honed grassroots strategies of former division members and their families which shaped political activism during the war were undermined. And it is to the changing set of circumstances that we must now turn.

Communities at Odds

By the 1960s and 1970s, the spirit of determined hope expressed by Jenkins and other 93rd veterans would be tempered by violence and intra-racial class conflict. Driving home to Washington, D.C., in the early morning hours of 11 July 1964 after two weeks of Army Reserves training at Georgia's Fort Benning, Lemuel Penn, John Howard, and Charles Brown—all decorated veterans of service with the U.S. 93rd Infantry Division and high-ranking reserve officers—encountered heavy gunfire from six Ku Klux Klan members on a highway bridge near Athens. Although Howard and Brown had escaped injury from the shotgun blasts, Penn, a director of adult and vocational education for the District of Columbia public school system, lay mortally wounded. After weeks of investigation, Georgia state investigators, CID, and FBI agents arrested, charged, and indicted four men in connection with Penn's murder, but an all-white jury acquitted three of the men of the charges less than two months later. Moreover, a U.S. district court judge in Georgia upheld a motion made by defense lawyers to dismiss the indictments brought against those convicted by the federal grand jury on the grounds that the actions of the men had not violated the rights of the deceased black officer under the Fourteenth Amendment.[82]

The fatal shooting of Lemuel Penn and the subsequent trial and acquittal of his assailants were part and parcel of the reign of terror that spread across the southern region during the early 1960s. Later that year, unarmed citizens in Americus, Georgia, were cattle-prodded and gassed by local police. Around the same time, civil rights demonstrators in Plaquemines, Louisiana, were tear-gassed and clubbed into submission by local law enforcement officials and Ku Klux Klan members. In Mississippi, Klan members carried out their own version of extralegal terrorism, staging numerous cross burnings, public whippings, kidnappings, house bombings, and gangland executions. In June 1963, Mississippi NAACP branch leader Medgar Evers was gunned down by an assassin in the driveway of his home in Jackson. A little over a year later, Michael Schwerner, James Chaney, and Andrew Goodman were murdered in Neshoba County.[83] And in ways similar to Penn's killing, the process of solving the murders and bringing the perpetrators to justice in each case was extremely slow.

Incensed by the verdict and the subsequent court decision in the Penn case, black leaders and daily newspapers wrote and published letters of outrage, as many linked the shooting of the army officer and the acquittal of his assailants to the social and political standing of black people in American society.[84] For example, the *Baltimore Afro-American* stated in an editorial entitled "Not Guilty, They Said": "With this kind of justice the rule, rather than the exception in too many states, there are still some Americans who pretend they do not understand why colored citizens insist on taking to the streets to air their disgust, anger and frustrations."[85] W. J. Hudson, president of the Athens, Georgia, NAACP branch, commented, "The Negro community of the area is more disturbed than you might think."[86] Two years later, federal attorneys appealed the case directly to the U.S. Supreme Court, which overturned the lower court's dismissal of the case and ordered further proceedings and a change of venue.[87] In 1969, another all-white jury, in Augusta, Georgia, found the men guilty of infringing upon the rights of the servicemen to pass through the state unharmed—rather than guilty of Penn's murder. Furthermore, they ordered the men to serve up to ten years' imprisonment, but the men managed to gain parole after serving only half of the sentence.[88]

Penn's death and the truncated sentences served by the men charged with his murder are vivid examples of how black men who defended their country during World War II were constantly reminded of their ambiguous roles as martyrs and symbols of the African American struggle for equality during the period. And these reminders were often extended to their family members. Less than a month after her husband's death, Georgia Penn received a steady stream of letters from Klan members like the following: "I am writing to tell you that I think your husband's death was justified and served as a good example of what happens to trespassers in the South. Him and other Niggers from up north have no business in a white man's land. If you were smart you would issue a statement justifying the action my fellow clansmen took. The Civil Rights Bill is a hoax and should be repealed. Your husband's companions should have been shot too."[89] Georgia Penn would not live to see the successful prosecution of the men who killed her husband, dying after contracting lupus less than a year later.[90]

For the two surviving car passengers in the harrowing experience, however, the incident also served to remind them of their place as black men in a racially stratified society. Recalling the incident several decades later, John Howard remarked, "First of all, they (the CID, FBI, and state investigators) did not believe that it had happened the way that it did. We had to go back to the scene of the crime, where they saw the skid marks along the highway before they started to believe that things had happened the way as we described them. Second, the state police chief told the CID that he wanted us to stay in Athens. I disagreed and told a CID sergeant that I was not going to stay in Athens and to take me to the nearest army post—which was Augusta, Georgia. When we arrived at the post, we were immediately interrogated. I deeply resented this because they made it seem like we were lying and had done something wrong."[91] When Charles Brown passed away in Washington, D.C., in 1978, the local paper punctuated his obituary with his race and his role in the ordeal in the following manner, "Colonel Brown, an Afro-American, school head, and a Reserve officer, was with Lemuel Penn, a D.C. and fellow Afro-American, school official, and Army Reserve Officer, when Penn was shot to death in the small Georgia town of Colbert."[92]

Race also continued to structure the lives of former division servicemen in other settings. Beginning in the 1950s, the country witnessed a fundamental shift from a manufacturing to a service-oriented to finally a deindustrialized state. By 1990, the reorganization of the nation's economy and labor markets along with the spatial redistribution of population especially affected young African Americans in the schoolrooms of the nation's largest cities. Washington, D.C., for instance, was deeply troubled by financial woes, drugs, guns, declining test scores, dilapidated buildings, and administrative corruption, and the dismal state of the District of Columbia's public school system raised grave concern among liberal and conservative observers alike. In November 1996, members of a congressionally appointed financial control board declared a state of emergency in the city's public schools, ordered the removal of the district's superintendent, and reduced the powers of the elected board of education. Issuing a scathing report that castigated the quality and management of the schools, the five-member board asserted that "this school system has allowed and fostered educational child abuse" and insisted that "strong action needed to be taken."[93]

Into the fray stepped Julius W. Becton Jr., a former U.S. 93rd Infantry Division member and retired army lieutenant general. After leaving the division as a second lieutenant in 1945, Becton continued his military career, serving in Korea and Vietnam and advancing steadily up the ranks before becoming the nation's highest-ranking African American general officer in the early 1980s. He served briefly as the director of the Federal Emergency Management Agency under President Ronald Reagan before taking over the presidency of the financially depressed Prairie View Agricultural and Mechanical University in the early 1990s. A self-described "can-do guy," Becton quickly grasped the situation and threw himself into the job, making a number of administrative changes to rectify the situation. Within months after he arrived at the Texas campus, Prairie View witnessed a swift reversal of its financial woes. By late 1996, news of his considerable managerial abilities began to spread throughout the country, reaching Washington, D.C., where it attracted the attention of control board chairman Andrew Brimmer. After meeting with several control board members and holding a series of discussions about the state of the District public school system, Becton elected to take the reins of what he described as "a wonderful opportunity to help the children." As he remarked during a taped interview with journalist Charlayne Hunter-Gault on PBS's *McNeil-Lehrer Newshour*, "No matter what we do, if we measure it against the idea of children first, and it works, fine." But he also warned that "if it doesn't work, then maybe we shouldn't be doing it."[94]

Guided by a philosophy of non-negotiable integrity and intense loyalty that served him since he entered the army in 1943, Becton plunged headfirst into a river whose political currents he neither understood nor liked. Not long after being appointed as the District's chief executive officer, the retired three-star army general encountered numerous bureaucratic snarls, obstructive action from city officials in the mayor's office, and backbiting complaints of overspending from board members in the media. After serving less than two years on the job, Becton resigned in April 1998, citing irreconcilable differences with the city's financial control board and budgeters and arguing that a lifetime of integrity and credibility had been impugned. In his letter of resignation, in which he referred to the District's public school situation, he stated, "This issue is no longer about children; it's about power politics."[95]

Becton's experience in the public arena and his remarks during his impending resignation echoed the sentiments that many African American veterans shared regarding their place in American society and their communities during the late twentieth century. During the period, black 93rd Division veterans frequently found themselves estranged from the communities in which they lived. Their feelings of community were similar to those expressed by noted historian and activist W. E. B. Du Bois some ninety years earlier. In his evocative piece published in 1903 titled *The Souls of Black Folk*, Du Bois brilliantly reminded the world of the veil that existed between African Americans and their surroundings: "After the Egyptian and Indian, the Greek and Roman, the Teuton and Mongolian, the Negro is a sort of seventh son, born with a veil, and gifted with second-sight in this American world,—a world which yields him no true self-consciousness, but only lets him see himself through the revelation of the other world. One ever feels his two-ness,—an American, a Negro; two souls, two thoughts, two unreconciled strivings; two warring ideals in one dark body, whose dogged strength alone keeps it from being torn asunder."[96] Increasingly, black World War II veterans and their communities appeared in the same public spaces relating to social reform, but they were worlds apart on strategies and politics. As Becton and other former GIs affirm, devising strategies to meet present and future challenges will require resolving seemingly irreconcilable differences and removing the veil on previously formulated equations of political, social, and economic empowerment.

Conclusion

The historical experiences of African Americans came full circle for the men who served in the U.S. 93rd Division and their families. As young men who entered the army in the early 1940s, they had already endured what seemed like a lifetime in the struggle for respect and human dignity. The poverty-ridden Great Depression and New Deal years of the 1930s had tempered their hope and expectations, but they moved forward with grim determination. Imbued with a hearth-forged class-consciousness and ethnic pride, they approached the militarized world of World War II America and service in the segregated army with youthful aspiration and healthy skepticism. For many of them, fighting fascism and fighting racism were not discrete categories but a dual struggle leading to a better way of life.

With the wartime emergency and subsequent military service, black soldiers and their families adopted a political stance that allowed them to embrace the Double Victory strategies enunciated by prominent black organizations and figures while keeping their distance when elements of these strategies clashed with their own interests. And throughout the war, army commanders, policymakers, and the black press slowly came to terms with the shadowy politics that structured the lives of division members as they wrestled with issues relating to the employment of African American troops. Much of this perspective was grounded in the military barracks culture and grassroots garrison politics of Fort Huachuca, Arizona; Camp Polk, Louisiana; and Camp Clipper, California. But by summer of 1943, their attitudes toward military service became more complex as concerns over race riots involving African American military personnel and their families grew.

In addition, controversies surrounding the deployment of black soldiers into action animated discussion among black division members and their families both at home and on the training field about their place in American society and the general state of American democracy in the worldwide conflict. When the men of the division walked up the gangplanks of Camp Stoneman, California, later that year, little did they realize that the combination of training-field culture and home front politics would shape their experiences long after they departed. While overseas, black GIs discovered that the Janus-faced politics of the Pacific war and the island deployment of black soldiers frequently pivoted on the interconnected dimensions of race, gender, and rumor. In response, black division members and their loved ones shifted their strategy of empowerment from one that directly sought first-class democracy through military service at home to one that employed cryptic language to ensure individual and collective respectability abroad. All the while, concerns over the conditions of their communities of origin continued to shape their efforts.

African Americans' political struggles in World War II underwent a transformation as the 1940s gave way to the civil rights struggles of the 1950s and 1960s. Most returning division members and their families found that although racial injustice was still a part of postwar life, the strategies they had devised to fight it during the war required recalibration, this time to meet the racial and gender conventions of postwar America and the deteriorating economic conditions of their communities. Once most division members returned to American shores, they were determined to turn back the clock to the moment when they first entered military service as a way of recapturing the time lost in duty to their country. Yet nearly all of them also desired to apply the lessons of measured resistance learned while in uniform where it counted the most. As one veteran put it after returning to his hometown of Monroe, Georgia, "I got through fighting in the P.T.O (Pacific Theater of Operations) and now I've got to fight in the S.T.O, U.S.A (Southern Theater of Operations in the United States)."[97] Indeed, black former GIs staged new campaigns on the streets of Chicago, Atlanta, Washington, D.C., and New York City in the immediate postwar years. But making the transition to civilian life was not easy for most division veterans. From the moment they returned to their old communities, the social climate of postwar America and the shifts in the social calculus challenged their war-born political sensibilities at every turn. As they shed their youthful energy for more seasoned politics at the end of the twentieth century, they began to realize that military service alone was not enough to overcome racial discrimination; they needed to sharpen the tools they had forged in the wartime struggle.

Meanwhile, the legacy of African Americans associated with the U.S. 93rd Infantry Division became inextricably tied to the broader fabric of American life as members of the division themselves became the subjects of nostalgia and memory. For example, throughout the 1970s and 1980s, former members of the division gathered at Fort Huachuca, Arizona, to reflect on their wartime experiences. With wives, children, and grandchildren, they came from Georgia, New York, Washington, California, Ohio, Michigan, and other states. Among them stood Frank and Alvirita Little. During their visits, the Little family heard the testimonials given by dignitaries and political officials extolling the contributions that black GIs made to the war. What the couple thought of these gatherings is unknown. But the World

War II veteran was astonished when he discovered that the base museum had enshrined his military career with a life-size exhibit of his office with his old nameplate, "First Sergeant Little—The Buck Stops Here." When asked about his own wartime service, Little merely shrugged and stated, "What my men and I did was what any Negro would have done during the period. We don't want to be remembered as heroes, but merely as servicemen in the army," he later explained.[98]

But perhaps the true meaning of their wartime and postwar past was captured thirty years later. In 2004, members of the Lemuel Penn Memorial Committee met at a Comer, Georgia, Baptist church to get Highway 72 renamed to preserve the memory of the slain World War II veteran. During the gathering, Dena Chandler, the committee chairperson, may have said it best when she stated, "Though the South's racial climate has changed, more healing needs to be done. Not enough people know about Penn's story and this is part of the reason why the committee wants the marker. People need to understand the past so that they won't repeat it."[99] The wishes of Chandler and other supporters became reality on 7 October 2006, when a crowd of local residents gathered along Highway 72 to again pay tribute to the man who was gunned down while returning home from military service more than forty years earlier. There, prayer, music, and memory met with considerable force as a bronze historical marker was erected on the Broad River Bridge, calling attention to Penn's murder as well as commemorating the Washington, D.C., resident's lifetime of military service.[100] During the service, a color guard marched forward, presenting the 93rd Infantry Division flag to honor Penn's World War II service. What members of the audience may have thought about his military past has not been recorded. Little did they realize it, but as black and white members of the dedication committee moved along the highway toward the designated marker, they were also marching, albeit slowly, toward a consciously interracial future fashioned from a haunting memory of a past never to be forgotten.

Abbreviations

AGF	Army Ground Forces
AGF Records	RG 337, Records of Headquarters Army Ground Forces, National Archives and Records Administration, College Park, Md.
AGO	Office of the Adjutant General
AGO Records	RG 407, Records of the Adjutant General's Office, National Archives and Records Administration, College Park, Md.
ARC Records	RG 200, Records of the American Red Cross, National Archives and Records Administration, College Park, Md.
Barnett Papers	Claude A. Barnett Papers, Chicago Historical Society, Chicago, Ill.
Boyd Collection	Leonard R. Boyd Collection, Hoover Institution, Stanford University, Stanford, Calif.
CCC Records	RG 35, Records of the Civilian Conservation Corps, Civilian Branch, National Archives and Records Administration, Washington, D.C.
Davis Papers	Benjamin O. Davis Sr. Papers, Archives, U.S. Army Military History Institute, Carlisle, Pa.
Du Bois Papers	W. E. B. Du Bois Papers, Special Collections and University Archives, W. E. B. Du Bois Library, University of Massachusetts at Amherst, Amherst, Mass.
FDRL	Franklin D. Roosevelt Library, Hyde Park, N.Y.
FHHM	Fort Huachuca Historical Museum, Fort Huachuca, Ariz.
HIA	Hoover Institution Archives, Stanford, Calif.
Lee Papers	Edwin Lee Papers, Archives and Special Collections, University of Illinois at Springfield, Springfield, Ill.
NAACP Papers, LOC	National Association for the Advancement of Colored People Papers, Manuscript Division, Library of Congress, Washington, D.C.
NARA	National Archives and Records Administration, Washington, D.C.
OCA Records	Records of the Office of the Civilian Aide to the Secretary of War, in RG 107, Records of the Office of the Secretary of War, National Archives and Records Administration, College Park, Md.

RG	Record Group
RGH	RG 496, Records of General Headquarters, Southwest Pacific Area and United States Army Forces, Pacific (World War II), National Archives and Records Administration, Washington, D.C.
Stimson Papers	Henry Lewis Stimson Papers, Yale University, New Haven, Conn.
TCF	Tuskegee Institute News Clipping File, University of California at Berkeley, Berkeley, Calif.
USACC Records	RG 394, Records of the U.S. Army Continental Commands, National Archives and Records Administration, Washington, D.C.
USAJ	U.S. Army Judiciary, Nassif Building, Falls Church, Va.
USAMHI	U.S. Army Military History Institute, Carlisle, Pa.
USOR	Records of the USO, University of Minnesota, St. Paul, Minn.
WDGS/WDSS Records	RG 165, Records of the War Department General and Special Staffs, National Archives and Records Administration

Interviews with the Author

Briggs, Clenon, Chicago, Ill., 12 February 1993

Browne, Vincent J., Washington, D.C., 28 July 1993

Carr, Edward, Detroit, Mich., 15 March 1998

Coggs, Pauline Redmond, Milwaukee, Wis., 12 February 2000; 13 February 2000

Davis, Edgar, Montclair, N.J., 4 August 1994

Ellis, Francis, Ann Arbor, Mich., 1 March 1995

Etters, Bennie, Cleveland, Ohio, 17 January 1995

Fentress, William F., Taylorville, Ill., 26 January 1993

Fraser, Reuben E., Jr., Apple Valley, Minn., 5 May 1993

Freeman, Edward A., Kansas City, Kans., 9 July 1993

Gaines, Clarence L., Cleveland, Ohio, 6 February 1993

Galley, Robert, Palestine, Tex., 22 April 1993

Greene, Freida Bailey, Phoenix, Ariz., 19 March 1998; 26 March 1998

Griffey, Durward P., Cleveland, Ohio, 9 May 1991

Griffin, Curtis, Cincinnati, Ohio, 3 August 1991

Hall, Herbert, Cleveland, Ohio, 6 February 1993

Hartsfield, Arnett, Los Angeles, 8 December 1994

Howard, John D., Washington, D.C., 20 July 1993

Howard, Marguerite, Washington, D.C., 20 July 1993

Hurst, Richard, Tavares, Fla., 13 April 1991

Isaacs, Andrew, Inglewood, Calif., 2 November 1994

Jarrett, Willard L., Asheville, N.C., 30 March 1993; 19 July 1993

Jenkins, Raymond, Detroit, Mich., 28 February 1990; 1 March 1990

Johnson, Isaiah A., Sr., Hampton, Va., 3 July 1993

Johnson, Robert J., Los Angeles, Calif., 3 November 1994

Layton, Benjamin T., Kensington, Md., 30 April 1991

Little, Alvirita, Seattle, Wash., 8 May 1993

Logan, Leo, Fresno, Calif., 19 June 1993

Marshall, John W., Cleveland Heights, Ohio, 2 July 1991

McGriff, Asberry, San Jose, Calif., 31 March 1993

Nicholas, George, Philadelphia, Pa., 8 February 1993

Peery, Nelson, Chicago, Ill., 4 December 1994; 9 December 1994

Pendergrass, Thomas S., Columbia, Md., 3 May 1994

Quinn, Edward G., Rome, N.Y., 13 March 1993

Roberts, Percy S., Three Rivers, Mich., 3 May 1993

Ross, Clarence R., Stockton, Calif., 28 April 1993

Sanderson, Walter B., Jr., Adelphi, Md., 29 July 1993

Shuffer, George M., Jr., El Paso, Tex., 4 June 1993; 14 June 1993

Smith, Frank E., Cleveland, Ohio, 3 August 1991

Thompson, Julius G., Newark, N.J., 5 March 1993; 3 May 1993

Toles, Marke, Dallas, Tex., 7 April 1992

Wertz, Irma Jackson Cayton, Detroit, Mich., 16 March 1998

White, Thomas M., Cleveland, Ohio, 15 February 1991; 6 February 1993

Whittico, James M., St. Louis, Mo., 2 April 1993

Williams, Bismark, Jr., Asheville, N.C., 12 April 1993

Williams, Elliotte J., Fort Washington, Md., 8 June 1992

Williams, Henry L., Cleveland, Ohio, 3 August 1991; 4 February 1993; 7 February 1993

Young, Arline, Wilmington, Del., 17 February 1995

Young, Julius B., Wilmington, Del., 17 February 1995

Preface

1. Brent Staples, "Celebrating World War II—and the Whiteness of American History," *New York Times*, 9 December 2001, 12.

Introduction

Epigraphs: George N. Leighton to James M. Nabritt, 20 June 1945, box 122-2, Correspondence, J-RE, Howard University Men and Women in the Armed Forces Papers, Howard University Founders Library, Washington, D.C.; W. E. B. Du Bois, "As the Crow Flies," *New York Amsterdam News*, 26 June 1943, 10.

1. *Detroit Tribune*, 8 September 1945.

2. "Bowen and Greene to Vet Administration," *Michigan Chronicle*, 19 March 1946, 5; Walter R. Greene Clipping File (in author's possession); Francis Ellis interview with author; Freida Bailey Greene interview with author, 26 March 1998.

3. Bell I. Wiley, *The Training of Negro Troops* (Washington, DC: Army Ground Forces Historical Section, 1946); Samuel Stouffer et al., *The American Soldier: Adjustment during Army Life*, vol. 1 (Princeton, NJ: Princeton University Press, 1949); Jean Byers, *A Study of the Negro in Military Service* (Washington, DC: U.S. Department of Defense, 1950); Morris J. MacGregor, *The Integration of the Armed Forces, 1940–1965* (Washington, DC: Center of Military History, 1981); Sherie Mershon and Steven Schlossman, *Foxholes and Color*

Lines: Desegregating the U.S. Armed Forces (Baltimore: Johns Hopkins University Press, 1998).

4. Ulysses G. Lee Jr., *United States Army in World War II, Special Studies: The Employment of Negro Troops* (Washington, DC: Office of the Chief of Military History, 1966); Bernard C. Nalty, *Strength for the Fight: A History of African Americans in the Military* (New York: Free Press, 1986); Gerald Astor, *The Right to Fight: A History of African Americans in the Military* (Novato, CA: Presidio Press, 1998).

5. Examples include Geoffrey Perrett, *Days of Sadness, Years of Triumph: The American People, 1939–1945* (Madison: University of Wisconsin Press, 1985); Richard M. Dalfiume, *Desegregation of the U.S. Armed Forces: Fighting on Two Fronts, 1939–1953* (Columbia: University of Missouri Press, 1969); William H. Chafe, *The American Woman: Her Changing Social, Economic, and Political Roles, 1920–1970* (New York: Oxford University Press, 1972); John Costello, *Virtue under Fire: How World War II Changed Our Social and Sexual Attitudes* (Boston: Little, Brown, 1985); Richard Polenberg, *War and Society: The United States, 1941–1945* (Philadelphia: Lippincott, 1972); Tom Brokaw, *The Greatest Generation* (New York: Random House, 1998); and John Morton Blum, *V Was for Victory: Politics and American Culture during World War II* (New York: Harcourt Brace Jovanovich, 1976). There are some important exceptions, however. See especially Harvard Sitkoff, "American Blacks in World War II: Rethinking the Militancy-Watershed Hypothesis," in *The Home Front and War in the Twentieth Century,* ed. James Titus (Washington, DC: GPO, 1984); D'Ann Campbell, *Women at War with America: Private Lives in a Patriotic Era* (Cambridge: Harvard University Press, 1984); John Dower, *War without Mercy: Race and Power in the Pacific War* (New York: Pantheon, 1986); Paul Fussell, *Wartime: Understanding and Behavior in the Second World War* (New York: Oxford University Press, 1989); Richard Polenberg, "The Good War? A Reappraisal of How World War II Affected American Society," *Virginia Magazine of History and Biography* 100 (July 1992); John Morton Blum, *Liberty, Justice, Order* (New York: Norton, 1993); Michael C. C. Adams, *The Best War Ever: America and World War II* (Baltimore: Johns Hopkins University Press, 1994); Roger Daniels, "Bad News from the Good War: Democracy at Home during World War II," in *The Home-Front War: World War II and American Society,* ed. Kenneth Paul O'Brien and Lynn Hudson Parsons (Westport, CT: Greenwood Press, 1995); and John W. Jeffries, *Wartime America: The World War II Home Front* (Chicago: Ivan R. Dee, 1996).

6. See, for example, Beth Bailey and David Farber, *The First Strange Place: Race and Sex in World War II Hawaii* (Baltimore: Johns Hopkins University Press, 1994); Maggi M. Morehouse, *Fighting in the Jim Crow Army: Black Men and Women Remember World War II* (Lanham, MD: Rowman and Littlefield, 2000); Brenda L. Moore, *To Serve My Country, To Serve My Race: The Story of the Only African American WACs Stationed Overseas during World War II* (New York: New York University Press, 1996).

7. My book builds upon recent general studies that have begun to explore this avenue of inquiry. Among these works are George Lipsitz, *A Life in the Struggle: Ivory Perry and the Culture of Opposition* (Philadelphia: Temple University Press, 1988); Brenda Gayle Plummer, *Rising Wind: Black Americans and U.S. Foreign Affairs, 1935–1960* (Chapel Hill: University of North Carolina Press, 1996); George Lipsitz, "'Frantic to Join . . . the Japanese Army': The Asia Pacific War in the Lives of African American Soldiers and Civilians," in

The Politics of Culture in the Shadow of Capital, ed. Lisa Lowe and David Lloyd (Durham, NC: Duke University Press, 1997); Marc Gallicchio, *The African American Encounter with Japan and China: Black Internationalism in Asia, 1895–1945* (Chapel Hill: University of North Carolina Press, 2000); and Sean Brawley and Chris Dixon, "Jim Crow Downunder? African American Encounters with White Australia, 1942–1945," *Pacific Historical Review* 71 (Fall 2002). Of special note is Chris Dixon and Sean Brawley, "Tan Yanks and a 'Semblance of Civilization': African American Encounters with the South Pacific, 1941–45," in *Through Depression and War: The United States and Australia,* ed. Peter Bastian and Roger Bell (Sydney, Australia: Australian-American Fulbright Commission and the Australian and New Zealand American Studies Association, 2002). I would like to thank Chris Dixon for sharing this timely piece with me.

Part One • The Crucible

Epigraph: George M. Shuffer Jr., *My Journey to Betterment: An Autobiography* (New York: Vantage Press, 1999), 28.

One • The Great Depression and African American Youth Culture

Epigraph: Mary McLeod Bethune, "I'll Never Turn Back No More!" Southern Regional Office, General Office File, box A61, 1939–Miscellany, National Urban League Papers, Manuscript Division, Library of Congress, Washington, D.C.

1. Leo Logan interview with author.

2. Mary McLeod Bethune, "I'll Never Turn Back No More!," Southern Regional Office, General Office File, box A61, 1939–Miscellany, National Urban League Papers, Manuscript Division, Library of Congress, Washington, D.C.

3. Richard Sterner, *The Negro's Share: A Study of Income, Consumption, Housing, and Public Assistance* (New York: Harper and Brothers, 1943), 34.

4. Bernard Karpinos, *The Socio-Economic Status and Employment Status of Urban Youth in the United States, 1935–36* (Washington, DC: GPO, 1941), 15.

5. United States Works Projects Administration, *Youth on Relief* (Washington, DC: GPO, 1936); Bruce L. Melvin and Elna N. Smith, *Rural Youth: Their Situation and Prospects* (Washington, DC: GPO, 1938), 29.

6. United States Works Projects Administration, *Statistics on Youth* (Washington, DC: GPO, 1935).

7. Ibid.; George P. Rawick, "The New Deal and Youth: The Civilian Conservation Corps, the National Youth Administration, and the American Youth Congress" (Ph.D. diss., University of Wisconsin, 1957), 23.

8. U.S. Bureau of the Census, *Census of Partial Employment, Unemployment and Occupations: 1937,* vol. 1, *United States Summary, Geographic Divisions, and States from Alabama to Indiana* (Washington, DC: GPO, 1938); U.S. Bureau of the Census, *Census of Partial Employment, Unemployment and Occupations: 1937,* vol. 2, *States from Iowa to New York* (Washington, DC: GPO, 1938); U.S. Bureau of the Census, *Census of Partial Employment, Unemployment and Occupations: 1937,* vol. 3, *States from North Carolina to Wyoming, Alaska, and*

Hawaii (Washington, DC: GPO, 1938); U.S. Bureau of the Census, *Census of Partial Employment, Unemployment and Occupations: 1937*, vol. 4, *Final Report on Total and Partial Unemployment*, prepared by the Office of Administrator of the Census of Partial Employment, Unemployment, and Occupations (Washington, DC: GPO, 1938); United States Works Progress Administration, *Statistics on Youth* (Washington, DC: GPO, 1935).

9. Henry L. Williams interview with author, 7 February 1993.

10. Raymond Jenkins interview with author, 28 February 1990.

11. Col. Duncan K. Major Jr., Acting Assistant Chief of Staff, G-3, to C. A. Barnett, Associated Negro Press, 7 June 1933, Administrative Files, folder: Correspondence, USACC Records.

12. William F. Fentress interview with author; J. Fred Kurtz, Assistant to the Director, Relief Division, Pennsylvania State Emergency Relief Board, to W. Frank Persons, 19 March 1935, Administrative Files, USACC Records.

13. W. Frank Persons to Roy Wilkins, NAACP Assistant Secretary, 2 June 1933, Administrative File, box C-223, group I, folder: Civilian Conservation Corps, 1933, NAACP Papers, LOC; C. W. Spofford, Veterans Administration, to Roy Wilkins, NAACP Assistant Secretary, 21 October 1933, Administrative File, box C-223, group I, folder: Civilian Conservation Corps, 1933, NAACP Papers, LOC; "U.S. Labor Dept Assures No J.C. in Reforesting," *Baltimore Afro-American*, 16 April 1933, 22.

14. Charles W. Johnson, "The Civilian Conservation Corps: The Role of the Army" (Ph.D. diss., University of Michigan, 1968), 143.

15. Howard Oxley, "The Civilian Conservation Corps and the Education of the Negro," *Journal of Negro Education* 7 (July 1938), 148.

16. "276 Foresters from Baltimore in Camps," *Baltimore Afro-American*, 22 April 1933.

17. Johnson, "Civilian Conservation Corps," 150.

18. Ibid., 154.

19. Ibid., 150.

20. "49,000 Negro Enrollees in CCC," *New York Age*, 26 October 1935, 3.

21. Percy S. Roberts interview with author; Camp Inspection Report of William P. Hannon, CCC Special Investigator, 3, 4, 5 February 1937, Division of Investigations, Camp Inspection Reports, 1933–42, folder: Illinois, CP2, Winnetaka (formerly SP-15), CCC Records.

22. For more on the army's involvement in the Civilian Conservation Corps, see John A. Salmond, *The Civilian Conservation Corps, 1932–1942: A New Deal Case Study* (Durham, NC: Duke University Press, 1967); Johnson, "Civilian Conservation Corps," chap. 8; Rawick, "New Deal and Youth," chaps. 3, 6; and Michael W. Sherraden, "The Civilian Conservation Corps: Effectiveness of the Camps" (Ph.D. diss., University of Michigan, 1979).

23. "276 Foresters From Baltimore in Camps."

24. Eugene Boykin, "Genius of the Civilian Conservation Corps," January 1938, Administrative File, box 223, group I, folder: Civilian Conservation Corps, Eugene Boykin, 1937–1938, NAACP Papers, LOC.

25. Howard Oxley to Adjutant General, 15 March, box 17, folder: Office of Education, CCC, CCC Records; Charles Rutter, "CCC Boasts Model Educational Plan," *Pittsburgh Courier*, 28 November 1936.

26. William F. Fentress interview with author; Percy S. Roberts interview with author;

Leo Logan interview with author; CCC Camp Educational Report, Camp Lone Star, Kansas, Assistant Camp Education Adviser James Jones, 26 July 1938, Division of Investigations, Camp Inspection Reports, 1933–42, Kansas SCS-9 to SE-235, box 72, folder: Kansas, SES, Lone Star, Co. 2734, CCC Records.

27. "Camp Benezett," *Pittsburgh Courier*, 15 September 1934, 6; "Benezett, PA," *Pittsburgh Courier*, 29 September 1934, 7.

28. "Jail Harlem Negroes at Conservation Site, *New York Times*, 8 July 1933, Administrative File, box C-223, group I, folder: Civilian Conservation Corps, 1933, NAACP Papers, LOC.

29. "Inhuman Treatment of CCC Camp, Vets Charged," *Pittsburgh Courier*, 26 October 1935.

30. Percy S. Roberts interview with author; memorandum, Harold G. Chafey, Special CCC Investigator, to CCC Director, 19 May 1940, Division of Investigations, Camp Inspection Reports, 1933–42, Idaho SCS-7 to Illinois CP-2, box 57, folder: Illinois, Winnetaka (formerly SP-14), CCC Records.

31. War Department representative on CCC Advisory Council to Director, Civilian Conservation Corps, 13 September 1940, Division of Investigations, Camp Inspection Reports, 1933–42, Idaho SCS-7 to Illinois CP-2, box no. 57, folder: Illinois, Winnetaka (formerly SP-14), CCC Records.

32. "Discharge CCC Boys for Asking for Food," *Pittsburgh Courier*, 12 October 1935.

33. Report of Investigation Relative to Alleged Condition at Camp Pomona, Joseph A. Atkins, District Commander, to Adjutant General, 25 January 1938, Division of Investigations, Camp Inspection Reports, 1933–42, DF8-F2, box 59, folder: Illinois, F2, Pomona Co. 620, CCC Records.

34. Supplemental Report, Camp CP-2, Company 605, Glenview, Illinois, Camp Skokie Valley, 19 May 1940, Division of Investigations, Camp Inspection Reports, 1933–42, Idaho SCS-7 to Illinois CP-2, box 57, folder: Illinois, Winnetaka (formerly SP-14), CCC Records.

35. CCC Camp Educational Report, Ralph L. Mabry, Educational Adviser, 620th Post Office–Pomona, Illinois, 23 January 1941, Division of Investigations, Camp Inspection Reports, 1933–42, DF8-F2, box 59, folder: Illinois, F2, Pomona Co. 620, CCC Records.

36. Camp Inspection Report of Pomona Illinois Company 620, F-2, District Special Investigator Harold G. Chafey, 12 January 1940, Division of Investigations, Camp Inspection Reports, 1933–42, DF8-F2, box 59, folder: Illinois, F2, Pomona Co. 620, CCC Records; Distribution of Man-Days for Three Preceding Months, Ponoma Camp F-2, CCC Special Investigator Harold G. Chafey, 23 January 1941, Division of Investigations, Camp Inspection Reports, 1933–42, DF8-F2, box 59, folder: Illinois, F2, Pomona Co. 620, CCC Records.

37. William F. Fentress interview with author.

38. "Youths Urged to Join CMTC," *Philadelphia Afro-American*, 27 May 1939; memorandum, Information for Blue Course Trainees Relative to Commissions in the Officers' Reserve Corps, Adjutant, 8th Infantry, CMTC Headquarters, 22 July 1940, 2nd Corps Area Citizens' Military Training Camp, Annual Report, 1930–40, Fort Dix–Pine Camp, N.Y., box 7, 5 July–3 August 1940, USACC Records.

39. "Select Reserve Officers for Citizen's Camp," *Pittsburgh Courier*, 25 July 1936; West A. Hamilton, Oral History Interview, Moorland-Spingarn Research Center, Howard Univer-

sity, Washington, D.C.; William C. Matney, ed., *Who's Who among Black Americans*, 1st ed., *1975–1976* (Northbrook, IL: Who's Who Among Black Americans, 1976), 1:512.

40. John D. Howard interview with author.

41. Charles Johnson Jr., "Black Soldiers in the National Guard, 1877–1949" (Ph.D. diss., Howard University, 1976), 378.

42. "Interest in Citizens' Military Training Camp at Fort Howard," *Philadelphia Afro-American*, 23 July 1938.

43. Claude Ferebee to Walter White, 19 August 1945, Administrative File, box G-648, 93rd Division, 1943–46, group II, NAACP Papers, LOC.

44. Henry E. Dabbs, *A First Edition Reference Work on Black Brass: Black Generals and Admirals in the Armed Forces of the United States* (Freehold, NJ: Afro-American Heritage House, 1984), 180; Matney, *Who's Who among Black Americans*, 1st ed., *1975–1976* 1:314.

45. John D. Howard interview with author.

46. Reuben E. Fraser Jr. interview with author.

47. John D. Howard interview with author.

48. Annual Report of Operating Costs, Washington, D.C., High Schools (Colored), Fiscal Year 1939, entry 121.2–ROTC, Annual Report, Third Corps Area ROTC General Correspondence, 1925–40, box 15, USACC Records.

49. "Officer Out in Front," *The 6's Review*, 1 March 1945, 2, entry 188, box 260, folder: 332nd Fighter Group to 761 Tank Destroyer Battalion, OCA Records.

50. Dutton Ferguson, "N. A. A. C. P. Aid Sought to Curb Vanishing Ranks among Race Soldiers," *Pittsburgh Courier*, 26 May 1934.

51. John D. Howard interview with author.

52. Questionnaire, Howard University, 13 October 1927, War Department, Office of the Chief of Infantry, file: 1927, Third Service Command, ROTC, box 451, entry 96, USACC Records.

53. Annual Report of Operating Costs, Howard University, Fiscal Year 1939, entry 121.2–ROTC, Third Corps Area, ROTC General Correspondence, 1925–40, box 15, USACC Records.

54. "W. Virginia State to Provide Military Training for Youths," *Pittsburgh Courier*, 20 February 1937.

55. Walter B. Sanderson Jr. interview with author; Vincent J. Browne interview with author; Questionnaire, Howard University, 13 October 1927.

56. Walter B. Sanderson Jr. interview with author.

57. Vincent J. Browne interview with author; Iris Cloyd, ed., *Who's Who among Black Americans: 1990–1991* (Detroit: Gale Research, 1991), 167.

58. Vincent J. Browne, "A Program for Negro Preparedness," *Opportunity* 18 (August 1940), 230–31.

Two • *Why Should I Fight?*

Epigraphs: Horace R. Cayton, "Negro Morale," *Opportunity* 19 (December 1941), 371; Ulysses G. Lee, *United States Army in World War II, Special Studies: The Employment of Negro Troops* (Washington, DC: Office of the Chief of Military History, 1966), 45.

1. Judith Stein, *The World of Marcus Garvey: Race and Class in Modern Society* (Baton

Rouge: Louisiana State University Press, 1986), chap. 13; E. David Cronon, *Black Moses: The Story of Marcus Garvey and the Universal Negro Improvement Association* (Madison: University of Wisconsin Press, 1955), chaps. 2, 7; Gerald Gill, "Dissent, Discontent and Disinterest: Afro-American Opposition to the United States Wars of the Twentieth Century" (manuscript in the possession of Robin D. G. Kelley), 128–29. I wish to thank Robin Kelley for bringing this important work to my attention.

2. St. Clair Drake, *Churches and Voluntary Associations in the Chicago Negro Community* (Chicago: Works Projects Administration, 1940), 238.

3. George Shepperson, "Ethiopianism: Past and Present," in *Christianity in Tropical Africa: Studies Presented and Discussed at the Seventh International African Seminar, University of Ghana, April 1965*, ed. C. G. Baeta (London: Oxford University Press, 1968), 249.

4. Roi Ottley, *"New World A-Coming": Inside Black America* (Boston: Houghton Mifflin, 1943), 107.

5. "A Committee for Ethiopia Is Formed; Rev. A. C. Powell Made Vice Chairman of New Group," *Norfolk Journal & Guide*, 27 July 1935.

6. "New York Man Sails to Work for Ethiopia; Dr. Willis N. Huggins to Help Shape World Opinion," *Norfolk Journal & Guide*, 3 August 1935.

7. "Italian-Ethiopian War Scare Boom to Numerous Religious Cult Leaders," *Norfolk Journal & Guide*, 27 July 1935.

8. Drake, *Churches and Voluntary Associations*, 237.

9. Ottley, *"New World A-Coming,"* 98.

10. Richard Wright, "Joe Louis Uncovers Dynamite," *New Masses*, 8 October 1935, 18–19.

11. Frank Little Clipping File (in author's possession); Alvirita Little interview with author.

12. Reuben E. Fraser Jr. interview with author.

13. Nelson Peery interview with author, 4 December 1994.

14. George M. Shuffer Jr. interview with author, 14 June 1993.

15. Gill, "Dissent, Discontent and Disinterest," 131.

16. George Padmore, "The Second World War and the Darker Races," *Crisis* (November 1939), 327–28.

17. Byron R. Skinner, "The Double 'V': The Impact of World War II on Black America" (Ph.D. diss., University of California, Berkeley, 1978), 14.

18. J. R. Johnson [C. L. R. James], *Why Negroes Should Oppose the War* (New York: Pioneer Publishers, 1939), 5.

19. Horace Mann Bond, "Should the Negro Care Who Wins the War?" *Annals of the American Academy of Political and Social Science* 223 (September 1942), 81–84; E. E. Johnson, "Should Negroes Save Democracy?" *Scribner's Commentator* 11 (November 1941), 57–62; "What Have Negroes to Fight For?" *PM*, 7 May 1941, 16–17; Adam C. Powell Jr., "Is This a White Man's War?" *Common Sense* 11 (April 1942), 111–13; Roi Ottley, "A White Folks' War?" *Common Ground* 11 (Spring 1942), 29.

20. St. Clair Drake and Enoch Waters, "Blitz over Georgia," *Chicago Defender*, 25 September 1940.

21. "American Nazism," *Opportunity* 19 (February 1941), 35.

22. Walter White, "What the Negro Thinks of the Army," *Annals of the American Academy of Political and Social Science* 223 (September 1942), 67.

23. Horace Cayton, "Negro Morale," *Opportunity* 19 (December 1941), 373.

24. William N. Jones, "What Will Adolf Hitler Do to Us If He Wins?" *Philadelphia Afro-American*, 9 September 1939.

25. Ralph Matthews, "Watching the Big Parade," *Baltimore Afro-American*, 30 March 1940.

26. *Pittsburgh Courier*, 20 December 1941.

27. National Conference on Problems of the Negro and Negro Youth, 6–8 January 1937, Southern Regional Office, General Office File, 1919–79, box A61, 1939, National Urban League Papers, Manuscript Division, Library of Congress, Washington, D.C.

28. "Launch Campaign for Army, Navy Recognition," *Pittsburgh Courier*, 19 February 1938.

29. Robert L. Vann to President Franklin D. Roosevelt, 19 January 1939, OF 93, Colored Matters (Negroes), X-Refs, 1938–39, FDRL; editorial, "A Negro Division," *Pittsburgh Courier*, 19 February 1938.

30. "Only 3,604 Colored in U.S. Army," *Philadelphia Afro-American*, 28 October 1939.

31. Levi Pierce to Secretary of War Harry H. Woodring, 10 October 1939, Barnett Papers, Part 3: Subject Files on Black Americans, 1918–67, Series F: The Military, 1925–65, reel 1; "U.S. Army Men Get Sissy Jobs," *Philadelphia Afro-American*, 14 October 1939; "1,208 Race Troops Carry Guns, Rest Chambermaids," *Pittsburgh Courier*, 30 April 1938.

32. Levi Pierce to Secretary of War Harry H. Woodring, 10 October 1939, Barnett Papers.

33. Transcripts of West A. Hamilton, Oral History Interview, Moorland-Spingarn Research Center, Howard University, Washington, D.C.; Louis Lautier, "1350 Commissioned in Army; Only 5 Colored," *Baltimore Afro-American*, 4 May 1940.

34. Louis Lautier, "Only 7 States Have Units of National Guard," *Philadelphia Afro-American*, 23 July 1938; "Fear Shift of N.G. Units to Labor Status," *Baltimore Afro-American*, 13 April 1940; Charles Johnson Jr., "Black Soldiers in the National Guard, 1877–1949" (Ph.D. diss., Howard University, 1976), 448–49.

35. *Pittsburgh Courier*, 19, 26 March, 2, 9, 16, 23, 30 April 1938.

36. Augusta Strong, "Southern Youth's Proud Heritage," *Freedomways* (First Quarter 1964), 40–42; "Youth Congress Endorses Courier Drive," *Pittsburgh Courier*, 16 April 1938.

37. "Steering Committee Set Up to Guide Army Bills through House, Senate," *Pittsburgh Courier*, 16 April 1938; "Courier Equality Fight to Congress," *Pittsburgh Courier*, 2 April 1938; "Fish Introduces Courier Bill," *Pittsburgh Courier*, 9 April 1938.

38. "We Will Have to Fight," *Pittsburgh Courier*, 12 March 1938.

39. Diary 1940, 1–10 June, 14–21 September 1940, box 3, Rayford Logan Papers, Manuscript Division, Library of Congress, Washington, D.C.

40. Diary 1940, 4 September 1940, box 3, Rayford W. Logan Papers, Manuscript Division, Library of Congress, Washington, D.C.; "Fish Amendment Covers Draftees and Volunteers," *Pittsburgh Courier*, 14 September 1940.

41. U.S. Congress, *United States Statutes at Large*, 76th Cong., 2nd and 3rd sess., 54 (1939–40) (Washington, DC: GPO, 1940), 887.

42. Diary 1940, 31 August 1940, box 3, Rayford W. Logan Papers, Manuscript Division, Library of Congress, Washington, D.C.

43. Ulysses G. Lee, *United States Army in World War II, Special Studies: The Employment of Negro Troops* (Washington, DC: Office of the Chief of Military History, 1966), 74.

44. "Executive Board of NMA Supports Army-Navy Fight," *Pittsburgh Courier,* 23 April 1938; telegram, Dr. William M. Thomas to Franklin D. Roosevelt, 5 July 1938, Official File 93, Colored Matters (Negroes), X-Refs., 1938–39, FDRL.

45. "Philly's Men Favor Draft," *Baltimore Afro-American,* 17 August 1940.

46. Ibid.; "The Inquiring Reporter; Are You in Favor of Conscription for Peace-Time Military Training?" *Baltimore Afro-American,* 7 September 1940.

47. "Refuse to Fight Unless Trained, Diggs Urges," *Baltimore Afro-American,* 29 June 1940.

48. "A Few of 463,835 Who Registered Here for Selective Service," *Chicago Defender,* 26 October 1940; U.S. Bureau of the Census, *Sixteenth Census of the United States: 1940, Population; Second Series: Characteristics of the Population, United States Summary* (New York: Arno Press, 1976), 117.

49. U.S. Selective Service System, *Special Monograph no. 10: Special Groups,* vol. 1 (Washington, DC: GPO, 1953), 86; "U.S. Calls Million Men," *Baltimore Afro-American,* 19 October 1940.

50. Thomas M. White interview with author, 6 February 1993; "Volunteers Make Up Major Part of Draft Board's Negro Quota," *Cleveland Call & Post,* 22 February 1941; Special Orders, Grad Officer Candidate Course, Thornton Chase, Colonel, Adjutant General, Headquarters, the Infantry School, Fort Benning, Ga., 21 July 1942 (in author's possession).

51. U.S. Selective Service System, *Special Monograph no. 10: Special Groups,* vol. 2 (Washington, DC: GPO, 1953), 101; Willard L. Jarrett interview with author, 19 July 1993 and 30 March 1993; Bismark Williams Jr. interview with author.

52. U.S. Selective Service System, *Special Monograph no. 10: Special Groups,* 2:103; U.S. Selective Service, *Special Monograph no. 10: Special Groups,* 1:85.

53. Director of the Selective Service System, *Selective Service as the Tide of War Turns: The Third Report of the Director of Selective Service, 1943–1944* (Washington, DC: GPO, 1945), 593.

54. "Fourth Corps Area Leads in Number of Draftees," *Chicago Defender,* 22 March 1941; "4,780 from Illinois in First Draft," *Chicago Defender,* 26 October 1940.

55. Memorandum, Executive Assistant to the Director of Selective Service for William Hastie, Civilian Aide to the Secretary of War, 28 January 1941, in *Special Monograph no. 10: Special Groups,* 1:92.

56. "Local Boards Send 191 Draftees to Army Camp," *Chicago Defender,* 22 March 1941.

57. "Toledo Draft Boards Induct 63 Negroes for Uncle," *Cleveland Call & Post,* 9 January 1942; "Lucas County Draft Board Inducts More Recruits," *Cleveland Call & Post,* 13 June 1942.

58. U.S. Selective Service, *U.S. Selective Service in Peacetime: First Report of the Director of Selective Service, 1940–31* (Washington, DC: GPO, 1942), 254–56.

59. Major Lewis B. Hershey to Henry L. Stimson, Secretary of War, 14 February 1941, Official Papers, Lewis Hershey Papers, Archives, USAMHI.

60. "Draft Machinery Goes into High in Negro Wards," *Cleveland Call & Post,* 25 January 1941; "Watching the 'Draft Induction Mill' at Central Armory," *Cleveland Call & Post,* 29 March 1941, 8; "Ohio Draftees Are Inducted at Cleveland; First of State's Soldiers Become Guardians of Country's Welfare," *Cleveland Call & Post,* 1 March 1941.

61. Clarence L. Gaines interview with author.

62. Frank E. Smith interview with author.

63. Henry L. Williams interview with author, 7 February 1993.

64. "Legion Post Plans 'Farewell' Dance for Race Draftees," *Cleveland Call & Post*, 15 February 1941.

65. "Plan 'Farewell Dance' for National Guard; Guardsmen and Friends to Get Send-Off March 8th," *Cleveland Call & Post*, 1 March 1941.

66. "9,000 Jam Station, Streets As Record Group of Negro Draftees Join Armed Forces," *Cleveland Call & Post*, 11 July 1942.

67. "Volunteers Fill State's First Draft Quota of 157," *Baltimore Afro-American*, 16 November 1940; "Protest Scheme to Defer Colored Draftees," *Pittsburgh Courier*, 28 December 1940.

68. "Army Opening Doors to New Group of Men; Fulton Is Sending 49 Negro Youths," *Atlanta Daily World*, 6 August 1941.

69. "Band Plays 'Tuxedo Junction' As 23 Alabama Draftees Go to Camp," *Pittsburgh Courier*, 21 December 1940.

70. "Draft Board 18 in Hunt for Delinquents," *Cleveland Call & Post*, 11 October 1941; "20 Delinquents in Draft Board No. 13," *Cleveland Call & Post*, 14 March 1943; "Draft Board 13 Seeks Registrants Who Ducked Exams," *Cleveland Call & Post*, 21 March 1942; "Draft Board 18 Seeks Delinquents," *Cleveland Call & Post*, 14 March 1943.

71. "Release of 500 Martyrs Is Demanded," *Chicago Defender*, 25 September 1940, 4; Phillip McGuire, "Black Civilian Aides and the Problems of Racism and Segregation in the United States Armed Forces: 1940–1950" (Ph.D. Diss., Howard University, 1975), 50.

72. Memorandum, Selective Service Statistics, Colonel Campbell C. Johnson, 25 October 1945, box 442, G-1, Personnel, entry 43, WDGS/WDSS Records; Selective Service System, *Selective Service in Wartime: Second Report of the Director of Selective Service, 1941–1942* (Washington, DC: GPO, 1943), 291.

73. "15 Jailed in Draft Evasion Roundup Here," *Michigan Chronicle*, 22 May 1943.

74. Raymond Jenkins interview with author, 28 February 1990.

75. Leo Logan interview with author.

76. Durward P. Griffey interview with author.

77. Elliotte J. Williams interview with author.

78. John W. Marshall interview with author.

79. Edward A. Freeman interview with author; Florence Murray, ed., *The Negro Handbook: 1941* (New York: Wendell Malliet and Co., 1942), 2; "Back to Arizona," *Atlanta Daily World*, 3 February 1943; G. James Fleming and Christian E. Burckel, eds., *Who's Who in Colored America: An Illustrated Biographical Directory of Notable Living Persons of African Descent in the United States* (Yonkers-on-Hudson, NY: Christian E. Burckel and Assoc., 1950), 196.

80. Memorandum, G-1 for the Chief of Staff, Subject: Use of Negro Manpower in Time of Emergency, 26 April 1937, entry 43, box 442, G-1 Personnel, WDGS/WDSS Records; Memorandum, Robert P. Patterson, Assistant Secretary of War, for Franklin D. Roosevelt, 8 October 1940, Official File 93, Colored Matters (Negro), October–December 1940, FDRL.

81. "Negro Reserve Officers Not Called; Only Whites Called for Active Duty," *Baltimore Afro-American*, 28 September 1940.

82. Johnson, "Black Soldiers in the National Guard, 1877–1949," 468.

83. Nina E. Mueller, "The Negro in World War II and Implications for Status Change" (master's thesis, University of Texas at Austin, 1947), 39.

84. Survey and Recommendations Concerning the Integration of the Negro Soldier into the Army, Submitted to the Secretary of War by the Civilian Aide to the Secretary of War, Memorandum, Civilian Aide to the Secretary of War to the Secretary of War through the Undersecretary of War, 22 September 1941, entry 236, box 259, OCA Records.

85. Ibid.

86. Ibid.

87. Memorandum, Chief of Staff George C. Marshall for Secretary of War Stimson, 1 December 1941, OCA Records.

88. C. C. Ballou to the Assistant Commandant, General Staff College, 14 March 1920, Army War College, USAMHI.

89. Allen J. Greer to Assistant Commandant, General Staff College, Subject: Use to Be Made of Negroes in the U.S. Military Service, 13 April 1920, Army War College, USAMHI.

90. Colonel Herschel Tupes to Colonel Allen J. Greer, General Staff, War Plans Division, Subject: Employment of Negroes in Our Military Establishment, 26 March 1919, Army War College, USAMHI.

91. William P. Jackson to Assistant Commandant, General Staff College, Subject: Use to Be Made of Negroes in the U.S. Military Service, 28 March 1920, Army War College, USAMHI.

92. Major Thomas A. Roberts to Assistant Commandant, General Staff College, 5 April 1920, Army War College, USAMHI.

93. Colonel Vernon A. Caldwell to Assistant Commandant, General Staff College, Subject: Use to Be Made of Negroes in the U.S. Military Service, 14 March 1920, Army War College, USAMHI.

94. Memorandum, G-3 for Chief of Staff, 28 November 1922, entry 43, box 127, WDGS/WDSS Records.

95. The Adjutant General to the Commanding Generals of all Corps Areas, Subject: The Use of Negro Manpower in the Event of Complete Mobilization, 12 July 1923, entry 43, box 442, G-1 Personnel, WDGS/WDSS Records.

96. Memorandum, Malin Craig, Assistant Chief of Staff, to the Chief of Staff, Subject: The Use of Negro Manpower in the Event of a Mobilization for a Major Emergency, 26 March 1927, entry 43, box 442, G-1 Personnel, WDGS/WDSS Records.

97. Memorandum, G-1 for the Chief of Staff, Subject: Use of Negro Manpower in Time of Emergency, 26 April 1937, entry 43, box 442, G-1 Personnel, WDGS/WDSS Records.

98. The Adjutant General's Office, *Official Army Register: January 1, 1946* (Washington, DC: GPO, 1946), 677; A. N. Marquis Company, *Who Was Who in America: A Companion Biographical Reference Work to Who's Who in America* (Chicago: A. N. Marquis Co., 1963), 3:359; Roger Spiller, ed., *Dictionary of American Military Biography* (Westport, CT: Greenwood Press, 1984), 1:6–7.

99. Robert R. Sears, "Lewis Madison Terman," in *Dictionary of American Biography, Supplement 6: 1956–1960*, ed. John A. Garraty (New York: Charles Scribner's Sons, 1980), 626–27.

100. Henry Clay Smith, "Walter Van Dyke Bingham," in *Dictionary of American Biography, Supplement 5: 1951–1955*, ed. John A. Garraty (New York: Charles Scribner's Sons, 1977), 58–59; "Dr. Walter V. Bingham, Psychologist, 72," *New York Times*, 9 July 1952.

101. May V. Seagoe, *Terman and the Gifted* (Los Altos, CA: William Kaufmann, 1988), 64–65.

102. Classification and Enlisted Replacement Branch, AGO, "Personnel Research in the Army: I, Background and Organization," *Psychological Bulletin* 40 (February 1942), 133.

103. Classification and Enlisted Replacement Branch, AGO, "The Army General Classification Test," *Psychological Bulletin* 42 (December 1945), 760–66.

104. Memorandum, Joseph R. Dorsey for the 93rd Commanding General, 25 April 1943, Subject: Notes on the Distribution of AGCT Scores in the 93rd Infantry Division and the Disposition of Grade V Enlisted Men, box: Inspection Tours, United States, Texas–Virginia, Numbered Units, Davis Papers.

105. Lieutenant General Courtney H. Hodges to Lesley J. McNair, Headquarters, Army Ground Forces, 8 April 1943, file 322, AGF, 93rd Infantry Division, Organization & Tactical Units, binder I, AGF Records.

106. Walter V. Bingham, "Personnel Classification Testing in the Army," *Science*, 29 September 1944, 276.

107. Staff, Personnel Research Section, Classification and Enlisted Replacement Branch, AGO, "Personnel Research in the Army; II: The Classification System and the Place of Testing," *Psychological Bulletin* 40 (March 1943), 207.

108. "War to Figure in NAACP Agenda; Conference to Consider Relation to Our Rights," *Baltimore Afro-American,* 15 June 1940.

109. "Philly Host to NAACP Conference," *Baltimore Afro-American,* 22 June 1940.

110. "Mass Protests against Army Jim Crow Urged," *Baltimore Afro-American,* 22 June 1940.

111. "Memorandum, Negro Participation in Armed Forces," Mary McLeod Bethune to President Franklin D. Roosevelt, undated (circa July 1940), Official File 93, Colored Matters (Negroes), 1940, FDRL.

112. *Pittsburgh Courier, Baltimore Afro-American,* 13, 27 April 1940; 18 May 1940; 1, 15, 22 June 1940; 13 July 1940; 17, 24 August 1940; 7, 14, 21 September 1940; 19 October 1940.

113. *Baltimore Afro-American,* 31 August 1940.

114. "Military Policy and the Negroes," *Socialist Appeal,* 9 November 1940, quoted in C. L. R. James et. al., *Fighting Racism in World War II* (New York: Monad Press, 1980), 60–61.

115. Eugene Kinckle Jones to President Franklin D. Roosevelt, September 1940, Official File 93, Colored Matters (Negroes), January–September 1940, FDRL.

116. "NAACP and Youth Disagree on War; Two Groups Divide over Army Draft," *Baltimore Afro-American,* 29 June 1940; "NAACP Turns Thumbs Down on Youth Protest against Compulsory Enlistment," *Baltimore Afro-American,* 29 June 1940.

117. "'You're Wrong,' Says Mitchell," *Baltimore Afro-American,* 17 August 1940.

118. Memorandum, Brigadier General F. M. Andrews, G-3 for the Chief of Staff, Subject: Employment of Negro Manpower, 3 June 1940, entry 43, box 442, G-3, Operations and Training, WDGS/WDSS Records.

119. Memorandum, Major General Henry H. Arnold for the Assistant Chief of Staff, G-3, 31 May 1940, box 442, G-3, Operations and Training, WDGS/WDSS Records.

120. Memorandum, Colonel Clyde L. Eastman for the Assistant Chief, G-3, 28 May 1940, box 442, G-3, Operations and Training, WDGS/WDSS Records.

121. Henry Stimson Diary, 27 September 1940, Stimson Papers.

122. Ibid., 25 October 1940.

123. George C. Marshall, interview by Forrest C. Pogue, in *George C. Marshall: Interviews and Reminiscences for Forrest C. Pogue*, ed. Larry I. Bland (Lexington, VA: George C. Marshall Foundation, 1991), 438, 501.

124. Memorandum, Brigadier General William E. Shedd for the Assistant Chief of Staff, G-3, 20 June 1940, box 442, G-3, Operations and Training, WDGS/WDSS Records.

125. Memorandum, Brigadier General George V. Strong for the Assistant Chief of Staff, G-3, 29 June 1940, box 442, G-3, Operations and Training, WDGS/WDSS Records.

126. Memorandum, Orlando Ward, Secretary of the General Staff, for the G-1, 5 September 1940, box 442, G-3, Operations and Training, WDGS/WDSS Records.

127. Press Release, "Expansion of Colored Organizations Planned," 16 September 1940, Official File 93, Colored Matters (Negro), January–September 1940, FDRL; "U.S. Orders 8 New Units," *Baltimore Afro-American,* 28 September 1940.

128. Memorandum, General George C. Marshall, Chief of Staff for the G-1, 14 September 1940, in Morris J. MacGregor and Bernard C. Nalty, eds., *Blacks in the United States Armed Forces: Basic Documents,* vol. 5, *Black Soldiers in World War II* (Wilmington, DE: Scholarly Resources, 1977), 25.

129. General George C. Marshall, Chief of Staff, to Senator Henry Cabot Lodge Jr., 27 September 1940, in Larry I. Bland, ed., *The Papers of George C. Marshall,* vol. 2, *"We Cannot Delay," July 1, 1939–December 6, 1941* (Baltimore: Johns Hopkins University Press, 1986), 336–37.

130. Press Release, NAACP, 5 October 1940, Official File 93, Colored Matters (Negro), October–December 1940, FDRL; Memorandum, Robert P. Patterson, Assistant Secretary of War, for Franklin D. Roosevelt, 8 October 1940, Official File 93, Colored Matters (Negro), October–December 1940, FDRL.

131. Remarks, George C. Marshall and Eugene R. Householder during Conference of Negro Newspaper Representatives, 8 December 1941, Barnett Papers, Part 3: Subject Files on Black Americans, 1918–60, Series F: The Military, 1925–65, reel 1.

132. "Plans Definitely Underway for Colored Army Division in Arizona," *Baltimore Afro-American,* 20 December 1941; "Rush New Jim Crow Army Plan; Select Base, Appeal for Volunteers," *Chicago Defender,* 20 December 1941; "Army Announces Plans for Formation of Ninety-third Infantry Division and New Air Squad," *Cleveland Call & Post,* 31 January 1942.

133. Walter White to Army Chief of Staff George C. Marshall, 22 December 1941, Barnett Papers, Part 3: Subject Files on Black Americans, 1918–60, Series F: The Military, 1925–65, reel 1.

134. Editorial, "For Democracy and Unity," *Chicago Defender,* 13 December 1941.

135. Editorial, "Sweet Nothings to 24 Editors," *Baltimore Afro-American,* 20 December 1941.

136. P. L. Prattis, "The Horizon: Conference of Negro Editors Was Challenge to War Department Officials," *Pittsburgh Courier,* 18 December 1941.

Three • Of Sage and Sand

Epigraph: Truman Gibson to Earl B. Dickerson, 23 November 1942, entry 188, box 207, folder: Fort Huachuca, Arizona, 1942–44, OCA Records.

1. General Court Martial Orders 68, Headquarters–93d Infantry Division, *United States v. Jerry Johnson,* General Court Martial 226766, 16 October 1942, Department of the Army, USAJ.

2. Findings of the Judge Advocate General, Office of the Judge Advocate, *United States v. Jerry Johnson,* 16 October 1942, 1–2.

3. George H. Allen, certificate of testimony, Holding by the Board of Review, *United States v. Jerry Johnson,* 25 July 1942, 1.

4. Edward F. Moran, certificate of testimony, Holding by the Board of Review, *United States v. Jerry Johnson,* 25 July 1942.

5. Lee E. Moore, certificate of testimony, Holding by the Board of Review, *United States v. Jerry Johnson,* 25 July 1942, 1–2.

6. Verbatim record of the trial, *United States v. Jerry Johnson,* 30 September 1942, Office of the Judge Advocate, Department of the Army, USAJ, 9–10.

7. "Start Work on Home for Negro Army Division; Twenty-fifth and 368th U.S. Army Regiments to Be Expanded to Total of 17,903 Men," *Cleveland Call & Post,* 20 December 1941. Based on the army's long-standing policy of racial segregation, Fort Huachuca was one of the few defense installations where black soldiers who served in the U.S. Army could receive military training. Located at the base of the Huachuca Mountains, the post was established during the last half of the nineteenth century and served as an advance headquarters and supply base for military personnel and settlers during the Indian Wars of the 1870s and 1880s. The fort later served as the home of the men of the 10th Cavalry while they guarded the United States–Mexico border during World War I. By the beginning of World War II, the cantonment area underwent massive construction in order to house the extra 11,309 soldiers who, combined with the 25th and 368th infantries, constituted the remainder of the U.S. 93rd Infantry Division.

8. Memorandum, Edward M. Almond to the Commanding General, 93rd Infantry Division, 30 June 1942, Subject: Reception System for Filler Replacements, Activation of 93rd Infantry Division, folder: Colonel Edward M. Almond–93rd Infantry Division, box: World War II–93rd and 92nd Division and Personal Papers, Edward Almond Papers, Archives, USAMHI.

9. *Ninety-third Blue Helmet,* 26 March 1943; Robert F. Cocklin, survey questionnaire correspondence, Arlington, Va., 11 May 1992. The personnel makeup for World War II infantry divisions was as follows: three regiments with each unit composed of approximately 3,000 men; each regiment was made up of three battalions along with a cannon company and an intelligence and reconnaissance platoon. The battalions, in turn, consisted of four companies, each constituting 190 or more men; each company normally had four platoons of 48 servicemen. Finally, platoons were broken down into two sections and two squads,

with 12 men constituting a regular squad. The division's total numbers were rounded out by large numbers of Headquarters, Heavy Weapons, Engineering, and Medical personnel.

10. Clarence L. Gaines interview with author; Clarence L. Gaines, "With Ohio's Soldiers," *Cleveland Call & Post*, 15 March 1941.

11. "Army Radioman Tells about Trip," *Baltimore Afro-American*, 22 March 1941.

12. Clarence L. Gaines, "With Ohio's Soldiers," *Cleveland Call & Post*, 22 March 1941; Henry L. Williams interview with author, 4 February 1993.

13. Walter B. Sanderson Jr. interview with author.

14. "New Family at Fort Huachuca," *Pittsburgh Courier*, 4 July 1942.

15. Reuben E. Fraser Jr. interview with the author.

16. "50 Draftees Ordered to Fort Custer," *Chicago Defender*, 8 March 1941; "20 Students to Officers Schools," *Baltimore Afro-American*, 4 April 1942; "Transfer 27 Officers to Ninety-third Division," *Chicago Defender*, 31 October 1942.

17. "Ninety-third Division Officers Visit West Medford," *Boston Guardian*, 8 December 1942.

18. Carter G. Woodson, *The Negro Professional Man and the Community* (Washington, DC: Association for the Study of Negro Life and History, 1934); "144 Negro Chaplains Serve in Armed Forces," *Pittsburgh Courier*, 12 December 1942; Luther M. Fuller, "The Chaplain and Army Morale Building" (n.d., 1942?), Schomburg Clipping File, New York Public Library, Schomburg Center for Research in Black Culture, New York; The Advisory Group of Church Representatives of the Joint Army and Navy Committee on Welfare and Recreation, "The Chaplain and the Negro in the Armed Services," 4 September 1944, enclosed in memorandum from Major General Luther D. Miller, Chief of Chaplains, to the Army Service Forces Director of Personnel, 4 January 1946, entry 188, box 187, folder: Chaplains-Departmental, OCA Records; Ulysses G. Lee, *United States Army in World War II, Special Studies: The Employment of Negro Troops* (Washington, DC: Office of the Chief of Military History, 1966); Edwin Lee, interview by Georgia Rountree, Winter 1972–73, Lee Papers; Hildrus A. Poindexter, *My World of Reality: An Autobiography* (Detroit: Balamp Publishing, 1973); Bernard C. Nalty, *Strength for the Fight: A History of Black Americans in the Military* (New York: Free Press, 1986); Donald F. Crosby, *Battlefield Chaplains: Catholic Priests in World War II* (Lawrence: University Press of Kansas, 1994).

19. Report of Detached Service by Chaplain Charles T. Watkins, 29 September 1942, Charles T. Watkins Career 201 File, RG 247, Records of the Office of the Chief of Chaplains, NARA.

20. James M. Whittico interview with author; Arthur Bunyan Caldwell, *History of the American Negro: West Virginia Edition* (Atlanta: A. B. Caldwell Publishing Co., 1923), 268–70; telegram, Wallace B. Christian to William H. Hastie, Civilian Aide to the Secretary of War, 8 May 1942, entry 188, box 215, March-on-Washington (Negro) to Medical School, OCA Records; Lawrence D. Reddick, "Letters from the Jim Crow Army," *Twice a Year* 14–15 (Fall–Winter 1946–47), 377. Further information about Whittico's family in West Virginia may be gleaned from Joe William Trotter's insightful book *Coal, Class, and Color: Blacks in Southern West Virginia, 1915–1931* (Urbana: University of Illinois Press, 1990).

21. Mary P. Motley, ed., *The Invisible Soldier: The Experience of the Black Soldier, World War II* (Detroit: Wayne State University Press, 1987), 89.

22. Edwin Lee interview by Georgia Rountree.

23. "Fort Huachuca," *Cleveland Call & Post,* 6 December 1941.

24. "Old Non-coms Annoy Fort Huachuca Recruits," *Baltimore Afro-American,* 18 November 1941.

25. Elliotte J. Williams interview with author.

26. Motley, *Invisible Soldier,* 74–75.

27. John W. Marshall interview with author.

28. Marke Toles interview with author.

29. Memorandum, unsigned, Subject: Morale at Low Ebb in Ninety-third Infantry division, entry 188, box 207, Fort Eustis, Va., to Fort Huachuca, Ariz., OCA Records; Nelson Peery, *Black Fire: The Making of an American Revolutionary* (New York: New Press, 1994), 155.

30. Proceedings, 29 August 1942, in *United States v. James D. Green,* General Court Martial 226860, transcript of the trial, Department of the Army, USAJ.

31. Proceedings, 24 August 1942, in *United States v. Leonard Holmes,* General Court Martial 224747, transcript of the trial, Department of the Army, USAJ.

32. Proceedings, 30 June 1942, in *United States v. Private James Rowe,* General Court Martial 34204378, transcript of the trial, Department of the Army, USAJ; Henry L. Stimson Diary, 13 October 1942, Stimson Papers; Secretary of War Henry L. Stimson to the President, 15 October 1942, Department of the Army, USAJ; directive, Franklin Delano Roosevelt to the Commanding General, 93rd Infantry Division, 17 October 1942, Department of the Army, USAJ; memorandum, Edwin N. Hardy to the Commanding General, 93rd Infantry Division, 6 November 1942, Department of the Army, USAJ.

33. "Akron Soldiers Do Miss Ohio's Fastest Growing Weekly," *Cleveland Call & Post,* 24 May 1941; Sgt. Wilson Isabell, "Fort Huachuca," *Cleveland Call & Post,* 26 June 1941; "Sergeant King Visits Aunt in Barberton," *Cleveland Call & Post,* 9 January 1943.

34. Edward R. Jones, "Fort Huachuca," *Cleveland Call & Post,* 21 June 1941; Benjamin Bolton, "Fort Huachuca," *Cleveland Call & Post,* 5 July 1941; Henry L. Williams interview with author, 4 February 1993; Thomas Counts, "Fort Huachuca," *Cleveland Call & Post,* 26 July 1941; William J. Slade, "News from Company L," *Cleveland Call & Post,* 26 July 1941.

35. William Slade, "Fort Huachuca," *Cleveland Call & Post,* 2 August 1941.

36. Edward Ross and Lewis D. Todd, "Company I," *Cleveland Call & Post,* 21 June 1941; Lewis D. Todd, "Fort Huachuca," *Cleveland Call & Post,* 9 August 1941.

37. Benjamin T. Layton interview with author.

38. "Fort Huachuca," *Cleveland Call & Post,* 26 July 1941; "Company I, Fort Huachuca," *Cleveland Call & Post,* 30 August 1941; "Soldiers in Uncle Sam's New Ninety-third Division," *Cleveland Call & Post,* 13 June 1942; "Soldiers Enjoy United States Army," *Houston Informer and Texas Freeman,* 13 June 1942.

39. "Twenty-fifth Infantry Band 74 Years Old," *Ninety-third Blue Helmet,* 16 October 1942.

40. Julius G. Thompson interview with author, 5 March 1993; Peter Dana, "Billy Kyle—Philly Boy—Makes Good in Big Way in 'Big Town' Whirl," *Philadelphia Tribune* 2 May 1942; Ole J. Astrup, "The Forgotten Ones: Billy Kyle," *Jazz Journal International* 37, no. 8 (1984), 10; "Uncle Sam Really Got a Bargain at Fort Huachuca," *Atlanta Daily World,* 14 January 1943.

41. Ollie Stewart, "Fort Huachuca Is Cluttered with Morale Missionaries," *Baltimore Afro-American*, 18 November 1941; Ollie Stewart, "Fort Huachuca, Army's Siberia, Gets Ready to Receive New Division," *Baltimore Afro-American*, 11 April 1942.

42. "Mrs. Dillon in Charge of Service Club," *Ninety-third Blue Helmet*, 2 October 1942.

43. "With Ohio Soldiers: Fort Huachuca," *Cleveland Call & Post*, 6 July 1941; Gus Clark, "With Ohio Soldiers–Fort Huachuca," *Cleveland Call & Post*, 25 October 1941.

44. Roy Wilkins, "Nurses Go to War," *Crisis* (February 1943), 42–43; Zola Mae Lang Fraser Personal Papers, Apple Valley, Minn. (in author's possession courtesy of Reuben Fraser).

45. "Miss Hawes with Red Cross Here," *Ninety-third Blue Helmet*, 30 October 1942; "Miss Hawes to Fort Huachuca," *Baltimore Afro-American*, 14 November 1942; "Red Cross Names Huachuca Assistant," *Pittsburgh Courier*, 14 November 1942.

46. "Joins Red Cross at Fort Huachuca," *Pittsburgh Courier*, 29 August 1942; "Helps Troops," *Detroit Tribune*, 22 August 1942; memorandum, Leonore Cox, Field Worker, to Perle Dow, Assistant Military and Naval Welfare Director, 3 August 1942, Subject: Recreational Report, Chronological Files, FHHM.

47. Memorandum, Cox to Dow, 3 August 1942.

48. Shirley Graham to W. E. B. Du Bois, 2 May 1942, Du Bois Papers, reel 53; Shirley Graham to Claude A. Barnett, 19 June 1942, box 318, folder 2, Barnett Papers; Shirley Graham to W. E. B. Du Bois, 30 October 1942, Du Bois Papers, reel 53.

49. Shirley Graham, "Negroes Are Fighting for Freedom," *Common Sense* 12 (February 1943), 45–50; Shirley Graham, "A Letter to the President," *PM Daily*, 24 June 1943.

50. Shirley Graham to W. E. B. Du Bois, 9 November 1941, Du Bois Papers, reel 53; Thomas M. White interview with author, 15 February 1991; "'Tenshun! Front and Center!" *Pittsburgh Courier*, 6 June 1942; Anna Rothe, "Shirley Graham," *Current Biography*, October 1946, 17–18; "Shirley Graham Du Bois, 69, Writer and Widow of Civil Rights Leader," *New York Times*, 5 April 1977.

51. "WAAC Companies Will Report to Fort Huachuca," *Atlanta Daily World*, 11 September 1942; "Lieutenant Sherard Heads WAAC Unit Reporting at Fort Huachuca; 10,000 Greet First Detail of Auxiliaries," *Atlanta Daily World*, 6 December 1942; "When WAACs Invaded Fort Huachuca," *Atlanta Daily World*, 24 December 1942.

52. "Two Companies of WAACs Arrive at Fort Huachuca," *Atlanta Daily World*, 9 December 1943.

53. "Des Moines Scene Unparalleled in History," *Pittsburgh Courier*, 1 August 1942; "Talk of the Troops," *Cleveland Call & Post*, 6 February 1943.

54. Irma Cayton, "W.A.A.C's," *Special Service Bulletin* 1 (March 1943), 10, 19.

55. Memorandum to Colonel Catron, 5 January 1943, ref: Negro WAAC Companies for duty with Ninety-third Division, entry 320.2, 1 January 1943, box 74, file: Activation of Post Headquarters Companies and Photographic Lab Companies, Sec. 2, S54, WDGS/WDSS Records.

56. Irma Jackson Cayton Wertz, "A First WAC" (MS in author's possession); Irma Jackson Cayton Wertz interview with author.

57. Gus Clark, "Fort Huachuca," *Cleveland Call & Post*, 21 June 1941; "'Cabin in Sky' Group Entertains Huachuca Soldiers," *Atlanta Daily World*, 5 October 1942; "Etta Moten Sings for

Soldiers at Fort Huachuca," *Pittsburgh Courier,* 31 January 1942; "Famous Movie Star Fetes Fort Huachuca Soldiers," *Pittsburgh Courier,* 13 March 1943.

58. "Noble Sissle to Play Here Christmas Day," *Ninety-third Blue Helmet,* 18 December 1942.

59. "Top Entertainment Labor Day for Ninety-third Soldiers," *Atlanta Daily World,* 5 September 1942.

60. "Negro Leader to Be Here Friday," *Arizona Daily Star,* 29 July 1942.

61. "Branch News," *Crisis* (January 1943), 28; Roy Wilkins, Assistant NAACP Secretary, to Captain John H. Healy, Public Relations Officer, 5 December 1942, Chronological Files, FHHM.

62. "Ninety-third Division Now Has Its Own Paper," *Baltimore Afro-American,* 26 September 1942; box: Unit Newspaper–*The Blue Helmet,* Warren McNaught Papers, Archives, USAMHI.

63. Charles T. Watkins, "Brotherhood Week," *Special Service Bulletin* 1 (March 1943), 14.

64. For example, see *Pittsburgh Courier,* 30 May; 6, 20 June; 4, 18 July; 5, 26 September; 3, 10, 17, 31 October; 14 November; 12, 19 December 1942; *Chicago Defender,* 13, 27 June; 18 July; 8 August; 5 September; 31 October 1942; 9, 23 January 1943; *Atlanta Daily World,* 1, 10 July; 17, 24 August; 1 September; 25 October 1942.

65. *Cleveland Call & Post,* 15, 22 March; 6, 26 April; 10, 17, 31 May; 7, 21 June; 19 July; 2 August; 11, 25 October; 8 November; 6 December 1941; 10, 17 January; 9 May; 6, 13, 27 June 1942.

66. *Baltimore Afro-American,* 22 March; 12 April; 3 May 1941.

67. *Chicago Defender,* 6 March; 3, 10 April 1943.

68. Truman K. Gibson to Claude A. Barnett, 11 May 1942, box 315, Barnett Papers; memorandum, Homer B. Roberts, Assistant Public Relations Officer, to Post Commander, Fort Huachuca, Arizona, 3 December 1942, Subject: Negro Newspaper Control, entry 188, box 207, Fort Eustis, Va., to Fort Huachuca, Ariz., OCA Records; Roy Wilkins, Assistant NAACP Secretary, to Captain John H. Healy, Public Relations Officer, 5 December 1942, Chronological Files, FHHM; Gunnar Myrdal, *An American Dilemma: The Negro Problem and Modern Democracy* (New York: Harper and Row, 1944); Richard M. Dalfiume, "The Forgotten Years' of the Negro Revolution," *Journal of American History* 55 (June 1968), 90–106; Lee Finkle, "The Conservative Aims of Militant Rhetoric: Black Protest during World War II," *Journal of American History* 60 (December 1973), 692–713; Neil Wynn, *The Afro-American and the Second World War* (New York: Holmes and Meier, 1976); Patrick Washburn, *A Question of Sedition: The Federal Government's Investigation of the Black Press during World War II* (New York: Oxford University Press, 1986); Robert Hill, introduction to *The FBI's RACON: Racial Conditions in the United States during World War II,* ed. Robert A. Hill (Boston: Northeastern University Press, 1995), 1–72.

69. Memorandum, unsigned, Subject: Morale at Low Ebb in Ninety-third Division, OCA Records.

70. Memorandum, Major General James C. Magee, Surgeon General to the U.S. Army Chief of Staff, 17 February 1943, Subject: Fort Huachuca–A Survey of Venereal Disease and Social Hygiene Conditions, file 322, AGF, 93rd Infantry Division, Organization & Tactical Units, binder I, AGF Records; "40-Mile State Speed Limit Is Set Up, Moore Asks 35 Or-

der," *Arizona Daily Star*, 23 September 1942; "35-Mile Limit on Auto Speed Will Be Arizona Rule," *Arizona Daily Star*, 1 October 1942.

71. "Motorists Are Defying Limits," *Arizona Daily Star*, 21 October 1942.

72. General Court-Martial Orders 30, Headquarters–93rd Infantry Division, *United States v. William Curry*, General Court Martial 223949, 1 August 1942, Department of the Army, USAJ; "Trial Awaited after Battle," *Arizona Daily Star*, 17 June 1942; "Huachuca Soldiers Battle Tucson Cops," *Indianapolis Recorder*, 27 June 1942; "Two Soldiers Held for Fort Huachuca Assaults," *Chicago Defender*, 4 July 1942.

73. Homer Roberts to Truman Gibson, Assistant Civilian Aide to the Secretary of War, 5 December 1944, entry 188, box 207, Fort Eustis, Va., to Fort Huachuca, Ariz., OCA Records; "Reports Conflict on Arizona Army Riot," *Chicago Defender*, 18 July 1942; "Race Soldiers at Guinea Southwest Theatre of War," *Indianapolis Recorder*, 18 July 1942; "Arizona Posse Kills Negro Soldier," *New York Age*, 18 July 1942; "Facts Withheld in Slaying of Soldier," *Baltimore Afro-American*, 25 July 1942; "Link Old Grudge against 368th with Killing of Soldier," *Baltimore Afro-American*, 25 July 1942.

74. Nelson Peery, interview by Terri Gross, National Public Radio Program: "Fresh Air," August 1994; Nelson Peery interview with author, 9 December 1994.

75. "2 Slain, 12 Hurt in Arizona Rioting," *Baltimore Afro-American*, 5 December 1942; "Jail 180 Soldiers in Arizona Riot, 2 Killed," *New York Age*, 5 December 1942; "Inside Story of Arizona Riot!" *Chicago Defender*, 5 December 1942; "General Davis Probes Phoenix Riot," *Pittsburgh Courier*, 5 December 1942.

76. Memorandum, unsigned, Subject: Morale at Low Ebb in Ninety-third Division, OCA Records; memorandum, Benjamin O. Davis Sr. to the Inspector General, 7 August 1942, Subject: Special Inspection of the Ninety-third Infantry Division, box: Inspection Tours, United States, Texas-Virginia, Numbered Units, Davis Papers.

77. "Arizona Girls Bemoan Troop Movements," *Baltimore Afro-American*, 11 April 1942.

78. Memorandum, unsigned, undated (possibly July 1942), entry 188, box 207, Fort Eustis, Va., to Fort Huachuca, Ariz., OCA Records.

79. "Sweeping Action to Halt Vice in Fry, Adjacent to Huachuca Is Taken by County Attorney," *Douglas Daily Dispatch*, 6 August 1944, Chronological Files, FHHM.

80. Nelson Peery, interview by Terri Gross, National Public Radio Program: "Fresh Air," August 1994.

81. Robert J. Johnson interview with author.

82. Memorandum, Major General James C. Magee, Surgeon General for the U.S. Army Chief of Staff, 17 February 1943, Subject: Fort Huachuca–A Survey of Venereal Disease and Social Hygiene Conditions, file 322, AGF, 93rd Infantry Division, Organization & Tactical Units, binder I, AGF Records.

83. Ibid.

84. Memorandum, Lesley J. McNair for the Assistant Chief of Staff, G-3, 9 March 1943, Subject: Ninety-third Division, file 322, AGF, 93rd Infantry Division, Organization & Tactical Units, binder I, AGF Records; Edwin Hardy, Fort Huachuca Post Commandant, to Lesley J. McNair, 17 March 1943, file 322, 93rd Infantry Division, Organization & Tactical Units, binder I, AGF Records.

85. Hardy to J. McNair, 17 March 1943.

86. Office Notes, Edwin Hardy, Conferences with Truman Gibson Jr., Charles Jackson, Mr. Robinson, George Bynum, Truman K. Gibson Sr., 9 July 1942, Subject: Development of Fry, Arizona, with Negro Capital, entry 188, box 207, Fort Eustis, Va., to Fort Huachuca, Ariz., OCA Records.

87. Truman K. Gibson Jr., Assistant Civilian Aide to the Secretary of War, to Truman K. Gibson Sr., 20 July 1942, entry 188, box 207, Fort Eustis, Va., to Fort Huachuca, Ariz., OCA Records; Truman K. Gibson Jr., Assistant Civilian Aide to the Secretary of War, to Edwin Hardy, Fort Huachuca Post Commander, 24 June 1942, entry 188, box 207, Fort Eustis, Va., to Fort Huachuca, Ariz., OCA Records.

88. Office Notes, Edwin Hardy, Conferences with Truman Gibson Jr., Charles Jackson, Mr. Robinson, George Bynum, Truman K. Gibson Sr., 9 July 1942, Subject: Development of Fry, Arizona, with Negro Capital; Truman K. Gibson, Civilian Aide to the Secretary of War, to William J. Trent Jr., Federal Works Administration, 27 July 1942, entry 188, box 207, Fort Eustis, Va., to Fort Huachuca, Ariz., OCA Records; "New Army Nite Club to Accommodate a Thousand," *Baltimore Afro-American*, 1 August 1942; "To Start Building near Fort Huachuca," *Atlanta Daily World*, 17 August 1942; Edwin Hardy, Fort Huachuca Post Commander, to Truman K. Gibson, Civilian Aide to the Secretary of War, 23 November 1942, entry 188, box 207, Fort Eustis, Va., to Fort Huachuca, Ariz., OCA Records; Hardy to McNair, 17 March 1943.

89. Truman K. Gibson Jr. to Field Recreation Representative James W. Geator, Federal Security Agency, 10 September 1944, entry 188, box 207, Fort Eustis, Va., to Fort Huachuca, Ariz., OCA Records; Letter, Truman K. Gibson Jr. to Colonel Edwin N. Hardy, Fort Huachuca Post Commander, 13 September 1944, entry 188, box 207, Fort Eustis, Va., to Fort Huachuca, Ariz., OCA Records.

90. "To Start Building near Fort Huachuca," *Atlanta Daily World*, 17 August 1942; "Fort Huachuca Is Incentive Enough for Nearby Fry City," *Oklahoma Eagle*, 14 November 1942; "Fort Huachuca Says Goodbye to Bad Fry," *Baltimore Afro-American*, 14 November 1942; "Fry Amusement Center; Williams Is a Designer of Structure," *California Eagle*, 24 March 1943; J. F. Weadock, "Squalid Village of Fry to Be Replaced by New Negro Center," *Arizona Daily Star*, 9 October 1942.

91. Memorandum, John Harlan, Inspector General's Department, to the Inspector General, 26 October, Subject: Investigation of Alleged Conditions at Fort Huachuca, Arizona, entry 26F, box 44, RG 159, Records of the Office of the Inspector General, Secret FBI Reports, NARA.

92. Truman K. Gibson Jr. to Claude A. Barnett, 24 October 1942, box 315, Barnett Papers.

93. Several works relating to the history of American sexuality have influenced my thinking on this score. These studies include Kathy Peiss, "'Charity Girls' and City Pleasures: Historical Notes on Working Class Sexuality, 1880–1920," in *Powers of Desire: The Politics of Sexuality*, ed. Ann Snitow (New York: Monthly Review Press, 1983), 74–87; Allan Berube, *Coming Out under Fire: The History of Gay Men and Women in World War II* (New York: Penguin Books, 1990); Beth Bailey and David Farber, *The First Strange Place: Race and Sex in World War II Hawaii* (Baltimore: Johns Hopkins University Press, 1994); Timothy J. Gilfoyle, *City of Eros: New York City, Prostitution, and the Commercialization of Sex, 1790–1920* (New York: Norton, 1992); George Chauncey, *Gay New York: Gender, Urban Culture, and the*

Making of the Gay Male World, 1890–1940 (New York: Basic Books, 1994); and Leisa D. Meyer, *Creating GI Jane: Sexuality and Power in the Women's Army Corps during World War II* (New York: Columbia University Press, 1996).

94. Biff Blake, "369th Infantry Marches More than Sixty Miles Last Week on Four Day Tactical March," *Ninety-third Blue Helmet*, 25 September 1942.

95. Memorandum for Brigadier General, Benjamin O. Davis Sr., Combat Firing Course at Charleston, 4 January 1943, box: Inspection Tours, United States, Alabama-Indiana, Davis Papers; "Combat Course at Charleston Offers Many Thrills for Soldiers, *Ninety-third Blue Helmet*, 26 February 1943; E. W. Baker, "Real Bullets Fly and Dynamite Bursts As Ninety-third 'Captures' Ghost Mining Town," *Pittsburgh Courier*, 27 February 1943.

96. Michael H. F. Mahoney, "Mervyn Freeman, Who Put Ninety-third in News Reels Last Week, Has Made Movies since He Was 16," *Ninety-third Blue Helmet*, 1 January 1943.

97. Michael H. F. Mahoney, "Earl Brown, Writer for Life, Doing Story on Ninety-third Infantry Division," *Ninety-third Blue Helmet*, 15 January 1943; "Negro Division; It Prepares to Go Overseas," *Life Magazine*, 9 August 1943, 37–41.

98. "Negro Division Eager to Fight," *Arizona Daily Star*, 17 January 1943; "Ninety-third 'Almost Ready,'" Says General Miller," *Baltimore Afro-American*, 23 January 1943.

99. "Lt. Krueger Inspects Ninety-third," *Pittsburgh Courier*, 17 October 1942, Chronological Files, FHHM; "Unit Draws Praise from High Command," *Pittsburgh Courier*, 17 October 1942; "General Inspects Men at Huachuca," *Arizona Daily Star*, 6 January 1943.

100. Memorandum, Benjamin O. Davis Sr. to the Inspector General, August 7, 1942, Subject: Special Inspection of the Ninety-third Infantry Division, Davis Papers; Vincent Tubbs, "General Davis Reviews New 369th Regiment," *Baltimore Afro-American*, 1 August 1942; "Negro General Inspects Fort," *Arizona Daily Star*, 23 July 1942.

101. Curtis Griffin interview with author; Thomas S. Pendergrass interview with author; Julius G. Thompson interview with author, 3 May 1993; Robert Galley interview with author.

102. Benjamin O. Davis Sr. to Sadie, 28 July 1942, folder: Personal letters to wife written in the United States, 13 January–20 August 1942, box: Personal Letters, Diary, 1941–45, Davis Papers.

103. Memorandum, Benjamin O. Davis Sr. to Commanding General, Fort Huachuca, 28 July 1942, Subject: Complaints, Prisoners, folder: Inspection Report from Office of the Inspector General for 93rd Infantry Division, box: Inspection Tours, United States, Texas-Virginia, Numbered Units, Davis Papers.

104. Ibid.

105. Peery, *Black Fire*, 144.

106. For more on this policy, see Bell I. Wiley, *The Training of Negro Troops* (Washington, DC: Army Ground Forces Historical Section, 1946); Jean Byers, *A Study of the Negro in Military Service* (Washington, DC: U.S. Department of Defense, 1950); Lee, *United States Army in World War II*, chap. 7; Nalty, *Strength for the Fight*, 163–64.

107. The A. N. Marquis Company, *Who Was Who in America: A Companion Biographical Reference Work to Who's Who in America* (Chicago: A. N. Marquis Co., 1963), 3:359; E. W. Baker, "Mississippian to Head Ninety-third Division," *Pittsburgh Courier*, 14 March 1942, 1.

108. Conversations between Lieutenant General (Ret.) Edward M. Almond and Cap-

tain Thomas G. Fergusson, Transcribed Manuscript, 25 March 1975, Anniston, Ala., p. 80, courtesy of the Senior Officers Debriefing Program, USAMHI.

109. John D. Howard interview with author.

110. Proceedings, 26 October 1942, in *United States v. Rudolph H. Porter,* General Court Martial 227912, transcript of the trial, Department of the Army, USAJ.

111. Leo Logan interview with author.

112. Ibid.

113. Reuben E. Fraser Jr. interview with author.

114. Memorandum, C. E. Nelson to All Officers at Fort Huachuca, 4 June 1942, Subject: Fort Huachuca Officers Clubs, folder: Inspection Reports for the Office of the Inspector General–Fort Huachuca, Ariz., box: Inspection Tours, United States, Alabama-Indiana, Davis Papers.

115. Ibid.; "Segregation at Fort Huachuca, One Clubhouse for White Army Officers; Another for Colored," *Pittsburgh Courier,* 4 July 1942.

116. Cornelius Smith, "Fort Huachuca: A Brief History" (manuscript in author's possession), 28.

117. "Arizona's Huge Long Staple Crop Requires Many Pickers," *Arizona Daily Star,* 29 May 1942.

118. Howard Welty, "Lack of Labor Growing Acute," *Arizona Daily Star,* 22 May 1942.

119. "Schools to Aid Cotton Picking," *Arizona Daily Star,* 30 May 1942; "State Cotton Crop Will Be Left in Field," *Arizona Daily Star,* 28 August 1942; "Cotton Picking Problem Acute," *Arizona Daily Star,* 29 August 1942; "Labor Import Plan Cleared," *Arizona Daily Star,* 15 September 1942; "Japs Will Aid Cotton Picking," *Arizona Daily Star,* 15 September 1942; "Weary Japanese Disappointed by First Day in Cotton Fields," *Arizona Daily Star,* 22 September 1942; "Cotton Picking Still Problem," *Arizona Daily Star,* 25 September 1942; Lack of Cotton Pickers Hikes Loss to Thousands Each Day," *Arizona Daily Star,* 30 September 1942; "Indians Treble Aid in Harvest," *Arizona Daily Star,* 2 October 1942; "Judges Approve Use of Convicts in Cotton Fields," *Arizona Daily Star,* 9 October 1942; "Cotton Picker Response Poor," *Arizona Daily Star,* 14 October 1942.

120. Governor Sidney Osborn to Walter White, 12 November 1942, group II, box 150, Soldier Complaints, 1942–43, NAACP Papers, LOC.

121. Henry L. Stimson Diary, February 26, 1943, Stimson Papers; Senate Committee on Agriculture and Forestry, *Food Supply of the United States,* pt. 1, 78th Cong., 1st sess., 23 February 1943, 266.

122. Senate Committee on Agriculture and Forestry, *Food Supply of the United States,* 274; Nathan Robertson, "Uses Draftees; Soldiers Pick Arizona Cotton, *PM Daily,* 24 February 1943; "Say Race Regiment to Become Cotton Pickers," *Michigan Chronicle,* 6 March 1943.

123. Peri Arnold, *Making the Managerial Presidency* (Princeton, NJ: Princeton University Press, 1986); Ira Katznelson, "Was the Great Society a Lost Opportunity?" in *The Rise and Fall of the New Deal Order, 1930–1980,* ed. Steve Fraser and Gary Gerstle (Princeton, NJ: Princeton University Press, 1989), 185–211; Desmond King, *Separate and Unequal: Black Americans and the U.S. Federal Government* (New York: Oxford University Press, 1995); Daniel

Kryder, *Divided Arsenal: Race and the American State during World War II* (Cambridge: Cambridge University Press, 2000).

124. Franklin D. Roosevelt, *Complete Press Conferences of Franklin D. Roosevelt, 1943* (New York: Da Capo Press, 1972), 21:179–80.

125. "Cotton Picking Assignment for Men in Army Is Frowned Upon; Fear Huachuca Would Be Chief Victims," *Atlanta Daily World,* 3 March 1943; St. Clair Bourne, "National Roundup," *People's Voice,* 6 March 1943.

126. "No Cotton Picking for Ninety-third," *Chicago Defender,* 6 March 1943.

127. NAACP Executive Secretary Walter White to Secretary of War Henry L. Stimson, 26 February 1943, Part 9: Discrimination in the Armed Forces, Series A: General Files on the Armed Forces' Affairs, 1918–55, file: U.S. Army, 93rd Division, 1943–46, NAACP Papers, LOC.

128. "Cotton Picking Assignment for Men in Army Is Frowned Upon; Fear Huachuca Would Be Chief Victims," *Atlanta Daily World,* 3 March 1943.

129. C. H. Douglass to NAACP Executive Secretary Walter White, 26 February 1943, Part 9: Discrimination in the Armed Forces, Series A: General Files on the Armed Forces' Affairs, 1918–1955, file: U.S. Army, 93rd Division, 1943–46, NAACP Papers, LOC.

130. Horace R. Cayton, "Cotton Pickers," *Pittsburgh Courier,* 6 March 1943, TCF.

131. Monthly Report of Chaplain Robert J. Smith, January 1943, Robert J. Smith Career 201 File, RG 247, Records of the Office of the Chief of Chaplains, NARA.

132. Everett Hodge to Walter White, 25 October 1942, group II, box 150, Soldier Complaints, 1942–43, NAACP Papers, LOC.

133. Midian O. Bousfield to Truman Gibson, 7 March 1943, entry 188, box 207, Fort Eustis, Va., to Fort Huachuca, Ariz., OCA Records.

134. Memorandum, James O'Neal to Benjamin O. Davis Sr., 17 December 1943, folder: Inspection Report from Office of the Inspector General for 93rd Infantry Division, box: Inspection Tours, United States, Texas-Virginia, Numbered Units, Davis Papers.

135. "Army Cotton Job Will Be Delayed Officials State," *Arizona Daily Star,* 25 February 1943; "Cotton Losses Are Predicted," *Arizona Daily Star,* 25 February 1943; "Change in Army Cotton Crop Order Stirs Up Controversy," *Arizona Daily Star,* 26 February 1943.

136. "Secretary Stimson States 'Emergency' Found Non-Existent; Previous Announcement Involving Ninety-third Had Stirred Up More Charges of Discrimination," *Baltimore Afro-American,* 6 March 1943, "No Cotton Picking for Ninety-third," *Chicago Defender,* 6 March 1943.

137. Midian O. Bousfield to Truman Gibson, 7 April 1943, entry 188, box 207, Fort Eustis, Va., to Fort Huachuca, Ariz., OCA Records.

138. Nelson Peery interview with author, 9 December 1994.

139. Bousfield to Gibson, 7 April 1943, OCA Records.

Part Two • *The Hand That Rocks the Cradle Holds the Shield*

Epigraphs: Pauli Murray, "Negro Youth's Dilemma," *Threshold* 2 (April 1942), 8–11; Barbara Omolade, "We Speak for the Planet," in *Living with Contradictions: Controversies in Feminist Social Ethics,* ed. Alison M. Jaggar (Boulder, Colo.: Westview Press, 1994).

Four • *Service Families on the Move*

Epigraph: Thelma T. Hawes, Assistant Field Director, American Red Cross, to Perle Dow, Assistant Director, Military and Naval Welfare Director, Subject: August Monthly Report, 31 August 1943, file 1000, box 1708, ARC Records.

1. Thelma Thurston Gorham, "Negro Army Wives," *Crisis* (January 1943), 21–22.

2. For a broader discussion of the adaptive strategies of families, see Darlene Clark Hine, "Black Migration to the Urban Midwest: The Gender Dimension, 1915–1945," In *The Great Migration in Historical Perspective: New Dimensions of Race, Class, and Gender*, ed. Joe William Trotter (Bloomington: Indiana University Press, 1991), 127–46; Sharon Harley, "For the Good of Family and Race: Gender, Work, and Domestic Roles in the Black Community, 1880–1930," *Signs: Journal of Women in Culture and Society* 15 (Winter 1990), 336–49; Kevin K. Gaines, *Uplifting the Race: Black Leadership, Politics, and Culture in the Twentieth Century* (Chapel Hill: University of North Carolina Press, 1996); and Deborah Gray White, *Too Heavy a Load: Black Women in Defense of Themselves, 1894–1994* (New York: Norton, 1999). For invaluable descriptions of World War II's effect on women and family life, see Karen Anderson, *Wartime Women: Sex Roles, Family Relations, and the Status of Women during World War II* (Westport, CT: Greenwood Press, 1981), chaps. 1, 3, 4; Elaine Tyler May, *Homeward Bound: American Families in the Cold War Era* (New York: Basic Books, 1988), esp. chap. 3; William M. Tuttle Jr., *"Daddy's Gone to War": The Second World War in the Lives of America's Children* (New York: Oxford University Press, 1993); and William H. Chafe, *The American Woman: Her Changing Social, Economic, and Political Roles, 1920–1970* (New York: Oxford University Press, 1972), 135–95.

3. Data used to determine net in-migration in areas surrounding the military facility were gathered from 175 survey questionnaires, black newspapers, the *Ninety-third Blue Helmet*, archival records at the Fort Huachuca Historical Museum, and the National Archives and Records Administration. I particularly focused on the years beginning with 1941 and ending with 1942 because I wanted to examine the migration patterns of service dependents that occurred during the initial training of the 93rd Infantry Division while stationed at Fort Huachuca in 1942 and the out-flow of service families after the unit's deployment to the 3rd Army Maneuver Area fourteen months later.

4. *New York Age*, 10 April 1943.

5. *Cleveland Call & Post*, 17 May 1941.

6. *Fort Huachuca Scout*, 1 September 1955, Biographical Sketches, Archives, FHHM.

7. Lillian Jones, interview by Muriel S. French, 22 July 1982, Sierra Vista Public Library, Sierra Vista, Ariz.; Jack Hein, *Herald Dispatch*, 10 March 1981, Fort Huachuca Biographical Sketches, Archives, FHHM.

8. *Fort Huachuca Scout*, 20 November 1986, Fort Huachuca Biographical Sketches, Archives, FHHM; *New York Age*, 25 June 1943. For a description of John A. De Veaux Sr., see James Fleming and Christian E. Burckel, eds., *Who's Who in Colored America: An Illustrated Biographical Directory of Notable Living Persons of African Descent in the United States*, 7th ed. (Yonkers-on-Hudson, NY: Christian Burckel and Assoc., 1950), 152, and John A. De Veaux Career 201 File, RG 247, Records of the Office of the Chief of Chaplains, NARA.

9. *Baltimore Afro-American*, 18 November 1941; *Ninety-third Blue Helmet*, 16 October 1942.

10. *Ninety-third Blue Helmet,* 2 October 1942; *Pittsburgh Courier,* 27 March 1943.

11. *Ninety-third Blue Helmet,* 18 September 1942.

12. Ibid., 20 November 1942.

13. Ibid.

14. Ibid., 23 December 1942.

15. Anderson, *Wartime Women,* 78–81; Tuttle, *"Daddy's Gone to War,"* 18–29. For a broader discussion of wartime marriages, family formation, and migration patterns, see John Modell and Duane Steffey, "Waging War and Marriage: Military Service and Family Formation, 1940–1950," *Journal of Family History* 13, no. 2 (1988), 200–206; John Modell, *Into One's Own: From Youth to Adulthood in the United States, 1920–1975* (Berkeley: University of California Press, 1989); John D'Emilio and Estelle B. Freedman, *Intimate Matters: A History of Sexuality in America* (New York: Harper and Row, 1988); and Jacqueline Jones, *The Dispossessed: America's Underclasses from the Civil War to the Present* (New York: Basic Books), 224–29.

16. *Washington Tribune,* 27 June 1942; Biographical Sketches of First Committee of Management Members of Twelfth Avenue USO Club, Tucson, Ariz., 22 March 1945, box 19, YMCA of the USA Archives, USOR; George N. Leighton, survey questionnaire correspondence, Chicago, 11 April 1995.

17. *Baltimore Afro-American,* 29 August 1942; *Ninety-third Blue Helmet,* 8 January 1943; Arline Young interview with author; Julius B. Young interview with author.

18. "Many Marriage Licenses Are Going to Military Men Here," *Arizona Daily Star,* 21 March 1943, 2.

19. *Pittsburgh Courier,* 4 July 1942.

20. *Baltimore Afro-American,* 28 March 1942.

21. *Ninety-third Blue Helmet,* 2 October 1942.

22. Irma Jackson Cayton Wertz, "A First WAC" (MS in author's possession), 7; Irma Jackson Cayton Wertz interview with author; for biographical background on Hardy, see *Ninety-third Blue Helmet,* 23 December 1942.

23. Ulysses G. Lee, *United States Army in World War II, Special Studies: The Employment of Negro Troops* (Washington, DC: Office of the Chief of Military History, 1966); memorandum, Colonel E. B. Maynard, Post Surgeon, to the Commanding General, Services of Supply, Attention: the Surgeon General, War Department, 10 February 1943, Subject: Annual Report of Medical Department Activities at Fort Huachuca, Arizona, 1942, entry 54A, box 170, folder: Post Surgeon Annual Records, Fort Huachuca, Ariz., 1942–43, RG 112, Records of the Office of the Surgeon General, Military Field Branch, NARA.

24. Memorandum, LTC Henry L. Love and LTC John H. Amen, Inspectors General, to Office of the Commanding General, Ninth Service Command, 9 October 1944, Subject: Report of Investigation of Alleged Prostitution at Fort Huachuca, Arizona, entry 26F, box 44, folder: General Correspondence, Secret, Fort Huachuca, Ariz., 1939–47, RG 159, Records of the Office of the Inspector General, Military Field Branch, NARA.

25. Medical Department, U.S. Army, *Preventive Medicine in World War II,* vol. 5, *Communicable Diseases Transmitted through Contact or by Unknown Means* (Washington, DC: Office of the Surgeon General, 1960), 140–41.

26. Allan M. Brandt, *No Magic Bullet: A Social History of Venereal Disease in the United*

States Since 1880, expanded ed. (New York: Oxford University Press, 1987); Allan Berube, *Coming Out under Fire: The History of Gay Men and Women in World War II* (New York: Penguin Books, 1990); and Lee, *United States Army in World War II,* 279–86. A deeper understanding of this wartime ideology might be gained from a careful reading of Leisa D. Meyer, *Creating GI Jane: Sexuality and Power in the Women's Army Corps during World War II* (New York: Columbia University Press, 1996); and Beth Bailey and David Farber, *The First Strange Place: Race and Sex in World War II Hawaii* (Baltimore: Johns Hopkins University Press, 1994), 162–64. Also see Adele Logan Alexander, "'She's No Lady, She's a Nigger': Abuses, Stereotypes, and Realities from the Middle Passage to Capitol (and Anita) Hill," in *Race, Gender, and Power in America: The Legacy of the Hill-Thomas Hearings,* ed. Anita Faye Hill and Emma Coleman Jordan (New York: Oxford University Press, 1995), 3–25.

27. Arthur Miller, *Situation Normal* (New York: Reynal and Hitchcock, 1944), 28.

28. Verbatim record of the trial, *United States v. Jerry Sykes,* 16 September 1942, Office of the Judge Advocate General, Department of the Army, USAJ, 12.

29. H. Leonard Richardson to Walter White, NAACP Executive Secretary, 24 November 1942, group II, box 150, Soldier Complaints, 1942–43, NAACP Papers, LOC.

30. "Dr. M. O. Bousfield, Chicago Physician," *New York Times,* 17 February 1948; memorandum, Midian O. Bousfield, 8 July 1942, Zola Mae Lang Fraser Clipping File (in the possession of the author).

31. *Baltimore Afro-American,* 29 November 1942; *Sunday Chicago Bee,* 23 May 1943; *Baltimore Afro-American,* 11 April 1943.

32. "'Surprises' Just Headaches for Soldier Hosts at Camps," *Baltimore Afro-American,* 20 February 1943, 13.

33. "Correspondence from William E. Allen, Jr.," *Journal of the National Medical Association* 34 (July 1942), 164.

34. "Captain Robert Bennett Weds Pretty Actress in Arizona," *Detroit Tribune,* 20 December 1942, 5; Bill Michelmore, "Gypsy Violins Mourn a Friend," *Detroit Free Press,* 13 February 1975, 3, 12A.

35. "Chaplain and Wife," *Pittsburgh Courier,* 5 June 1942, 15; Biographical Data, John R. Wesley, 31 August 1944, John R. Wesley Career 201 File, RG 247, Records of the Office of the Chief of Chaplains, NARA.

36. "Planned Parenthood Fits in with Health Week," *Philadelphia Tribune,* 11 April 1942, 8; "Washington Notes," *Chicago Defender,* 25 July 1942, 18.

37. Clarence L. Gaines interview with author; "Social Whirl," *Arizona's Negro Journal,* 26 June 1942, 4; "Three Generations of Gaines," Public Affairs News Release, 12 August 1971, Biographical Sketches, FHHM. For more on adaptive visiting strategies, see Earl Lewis, *In Their Own Interests: Race, Class, and Power in Twentieth Century Norfolk* (Berkeley: University of California Press, 1991), and Earl Lewis, "Afro-American Adaptive Strategies," *Journal of Family History* 12 (Winter 1987), 407–20.

38. Memorandum, Roland R. Bach to Harry L. Walden, Military and Naval Welfare Service Director, 1 July 1942, Subject: Bi-monthly Narrative Report for Period April 30 to June 30, 1942, box 1708, Arizona-Davis, Monthan Field—Kingman Army Air Field Station Hospital, ARC Records.

39. Memorandum, Thelma Hawes, ARC Field Worker, to Perle Dow, Assistant Mili-

tary and Naval Welfare Director, 31 October 1943, Subject: Annual Report, box 1708, Arizona-Davis, Monthan Field—Kingman Army Air Field Station Hospital, ARC Records.

40. John Byng-Hall, *Rewriting Family Scripts: Improvisation and Systems Change* (New York: Guilford Press, 1995), 23–96; Carol B. Stack and Linda M. Burton, "Kinscripts: Reflections on Family, Generation, and Culture," in *Mothering: Ideology, Experience, and Agency,* ed. Evelyn Nakano Glenn, Grace Chang, and Linda Rennie Forcey (New York: Routledge, 1994), 33–44; Katherine Nelson, "Social Cognition in a Script Framework," in *Social Cognitive Development: Frontiers and Possible Futures,* ed. John H. Flavell and Lee Ross (Cambridge: Cambridge University Press, 1981), 97–118.

41. Headman, Ferguson & Carollo, Invitation for Bids–War Department Office of the Construction Division, Quartermaster Corps, 8 December 1941, binder: Fort Huachuca History, 1936–41, FHHM; "Race Army Officers Occupy New Homes at Fort Huachuca," *Cleveland Call & Post,* 15 March 1941, 2.

42. "Huachuca Gets 35,000 Troops," *Arizona Daily Star,* 2 May 1942, Chronological Files, FHHM.

43. "Start Work on Home for Negro Army Division," *Cleveland Call & Post,* 20 December 1941, 1.

44. Memorandum, Midian O. Bousfield to Truman Gibson Jr., 11 August 1944, Subject: Civilian Housing at Fort Huachuca, entry 188, box 207, Fort Eustis, Va., to Fort Huachuca, Ariz., OCA Records.

45. Truman K. Gibson Jr. to P. L. Prattis, 25 June 1942, entry 188, box 207, Fort Eustis, Va., to Fort Huachuca, Ariz., OCA Records.

46. Truman K. Gibson, Jr. to Colonel Edwin N. Hardy, 24 June 1942, entry 188, box 207, Fort Eustis, Va., to Fort Huachuca, Ariz., OCA Records.

47. Notes for Historical Record of Twelfth Avenue USO, Tucson, Ariz., 22 March 1942, box 19, History of Tucson USO Club, 1942–46, USOR.

48. "Housing Project Pressed by City," *Arizona Daily Star,* 25 March 1942, 4.

49. Lieutenant Colonel G. H. McManus Jr., 93rd Adjutant General, to the Bisbee Chamber of Commerce, 25 May 1942; G. R. Michaels, Secretary of the Bisbee Chamber of Commerce, to Lieutenant Colonel G. H. McManus Jr., 29 May 1942; Wesley T. Allen, President, Bisbee Merchants' Association, Incorporated, to G. R. Michaels, Secretary of the Bisbee Chamber of Commerce, 23 April 1943, all in Chronological Files, FHHM.

50. Open letter, G. R. Michaels, Secretary of the Bisbee Chamber of Commerce, to Fort Huachuca Post Commander, 17 June 1943, Chronological Files, FHHM.

51. U.S. Bureau of the Census, *County Data Book: A Supplement to the Statistical Abstract of the United States, 1940* (Washington, DC: GPO, 1947), 64.

52. G. R. Michaels, Secretary of the Bisbee Chamber of Commerce, to the Adjutant General, 93rd Infantry Division, 29 May 1942, Chronological Files, FHHM.

53. "Flees Arizona Mines after Soldier Is Slain," *Chicago Defender,* 28 November 1942, 8; Gordon Rucker to William Hastie, Civilian Aide to the Secretary of War, 16 November 1942, entry 188, box 207, OCA Records.

54. "Fort Huachuca Area Landlords Must File Lists," *Arizona Daily Star,* 4 November 1942, 4.

55. "Consolidated's Hiring Halted," *Arizona Daily Star,* 20 November 1942, 3.

56. U.S. Bureau of the Census, *Sixteenth Census of the United States, 1940*, vol. 2 (Washington, DC: GPO, 1943), 345, table 1; U.S. Bureau of the Census, *County Data Book*, 64, table 3; U.S. Bureau of the Census, *Seventeenth Census of the United States, 1950*, vol. 2: Arizona (Washington, DC: GPO, 1952), 3–9, table 8; "Population of Tucson Higher," *Arizona Daily Star*, 2 September 1942, 14.

57. Press Release, Fort Huachuca Public Relations Office, 16 May 1942, entry 188, box 207, Fort Eustis, Va., to Fort Huachuca, Ariz., OCA Records.

58. Harry T. Getty, "Interethnic Relationships in the Community of Tucson" (Ph.D. diss., University of Chicago, 1950), 21.

59. U.S. Bureau of the Census, *County Data Book*, 69; U.S. Bureau of the Census, *2006 American Community Survey* (Washington, DC: GPO, 2006), Selected Housing Characteristics, table 3.

60. "Mayor Favors Housing Delay," *Arizona Daily Star*, 28 February 1942, 1, 6.

61. "Tucson Housing Plan Proposed," *Arizona Daily Star*, 5 September 1942, 3.

62. "Housing Inquiries Heavy at Chamber of Commerce; Room Listings Asked," *Arizona Daily Star*, 15 September 1942, 4, "Tucson Housing Called Critical," *Arizona Daily Star*, 11 August 1942, 2.

63. "Low-Cost Housing," *Arizona Daily Star*, 6 March 1942, 8; Jean C. Hunton, survey questionnaire correspondence, U.S. Virgin Islands, 22 March 1993.

64. "Housing Project for Tucson War Workers Is Considered," *Arizona Daily Star*, 3 December 1942, 2.

65. June Caldwell, "Tucson: The Folk Industry," in *Rocky Mountain Cities*, ed. Ray West Jr. (New York: Norton, 1949), 224.

66. Henry Jethro, "Arizona Cops Keep Busy Separating Three Races," *Baltimore Afro-American*, 26 August 1944, 11.

67. "Negro Center," *Arizona Daily Star*, 27 January 1942, 4.

68. "Trial Awaited after Battle," *Arizona Daily Star*, 17 June 1942, 12; "Two Women Given 60 Days for Part in Negro Battle," *Arizona Daily Star*, 26 June 1942, 6.

69. "Negroes Jailed in Assault Case," *Arizona Daily Star*, 2 July 1942, 14.

70. Gordon T. Rucker to Judge William H. Hastie, 16 November 1942, entry 188, box 207, Fort Eustis, Va. to Fort Huachuca, Ariz., OCA Records.

71. Memorandum, Lieutenant Colonel William Slater for Judge William H. Hastie, undated, entry 188, box 207, Fort Eustis, Va., to Fort Huachuca, Ariz., OCA Records; "Murder Cases to Be Set for Trial," *Arizona Daily Star*, 23 January 1943, 4.

72. Truman K. Gibson Jr. to Gordon T. Rucker, 26 November 1942, entry 188, box 207, Fort Eustis, Va., to Fort Huachuca, Ariz., OCA Records.

73. Rucker to Hastie, 16 November 1942, OCA Records.

74. Memorandum, G. R. Michaels to Edwin Cooley, Regional Supervisor, 17 June 1943, Chronological Files, FHHM.

75. Allen to Michaels, 23 April 1943, FHHM. For more on this, see Lee, *United States Army in World War II*, 281–82.

76. "Police Don't Like 'Zoot Suits'; Nab Trio of Wearers," *Arizona Daily Star*, 17 March 1943, 9.

77. "Zoot Suit Gangs Drawing Ire of Sheriff, Checkup Planned," *Arizona Daily Star*, 16 March 1942, 3; "Nine Are Held in Zoot' Round-Up," *Arizona Daily Star*, 5 April 1943, 4.

78. Robert B. Elliott, "Policewoman Separates Mexicans and Whites at USO Dances in Arizona," *Baltimore Afro-American*, 26 August 1944, 14.

79. Jethro, "Arizona Cops Keep Busy Separating Three Races," 11.

80. "Ranch Named in Honor of 'Double V,'" *Pittsburgh Courier*, 15 August 1942, 15.

81. "Church at Fry to Serve as School," *Arizona Daily Star*, 30 January 1942, 9.

82. "White Arizona Community Accepts Race Residents," *Pittsburgh Courier*, 5 September 1942, 14; "Military Setting for Arizona Rites," *Pittsburgh Courier*, 3 October 1942, 10.

83. Edwin Lee, interview by Georgia Rountree, Winter 1972–73, Lee Papers; "Edwin Lee," in *Who's Who in the Midwest: 1972–1973*, 13th ed. (Chicago: Marquis Who's Who, 1972), 50; "Visitors to the Guest Houses," *Ninety-third Blue Helmet*, 20 November 1942, 8; Arline Young interview with author.

84. Jean C. Hunton, survey questionnaire correspondence.

85. Freida Bailey Greene interview with author, 26 March 1998.

86. Pauline Redmond Coggs interview with author, 12 February 2000.

87. This important duty was not unlike the duties performed by black women in other settings during this period. For example, see Adrienne Lash Jones, *Jane Edna Hunter: A Case Study of Black Leadership, 1910–1950*, vol. 12 of *Black Women in the United States History*, ed. Darlene Clark Hine (Brooklyn, NY: Carlson Publishing, 1990); White, *Too Heavy a Load*, 30–31; and Hine, "Black Migration to the Urban Midwest," 137.

88. "Cleveland Ladies Organize to Aid Negro Soldiers in Camps," *Cleveland Call & Post*, 7 February 1942, 9.

89. Historical Report of G Avenue USO, Douglas, Ariz., 1946, box 4, USOR.

90. "USO Discuss Recreation for WAAC's," *Ninety-third Blue Helmet*, 30 October 1942, 7; "Principal Chief Nurse at Fort Seeks Overseas Duty; Career in Army Hospital Noteworthy," *Douglas Daily Dispatch*, 9 January 1943, Chronological Files, FHHM; Frank E. Bolden, "Workers at Huachuca Deserve Recognition for Their War Efforts," *Pittsburgh Courier*, 5 December 1942, 11.

91. Paula Giddings, *When and Where I Enter: The Impact of Black Women on Race and Sex in America* (New York: Bantam Books, 1984), 199–258; Elaine M. Smith, "Mary McLeod Bethune and the National Youth Administration," in *Clio Was a Woman: Studies in the History of American Women*, ed. Mabel E. Deutrich and Virginia C. Purdy (Washington, DC: Howard University Press, 1980); B. Joyce Ross, "Mary McLeod Bethune and the National Youth Administration: A Case Study of Power Relationships in the Black Cabinet of Franklin D. Roosevelt," *Journal of Negro History* 60 (January 1975), 1–28; Linda Gordon, "Black and White Visions of Welfare: Women's Welfare Activism, 1890–1945," *Journal of American History* 78 (September 1991), 559–90; Also see Susan M. Hartmann, "Women's Organizations during World War II: The Interaction of Class, Race, and Feminism," in *Woman's Being, Woman's Place: Female Identity and Vocation in American*, ed. Mary Kelley (Boston: Hall, 1979), and Karen Tucker Anderson, "Last Hired, First Fired: Black Women Workers during World War II," *Journal of American History* 69 (June 1982), 82–97.

92. White, *Too Heavy a Load*, 150–52.

93. For more on this strategy, see Charles Payne, "Men Led, but Women Organized: Movement Participation of Women in the Mississippi Delta," in *Women in the Civil Rights Movement: Trailblazers and Torchbearers, 1941–1965*, ed. Vicki L. Crawford, Jacqueline A. Rouse, and Barbara Woods (Bloomington: Indiana University Press, 1993), 1–11; Carol Mueller, "Ella Baker and the Origins of 'Participatory Democracy,'" in *Women in the Civil Rights Movement: Trailblazers and Torchbearers, 1941–1965*, ed. Vicki L. Crawford, Jacqueline A. Rouse, and Barbara Woods (Bloomington: Indiana University Press, 1993), 51–70; Charles Payne, *I've Got the Light of Freedom: The Organizing Tradition and the Mississippi Freedom Struggle* (Berkeley: University of California Press, 1995); Belinda Robnett, *How Long? How Long?: African American Women in the Struggle for Civil Rights* (New York: Oxford University Press, 1997); and Cheryl Townsend Gilkes, "Together and in Harness: Women's Traditions in the Sanctified Church," *Signs: Journal of Women in Culture and Society* 10 (Summer 1985), 678–99.

94. "'41 Saw Tucson Ready; '42 Finds It More So," *Arizona Daily Star*, 1 January 1942, 1, 14.

95. Edward Carr interview with author.

96. History of Tucson USO Club, 1942–46, box 19, USOR.

97. "Negro Center Idea Dropped," *Arizona Daily Star*, 15 January 1942, 1.

98. Hazel Merrill to NAACP Executive Secretary Walter White, 5 June 1942, Part 9: Discrimination in the Armed Forces, Series B: Armed Forces Files, 1940–1950, group II, box B-191, United Service Organization, NAACP Papers, LOC; "An Open Letter," *Arizona Daily Star*, 18 January 1942, 7.

99. "Topics of Tucson," *Arizona Daily Star*, 22 January 1942, 4.

100. "An Open Letter," *Arizona Daily Star*, 18 January 1942, 7.

101. Ellen Stuart Russell, "Negro Center," *Arizona Daily Star*, 7 February 1942, 9.

102. L. W. Mays, "It Is Not Their Wrong," *Arizona Daily Star*, 23 January 1942, 9.

103. S. R. Hudson, "Let Us Not Forget," *Arizona Daily Star*, 23 January 1942, 9.

104. "Women Voters to Hear Recreation Center Discussed," *Arizona Daily Star*, 22 January 1942, 7; "Topics of Tucson," *Arizona Daily Star*, 6 February 1942, 18; "The Social Whirl," *Arizona's Negro Journal*, 22 January 1942, 7; "The Social Whirl," *Arizona's Negro Journal*, 29 January 1942, 7; "The Social Whirl," *Arizona's Negro Journal*, 1 March 1942, 7; "The Social Whirl," *Arizona's Negro Journal*, 8 March 1942, 7.

105. "Look at Conditions," *Arizona Daily Star*, 11 April 1942, 2.

106. Henry McClaine, "Wake Up Tucson," *Arizona Daily Star*, 6 February 1942, 2.

107. Holton H. Collins Jr., "Negro Center," *Arizona Daily Star*, 8 February 1942, 7.

108. "Topics of Tucson," *Arizona Daily Star*, 29 March 1942, 4.

109. "Legion Will Hear about Negro USO," *Arizona Daily Star*, 22 May 1942, 3; "Topics of Tucson," *Arizona Daily Star*, 11 June 1942, 2.

110. "Topics of Tucson," *Arizona Daily Star*, 29 July 1942, 3.

111. History of Tucson USO Club, 1942–46, box 19, USOR.

112. "Negro USO Work Is Started Here," *Arizona Daily Star*, 22 May 1942, 3.

113. Goldie D. Carter, "The Same Blue Sky: The Story of the Tucson USO," *Woman's Press: The National Magazine for Young Women's Christian Association* 41 (March 1947), 35–36.

114. Merrill to White, 5 June 1942, Part 9, NAACP Papers, LOC.

115. *New York Amsterdam Star-News*, 18 July 1942; *Kansas City Call*, 28 July 1942; *Pittsburgh Courier*, 18 July 1942; *Atlanta Daily World*, 15 July 1942; *Houston Negro Labor News*, 18 July 1942, all in TCF.

116. "NAACP Flays War Department," *Baltimore Afro-American*, 25 July 1942, 19.

117. "Wanted to Send Telegram," *Kansas City Call*, 28 July 1942, TCF.

Five • War Maneuvers and Black Division Personnel

Epigraphs: *Pittsburgh Courier*, 18 April 1942, 5; Elliotte J. Williams interview with author.

1. Ralph Ellison, "Editorial Comment," *Negro Quarterly: A Review of Life and Culture* 1 (Winter 1943), 295–302.

2. Carl Murphy, "30,000 Troops Maneuver in Louisiana Bad Lands," *Baltimore Afro-American*, 15 May 1943, 1, 11.

3. Memorandum, Benjamin O. Davis Sr. to the Inspector General, 3 May 1945, Subject: Special Inspection, Ninety-third Infantry Division, file 333.1, AGF, 93rd Infantry Division, Inspection, binder 1, AGF Records.

4. E. W. Baker, "River Crossing Problems End Two Months of Louisiana Maneuvers," *Pittsburgh Courier*, 19 June 1943, 14.

5. Memorandum, Davis to the Inspector General, 3 May 1945, AGF Records.

6. Ben Burns, "93rd Division Nearing Combat Shape, Louisiana Battle Shows," *Chicago Defender*, 15 May 1943, 2; Carl Murphy, "30,000 Troops Maneuver in Louisiana Bad Land," *Baltimore Afro-American*, 15 May 1943, 1–11; Robert M. Ratcliffe, "Newsmen Thank War Department for Trip to Louisiana," *Atlanta Daily World*, 11 May 1943, 1, 6; William O. Walker, "Personal Notes on the Third Army Louisiana Maneuvers," *Cleveland Call & Post*, 15 May 1943, 12; William G. Nunn, "General Lauds Troops for Skill in Maneuvers Test," *Pittsburgh Courier*, 15 May 1943, 1, 8; Paul Keen, "Detroit Soldiers Play Big Role in War Maneuvers," *Michigan Chronicle*, 15 May 1943, 2.

7. Roy Wilkins, "Maneuvers Show 93rd Is Ready," *Crisis* (June 1943), 170–71.

8. "Southern Maneuvers—Sketched by PV's Ol Harrington," *People's Voice*, 15 May 1943, 8; "Southern Maneuvers Seen through the Eyes and Pen of PV's Ol Harrington," *People's Voice*, 22 May 1943, 8.

9. Ben Burns, "Lack of Race Officers in 93rd Hit by Scribe—Promotions Slow," *Chicago Defender*, 22 May 1943, 2.

10. Christo Waller and Ernest Davenport, "Maneuver Lament," *Baltimore Afro-American*, 26 June 1943, 14.

11. Thyr Byrd, "93rd Division Psalms," *Pittsburgh Courier*, 19 June 1943, 3.

12. "Both Maneuvers Force 'Winners,'" *New Orleans Times Picayune*, 30 April 1943, 2; "Crack Ninety-third Division on Maneuvers in Louisiana," *Louisiana Weekly*, 22 May 1943, 1, 6.

13. Charles S. Johnson, *To Stem This Tide: A Survey of Racial Tension Areas in the United States* (Boston: Pilgrim Press, 1943), 81.

14. Ibid., 65; Adam Fairclough, *Race and Democracy: The Civil Rights Struggle in Louisiana, 1915–1972* (Athens: University of Georgia Press, 1995), 80.

15. Alvin E. White, "Louisiana Congressman Fears 'Best Blood of America' to be Sacrificed for Undrafted Negroes," *Oklahoma City Black Dispatch*, 26 September 1942, TCF.

16. James A. Burran III, "Racial Violence in the South during World War II" (Ph.D. diss., University of Tennessee, Knoxville, 1977), 60; Florence Murray, ed., *The Negro Handbook, 1944* (New York: Current Reference Publications, 1944), 95; "Declares Presence May Lead to Riots," *Pittsburgh Courier*, 8 August 1942, 1, 4.

17. "Army Chief of Staff Tells Alabama Senator Negro Soldiers Will Remain in the South," *New York Age*, 22 August 1942, 1.

18. Communiqué, William G. Nunn, Managing Editor of the *Pittsburgh Courier*, Bureau of Public Relations, War Department, entry 188, box 214, Lawyers–Opportunities in the Army to March Field, California, OCA Records.

19. Edwin Lee, interview by Georgia Rountree, Winter 1972–73, Lee Papers.

20. Bismark Williams Jr. interview with author.

21. Nelson Peery interview with author, 9 December 1994.

22. Ulysses G. Lee, *United States Army in World War II, Special Studies: The Employment of Negro Troops* (Washington, DC: Office of the Chief of Military History, 1966), 366–67.

23. Fairclough, *Race and Democracy*, 77–79.

24. Daniel Kryder, *Divided Arsenal: Race and the American State during World War II* (Cambridge: Cambridge University Press, 2000), chap. 6; Robin D. G. Kelley, "Congested Terrain: Resistance on Public Transportation," cited in Robin D. G. Kelley, *Race Rebels: Culture, Politics and the Black Working Class* (New York: Free Press, 1994), 55–75; Pete Daniel, "Going among Strangers: Southern Reactions to World War II," *Journal of American History* 77 (December 1990), 886–911; Phillip McGuire, *He, Too, Spoke for Democracy: Judge Hastie, World War II, and the Black Soldier* (Westport, CT: Greenwood Press, 1988), chap. 3; Howard Odum, *Race and Rumors of Race: Challenge to American Crisis* (Chapel Hill: University of North Carolina Press, 1943), 113–28.

25. Federal Bureau of Investigation, Survey of the Racial Conditions in the United States, Section III: Southern Section in the United States, cited in *The FBI's RACON: Racial Conditions in the United States during World War II*, ed. Robert A. Hill (Boston: Northeastern University Press, 1995), 327.

26. Communiqué, William G. Nunn, OCA Records.

27. Isaiah A. Johnson Sr. interview with author.

28. "Chi Soldier Refuses to 'Shut Up'; Beaten by Bus Driver," *Chicago Bee*, 16 May 1943, 1, 2.

29. Sara F. Normant to Eleanor Roosevelt, 23 May 1943, ER 100.1, Letters from Servicemen, box 70, 1943, Eleanor Roosevelt Papers, FDRL.

30. Cyril R. Powell to the *Chicago Defender*, 1 October 1943, Veterans Affairs File, 1940–50, box G-16, Soldier Complaints, 1942–43, NAACP Papers, LOC.

31. Memorandum, Garland Adamson to the Commanding Officer, 9 January 1943, Subject: Preliminary Report of Survey on Venereal Disease Control in and around Camp Polk Area, box 11, USOR; John Neal to Lieutenant Colonel William G. Gilks, 26 August 1942, box 11, USOR.

32. An Afro-American Soldier to Walter White, 7 May 1943, Part 9, Discrimination in

the U.S. Armed Forces, 1918–1955, Series B, Armed Forces Legal Files, 1940–1950, Folder: Soldier Travel, 1942–50, NAACP Papers, LOC.

33. Inspection Data Prepared by the G-2 for General Benjamin O. Davis Sr., 25 April 1943, box: Inspection Tours, United States, Texas-Virginia, Numbered Units, Davis Papers.

34. Memorandum, 93rd Adjutant General to Brigadier General Benjamin O. Davis Sr., 25 April 1943, and memorandum, 93rd Adjutant General to Brigadier General Benjamin O. Davis Sr., 26 April 1943, both in folder: Inspection Reports for the Office of the Inspector General, box: Inspection Tours, United States, Texas-Virginia, Numbered Units, Davis Papers.

35. Brigadier General Benjamin O. Davis Sr. to Sadie Davis, 24 April 1943, folder: Personal letters written to wife in the United States, 24 January–15 December 1943, box: Personal Letters, Diary, 1941–45, Davis Papers.

36. Clenon Briggs interview with author.

37. Julius G. Thompson interview with author, 3 May 1993.

38. Elliotte J. Williams, survey questionnaire correspondence, Fort Washington, Md., 8 June 1992.

39. Memorandum, Reuben E. Fraser Jr., "An Analysis and Inside Story of the Ninety-third Infantry Division," May 1942–July 1944 (in author's possession).

40. William O. Walker, "Personal Notes on the Third Army's Louisiana Maneuver," *Cleveland Call & Post*, 15 May 1943, 12.

41. Paul Keen, "Detroit Soldiers Play Big Role in War Maneuvers; Captain Bennett in Louisiana War Practice," *Michigan Chronicle*, 15 May 1943, 2.

42. Nelson Peery interview with author, 9 December 1994.

43. Burns, "Lack of Race Officers in Ninety-third Hit by Scribe—Promotions Slow," 2.

44. Truman K. Gibson to Monroe Dowling, 20 April 1943, entry 188, box 207, Fort Eustis, Va., to Fort Huachuca, Ariz., OCA Records.

45. Michael Carter, "An Interview with Truman K. Gibson," *Baltimore Afro-American*, 17 July 1943, 6.

46. Daniel Kryder, *Divided Arsenal*, 144–46; Lee, *United States Army in World War II*, 174–78.

47. Memorandum, Truman K. Gibson Jr. to John J. McCloy, Assistant Secretary of War, 5 September 1944, in *Blacks in the United States Armed Forces: Basic Documents*, vol. 7, *Planning for the Postwar Employment of Black Personnel*, ed. Morris J. MacGregor and Bernard C. Nalty (Wilmington, DE: Scholarly Resources, 1977), 8–9.

48. Ann Petry, "In Darkness and Confusion," in *Cross Section 1947: A Collection of New American Writing*, ed. Edwin Seaver (New York: Simon and Schuster, 1947), 105.

49. "What the People Say; Objects to the Story on the 93rd Division," *Chicago Defender*, 5 June 1943, 14.

50. Robert Galley interview with author.

51. Asberry McGriff interview with author.

52. Frank Bolden to Truman K. Gibson Jr., 2 June 1943, entry 188, box 207, Fort Eustis, Va., to Fort Huachuca, Ariz., OCA Records.

53. Memorandum, Major General C. P. Hall to the Army Ground Forces Command-

ing General, 11 August 1942, Subject: Assignment of Second Lieutenants to the Ninety-third Infantry Division, file 210.31, AGF, 93rd Infantry Division, binder 1, AGF Records.

54. Ibid.

55. Memorandum, Headquarters, Army Assistant Ground Adjutant General R. A. Meredith to the 3rd Army Commanding General, 19 August 1942, file 210.31, AGF, 93rd Infantry Division, binder 1, AGF Records; Reuben E. Fraser Jr. interview with author.

56. "Fort Huachuca, Arizona," *Cleveland Call & Post*, 20 February 1943, 11B; Julius B. Young interview with author.

57. George Nicholas interview with author.

58. Memorandum, G-1 for the Chief of Staff, Subject: Use of Negro Manpower in Time of Emergency, 26 April 1937, entry 43, box 442, G-1 Personnel, WDGS/WDSS Records.

59. Memorandum, Acting Adjutant General to the Commanding Generals, Subject: Policy on Assignment of Negro Officer Personnel, 10 January 1943, entry 43, box 443, G-1 Personnel, WDGS/WDSS Records.

60. Edwin A. Lee interview by Georgia Rountree.

61. Freida Bailey Greene interview with author, 19 March 1998; Jean Byers, *A Study of the Negro in Military Service* (Washington, DC: U.S. Department of Defense, 1950), 127.

62. Erwin A. Jones to Benjamin O. Davis Sr., 24 April 1943, folder: Official and Semi-Official Correspondence, January–June 1943, box: Correspondence, 1943–45, Davis Papers; Robert W. Grant to Truman Gibson, 27 September 1943, Entry 188, box 251, folder: Transfers, OCA Records.

63. Grant to Gibson, 27 September 1943, OCA Records.

64. "Stop Negroes at First Looeys in 93rd," *Chicago Bee*, 28 February 1943, 1–2.

65. Elliotte J. Williams interview with author.

66. Leo Logan interview with author.

67. "Stop Negroes at First Looeys in 93rd," 2.

68. "Is the 93rd a Token Unit?" *Baltimore Afro-American*, 6 March 1943, 5; "Order Limiting Officers to First Lieutenant Protested," *Baltimore Afro-American*, 20 March 1943, 21; Roy Wilkins, "First Lieutenant Top Rank?" *Crisis* (March 1943), 72; Charley Cherokee, "National Grapevine," *Chicago Defender*, 20 March 1943, 15.

69. Charlie Cherokee, "National Grapevine," *Chicago Defender*, 6 March 1943, 15; "Negro in Army Quiz Irks Stimson; Cotton Picking Off," *Chicago Bee*, 7 March 1943, 1–2; "Stimson Riled by Questions Reveal Unit," *New York Amsterdam Star-News*, 6 March 1943, 3.

70. "Edward S. Greenbaum, Lawyer, Is Dead at 80," *New York Times*, 13 June 1970, 31.

71. Memorandum for Files, Colonel Edward S. Greenbaum, 8 March 1943, entry 43, box 441, G-1 Personnel, WDGS/WDSS Records.

72. Report, Special Inspection, 93rd Infantry Division, Brigadier General B. O. Davis to the Inspector General, 3 May 1943, file 333.1, AGF, 93rd Infantry Division Inspection, binder 1, AGF Records.

73. "General Miller Promoted," *93rd Blue Helmet*, 27 November 1942, 1; Bell I. Wiley, *The Training of Negro Troops* (Washington, DC: Army Ground Forces Historical Section, 1946), in Nalty and MacGregor, *Blacks in the United States Armed Forces: Basic Documents*, vol 7, *Planning for the Postwar Employment of Black Personnel*, 253.

74. A. N. Marquis Company, *Who Was Who in America: A Companion Biographical Reference Work to Who's Who in America*, vol. 2 (Chicago: A.N. Marquis Co., 1950), 373.

75. U.S. War Department, *The Adjutant General's Office, Official Army Register, 1 January 1946* (Washington, DC: GPO, 1946), 677.

76. Elliotte J. Williams interview with author.

77. John D. Howard interview with author.

78. Ibid.

79. Reuben E. Fraser Jr. interview with author; "Major Blackwood Special Service Chief at Huachuca," *California Eagle*, 17 February 1943, 4.

80. Ibid.

81. Memorandum, Fraser, "Analysis and Inside Story of the Ninety-third Infantry Division."

82. Memorandum, Acting Adjutant General to the Commanding Generals, Subject: Policy on Assignment of Negro Officer Personnel, 10 January 1943, WDGS/WDSS Records.

83. Memorandum, C. H. McManus Jr. to the 1st Battalion, 369th Infantry, 30 June 1943, box: Inspection Tours, United States, Alabama-Indiana, folder: Inspection Reports for the Office of the Inspector General–Fort Huachuca, Ariz., Davis Papers.

84. U.S. War Department, *The Adjutant General's Office, Official Army Register, 1 January 1946*, 677.

85. Monroe Dowling to Truman Gibson, undated (July 1943?), entry 188, box 207, Fort Eustis, Va., to Fort Huachuca, Ariz., OCA Records.

86. Clarence R. Ross interview with author.

87. Clenon Briggs interview with author.

88. Nelson Peery interview with author, 9 December 1994.

89. "Women in War Meeting Topic," *New York Amsterdam Star-News*, 27 March 1943, 12.

90. "Georgia Negro Army Mothers Call on White Mothers to Help Create Democracy," *Sunday Chicago Bee*, 18 April 1943, 33.

91. Percy Hines, "Postal Alliance News," *Sunday Chicago Bee*, 28 March 1943, 11, John E. Rousseau Jr., "Postal Convention Adopts Program to Combat All Racism," *Houston Informer*, 28 August 1943, 1, 3.

92. Memorandum, James N. Reese for Benjamin O. Davis Sr., 26 April 1943, folder: Inspection Reports for the Office of the Inspector General, box: Inspection Tours, United States, Texas-Virginia, Numbered Units, Davis Papers.

93. Memorandum, James N. Reese for Benjamin O. Davis Sr., 25 April 1943, folder: Inspection Reports for the Office of the Inspector General, box: Inspection Tours, United States, Texas-Virginia, Numbered Units, Davis Papers; William O. Walker, "Army Promotions Based on Merit of Individuals," *Cleveland Call & Post*, 15 May 1943, 12B.

94. Memorandum, 93rd Adjutant General for the Commanding General, 19 August 1943, Subject: Officers Overstrength in Ninety-third Infantry Division, file 322, AGF, 93rd Infantry Division, Organization & Tactical Units, binder I, AGF Records; Monroe Dowling to Truman K. Gibson, 14 August 1943, entry 236, box 359, folder: 93rd Division, OCA Records; John E. Royston to Truman Gibson, 17 October 1943, entry 236, box 359, folder: 93rd Division, OCA Records.

95. Monroe Dowling to Truman K. Gibson, 23 September 1943, entry 236, box 359, folder: 93rd Division, OCA Records.

96. Burns, "Lack of Race Officers in 93rd Hit By Scribe," 2; Byers, *Study of the Negro in Military Service,* 126–27.

97. Truman Gibson to Monroe D. Dowling, 23 September 1943, entry 236, box 359, folder: 93rd Division, OCA Records; 93rd Division Adjutant General to Monroe Dowling, 14 August 1943, entry 236, box 359, folder: 93rd Infantry Division, OCA Records.

98. Truman K. Gibson to George N. Leighton, 11 November 1943, entry 188, box 251, folder: Transfers, OCA Records.

99. Memorandum, William C. Elliott for the Troop Movements Branch (G-3), 11 May 1943, file 322, AGF, Organization & Tactical Units, binder 1, AGF Records.

100. Special Orders, Stanley M. Prouty for the 93rd Division Commander, 2 August 1943, Francis Ellis Clipping File (in author's possession); Francis Ellis interview with author.

101. Emmitt W. Baker, "Soldiers Sleep under Wet Towels to Keep Cool in Desert Training," undated, file 427, box 13698, folder 393-015, Press Releases, AGO Records.

102. Historical Section, 93rd Infantry Division, "93rd Infantry Division: Summary of Operations in World War II" (MS, Washington, D.C., March 1946), 3.

103. Freida Bailey Greene interview with author, 19 March 1998; Emmitt W. Baker, file 427, box 13698, folder 393-015, Press Releases, AGO Records; "Windy City Sophisticates," *Sunday Chicago Bee,* 21 November 1943, 12; Alyce Key, "Key Notes," *Los Angeles Tribune,* 17 January 1944, 15.

104. "Windy City Sophisticates," *Sunday Chicago Bee,* 25 July 1943, 12; "Windy City Sophisticates," *Sunday Chicago Bee,* 19 September 1943, "Windy City Sophisticates," *Sunday Chicago Bee,* 21 November 1943, 12.

105. L. R. Raibon, "San Bernardino," *California Eagle,* 4 November 1943, 5.

106. Edwin A. Lee interview by Georgia Rountree.

107. Rene Beauchamps, "The Gay Side," *California Eagle,* 28 October 1943, 4.

108. "Mrs. Laura Waller Joins Lieutenant in California," *Baltimore Afro-American,* 7 August 1943, 6.

109. L. R. Raibon, "San Bernardino," 5.

110. "Should I Sacrifice to Live Half-American?" *Pittsburgh Courier,* 31 January 1942, 3; "The Courier's Double 'V' for a Double Victory Campaign Gets Country-wide Support," *Pittsburgh Courier,* 14 February 1942, 1; "Readers Want Double 'V' Made into Pins, Emblems," *Pittsburgh Courier,* 24 February 1942, 2.

111. "Courier's 'Double V' Sweeps America from Coast to Coast . . . , Thousands Sanction War Slogan," *Pittsburgh Courier,* 28 February 1942, 24; "'VV' Clubs and Affiliate Members of the 'VV' Clubs of America," *Pittsburgh Courier,* 30 May 1942, 5; "'Double V' Club News," *Pittsburgh Courier,* 30 June 1942, 20.

112. "Courier War Slogan for 'Double Victory' Points Way for Race," *Pittsburgh Courier,* 14 March 1942, 12; "Evansville Negroes Mobilize Under 'VV' to Protest Jim Crow," *Pittsburgh Courier,* 14 March 1942, 14.

113. *Pittsburgh Courier,* 13 June 1942.

114. "NBC Baptists Endorse Courier's 'Double V' Drive," *Pittsburgh Courier,* 21 March

1942, 15; Byron R. Skinner, "The Double 'V': The Impact of World War II on Black America" (Ph.D. diss., University of California, Berkeley, 1978), 87.

115. Irene West, "The 'Double V' Crusaders!," *Pittsburgh Courier,* 18 April 1942, 5.

116. Skinner, "The Double 'V,'" 87.

117. Edgar T. Rouzeau, "Insist on Combat Duty, Rouzeau," *Pittsburgh Courier,* 1 January 1944, 1.

118. Walter White to Secretary of War Henry Stimson, 20 November 1943, file 322, AGF, Organization & Tactical Units, binder 1, AGF Records; "Asks Stimson to Issue Statement on Ninety-third Division," *Cleveland Call & Post,* 27 November 1943, 12.

119. "Along the NAACP Battlefront," *Crisis* 51 (January 1944), 20.

120. Memorandum, G-3 to 93rd Commanding General Raymond G. Lehman, 10 November 1943, Subject: Preparation of Unit for Overseas Service (Alert Instructions), file 322, AGF, Organization & Tactical Units, binder 1, AGF Records.

121. Joyce Thomas, "The 'Double V' Was for Victory: Black Soldiers, the Black Protest, and World War II" (Ph.D. diss., Ohio State University, 1993), 193.

122. Pauli Murray, "Negro Youth's Dilemma," *Threshold* 2 (April 1942), 8–11.

123. Pauli Murray, *Song in a Weary Throat: An American Pilgrimage* (New York: Harper and Row, 1987), 185.

124. Pauline Redmond Coggs interview with author, 12 February 2000.

125. "Dear Dad: What Am I to Adopt as My Philosophy of the War?" *Pittsburgh Courier,* 17 October 1942, 5.

126. "Son of Dee Cee Policeman Nips 3 Nips in Solomons," *Washington Tribune,* 13 May 1944, 30.

127. Nelson Peery to his mother, 20 November 1943 (in author's possession).

128. Nelson Peery interview with author, 9 December 1994.

129. Emmitt W. Baker, "Old Jobs and New Occupations Figure in Ninety-third Division GI Postwar Plans," undated, entry 427, box 13698, folder 393-015, Press Releases, AGO Records.

130. J. Robert Smith, "Ninety-third a 'Murder' Unit Soldiers Say," *Sunday Chicago Bee,* 30 January 1944, 1–2.

131. Edwin A. Lee interview by Georgia Rountree.

132. Reuben E. Fraser Jr. interview with author.

133. Nelson Peery interview with author, 9 December 1994.

134. Bismark Williams to his mother, 4 December 1943 (in author's possession); Bismark Williams Jr. interview with author.

135. General Court-Martial Orders 103, Headquarters, 93rd Infantry Division, *United States v. Adam Hutton,* General Court-Martial 245393, 25 November 1943, Department of the Army, USAJ.

136. General Court-Martial Orders 200, Headquarters, 93rd Infantry Division, *United States v. Cornelius J. Compton Jr.,* General Court-Martial 247302, 26 May 1944, Department of the Army, USAJ.

137. Cornelius Compton to Eleanor Roosevelt, 1 January 1944, ER 100.1, box 1784, Eleanor Roosevelt Papers, FDRL.

138. Edward H. Soulds, *Black Shavetail in Whitey's Army* (New York: Carlton Press, 1971), 59.

139. Alyce Key, "Key Notes," *Los Angeles Tribune,* 25 October 1943, 15.

140. Memorandum, Inspector General Virgil Peterson for the Deputy Chief of Staff, 29 December 1943, Subject: Overseas Readiness Status of the Ninety-third Infantry Division, entry 26F, box 12, Secret Correspondence, Overseas Reports, March 1943–January 1944, RG 159, Papers of the Office of the Inspector General, NARA.

141. Marguerite Howard interview with author.

142. Gwendolyn Williams, "Heart against the Wind," *Crisis* (January 1944), cited in *Bitter Fruit: African American Women in World War II,* ed. Maureen Honey. (Columbia: University of Missouri Press, 1999), 152–55.

143. Pauline Redmond Coggs interview with author, 12 February 2000.

144. Billy Rowe, "Mothers, Wives, Sweethearts," 22 February 1944, entry 427, box 13698, folder 393-015, Press Releases, AGO Records.

145. Ibid.

146. Arnett Hartsfield interview with author.

147. Edwin A. Lee interview by Georgia Rountree.

148. Nelson Peery to his mother, 25 December 1943 (in author's possession).

Part Three • Race and Sex Matter in the Pacific

Epigraphs: Walter White, *A Man Called White: The Autobiography of Walter White* (New York: Viking Press), 1948), 286; Gwendolyn Brooks, "Gay Chaps at the Bar," *Negro Story: Short Stories by or about Negroes for All Americans* 1 (March–April 1945), 49.

Six • War, Race, and Rumor under the Southern Cross

Epigraph: Gordon W. Allport and Leo Postman, *The Psychology of Rumor* (New York: Holt, Rinehart, and Winston, 1947), 31.

1. Edwin Lee, interview by Georgia Rountree, Winter 1972–73, Lee Papers.

2. Vincent Tubbs, "West Pointer Killed in Action," *Baltimore Afro-American,* 10 June 1944, 1, 14.

3. Historical Section, 93rd Infantry Division, "93rd Infantry Division: Summary of Operations in World War II" (MS, Washington, D.C., March 1946), 4.

4. Ninety-third Division Special Troops, 5–19 March 1944, box no. 13723, entry 427, 393-SP2-0.3.0 Daily Diary–Medical Detachment, 1 January–31 December 1944, AGO Records; Walter B. Sanderson Jr. interview with author.

5. Edwin Lee, Interview by Georgia Rountree, Winter 1972–73, Lee Papers.

6. Bismark Williams Jr. interview with author.

7. Asberry McGriff interview with author.

8. Andrew Isaacs interview with author; Robert J. Johnson interview with author.

9. "Evening in the Southwest Pacific," 38th Engineering Battalion, 28 May 1944, box 13706, entry 427, 393-Eng-O, 93rd Infantry Division Files, AGO Records.

10. Memorandum, Christo L. Waller to 368th Public Relations Office, Subject: Men in

the Service, 26 October 1945, box 13719, entry 427, 393–Inf (368)-5-0.20, 93rd Infantry Division Files, AGO Records.

11. "All Negro USO Unit in South Pacific Area," *Michigan Chronicle*, 8 July 1944, 13.

12. "New Guinea," *California Eagle*, 17 May 1945, 10; "E. Mordecai Runs Radio Show Overseas Titled 'The Groove,'" *California Eagle*, 12 July 1945, 14.

13. Thomas M. White and Herbert Hall interviews with author, 6 February 1993; Nelson Peery interview with author, 9 December 1994; Conrad Clark, "Lena Horne Number 1 on Pin-up Parade of Troops in Pacific," *Atlanta Daily World*, 5 September 1944, 2.

14. "Wants Morale Builders," *New York Amsterdam Star-News*, 30 January 1945, 12.

15. Robert B. Westbrook, "'I Want a Girl, Just like the Girl That Married Harry James': American Women and the Problem of Political Obligation in World War II," *American Quarterly* 42 (December 1990), 599–600; George Lipsitz, "'Frantic to Join . . . the Japanese Army': The Asia Pacific War in the Lives of African American Soldiers and Civilians," in *The Politics of Culture in the Shadow of Capital*, ed. Lisa Lowe and David Lloyd (Durham, NC: Duke University Press, 1997).

16. John Costello, *Virtue under Fire: How World War II Changed Our Social and Sexual Attitudes* (Boston: Little, Brown, 1985), 153.

17. Henry Elkin, "Aggressive and Erotic Tendencies in Army Life," *American Journal of Sociology* 51 (March 1946), 412.

18. "This Should Help Morale of Boys Overseas," *California Eagle*, 20 September 1945, 8; *Atlanta Daily World*, 18 October 1944, 5; "For the Boys at the Front," *Cleveland Call & Post*, 16 September 1944, 12.

19. "Wanted: Pinup Girls," *Baltimore Afro-American*, 3 June 1944, 4.

20. "Free Pinups for Soldiers," *Chicago Defender*, 11 December 1943, 1; "Says Hello to GI's Overseas," *New York Amsterdam Star-News*, 20 January 1945, 3; "Winsome," *Atlanta Daily World*, 5 August 1945, 1, 6; "Lonely Pinup," *Pittsburgh Courier*, 26, February 1944, 11.

21. John D. Howard interview with author; Arnett Hartsfield interview with author; Julius B. Young interview with author.

22. Raymond Jenkins interview with author, 1 March 1990; Julius G. Thompson interview with author, 3 May 1993.

23. Memorandum, Company A, 318th Engineering Battalion to Commanding General, 93rd Infantry Division, 28 May 1944, Subject: Lessons Learned on Bougainville, box 1, folder: Bougainville, Boyd Collection.

24. Edward H. Soulds, *Black Shavetail in Whitey's Army* (New York: Carlton Press, 1971), 59.

25. Harry A. Gailey, *Bougainville, 1943–1945: The Forgotten Campaign* (Lexington: University Press of Kentucky, 1991), 95.

26. Ibid., 34–35.

27. In many ways, my thinking on the racialized nature of the Pacific war has been influenced by John Dower's brilliant study *War without Mercy: Race and Power in the Pacific War* (New York: Pantheon, 1986).

28. Ulysses G. Lee, *United States Army in World War II, Special Studies: The Employment of Negro Troops* (Washington, DC: Office of the Chief of Military History, 1966), 497–98.

29. Theodore Coggs, interview with Fletcher Martin, 7 February 1945, Reference: 93rd Division, entry 236, box 359, folder: 93rd Infantry Division, OCA Records.

30. John D. Howard interview with author.

31. Clarence Ross interview with author.

32. Bismark Williams Jr. interview with author.

33. Mary P. Motley, ed., *The Invisible Soldier: The Experience of the Black Soldier, World War II* (Detroit: Wayne State University Press, 1987), 90.

34. Telegram, William G. Nunn to Truman Gibson, 22 November 1944, entry 236, box 359, Folder: 93rd Infantry Division, OCA Records.

35. Clenon Briggs interview with author.

36. Statement of Major General Harry H. Johnson, 93rd Division Headquarters, 26 February 1945, entry 236, box 359, Folder: 93rd Infantry Division, OCA Records.

37. Daily Record of Events, 28 April 1944, Leonard R. Boyd, Personal File: Bougainville, 93rd Infantry Division, box 1, folder: Bougainville, Boyd Collection.

38. Daily Record of Events, 10 May 1944, Leonard R. Boyd, Personal File: Bougainville, 93rd Infantry Division, box 1, folder: Bougainville, Boyd Collection.

39. Ninety-third Division Special Troops, 12 June 1944, box 13723, entry 427, 393-SP2-0.3.0 Daily Diary–Medical Detachment, 1 January–31 December 1944, AGO Records.

40. Reuben E. Fraser Jr. interview with author.

41. Ninety-third Division Special Troops, 18 May–17 June 1944, box 13723, entry 427, 393–SP2-0.3.0 Daily Diary–Medical Detachment, 1 January–31 December 1944, AGO Records.

42. "Cards Stacked against Negro Combat Units," *Houston Informer,* 23 October 1943, 9.

43. "Fish Asking Facts on Breaking Up of Combat Units," *Pittsburgh Courier,* 26 February 1944, 11.

44. Secretary of War Henry L. Stimson to Representative Hamilton Fish of New York, 19 February 1944, *Congressional Record,* 78th Cong., 2d sess., 1944, vol. 90, pt. 2 (Washington, DC: GPO, 1944) 2007–8.

45. Memorandum, Lenna B. Childers for Chief of the Analysis Branch, Negro Press Intelligence, 25 March 1944, Subject: Negro Press Trend for Week of March 13–18, entry 183, 291.2, box 127, General Correspondence of John J. McCloy, OCA Records.

46. John P. Davis, "Secretary of War Attacks Record of Race Combat Units," *Pittsburgh Courier,* 4 March 1944, 1, 4.

47. Roy Wilkins, "Army Labor Battalions," *Crisis* (April 1944), 104.

48. Memorandum, Lenna B. Childers for Chief of the Analysis Branch, Negro Press Intelligence, 25 March 1944, Subject: Negro Press Trend for Week of March 13–18, OCA Records.

49. "Bulletin," *Pittsburgh Courier,* 4 March 1944, 1; "Chicagoans Ask President Roosevelt to Oust Stimson," *Chicago Defender,* 4 March 1944, 3.

50. "Stimson 'Explains' Smear on Troops," *Chicago Defender,* 11 March 1944, 1, 3.

51. "White House Concerned over New Conversion of Race Units," *Pittsburgh Courier,* 15 March 1944, 1, 4; Walter White, *A Rising Wind* (New York: Doubleday, Doran and Co., 1945), 76.

52. Henry Stimson Diary, 6 March 1944, Stimson Papers.

53. Memorandum, Secretary of the Advisory Committee for the Members of the Advisory Committee on Negro Troop Policies, 29 February 1944, and memorandum, John J. McCloy for the Secretary of War, 2 March 1944, both in entry 188, 291.2, box 215, Negro Troops–Combat, OCA Records.

54. Radio message, George Marshall to Millard Harmon, 7 March 1944, entry 291.2, box 13704, file 393-3.11, AGO Records.

55. Radio message, Millard Harmon to George Marshall, 9 March 1944, entry 291.2, box 13704, file 393-3.11, AGO Records.

56. Lee, *United States Army in World War II*, 484–85; Gailey, *Bougainville*, 99; Maggi M. Morehouse, *Fighting in the Jim Crow Army: Black Men and Women Remember World War II* (Lanham, MD: Rowman and Littlefield, 2000), 131–33.

57. Lee, *United States Army in World War II*, 502.

58. "Stimson Confirms 93rd in South Pacific," *Baltimore Afro-American*, 8 April 1944, 7.

59. "Negro Infantry and Anticraft Units Plentiful in South Pacific," *Michigan Chronicle*, 26 February 1944, 11; Frank Kluckhorn, "U.S. Troops Crack Bougainville Foe; Some from Harlem in Spirited Action," *New York Times*, 17 March 1944, 7; Fletcher Martin, "Negro Gunners Blast Japs," *Norfolk Journal & Guide*, 18 March 1944, 1; Fletcher Martin, "Negro Troops Rout Japs on Bougainville Beach," *Cleveland Call & Post*, 6 May 1944, 1, 3.

60. Radio message, George C. Marshall to Millard Harmon, For Your Eyes Only, 18 March 1944, entry 291.2, box 13704, file 393-3.11, AGO Records.

61. Radio message, George C. Marshall to Millard Harmon, 22 March 1944, entry 291.2, box 13704, file 393-3.11, AGO Records.

62. South Pacific Force Commander to 14th Corps Commanding General, 23 March 1944, Leonard R. Boyd, Personal File: Bougainville, 93rd Infantry Division, box 1, folder: Bougainville, Boyd Collection.

63. Daily Record of Events, 26 March 1944, Leonard R. Boyd, Personal File: Bougainville, 93rd Infantry Division, box 1, folder: Bougainville, Boyd Collection.

64. Memorandum, 93rd Adjutant General for the 93rd Provisional Brigade Headquarters, 30 May 1944, Subject: Battle Casualties, Leonard R. Boyd, Personal File: Bougainville, 93rd Infantry Division, box 1, folder: Bougainville, Boyd Collection.

65. Edwin Lee interview by Georgia Rountree.

66. Memorandum, 93rd Assistant Division Commander for the 93rd Commanding General, 26 April 1944, Subject: Notes on Bougainville, 23–25 April 1944, Leonard R. Boyd, Personal File: Bougainville, 93rd Infantry Division, box 1, folder: Bougainville, Boyd Collection.

67. Nelson Peery, *Black Fire: The Making of an American Revolutionary* (New York: New Press, 1994), 240.

68. Marke Toles interview with author.

69. Julius B. Young interview with author.

70. Edwin Lee interview by Georgia Rountree.

71. Military Attaché Report for the Military Intelligence Division of the War Department General Staff, 10 October 1944, Subject: Japan—Japanese Intelligence Report on U.S. Negro Troops, entry 43, box 443, file 291.2, WDGS/WDSS Records.

72. For an extraordinary account of the controversy surrounding the wartime myth of

Tokyo Rose and the racial prejudice that the legend generated in American society in the aftermath of World War II, see Masayo Duus, *Tokyo Rose: Orphan of the Pacific* (New York: Kodansha International, 1979).

73. Memorandum, Philleo Nash, Assistant Deputy Director for the Office of War Information, 27 May 1944, Subject: Negro Troops in Axis Propaganda, entry 183, box 127, file 291.2–293.6, OCA Records.

74. Bennie Etters interview with author.

75. Daily Record of Events, 2 April 1944, Leonard R. Boyd, Personal File: Bougainville, 93rd Infantry Division, box 1, folder: Bougainville, Boyd Collection.

76. Memorandum, W. C. Dunckel for the Officers and Enlisted Men of the 593rd Artillery Battalion, 4 April 1944, entry 236, box 359, Folder: 93rd Infantry Division, OCA Records.

77. Memorandum, 93rd G-2 for the 93rd Division Headquarters, 4 April 1944, Personal File: Bougainville, 93rd Infantry Division, box 1, folder: Bougainville, Boyd Collection.

78. Daily Record of Events, 8 April 1944, Leonard R. Boyd, Personal File: Bougainville, 93rd Infantry Division, box 1, folder: Bougainville, Boyd Collection.

79. Memorandum, Adjutant General for First Sergeant Frank Little, 16 October 1947, Subject: Letter Orders, Frank Little Clipping File (in author's possession).

80. "Californian Commissioned from the Field," *Cleveland Call & Post,* 25 November 1944, 4.

81. Daily Record of Events, 8 April 1944, Leonard R. Boyd, Personal File: Bougainville, Ninety-third Infantry Division, Boyd Collection.

82. Daily Record of Events, 15–20 May 1944, Leonard R. Boyd, Personal File: Bougainville, 93rd Infantry Division, box 1, folder: Bougainville, Boyd Collection.

83. "Bronze Star Medal Given to Four Yanks on Bougainville; Cavalry Officer and Three Doughboys Cited for Action," *Atlanta Daily World,* 2 August 1944, 1.

84. Motley, *Invisible Soldier,* 91.

85. Patrol Report, John O. Trice to the 93rd G-2, 4 April 1944, 25th RCT (93rd Provisional Brigade), entry 393-2.11, box 13715, 93rd Division, AGO Records.

86. Memorandum, 93rd Adjutant General for the 93rd Provisional Brigade Headquarters, 30 May 1944, Subject: Battle Casualties, Leonard R. Boyd, Personal File: Bougainville, 93rd Infantry Division, box 1, folder: Bougainville, Boyd Collection.

87. Daily Record of Events, 31 March 1944, Leonard R. Boyd, Personal File: Bougainville, 93rd Infantry Division, box 1, folder: Bougainville, Boyd Collection.

88. Walter B. Sanderson Jr. interview with author; Fletcher Martin, "Young Army Doctors Getting Rare Experience in Pacific Jungles, Mission on Battlefields Is Two-Fold," *Atlanta Daily World,* 2 July 1944, 5.

89. Daily Record of Events, 19 April 1944, Leonard R. Boyd, Personal File: Bougainville, 93rd Infantry Division, box 1, folder: Bougainville, Boyd Collection; Memorandum, 93rd Division Psychiatrist for the 93rd Division Surgeon, 28 April 1944, Subject: Condition of the Area, 318th Medical Battalion Clearing Station, Leonard R. Boyd, Personal File: Bougainville, 93rd Infantry Division, box 1, folder: Bougainville, Boyd Collection.

90. General Orders no. 87, 22 September 1944, Administrative File, 1940–50, box A-648, 93rd Division, 1943–46, NAACP Papers, LOC.

91. Memorandum, George W. Little to 93rd Division Surgeon, 28 April 1944, Leonard R. Boyd, Personal File: Bougainville, 93rd Infantry Division, box 1, folder: Bougainville, Boyd Collection.

92. Daily Record of Events, 30 April 1944, Leonard R. Boyd, Personal File: Bougainville, 93rd Infantry Division, box 1, folder: Bougainville, Boyd Collection.

93. Leonard R. Boyd to War Department Operations Division, 17 May 1944, Leonard R. Boyd, Personal File: Bougainville, 93rd Infantry Division, box 2, folder: Bougainville, Boyd Collection.

94. Edward T. Hall Jr., "Prejudice and Negro-White Relations in the Army," *American Journal of Sociology* 52 (March 1947), 405.

95. Harry H. Johnson to Colonel McCook, 26 February 1945, entry 236, box 359, folder: 93rd Infantry Division, OCA Records.

96. Memorandum, Theodore J. Adamiak for the Commanding General, Island Command, 27 September 1944, Leonard R. Boyd, Personal File: Bougainville, 93rd Infantry Division, box 2, folder: Bougainville, Boyd Collection.

97. Memorandum, Robert C. Bennett for the U.S. Army Forces in the Far East (US-AFFE) Board, 24 January 1945, Subject: Report on the Performance and Efficiency of the Ninety-third Infantry Division, Administrative File, 1940–50, box A-18, Morale, 1941–45, NAACP Papers, LOC.

98. Memorandum, James M. Whittico for the U.S. Army Forces in the Far East (US-AFFE) Board, 25 January 1945, Subject: Report on the Performance and Efficiency of the Ninety-third Infantry Division, Administrative File, 1940–50, box A-18, Morale, 1941–45, NAACP Papers, LOC.

99. Memorandum, George W. Little for the 318th Medical Battalion, 26 April 1944, Subject: State of Morale within the Twenty-fifth Infantry Combat Team, box 1, folder: Bougainville, Boyd Collection.

100. Robert Galley interview with author.

101. Julius B. Young interview with author.

102. Nelson Peery to his mother, 11 May 1944 (in author's possession); Nelson Peery interview with author, 9 December 1994.

103. George Leighton to Eleanor Roosevelt, 28 April 1944, ER 100.1, Letters from Servicemen, box 1788, 1944, KN-L, Eleanor Roosevelt Papers, FDRL.

104. Robert C. Bennett to Truman Gibson Jr., 14 July 1945, entry 236, box 359, Folder: 93rd Infantry Division, OCA Records.

105. Officers of the 93rd Infantry Division to P. B. Young, 27 July 1945, Administrative File, 1940–50, box A-18, Morale, 1941–45, NAACP Papers, LOC.

106. Memorandum, William H. Considine to the 164th Infantry Commanding Officer, 12 April 1944, Subject: Report of Patrol and Combat Activities of Company K, Twenty-fifth Infantry, Leonard R. Boyd, Personal File: Bougainville, 93rd Infantry Division, box 2, folder: Bougainville, Boyd Collection.

107. Boyd Diary, 7 April 1944, box 1, folder: Bougainville, Boyd Collection.

108. Memorandum, Frank Lucas for the Commanding General, American Division, 2 May 1944, Subject: Report of Investigation of Company "K," Twenty-fifth Infantry Regiment, Ninety-third Division, patrol of 6 April 1944, HIA.

109. Patrol Report, Will D. Jones to Major C. E. Rasor, 7 April 1944, Patrol Reports—Bougainville, 2 April–12 May 1944, entry 393-2.11, box 6651, 93rd Division Files, AGO Records.

110. Memorandum, Arthur Mussett for the Adjutant General, Washington, D.C., 5 June 1944, Subject: Misbehavior before the Enemy of Sergeant Edward Dennis, Leonard R. Boyd, Personal File: Bougainville, 93rd Infantry Division, box 2, folder: Bougainville, Boyd Collection.

111. Memorandum, Frank Lucas for the Commanding General, Americal Division, 2 May 1944, Subject: Report of Investigation of Company "K," Twenty-fifth Infantry Regiment, Ninety-third Division, patrol of 6 April 1944, HIA.

112. Ibid.

113. Memorandum, 93rd Division Staff Judge Advocate and Inspector General for the 93rd Provisional Brigade Commanding General, 3 June 1944, Leonard R. Boyd, Personal File: Bougainville, 93rd Infantry Division, box 2, folder: Bougainville, Boyd Collection; Memorandum, Arthur T. Mussett for the Commanding General, 25th Infantry, 7 June 1944, Subject: Report of Investigation, Company "K," Twenty-fifth Infantry, Ninety-third Infantry Division, Leonard R. Boyd, Personal File: Bougainville, 93rd Infantry Division, box 2, folder: Bougainville, Boyd Collection.

114. Memorandum, Leonard R. Boyd for the 14th Corps Commanding General, 8 May 1944, Subject: Misconduct before the Enemy, Leonard R. Boyd, Personal File: Bougainville, 93rd Infantry Division, box 2, folder: Bougainville, Boyd Collection.

115. Memorandum, Leonard R. Boyd for 14th Corps Commander Oscar Griswold, 10 May 1944, Leonard R. Boyd, Personal File: Bougainville, 93rd Infantry Division, box 2, folder: Bougainville, Boyd Collection.

116. Leonard R. Boyd to Major General John E. Hull, 17 May 1944, Leonard R. Boyd, Personal File: Bougainville, 93rd Infantry Division, box 2, folder: Bougainville, Boyd Collection.

117. Richard Hurst interview with author.

118. Memorandum, Edwin M. Yon for Battalion and Detachment Commanders, 7 June 1944, Subject: Policies Relating to Officers and Non-Commissioned Officers of the Twenty-fifth Infantry, Leonard R. Boyd, Personal File: Bougainville, 93rd Infantry Division, box 2, folder: Bougainville, Boyd Collection.

119. *Congressional Record,* 79th Cong., 1st sess., vol. 91, pt. 5 (Washington, DC: GPO, 1945), 6994–96.

120. For example, see the following material related to the 92nd Division: Proceedings of the A Board of Review Appointed by Commanding General, 92nd Infantry Division, 24–25 June 1945, Subject: Combat Effectiveness of Negro Officers and Enlisted Men, Vicinity of Viareggio, Italy, 92nd Infantry Division Files, AGO Records, and memorandum, 92nd Infantry Division Board of Review to the Commanding General, 8 August 1945, Subject: Analysis of ETO Report, 92nd Infantry Division Files, AGO Records. For more detailed studies relating to the experiences of the 92nd Infantry Division in the European theater of operations, see Major Paul Goodman, *A Fragment of Victory in Italy during World War II, 1942–1945* (Carlisle Barracks, PA: Army War College, 1952); Lee, *United States Army in World War II,* chap. 14; Hondon Hargrave, *Buffalo Soldiers in Italy: Black Americans in World War II* (Jefferson, NC: McFarland, 1985); Bernard C. Nalty, *Strength for the Fight: A History of Black Americans in the Military* (New York: Free Press, 1986), 172–74; Robert W. Kesting, "Con-

spiracy to Discredit the Black Buffaloes: The Ninety-second Infantry in World War II," *Journal of Negro History* 72 (Winter–Spring 1987), 1–17; Daniel K. Gibran, *The 92nd Infantry Division and the Italian Campaign in World War II* (Jefferson, NC: McFarland, 2001); Christopher Paul Moore, *Fighting for America: Black Soldiers—The Unsung Heroes of World War II* (New York: Random House, 2005); and Morehouse, *Fighting in the Jim Crow Army*, 157–82.

121. Lieutenant Colonel (Ret.) Major Clark to 92nd World War II Association President John T. Flippen, 27 April 1992 (copy in author's possession).

122. Memorandum, Truman Gibson for Colonel H. A. Gerhardt, 2 September 1944, entry 236, box 359, folder: 93rd Infantry Division, OCA Records; memorandum, Walter White for President Franklin D. Roosevelt, the Undersecretary and Assistant Secretary of War, 12 February 1945, Subject: Ninety-third Infantry Division and Other Negro Combat Units, entry 236, box 359, folder: 93rd Infantry Division, OCA Records.

123. Radio message, Douglas MacArthur to George Marshall, 5 March 1944, RG 4, box 17, folder 3, C-N-C, USAFPAC, War Department Correspondence, 901–1000, 31 December 1944–29 April 1945, Douglas MacArthur Memorial Archives, Norfolk, Va.

124. Robert Eichelberger Diary, 19 July 1945, Robert Eichelberger Papers, Manuscript Department, Perkins Library, Duke University, Durham, N.C.

125. Lee, *United States Army in World War II*, 517.

126. Henry Stimson Diary, 21 February 1945, Stimson Papers.

127. Lee, *United States Army in World War II*, 512.

128. Ibid., 516–17.

129. "93rd Pushes On in Drive against Japs," *Chicago Defender*, 22 April 1944, 1, 15; "93rd in South Pacific," *Baltimore Afro-American*, 18 March 1944.

130. Enoch P. Waters, *An American Diary: A Personal History of the Black Press* (Chicago: Path Press, 1987), 385.

131. Charles H. Loeb, "Ninety-third Champs at Bit for Pacific 'Big Show'; Correspondent Loeb says Men Prefer Combat," *Atlanta Daily World*, 16 January 1945, 1; Charles Loeb, "Ninety-third Division Keeps Combat Integrity," *Atlanta Daily World*, 27 January 1945, 1; Charles Loeb, "Famed Ninety-third Unit Doing Hard Labor; Trained in States for Combat Duty, Ninety-third Far from the Front," *Cleveland Call & Post*, 27 January 1945, 1; cable message, Fletcher to the National Negro Press Affiliates, 7 December 1944, entry 236, box 359, folder: 93rd Infantry Division, OCA Records; telegram, William G. Nunn to Truman Gibson, 22 November 1944, entry 236, box 359, Folder: 93rd Infantry Division, OCA Records.

132. Memorandum, Walter White to President Franklin D. Roosevelt, Robert Patterson, Henry Stimson, and Truman K. Gibson, 12 February 1945, Subject: The Ninety-third Infantry Division and Other Negro Combat Units, entry 236, box 359, folder: 93rd Infantry Division, OCA Records.

133. Radio message, Army Chief of Staff George Marshall to Southwest Pacific Area Commander Douglas MacArthur, 1 March 1945, War Department Correspondence, RG 3, box 17, Douglas MacArthur Memorial Archives, Norfolk, Va.; radio message, General Douglas MacArthur to Army Chief of Staff George C. Marshall, 4 March 1945, War Department Correspondence, RG 4, box 17, Douglas MacArthur Memorial Archives, Norfolk, Va.

134. Robert F. Jefferson, "The Ninety-third Division: A Victim of Domestic Politics, 1938–1945" (master's thesis, Old Dominion University, 1989), 144–45.

135. Memorandum, Walter White to General Douglas MacArthur, 8 March 1945, entry 236, box 359, folder: 93rd Infantry Division, OCA Records.

136. Radio message, Douglas MacArthur to Chief of Staff George Marshall, 26 February 1945, War Department Correspondence, RG 3, box 17, Douglas MacArthur Memorial Archives, Norfolk, Va.

137. Francis Ellis interview with author.

138. Open letter, Sixteen 93rd Servicemen to the NAACP, 5 May 1945, Legal File, 1944–49, box B-150, Soldier Complaints, NAACP Papers, LOC.

139. Waters, *American Diary,* 389–90.

140. George N. Leighton to James M. Nabritt, 20 June 1945, folder: George N. Leighton, 1944–45 (typescript), box 122-2, Correspondence, J-RE, Howard University Men and Women in the Armed Forces Papers, Howard University Founders Library, Washington, D.C.

141. "Fort Huachuca Honors Soldier's Deeds," *California Eagle,* 18 January 1945, 5.

Seven • Relative Security in the Southwest Pacific

Epigraph: Gunnar Myrdal, *An American Dilemma: The Negro Problem and Modern Democracy* (1944), 2nd ed., 2 vols. (New York: Harper and Row, 1965), 586.

1. Grace Davis to Judge Advocate General Lee H. Cope, 23 November 1945, *United States v. Sergeant Samuel Hill,* Army Services, USAJ.

2. Holding by the Board of Review, Officers of the Judge Advocate General, Melbourne, Australia, *United States v. Sergeant Samuel Hill,* 2 May 1945, Army Service Forces, USAJ, 95.

3. Proceedings, 7–8 March 1945, in *United States v. Samuel Hill,* General Court-Martial 296823, transcript of the trial, Department of the Army, USAJ.

4. Report of Transfer of Samuel Hill, 5th Army Headquarters to the Adjutant General, 16 April 1947, USAJ.

5. Walter A. Luszki, *A Rape of Justice: MacArthur and the New Guinea Hangings* (Lanham, MD: Madison Books, 1991); J. Robert Lilly, "Dirty Details: Executing U.S. Soldiers during World War II," *Crime and Delinquency* 42 (October 1996), 491–516; J. Robert Lilly and J. Michael Thomson, "Executing US Soldiers in England, World War II: Command Influence and Sexual Racism," *British Journal of Criminology* 37 (Spring 1997), 262–87; Colonel Glen Felder, "A Long Way since Houston: The Treatment of Blacks in the Military Justice System," *Army Lawyer* (October 1987), 8–11.

6. Raymond Jenkins interview with author, 28 February 1990; Edgar Davis interview with author; Julius G. Thompson interview with author, 3 May 1993.

7. Ronald H. Spector, *Eagle against the Sun: The American War against Japan* (New York: Vintage Books, 1985), 289.

8. Robert Ross Smith, *The United States Army in World War II: The Approach to the Philippines* (Washington, DC: Office of the Chief of Military History, 1953), 13.

9. Mary P. Motley, ed., *The Invisible Soldier: The Experience of the Black Soldier, World War II* (Detroit: Wayne State University Press, 1987), 99.

10. Julius B. Young interview with author.

11. Claude Ferebee to Walter White, 19 August 1945, Legal File, 1944–49, box B-150, Soldier Complaints, NAACP Papers, LOC.

12. Edward Soulds, *Black Shavetail in Whitey's Army* (New York: Carlton Press, 1971), 63.

13. Robert W. Coakley and Richard M. Leighton, *Global Logistics and Strategy*, vol. 2, *1943–1945* (Washington, DC: Office of the Chief of Military History, 1968), 464.

14. Ibid.

15. Radiogram, George Marshall to General Douglas MacArthur, 27 February 1945, RG 3, SWPA, box 17, folder 3, War Department Messages, Archives, Douglas MacArthur Memorial Archives, Norfolk, Va.

16. Coakley and Leighton, *Global Logistics and Strategy*, 469; Maurice Matloff, *Strategic Planning for Coalition Warfare, 1943–1944* (Washington, DC: Office of the Chief of Military History, 1968), 460; D. Clayton James, *The Years of MacArthur*, vol. 2, *1941–1945* (Boston: Houghton Mifflin, 1975), 501.

17. Training Schedule, Division Officer School, Stirling Island, 14 September–30 September 1944, Francis Ellis Career 201 File (in author's possession); Francis Ellis interview with author.

18. Charles V. Lynn to the Veterans' Administration Personal Affairs Officer, 1 March 1946, box 241, entry 188, Randolph Field, Tex., to Recreation Facilities—Community—USO, OCA Records.

19. This paragraph and the next from Motley, *Invisible Soldier*, 92–94.

20. "Former Ninety-third Officer Fights Re-induction," *People's Voice*, 1 September 1945, 5.

21. U.S. Army Service Forces, Information and Education Division (Research Branch), "What the Soldier Thinks," Report no. 58 (August 1943), 2, 9; Lee Kennett, *G.I.: The American Soldier in World War II* (New York: Charles Scribner's Sons, 1987), 73–74.

22. Beth Bailey and David Farber, *The First Strange Place: Race and Sex in World War II Hawaii* (Baltimore: Johns Hopkins University Press, 1994); Joyce Thomas, "The 'Double V' Was for Victory: Black Soldiers, the Black Protest, and World War II" (Ph.D. diss., Ohio State University, 1993), 195; Wray R. Johnson, "Black American Radicalism and the First World War: The Secret Files of the Military Intelligence Division," *Armed Forces and Society* 26 (1999), 27–54; Sean Brawley and Chris Dixon, "Jim Crow Downunder? African American Encounters with White Australia, 1942–1945," *Pacific Historical Review* 71 (Fall 2002), 607–32.

23. Bailey and Farber, *First Strange Place*, 159.

24. Monthly Censorship Survey of Morale, Rumors, and Propaganda, APO 501, issue no. 5, September 1944, entry 551, box 24, RGH.

25. Addendum, Walter White to Undersecretary of War Robert P. Patterson, 12 February 1945, entry 236, box 369, OCA Records; memorandum, Bennett Saliman to Theater Censor, General Headquarters, AWPAC, APO 500, 10 August 1945, Subject: Supervision of Censorship, entry 551, box 12, RGH.

26. Memorandum, Office of the Theater Censor to the G-2, 93rd Infantry Division, APO 93, 11 April 1945, Subject: Censorship Report, entry 558, box 28, RGH.

27. E-mail correspondence with Nelson D. Peery, 20 June 2001 (in author's possession).

28. Thomas M. White, "Somewhere in the South Pacific" (in author's possession).

29. Thomas M. White interview with author, 6 February 1993.

30. William Couch, "To a Soldier" (in author's possession).

31. Abe Noel, "Bee Lines," *Chicago Bee*, 11 June 1944, 16.

32. Luszki, *Rape of Justice*, 1–11.

33. Ibid.

34. Ibid.

35. Ibid., 144.

36. Douglas MacArthur, *Reminiscences* (New York: McGraw-Hill, 1964), 192–93.

37. William Manchester, *American Caesar: Douglas MacArthur, 1880–1964* (Boston: Little, Brown), 431; D. Clayton James, *The Years of MacArthur*, vol. 2, *1941–1945* (Boston: Houghton Mifflin, 1975), 257–58.

38. Transcripts of Joseph L. Rauh Jr., Oral History Interview, Harry S. Truman Library, Independence, Mo.

39. Quoted in Kay Saunders and Helen Taylor, "The Reception of Black American Servicemen in Australia during World War II: The Resilience of 'White Australia,'" *Journal of Black Studies* 25 (January 1989), 335.

40. Monthly Censorship Survey of Morale, Rumors, and Propaganda, APO 501, issue no. 11, March 1945, entry 551, box 24, RGH.

41. National Association for the Advancement of Colored People Legal Defense and Educational Fund, *A United States Army Scottsboro Case* (New York: NAACP Legal Defense and Educational Fund, 1944); National Committee of the International Labor Defense, *For Equality of Military Justice: 1,100 Leaders and Organizations Join in Endorsing Appeal for Clemency for Privates Frank Fisher, Jr. and Edward R. Loury, Victims in the "Army Scottsboro Case"* (New York: International Labor Defense, 1944).

42. My thinking on this topic has been heavily influenced by the insights of Jacquelyn Dowd Hall, "The Mind That Burns in Each Body," *Southern Exposure* 12 (October–November 1984), 64–71, and Angela Davis, "Rape, Racism and the Myth of the Black Rapist," in *Women, Race and Class* (New York: Vintage Books, 1983), 172–201.

43. Clifford Bell to Dorothy Boyd, 1 February 1945, entry 551, box 35, RGH.

44. Verbatim record of trial by court-martial, *United States v. Sergeant Samuel Hill*, 7–8 March 1945, Branch Office of the Judge Advocate General, Melbourne, Victoria, Australia, NASSIF Building, Falls Church, Va., 1–4.

45. Chris Dixon and Sean Brawley, "'Tan Yanks' and a 'Semblance of Civilization': African American Encounters with the South Pacific, 1941–1945," in *Through Depression and War: The United States and Australia*, ed. Peter Bastian and Roger Bell (Sydney: Australian-American Fulbright Commission, 2002), 93–95. I wish to thank Chris Dixon for sharing this valuable article with me.

46. For example, Fletcher P. Martin, "Fijians Best Jungle Fighters, Japs Learn," *Baltimore Afro-American*, 27 May 1944, 5.

47. Dixon and Brawley, "'Tan Yanks' and a 'Semblance of Civilization,'" 94–95.

48. Lieutenant Cecil W. Davis, "Kids, Dogs, Pig Trail GIs Touring SWP Town," *Baltimore Afro-American*, 13 May 1944, 2.

49. Interview with Peter Lait, conducted by Dr. Iwamoto Hiromitsu and transcribed and translated by Pastor Jacob Aramans, 1 June 2004, Remembering the War in New

Guinea, http://ajrp.awm.gov.au/ajrp/remember.nsf/pages/NT0000311E (accessed 11 March 2007).

50. Verbatim record of trial by court-martial, *United States v. Sergeant Samuel Hill,* 7 March 1945, Branch Office of the Judge Advocate, Melbourne, Australia, NASSIF Building, Falls Church, Va., 2–3.

51. Ibid.

52. Memorandum, Chaplain Matthew A. Lowe to Commanding General, 93rd Infantry Division, Subject: Request for Appointment of a Special Colored Court, 22 February 1945; memorandum, Chaplain S. McMaster Kerr to Commanding General, 93rd Infantry Division, Subject: Request for Appointment of Special General Court, 23 February 1945, both in NASSIF Building, Falls Church, Va.

53. Memorandum, Douglas MacArthur to Commanding General, 6th Army, 4 August 1944; Memorandum, Alamo Force Commanding General Walter Krueger to Southwest Pacific General Headquarters, 4 August 1944, both in RG 4, box 14, folder: 6th Army Correspondence, Douglas MacArthur Memorial Archives, Norfolk, Va.

54. Charles Loeb, "Major General Johnson Challenges Writer to Presume His Texas Origin Makes Him Unfit to Lead Negro Soldiers," *Houston Informer and Texas Freeman,* 1 September 1945, 2.

55. Ibid.

56. Chaplain S. McMaster Kerr and Matthew A. Lowe to Commanding General, 93rd Infantry Division, 15 March 1945; memorandum, Chaplain Matthew A. Lowe to Assistant Judge Advocate General, APO 924, Subject: Review of Court-Martial Case of Sergeant Samuel Hill, 20 April 1945, both in NASSIF Building, Falls Church, Va. For an insightful study of the role of chaplains in the Second World War, see Donald F. Crosby, S.J., *Battlefield Chaplains: Catholic Priests in World War II* (Lawrence: University Press of Kansas, 1997).

57. Samuel Hill to Grace Davis and Theodore Hill, 15 March 1945, NASSIF Building, Falls Church, Va.; Theodore Hill to Franklin H. Williams, 28 January 1946, Part 9: Discrimination in the U.S. Armed Forces, 1918–1955, Series B: Armed Forces Legal Files, 1940–50, NAACP Papers, LOC.

58. Theodore Hill to the NAACP, 28 January 1946, Part 9: Discrimination in the U.S. Armed Forces, 1918–1955, Series B: Armed Forces Legal Files, 1940–50, NAACP Papers, LOC.

59. "Social Interlude at NAACP Confab," *Detroit Tribune,* 29 May 1945, 7.

60. Telegram, District of Columbia Branch President George E. C. Hayes to NAACP Branch Members, 20 June 1945, *Papers of the NAACP, Part 26: Selected Branch Files, 1940–1955, Series A: South,* ed. John Bracey and August Meier, folder: District of Columbia, Washington, January–July 1945 (Bethesda, MD: University Publications of America, 1992).

61. "Walter White to Speak," *Philadelphia Tribune,* 12 May 1945, 10.

62. "Walter White Reports to Army on Pacific Trip," *Philadelphia Tribune,* 24 April 1945, 2.

63. NAACP Assistant Special Counsel Franklin H. Williams to the Secretary of War, 21 February 1946, Part 9: Discrimination in the U.S. Armed Forces, 1918–1955, Series B: Armed Forces Legal Files, 1940–50, NAACP Papers, LOC.

64. "Army Men Send $93 to NAACP Fund," *Los Angeles Tribune,* 7 February 1944, 20.

65. "Pacific Soldiers send $1,895 for NAACP Work," *New York Age*, 12 August 1945, 3; "Along the NAACP Battlefront," *Crisis* (September 1944), 294; Walter White to Roy Wilkins, 9 March 1945, *Papers of the NAACP, Part 14: Race Relations in the International Arena, 1940–1955*, ed. John Bracey and August Meier, General Office File (Bethesda, MD: University Publications of America, 1992).

66. Oscar E. Holder, Monthly Newsletter, "To All Chaplains of the Ninety-third Infantry Division," 29 November 1944, Oscar E. Holder, 201 File, RG 247, Records of the Office of the Chief of Chaplains, NARA.

67. Walter White to Roy Wilkins, 9 March 1945, *Papers of the NAACP, Part 14: Race Relations in the International Arena, 1940–1955*, ed. John Bracey and August Meier, General Office File (Bethesda, MD: University Publications of America, 1992). For more on Walter White's trip to the Pacific theater of operations, see Kenneth R. Janken, *White: The Biography of Walter White, Mr. NAACP* (New York: New Press, 2003).

68. Robert F. Cocklin, survey questionnaire correspondence, Arlington, Va., 11 May 1992.

69. Robert Eichelberger to 93rd Commanding General, 5 July 1945, Francis Ellis Career Clipping File (in author's possession).

70. Robert C. Bennett to Walter White, 12 May 1945, Legal File, 1944–49, box B-150, Soldier Complaints, NAACP Papers, LOC.

71. George N. Leighton to James M. Nabritt, 20 June 1944, folder: Leighton, George N., 1944–45 (typescript), box 122-2, Correspondence J-RE, Howard University Men and Women in the Armed Forces Papers, Howard University Founder's Library, Washington. D.C.

72. Ibid.

73. Lloyd F. Graves to Miss Ovington, 7 November 1945, Administrative File, 1940–50, box G-15, Soldier Complaints, NAACP Papers, LOC.

74. John D. Howard interview with author.

75. General Julius W. Becton, survey questionnaire correspondence, Prairie View, Tex., 12 October 1992.

76. Office of the Theater Censor, APO 501, Censorship Survey of Morale, Rumors, and Propaganda, July 1944, entry 558, box 24, U.S. Army Force, Far East, G-2, Theater Censorship, RGH.

77. Edward G. Quinn interview with author.

78. *Congressional Record*, 79th Cong., 1st sess., pt. 5, 29 June 1945 (Washington, DC: GPO, 1945), 6994–95.

79. "Senators Back Eastland; War Department Says Charges 'Untrue'" *Sunday Chicago Bee*, 15 July 1945, 2.

80. "93rd Answers Eastland," *Pittsburgh Courier–Detroit Edition*, 4 August 1945, 7.

81. "GI Mother Rallies 2,500 against Senator Eastland," *Baltimore Afro-American*, 21 July 1945, TCF, reel 92, frame 356.

82. G-2 Weekly Report #88, "Wanted: One Jap Major," box 13700, folder 393-2.1, Periodic Report, no. 38-67, 93rd Infantry Division, May–July 1945, AGO Records.

83. "Ninety-third Off Morotai," *Daily Pacifican*, 1 July 1945, 2; "Japs Routed on Jolo Islands by Ninety-third Division," *Philadelphia Tribune*, 22 September 1945, 20; "26 New Ninety-third Heroes Awarded Bronze Stars," *Atlanta Daily World*, 6 January 1946, 1; Raymond Jenkins interview with author, 28 February 1990; James M. Whittico interview with author.

84. "On Patrol When News of Jap Surrender Was Announced," *Houston Informer and Texas Freeman,* 13 October 1945, 2.

85. Nelson Peery to his mother, 6 September 1945 (in author's possession); Nelson Peery interview with author, 9 December 1995.

86. Edwin Lee, interview by Georgia Rountree, Winter 1972–73, Lee Papers.

87. General Julius W. Becton, survey questionnaire correspondence, Prairie View, Tex., 12 October 1992.

88. "8,000 Japs Yield to Ninety-third Division," *Philadelphia Tribune,* 8 September 1945, 1.

89. "Army to Give Priority to Fathers, Overseas Veterans in Demobilizing," *New York Times,* 6 September 1944, 14; "Army's Outline of Preliminary Plans for Demobilizing When Reich Is Beaten," *New York Times,* 7 September 1944, 14.

90. Harry McAlpin, "Only 75 Negroes in 2,500 GIs Released," *Michigan Chronicle,* 26 May 1945, 3.

91. John C. Sparrow, *History of Personnel Demobilization in the United States Army* (Washington, DC: Office of the Chief of Military History, 1951), 154.

92. McAlpin, "Only 75 Negroes in 2,500 GIs Released," 3; "Army Point Rate Unfair to Non-combat Troops," "Army Admits Plan Unfair; Revelation Made in P.M. Article," *Houston Informer and Texas Freeman,* 28 July 1945, 1; *Philadelphia Tribune,* 9 June 1945, 1, 11; "Army Admits Point System Unfair to Negro," *Philadelphia Tribune,* 28 July 1945, 1, 10; "White Point System Protest Questioned," *Pittsburgh Courier–Detroit Edition,* 23 June 1945, 17; "Army Admits Point-Release Unfair to Negro Soldiers," *Pittsburgh Courier–Detroit Edition,* 28 July 1945; Ernest E. Johnson, "Many Negroes Due in Pacific Despite Peace," *New York Amsterdam News,* 25 August 1945, 3.

93. Nelson Peery interview with author, 9 December 1995.

94. Robert Johnson to his mother, 14 June 1945 (in author's possession).

95. "Soldier Says Colored Officers Left Behind," *Houston Informer and Texas Freeman,* 24 November 1945, 8.

96. Julius V. Merritt, "1063 Filipino Girls Become Brides of Colored Soldiers," *Baltimore Afro-American,* 2 February 1946, 2.

97. Enoch Waters Jr., "U.S. Army Installs Jim Crow in Manila," *Chicago Defender,* 13 October 1945, TCF.

98. "What the People Say; Negro Troops Can't Dance with Filipinos," *Chicago Defender,* 10 March 1945, 10.

99. "Reports U.S. Servicemen Planting Anti-Negro Bias in Philippines Confirmed," *California Eagle,* 20 September 1945, 1; "Tales about Tails," *Cleveland Call & Post,* 15 September 1945, 3.

100. Julius B. Young interview with author.

101. Reverend William H. Jernagin, *Christ at the Battlefront: Servicemen Accept the Challenge* (Washington, DC: Murry Brothers, 1946), 130.

102. "Hundreds of Negro Soldiers Hear Dr. Jernagin in Pasay Club Talk," *Daily Pacifican,* 7 November 1945, 4; Jernagin, *Christ at the Battlefront,* 88–91.

103. Carter Wesley, "Ram's Horn," *Houston Informer and Texas Freeman,* 24 November 1945, 14.

104. "Soldier Says Colored Officers Left Behind," 8.

105. "GIs Clash Near Manila: MPs End 3-Hour Battle," *Pittsburgh Courier–Detroit Edition,* 12 January 1946, 1.

106. Intelligence and Security Division Chief to the Office of the Chief of Transportation, 28 August 1945, RG 336, Office of the Chief of Transportation, box 53, Formerly Classified General Correspondence, 1941–46, folder 291-2-43ap, NARA.

107. "Rowe, ARC Worker Insulted," *Pittsburgh Courier–Detroit Edition,* 1 September 1945, 11.

108. Memorandum, 93rd Commanding General to Regimental, Battalion, Company, and Detachment Commanders, 28 August 1945, Subject: Policies Relating to Officers and Non-Commissioned Officers of the Ninety-third Infantry Division, box 4, folder: 93rd Division, Trip Home, Boyd Collection.

109. Brief, Chief, Intelligence and Security Division for General Marshall, and attached memo, Army Service Forces, 11 August 1945, RG 336, Office of the Chief of Transportation, box 53, Formerly Classified General Correspondence, 1941–46, folder: 291.2–43ap, NARA.

110. Civilian Aide Truman Gibson to Assistant Secretary of War John J. McCloy, 6 September 1945, entry 91, box 22, subject file, 1940–47, folder: NAACP, OCA Records.

111. "Stateside 85 Pointers to Be Discharged Immediately; Critical Score Due to Be Lowered after Jap Troops Are Disarmed," *Daily Pacifican,* 19 August 1945, 2; S. G. Henry and I. H. Edwards, Summary of Statements regarding the Demobilization of the Army, 28 August 1945, entry 91, box 22, subject file, 1940–47, folder: NAACP, OCA Records.

112. Summary of West Coast Port Commanders Conference on Returning Troops Movements, 6–7 September 1945, RG 336, Office of the Chief of Transportation, box 81, Historical Program Files, 1940–50, NARA; Phil Gordon, "142 Troopships Are Assigned to Speed Pacific Vets Home," *Daily Pacifican,* 24 November 1945, 1.

113. Nelson Peery, *Black Fire: The Making of an American Revolutionary* (New York: New Press, 1994), 335.

114. Edwin Lee interview by Georgia Rountree.

115. "Retiree Pays Nostalgic Museum Visit," *Huachuca Scout,* 2 July 1986, 5.

116. Raymond Jenkins to his mother, 2 January 1946 (in author's possession).

117. Nelson Peery to his mother, 6 September 1945.

118. William P. Hurd to Charles L. Cutler, 26 September 1961, *United States v. Sergeant Samuel Hill,* USAJ.

Epilogue

Epigraphs: Penn quoted in "Murdered Soldier-Educator Survived War, but Not in Georgia," *Baltimore Afro-American,* 18 July 1964, 1–2; Greene quoted in Clark Hallas, "Greene Says Detroit Must Quickly Root Out Seeds of Discontent," *Detroit News,* 2 November 1970, 13.

1. *High Society,* prod. and dir. Sol Siegel, MGM / United Artist Home Entertainment Group, 1985, videocassette.

2. For biographical background on Kyle, see John Chilton, *Who's Who of Jazz! Storyville*

to *Swing Street* (Philadelphia: Chilton, 1972), 190; Leonard G. Feather, *Encyclopedia of Jazz* (New York: Horizon, 1960), 304.

3. Ole J. Astrup, "The Forgotten Ones: Billy Kyle," *Jazz Journal International* 37, no. 8 (1984), 10.

4. Telegram, Commanding General Homer M. Groninger to the USAT *David C. Shanks*, 30 January 1946, box 4, folder: 93rd Infantry Division, Trip Home, Boyd Collection; "Last of Ninety-third Division Units Return from Pacific Theatre," *Cleveland Call & Post*, 16 February 1946, 4; "Last of 93rd Division Lands in California; Saw Its First Action in Solomons Fight," *Atlanta Daily World*, 16 February 1946, 1, 5.

5. Adjutant General to Commanding Generals of Boston, New York, Hampton Roads, New Orleans, Seattle, San Francisco, and Los Angeles Ports of Embarkation, 5 January 1946, Subject: Inactivation of Certain Army Ground and Service Forces Type Units, box 4, folder: 93rd Infantry Division, Trip Home, Boyd Collection.

6. "Happy Reunion after Two Long Years: Captain and Mrs. John E. Maupin," *Baltimore Afro-American*, 16 February 1946, 1.

7. Raphael R. Harris, "Gabbing in Richmond," *Baltimore Afro-American*, 16 February 1945, 15.

8. "Pacific Vets Parade in Nation's Capital," *Baltimore Afro-American*, 20 April 1946, 9.

9. Nelson Peery, *Black Fire: The Making of an American Revolutionary* (New York: New Press, 1994), 336.

10. John D. Howard interview with author.

11. "Taylorville Girl and San Antonio Vet Are Married," *Chicago Defender*, 16 March 1946, 11; William F. Fentress interview with author.

12. "Meriam Sanders Weds Former Army Chaplain," *Chicago Defender*, 6 July 1946, 9.

13. "Impressive Ceremony," *California Eagle*, 28 February 1946, 20.

14. Zola Fraser 201 Career File (in author's possession courtesy of Reuben Fraser).

15. What follows is based largely on a reading of Elaine Tyler May, *Homeward Bound: American Families in the Cold War Era* (New York: Basic Books, 1988), chap. 3.

16. "Gay Divorcees," *Ebony Magazine* (February 1950), 73; "Marrying Medico for Third Divorce," *Los Angeles Tribune*, 3 March 1951, 1, 14.

17. Dorothy Boulding Ferebee interview by Merze Tate, 28–31 December 1979, transcript, 451–52, Black Women Oral History Project, vol. 3, Schlesinger Library, Radcliffe College, Cambridge, Mass.

18. "Secret Ferebee Divorce Revealed As He Re-weds," *Baltimore Afro-American*, 30 June 1951, 1.

19. William C. Matney Jr., ed., *Who's Who among Black Americans*, 4th ed., *1985* (Lake Forest, IL: Educational Communications, 1985), 512.

20. Arthur P. Davis, J. Saunders Redding, and Joyce A. Joyce, eds., *The New Cavalcade: African American Writing from 1760 to the Present* (Washington, DC: Howard University Press, 1991), 866.

21. William T. Ray to Gloster Current, 7 June 1948, *Papers of the NAACP, Part 26: Selected Branch Files, 1940–1955, Series C: The Midwest*, ed. John Bracey and August Meier,(Bethesda, MD: University Publications of America, 2000).

22. Julius G. Thompson interview with author, 3 May 1993.

23. Julius B. Young interview with author.

24. See, for example, Herbert Shapiro, *White Violence and Black Response: From Reconstruction to Montgomery* (Amherst: University of Massachusetts Press, 1988); George Lipsitz, *Rainbow at Midnight: Labor and Culture in the 1940s* (Urbana: University of Illinois Press, 1994); Michael Goldfield, *The Color of Politics: Race and the Mainsprings of American Politics* (New York: New Press, 1997); Gerald Horne, *Communist Front? The Civil Rights Congress, 1946–1956* (Rutherford, NJ: Associated University Presses, 1988); John Egerton, *Speak Now against the Day: The Generation before the Civil Rights Movement in the South* (New York: Knopf, 1994); William Chafe, *The Unfinished Journey: America since World War II*, 3d ed. (New York: Oxford University Press, 1995); David H. Onkst, "'First a Negro . . . , Incidentally a Veteran': Black World War II Veterans and the GI Bill of Rights in the Deep South, 1944–1948," *Journal of Social History* 31 (Spring 1998), 517–43; Manning Marable, *Race, Reform, and Rebellion: The Second Reconstruction in Black America, 1945–1990*, 2nd ed. (Jackson: University Press of Mississippi, 1991); Steven Lawson, *Running for Freedom: Civil Rights and Black Politics in America since 1941* (Philadelphia: Temple University Press, 1991); Charles Payne, *I've Got the Light of Freedom: The Organizing Tradition and the Mississippi Freedom Struggle* (Berkeley: University of California Press, 1995); John Dittmer, *Local People: The Struggle for Civil Rights in Mississippi* (Urbana: University of Illinois Press, 1995); Arnold R. Hirsch, *Making the Second Ghetto: Race and Housing in Chicago, 1940–1960* (New York: Cambridge University Press, 1983); Thomas J. Sugrue, *The Origins of the Urban Crisis: Race and Inequality in Postwar Detroit* (Princeton, NJ: Princeton University Press, 1996); Gerald Horne, *Black and Red: W. E. B. DuBois and the Afro-American Response to the Cold War* (Albany: State University of New York Press, 1986); Martin Duberman, *Paul Robeson* (New York: Knopf, 1989); Gerald Horne, *Black Liberation / Red Scare: Ben Davis and the Communist Party* (Newark: University of Delaware Press, 1994); and Penny M. Von Eschen, *Race against Empire: Black Americans and Anticolonialism, 1937–1957* (Ithaca, NY: Cornell University Press, 1997).

25. "Berkeley Medic Fights Fascist Eviction Move," *California Eagle,* 28 February 1946, 1, 20; "Doctor Wages Fight to Keep Home," *Pittsburgh Courier,* 9 March 1946, 2.

26. Albert Washington, "Doctor Fights Eviction Suit," *Baltimore Afro-American,* 9 March 1946, 11.

27. "Berkeley Doctor Wins Right to Home in Exclusive District," *Los Angeles Tribune,* 18 December 1948, 5.

28. George M. Shuffer interview with author, 4 June 1993.

29. G. James Fleming and Christian E. Burckel, eds., *Who's Who in Colored America: An Illustrated Biographical Directory of Notable Living Persons of African Descent in the United States,* 7th ed., *1950* (Yonkers-on-Hudson, NY: Christian E. Burckel and Assoc., 1950), S 13.

30. Matney, *Who's Who among Black Americans,* 4th ed., *1985,* 488.

31. William C. Matney, *Who's Who among Black Americans,* 1st ed., *1975–1976* (Northbrook, IL: Who's Who among Black Americans, 1976), 1:314; Jean C. Hunton, survey questionnaire correspondence, U.S. Virgin Islands, 22 March 1993.

32. Asberry McGriff interview with author.

33. Memorandum, Melvin W. Ormes for Commanding Officer, Camp Stoneman, San Francisco Port of Embarkation, 16 July 1946, Subject: Recommendation for Army Commendation Ribbon, 16 July 1947; memorandum, G-3 for the Commanding General, 10th

U.S. Army Corps Headquarters, 13 October 1961, Reference: Recommendation for Promotion, both in Frank Little Clipping File (in author's possession).

34. "War Department to Study Tan Yanks' Utilization," *Baltimore Afro-American*, 6 October 1945, 12; Morris J. MacGregor, *The Integration of the Armed Forces, 1940–1965* (Washington, DC: Center for Military History, 1981), 130–32. For more on the army's postwar studies on the participation of African Americans in the U.S. Armed Forces, see Sherie Mershon and Steven Schlossman, *Foxholes and Color Lines: Desegregating the U.S. Armed Forces* (Baltimore: Johns Hopkins University Press, 1998); Gerald Astor, *The Right to Fight: A History of African Americans in the Military* (Novato, CA: Presidio Press, 1998); Bernard C. Nalty, *Strength for the Fight: A History of Black Americans in the Military* (New York: Free Press, 1986); Richard O. Hope, *Racial Strife in the U.S. Military: Toward the Elimination of Discrimination* (New York: Praeger, 1979); Neil A. Wynn, *The Afro-American and the Second World War* (New York: Holmes and Meier, 1975); Jack D. Foner, *Blacks and the Military in American History: A New Perspective* (New York: Praeger, 1974); Richard M. Dalfiume, *Desegregation of the U.S. Armed Forces: Fighting on Two Fronts, 1939–1953* (Columbia: University of Missouri Press, 1969); Richard Stillman, *Integration of the U.S. Armed Forces* (New York: Praeger, 1968); and the landmark study by Ulysses G. Lee, *United States Army in World War II, Special Studies: The Employment of Negro Troops* (Washington, DC: Office of the Chief of Military History, 1966).

35. Approving Action of Commanding General, 92nd Infantry Division of Proceedings of Board of Review Appointed by Letter Orders dated 23 June 1945 to Consider the Combat Effectiveness of Negro Officers and Enlisted Men, 2 July 1945, entry 291.2, file: "Top Secret: Ninety-second Infantry Division Combat Efficiency Analysis and Supplementary Report," AGO Records.

36. Memorandum, 92nd Commanding General, Major General Edward M. Almond, to John J. McCloy, undated, Subject: Expressions Showing Attitudes towards the Fighting Abilities of Negro Troops, box 359, entry 236, Folder: 93rd Division, OCA Records. For a fuller elaboration of the viewpoints that circulated among the 92nd Division high command during the period, see Paul Goodman, *A Fragment of Victory in Italy during World War II, 1942–1945* (Carlisle Barracks, PA: U.S. Army War College, 1952); Lee, *United States Army in World War II;* Ernest F. Fisher Jr., *Cassino to the Alps: United States Army in World War II* (Washington, DC: Office of the Chief of Military History, 1977); Robert W. Kesting, "Conspiracy to Discredit the Black Buffaloes: The Ninety-second Infantry in World War II," *Journal of Negro History* 72 (Winter–Spring 1987), 1–17; Hondon B. Hargrove, *Buffalo Soldiers in Italy: Black Americans in World War II* (Jefferson, NC: McFarland, 1985); and Dale Wilson, "Recipe for Failure: Major General Edward M. Almond and Preparation of the U.S. Ninety-second Infantry Division for Combat in World War II," *Journal of Military History* 56 (July 1992), 473–88.

37. For example, see Arnold M. Rose, "Army Policies toward Negro Soldiers," *Annals of the American Academy of Political and Social Science* 144 (March 1946); Rutherford B. Stevens, "Racial Aspects of Emotional Problems of Negro Soldiers," *Journal of Clinical Psychopathology* 103 (January 1947); Stewart Wolf, "Mental Illness among Negro Troops Overseas," *American Journal of Psychiatry* 103 (January 1947); Charles Dollard and Donald Young, "The Negro in the Armed Forces," *Survey Graphic* 36 (January 1947); Edward T. Hall Jr.,

"Prejudice and Negro-White Relations in the Army," *American Journal of Sociology* 52 (March 1947).

38. Warman Welliver, "Report on the Negro Soldier," *Harper's Magazine* (April 1946), 335.

39. "Addenda to a Report," *Harper's Magazine* (June 1946), 346.

40. Robert F. Cocklin, "Report on the Negro Soldier," *Infantry Journal* 54 (December 1946), 17.

41. *Pittsburgh Courier*, 22 January; 9, 23 February; 2, 9 March; *Baltimore Afro-American*, 23 March, 18 May, 27 July, 5 October, 16, 30 November 1946; 1 March, 7 May 1947; *Chicago Defender*, 5, 22, 13 June 1946; *Michigan Chronicle* 9 February 1946.

42. *Congressional Record*, 79th Cong., 1st sess., pt. 5, 29 June 1945 (Washington, DC: GPO, 1945), 7420–22; *Congressional Record*, 79th Cong., 2nd sess., 1 February 1946 (Washington, DC: GPO, 1946), 392–489; "Representative Gahagan Lauds Colored Servicemen," *Michigan Chronicle*, 2 February 1946, 13.

43. "93rd Answers Eastland," 7; "GI Mother Rallies 2,500 against Senator Eastland."

44. Lawrence D. Reddick, "Race Relations in the Army," *American Journal of Sociology* (July 1947), 41; "Dr. Reddick Hits Ex-Ninety-Second Officer's Anti-Negro Story," *Chicago Defender*, 20 April 1946, 9.

45. Henry L. Williams interview with author, 3 August 1991.

46. Clarence R. Ross interview with author.

47. Florence Murray, *The Negro Handbook: 1949* (New York: Macmillan, 1949), 284.

48. "Negro Vets Organize," *Los Angeles Tribune*, 4 May 1946, 8.

49. John Hudson Jones, "Lily White Housing Rapped by Vet Group," *Daily Worker*, 10 June 1946, 12.

50. "NPC Members Hail from Many States," *AVC Bulletin*, 15 July 1947, 7; "Vasco D. Hale of Bloomfield, Connecticut: World's Most Courageous Man," *Sepia Record* 10 (December 1953), 22–25.

51. Letters to AVC, *AVC Bulletin*, 1 September 1946, 5.

52. "Hit Gillem Report as Incomplete," *AVC Bulletin*, 15 May 1946, 6.

53. "Convention Elects 24 NPC Members of Various Backgrounds and Occupations," *AVC Bulletin*, 1 July 1946, 15; "Fordham Law Graduate among Top AVC Leaders," *Baltimore Afro-American*, 21 September 1946, 7; "Background of Vets' Lone Negro Official Told," *Los Angeles Tribune*, 21 September 1946, 4, Franklin H. Williams, "Democracy in Practice," *AVC Bulletin*, 15 May 1947, 3. For more on Williams, see Mark V. Tushnet, *Making Civil Rights Law: Thurgood Marshall and the Supreme Court, 1936–1961* (New York: Oxford University Press, 1994).

54. "Interracial Policy," *AVC Bulletin*, 29 August 1947, 8.

55. "New Coast Regional Officer Takes Over," *Los Angeles Tribune*, 9 September 1950, 7; Glenn Fowler, "Franklin H. Williams Dies at 72; Lawyer and Former Ambassador," *New York Times*, 22 May 1990, B11.

56. "National Negro Congress to Organize Vet Group," *Michigan Chronicle*, 12 January 1946, 13; "Vet Unit Backs Alabama Vote Attempt," *Baltimore Afro-American*, 16 February 1946, 9; "Veterans Set Up Nation-Wide Unit," *Baltimore Afro-American*, 13 April 1946, 17.

57. "The National Scene," *Daily Worker*, 2 July 1946, 3; "Michigan Special Session to Act on Rent Law," *Daily Worker*, 8 July 1946, 4.

58. "Anti-Lynch Crusade Gets Support of Veterans," *Daily Worker*, 8 September 1946, 7; "Lynch Protest will March on Capital," *Daily Worker*, 17 September 1946, 7.

59. Ruby Cooper, "Chicago Vet Squatters Welcome Negro to Project," *Daily Worker*, 18 November 1946, 4.

60. "Ex-Interns Conference Attended by 100 Doctors," *Baltimore Afro-American*, 15 June 1946, 3.

61. "Medico-Chi Officers and Committees for 1949," *Bulletin of the Medico-Chirurgical Society of the District of Columbia, Incorporated* 5 (December 1948), 5; "Medico-chi Officers and Committees, 1950," *Bulletin of the Medico-Chirurgical Society of the District of Columbia, Incorporated* 6 (December 1949), 3.

62. "Thomas on National Advisory Mental Health Council," *Journal of the National Medical Association* 47 (January 1955), 55–56; "The Distinguished Service Medal of the National Medical Association," *Journal of the National Medical Association* 47 (January 1955), 57–58; "Deaths," *Journal of the National Medical Association* 50 (May 1958), 221.

63. Paula Thorpe, "Fred J. Mabra, Sr.," *Sacramento Bee*, 1 September 1995, B5.

64. Walt Philbin, "Humidity, Heat Beat 18 Shriners," *Times-Picayune*, 19 August 1993, B1.

65. Matney, *Who's Who among Black Americans*, 1st ed., *1975–1976*, 1:284.

66. John D. Howard interview with author.

67. George N. Leighton, survey questionnaire correspondence, Chicago, 11 April 1995, Minutes of Boarding, Illinois State Conference of NAACP Branches, 11 September 1949, *Papers of the NAACP, Part 26: Selected Branch Files, 1940–1955, Series C: The Midwest*, ed. John Bracey and August Meier, September–December 1949 (Bethesda, MD: University Publications of America, 2000).

68. "Will Press Case in Cicero," *Pittsburgh Courier*, 1 September 1951, 4; Walter White, "This Is Cicero," *Crisis* (August–September 1951), 434–40; "Cicero Indictments," *Crisis* (October 1951), 530.

69. Ted Coleman, "Demand Federal Probe in Cicero," *Pittsburgh Courier*, 29 September 1951, 5; "This Must Be Fought!" *Pittsburgh Courier*, 29 September 1951, 6.

70. "Looking and Listening," *Crisis* (November 1951), 593–94: "Charges Dropped against Leighton," *Crisis* (November 1951), 603.

71. "U.S. to Probe Cicero Riot," *Pittsburgh Courier*, 6 October 1951, 1; "Rights Violation Studied; Federal Panel Opens Its Inquiry into Cicero Race Riots," *New York Times*, 6 November 1951; "U.S. Jury Indicts Seven in Cicero Race Riot," *New York Times*, 14 December 1951, 25.

72. "Race Riot Case Dropped; U.S. Clears Three Police of Cicero Civil Rights Charges," *New York Times*, 27 November 1954, 18.

73. Pauline Redmond Coggs, "Segregation Reconsidered," A People's Forum Based on *To Secure These Rights: The Report of the President's Civil Rights Committee*, 15 April 1948, *Milwaukee Urban League Newsletter*, 29 May 1950, Milwaukee Urban League Papers, reel 3, news clippings, the State Historical Society of Wisconsin, Madison, Wis.; Pauline Redmond Coggs interview with author, 13 February 2000.

74. Clarence L. Gaines interview with author.

75. James M. Whittico interview with author; Patricia W. Romero, ed., *In Black Amer-*

ica, 1968: The Year of Awakening (New York: Association for the Study of Negro Life and History, 1968), 304–5.

76. Larry G. Murphy, J. Gordon Melton, and Gary L. Ward, eds., *Encyclopedia of African American Religions* (New York: Garland Publishing, 1993), 40.

77. Matney, *Who's Who among Black Americans*, 1st ed., 1975–1976, 1:249.

78. Fleming and Burckel, *Who's Who in America*, 7th ed., 1950, 504, 152; Edwin Lee, interview by Georgia Rountree, Winter 1972–73, Lee Papers.

79. Nelson Peery interview with author, 9 December 1994.

80. Nelson Peery, *The Negro National Colonial Question* (Chicago: Workers Press, 1975).

81. Raymond Jenkins interview with author, 28 February 1990; Raymond Jenkins, "Reimburse Negroes for Slavery," *Detroit News*, 2 February 1967; Raymond Jenkins, "Reparations for African Americans Resolution" (undated), Raymond Jenkins Clipping File (in author's possession); Mitchell Landsberg, "Viewpoint: Reparations for Descendants of Slaves Discussed," *Memphis Commercial Appeal*, 5 June 1989; Tamara Audi, "Payback for Slavery: Growing Push for Reparations Tries to Fulfill Broken Promise," *Detroit Free Press*, 18 September 2000, 18; Chris L. Jenkins and Hamil R. Harris, "Descendants of Slaves Rally for Reparations," *Washington Post*, 18 August 2002, C1. For more on the question of reparations, see Raymond A. Winbush, ed., *Should America Pay? Slavery and the Raging Debate over Reparations* (New York: HarperCollins, 2003), and Ronald P. Salzberger and Mary C. Turck, eds., *Reparations for Slavery: A Reader* (Lanham, MD: Rowman and Littlefield, 2004).

82. *United States of America v. Herbert Guest et. al.*, U.S. District Court, Middle District, Georgia, Athens Division, Criminal no. 2232, 29 December 1964, *Race Relations Law Reporter* 9 (Winter 1964), 1692.

83. Marable, *Race, Reform, and Rebellion*, 72–73; Dittmer, *Local People*, chap. 10.

84. "Klansmen's Acquittal Spurs Race Discontent; Verdict in Penn Case Disgusts D.C. Negroes," *Pittsburgh Courier*, 12 September 1964, 1, 4; "Suspects Rounded Up, Freed, in Killer Hunt," *Brooklyn Amsterdam News*, 12 September 1964, 2; "All-White Jury Frees Klan Pair," *Baltimore Afro-American*, 12 September 1964, 1–2.

85. "Not Guilty, They Said," *Baltimore Afro-American*, 19 September 1964, 4.

86. "F.B.I. Scours Area of Negro Slaying," *New York Times*, 13 July 1964, 20.

87. *United States of America v. Herbert Guest et. al*, U.S. Supreme Court, no. 65, 25 March 1966, 86 S. Ct. 1170, *Race Relations Law Reporter* 11 (Summer, 1966), 593–94.

88. John D. Howard interview with author.

89. SAC Washington Field Office to Director, 8 August 1964 (PEMBIC), *FBI File on the Murder of Lemuel Penn* (Wilmington, DE: Scholarly Resources, 1997).

90. "Mrs. Lemuel A. Penn, Sniper Victim's Wife," *New York Times*, 22 July 1965, 31; Jim Thompson, "Highway 72 Revisted," *Athens Banner-Herald*, 11 July 2004, http://onlineathens.com/stories/071104/new_20040711120.shtml (accessed 6 January 2008).

91. John D. Howard interview with author.

92. "C. E. Brown, Ex-Principal of Bell High School, Dies," *Washington Post*, 22 October 1978, B6.

93. David A. Vise, "D.C. Control Board Takes Charge of Public Schools," *Washington Post*, 16 November 1996, 1.

94. Transcript, Army General Julius W. Becton, interview with Charlayne Hunter-Gault, *McNeil-Lehrer Newshour,* 2 December 1996.

95. Resignation letter of General Julius W. Becton as CEO/Superintendent of D.C. public schools, 14 April 1998, D.C. Watch, www.dcwatch.com/schools/ps980414.htm.

96. W. E. B. Du Bois, *The Souls of Black Folk,* ed. David W. Blight (Boston: Bedford / St. Martin's 1997), 38.

97. Oliver Harrington, *Where Is the Justice?* (Detroit: W. O. Evans, 1991), 2.

98. Lorena Edlen, "Retiree Pays Nostalgic Visit," *Huachucan Scout,* 15 April 1982, 4–5; Alvirita Little, correspondence with the author, 19 April 1993.

99. Beth Hatcher, "Community Pays Tribute to Man Killed by Klansmen," *Athens Banner-Herald,* 11 July 2004, www.onlineathens.com/stories/071104/new_penn.shtml (accessed 6 January 2008).

100. Julie Phillips, "Lemual Penn Dedication Service," *Athens Banner-Herald,* 7 October 2006, www.onlineathens.com/stories/100706/living_20061007026.shtml (accessed 7 January 2008).

I have used various sources and methods to reconstruct regimental, battalion, and company rosters as well as to compose career files for the individuals who make up the story. With the help of the staff members at the National Archives, Edward Carr, and the Freedom of Information Act, I was able to secure numerous personnel rosters of the U.S. 93rd Division for the years 1942 through 1946. As a former enlisted man with the finance section of the division, Carr taught me how to decipher the service numbers of the individuals listed on the rosters. Using the numerous interviews with veterans and collected questionnaire surveys, along with the personnel rosters as guides, I then sifted through hundreds of boxes of material in order to build an elaborate career database of individuals who were associated with the division during the wartime period. The most valuable records, located at the National Archives buildings at College Park, Maryland, and Washington, D.C., contained the bulk of this information, including Record Group 407 (Records of the Army Adjutant General), Record Group 337 (Records of Army Ground Forces Headquarters), Record Group 165 (Records of War Department General and Special Staffs, which include Records of the Military Intelligence Division), and Record Group 107 (Records of the Office of the Secretary of War, which include Records of the Civilian Aide to the Secretary of War). These papers contained important information about the unit such as individual names and service numbers as well as material relating to the promotion and transfer patterns of the pre-1948 military and the time-in-rank sequences of the World War II–era army.

Useful information regarding service families was also gleaned from Record Group 200 (Records of the American Red Cross). Additional rosters and other pertinent individual documents were found in Record Group 247 (Records of the Office of the Chief of Chaplains) and Record Group 112 (Office of the Surgeon General) at the archives. Finally, I also consulted the unit rosters in the papers of General Benjamin O. Davis Sr. and Edward Almond at the United States Military History Institute and the Leonard R. Boyd Collection at the Hoover Institution for War, Revolution, and Peace.

Information mined from the holdings of the National Military Personnel Records Center and other related materials supplemented the career information in my data set. The Freedom of Information Act allowed me to draw on the names and service numbers culled from the personnel rosters and elsewhere to request access to the career files of hundreds of surviving and deceased veterans which were either untouched or reconstructed after a fire in 1973. In most cases, my requests yielded valuable information relating to the veterans along with new leads on how to locate surviving former GIs. I was also able to secure critical documentation relating to the servicemen and their families from the biographical sketches and records at the Fort Huachuca Historical Museum in Arizona. Finally, using city directories of selected metropolitan areas between 1946 and 1960 housed at the Detroit Public Library, the Chicago Historical Society, and the Library of Congress, I was able to locate the addresses of servicemen and their families who had long since disappeared from the historical record. All told, my data set grew rapidly and now consists of 1,149 former GIs and family members with valuable life-history information including parents' names and occupations; dates of birth and, in many cases, death; points of origin; pre-war, wartime, and postwar migration movements; occupation; dates of service; marital status, and family sizes.

As I mentioned in the preface, many unpublished items (letters, diaries, photographs, service records, Officer Candidate School rosters, and other memorabilia) that appear throughout the book were received as a result of the open letters of inquiry sent to black weeklies and veterans newsletters and the numerous interviews conducted between 1991 and 2002. These sources were supplemented by the unpublished letters, autobiographies, and interviews located in the following collections: the National Association for the Advancement of Colored People Papers and the Veterans History Project at the Library of Congress; the Layle Lane Papers of the Schomburg Center for Research in Black Culture in the New York Public Library; the Edwin A. Lee Papers at the University of Illinois at Springfield Archives and Special Collection; the William H. Hastie Papers; the Eleanor Roosevelt Papers at the Franklin Delano Roosevelt Presidential Library; the Mary Penick Motley Papers at the Detroit Public Library; the Shirley Graham Papers in the Julius Rosenwald Collection at the Fisk University Library; the National Council of Negro Women Papers at the Mary McLeod Bethune Council House; the Tuskegee Institute News Clipping File, 1935–1960; and the major black weeklies published during the period. I have also drawn upon letters between service family members and GIs who requested their case files among the records of court-martial proceedings housed at the U.S. Army Judiciary.

To add greater texture to my study, I have also mined the published firsthand accounts in Phillip McGuire, ed., *Taps for a Jim Crow Army: Letters from Black Soldiers in World War II* (1983); Harry Maule, ed., *A Book of War Letters* (1943); Studs Terkel, ed., *The Good War* (1984); Edward Soulds, *Black Shavetail in Whitey's Army* (1971); Nelson Peery, *Black Fire: The Making of an American Revolutionary* (1994); Nelson Peery, *Black Radical: The Education of an American Revolutionary* (2007); Hildrus Poindexter, *My World of Reality: An Autobiography* (1973); Pauli Murray, *Song in a Weary Throat: An American Pilgrimage* (1987); William Jernagin, *Christ at the Battlefront: Servicemen Accept the Challenge* (1946); George M. Shuffer Jr., *My Journey to Betterment: An Autobiography* (1999); Jesse J. Johnson, *Ebony Brass: An Autobiography of Negro Frustration amid Aspiration* (1967); Truman K. Gibson Jr. with Steve Huntley, *Knocking Down Barriers: My Fight for Black America* (2005); and Walter White, *A Man Called White* (1948).

Various secondary sources helped me understand the rich social and cultural worlds that African American GIs and their families represented in the first half of the twentieth century. Readers interested in a broad overview of the black military experience should consult Ulysses G. Lee Jr., *The United States Army in World War II, Special Studies: The Employment of Negro Troops* (1966). Lee's study should be essential reading for anyone trying to grasp the relationship between military policy and race during the period. Also imperative are Gerald Astor, *The Right to Fight: A History of African Americans in the Military* (1998); Gail Buckley, *American Patriots: The Story of Blacks in the Military from the Revolution to Desert Storm* (2001); Jack D. Foner, *Blacks and the Military in American History: A New Perspective* (1974); Christopher Paul Moore, *Fighting for America: Black Soldiers—The Unsung Heroes of World War II* (2005); and Bernard C. Nalty, *Strength for the Fight: A History of African Americans in the Military* (1986).

Unit histories were very also instructive in the writing of this book. Maggi M. Morehouse, *Fighting in the Jim Crow Army: Black Men and Women Remember World War II* (2000); Daniel K. Gibran, *The 92nd Infantry Division and the Italian Campaign in World War II* (2001); Stanley Sandler, *Segregated Skies: All-Black Combat Squadrons of World War II* (1992); and Brenda L. Moore, *To Serve My Country, To Serve My Race: The Story of the Only African American WACs Stationed Overseas during World War II* (1996) provide a comprehensive portrait of the experiences of black men and women who served in the ranks of the segregated armies of the Pacific and Europe during the wartime period. Readers interested in understanding military racial policy during World War II should consult Richard M. Dalfiume, *Desegregation of the U.S. Armed Forces: Fighting on Two Fronts, 1939–1953* (1969); Sherie Mershon and Steven Schlossman, *Foxholes and Color Lines: Desegregating the U.S. Armed Forces* (1998); Phillip McGuire, *He, Too, Spoke for Democracy: Judge Hastie, World War II, and the Black Soldier* (1988); and Daniel Kryder, *Divided Arsenal: Race and the American State during World War II* (2000).

Throughout my research and writing, works such as Beth Bailey and David Farber, *The First Strange Place: Race and Sex in World War II Hawaii* (1992); William Tuttle, *"Daddy's Gone to War": The Second World War in the Lives of America's Children* (1993); and George Lipsitz, *A Life in the Struggle: Ivory Perry and the Culture of Opposition* (1988) forced me to think carefully about how World War II and the 1940s transformed the lives of African American GIs and their families and to read the sources against the grain in order to interpret the creative strategies they devised to offset the challenges they faced during the period. The inner worlds of black women's history and politics in the early twentieth century exemplified in the scholarship of Elsa Barkley Brown, Darlene Clark Hine, Hazel Carby, and Tera Hunter allowed me to recenter the context of *Fighting for Hope* in ways that simply were not possible beforehand. At the same time, the approaches adopted by Earl Lewis, Joe William Trotter, Kimberley Phillips, and James Grossman provided useful models for my study.

All the while, provocative works such as Leisa D. Meyer, *Creating GI Jane: Sexuality and Power in the Women's Army Corps during World War II* (1996); Karen Anderson, *Wartime Women: Sex Roles, Family Relations, and the Status of Women during World War II* (1981); John Dower, *War without Mercy: Race and Power in the Pacific War* (1986); John Costello, *Virtue under Fire: How World War II Changed Our Social and Sexual Attitudes* (1987); Allan Berube, *Coming Out under Fire: The History of Gay Men and Women in World War II* (1990); Ronald Takaki, *Double Victory: A Multicultural History of World War II* (2000); and Lewis A. Erenberg and Susan E. Hirsch, eds., *The War in American Culture: Society and Consciousness during World War II* (1996) allowed me to broaden my intellectual gaze to pose new questions about the connections of race, gender, sexuality, and culture in war as well as to reconfigure the very nature of my study. And books such as John Morton Blum, *V Was for Victory: Politics and American Culture during World War II* (1976); John W. Jefferies, *Wartime America: The World War II Home Front* (1996); and Richard Polenberg, *War and Society: The United States, 1941–1945* (1972), and articles written by Harvard Sitkoff, Kevin K. Gaines, Robin D. G. Kelley, and Beth Bailey spurred me to think in complex ways about war, political culture, and society during times of war.

The connections that I hoped to make between African Americans and U.S. foreign relations in the 1940s were greatly bolstered by recent books written by Brenda Gayle Plummer, Gerald Horne, Thomas Borstelmann, Penny Von Eschen, Carol Anderson, and Marc Gallicchio. As I set out to overhaul my dissertation, Von Eschen's *Race against Empire: Black Americans and Anti-colonialism, 1937–1957* (1997) appeared. Her sophisticated analysis of the ways that African Americans framed, interpreted, and refashioned their understandings of race and foreign relations during World War II and the Cold War eras altered my understanding of the period. Finally, Jennifer Brooks, *Defining the Peace: World War II Veterans and the Remaking of Southern Political Tradition* (2004); Mary Dudziak, *Cold War Civil Rights: Race and the Image of American Democracy* (2000); Philip A. Klinkner with Rogers M. Smith, *The Unsteady March: The Rise and Decline of Race Equality in America* (1999); and John Dittmer, *Local People: The Struggle for Civil Rights in Mississippi* (1994) provided me with a rich framework for thinking about the evolving political identities and consciousness of black World War II veterans and their families during the late 1940s and early 1950s.